ALSO BY GARY FISHGALL

Pieces of Time: The Life of James Stewart
Against Type: The Biography of Burt Lancaster

Gregory Peck

A BIOGRAPHY

Gary Fishgall

A LISA DREW BOOK
SCRIBNER
NEW YORK LONDON TORONTO SYDNEY SINGAPORE

SCRIBNER
1230 Avenue of the Americas
New York, NY 10020

For information about special discounts for bulk purchases,
please contact Simon & Schuster Special Sales:
1-800-456-6798 or business@simonandschuster.com

Designed by Colin Joh

Set in Caledonia

Manufactured in the United States of America

1 3 5 7 9 10 8 6 4 2

Library of Congress Cataloging-in-Publication Data is available.

ISBN 0-684-85290-X

For my mother, Sylvia Fishgall,
whose unflagging optimism and good spirits
are a wonder. With love and gratitude.

Contents

Acknowledgments

Biographers are somewhat like beggars. As they negotiate the twists and turns of their subjects' lives, they frequently find themselves with their hands out, asking for help. Fortunately for me, many heeded the call.

First and foremost, I must thank Gregory Peck. Disappointed with a previous biography published in 1980, he was not initially enthusiastic about someone new chronicling his life and times. Nevertheless, he graciously allowed friends and colleagues to speak with me if they so desired. Along the way, he warmed a bit to the project, consenting to provide written answers to written questions without asking for a single thing in return. After the manuscript was edited and copyedited, he reviewed the text and, to my great delight, was pleased with it, offering only a few minor corrections and additions, which I addressed. He also graciously provided a number of the images that appear in the photo insert. Thanks, as well, to Mr. Peck's secretary, Barbara Russel, who retired (for the second time) at the end of July 2001.

We are all products of our formative years, Peck perhaps even more than most. So I was particularly eager to chronicle the actor's experiences as a child and young man. Helping me accomplish this daunting task were La Jolla historical researcher and author Patricia A. Schaelchlin; Darlene John, School Historian, La Jolla Elementary School; Sister M. Petronilla and Sister Marilyn Gouailhardou of the Sisters of Mercy, Burlingame, California; Mary Jo Lamb-Ludwig and John C. Cash of the San Diego High School Alumni Association; John Panter and Dennis Sharp of the San Diego Historical Society; Bill Payne, Assistant Archivist, Special Collections and University Archives, Malcolm A. Love Library, San Diego State University; and Helen Wetzel Wood, Muriel Gutshall, and Lettie Knight Sullivan, Peck's classmates at San Diego High School. Particular thanks must go to Mary McKillop, Peck's second cousin on his mother's side, an avid family geneologist, who generously shared the fruits of her research as well as her own memories with me, and Sandra Spalding, a volunteer researcher at the La Jolla Historical Society, who not only helped me run down arcane bits of information but also suggested avenues of pursuit. A true research hound, Sandy went far beyond the call of duty to unearth wonderful tidbits about La Jolla and the Peck family.

The actor truly came into his own as a student at the University of California, Berkeley. The following individuals helped me flesh out these all-important college years: research assistant Wendy Stoltz; alumnus Lois O'Neil; John Kupersmith, Information Center, Doe Memorial Library; Mary Ajideh, Student Affairs Officer, Department of Dramatic Art; and Susanna A. Castillo-Robson, Registrar. Peck's rowing crew teammates Bob Andreson, John Collins, Linton Emerson, Jack Hoefer, Jack's wife, Kay, Dr. Benson Rowe, B. H. Schulte, and Kirk Smith were wonderful fonts of information on their sport and Peck's place on their team. Richard Barthel, Elizabeth Guest Berryhill, John Brenneis, Betty Cobb, Grace Fretter, Mindy McCorkle, and Bill Musladin were equally helpful with regard to Peck's involvement in campus dramatics.

For background information on the Neighborhood Playhouse in New York and the teachers with whom Peck studied, I am grateful to the school's director and librarian, respectively Harold Baldridge and David Seminon, as well as David Pressman, assistant to the renowned acting teacher Sanford Meisner during Peck's tenure, and Eli Wallach, who graduated from the program a year before Greg.

As readers of this book will discover, Peck devoted considerable time from the 1960s on to a variety of nonprofit endeavors, political, cultural, and medical. For helping me to understand the actor's contributions in this regard, I must thank the renowned film composer Elmer Bernstein; Ernest Dilihay, Director of Performing Arts for the City of Los Angeles Cultural Affairs Department; the incomparable Isaac Stern; the first director of the American Film Institute, George Stevens Jr.; screenwriter Daniel Taradash; Marsha Bronstein of the Motion Picture Television and Relief Fund; and Peter Pershick, public relations officer for the Los Angeles Public Library. For insights into the establishment and operations of the La Jolla Playhouse, I am grateful to Peck's friend and cofounder, Mel Ferrer, as well as to Norman Lloyd and Harry Carey Jr., both of whom worked several times with the company, and to Jessica Padilla of the current Playhouse staff.

Of course, the heart of the story is Peck's motion picture career. During the course of my research, I managed to view every one of the actor's feature and TV films. I couldn't have done so without the help of Donovan Brandt, manager, Eddie Brandt's Saturday Matinee Video in North Hollywood, who made available some very hard-to-locate pictures. As always, one must pay tribute to the specialty libraries in New York and Los Angeles that are so vital to an endeavor of this sort and to their caring, hardworking staffs, notably the Billy Rose Theatre Collection, the

New York Public Library for the Performing Arts; the Louis B. Mayer Library, American Film Institute, B. Caroline Sisneros, Librarian; the University of California, Los Angeles, Arts Library Special Collections, Young Research Library, UCLA, under the purview of Julie L. Graham and Lauren Buisson; and the Special Collections of the Doheny Library, University of Southern California, directed by Ned Comstock and home of the Warner Bros. Collection, under the supervision of Noelle Carter. Of particular importance to this project was the Academy of Motion Picture Arts and Sciences' Center for Motion Picture Study, housed in the beautiful Margaret Herrick Library, where Peck has donated a sizable collection of papers and scripts. Thanks to the library's Howard Prouty and Barbara Hall, not only for their usual kindness and assistance, but also for granting me access to portions of the Peck Collection that were not yet catalogued, and to Doug Johnson, who located requested material from the collection. I must also express my appreciation to the friends and colleagues of Mr. Peck's who shared their recollections with me: Eddie Albert, Philip Alford, Michael Ansara, Desi Arnaz Jr., Polly Bergen, Lois Bonfiglio, Aida Bortnik, Phil Bowles, David Brown, Betty Comden and Adolph Green, Jeff Corey, Gordon Davidson, Maurice Denham, Charles Durning, Marty Ewing, Ferdinand Fairfax, David Field, Rhonda Fleming, Jane Fonda, Robert Forster, Rita Gam, Ray Gosnell Jr., Ron Grow, Harold Herman, Anne Heywood, Celeste Holm, Claude Jarman Jr., Dean Jones, John T. Kretchmer, Harvey Laidman, Piper Laurie, Jerry London, Virginia Mayo, Andrew V. McLaglen, Jayne Meadows, J. P. Miller, Roger Moore, Terry Morse, Dan O'Herlihy, Estelle Parsons, Arthur Penn, Joseph Sargent, Walter Schallert, Peter Stone, David Warner, Jane Wyman, Richard Zanuck, Don Zepfel, and Jonathan Zimmerman. Thanks as well to the agents, managers, and publicists who helped me reach these individuals.

For help locating photos, thanks go to John and Meghan Collins; Bob Cozenza, the Kobal Collection; Evelyn Hoffman, the Library Foundation of Los Angeles; Jeremy Megraw, the New York Public Library; David Semonin and Peter King, the Neighborhood Playhouse; Michael Shulman, Archive Photos; and Greg Williams, the San Diego Historical Society.

Finally, for assistance with other pieces of the puzzle, I want to acknowledge the efforts of Carleton Davis, the Cape Playhouse, in Dennis, Massachusetts; Delphine, the American Society of Cinematographers; Gina Marchese, Agency Department, AFTRA; Henry W. Maxwell, Archives Specialist, Jersey City Public Schools; author Gerard Molyneaux, whose bio-bibliography of Peck is an awesome piece of scholarship; Gary Morrison, Assistant Registrar, Columbia University;

John J. Norton, Senior Library Assistant, and Bruce Brandt, Supervising Library Assistant, New Jersey Room, Jersey City Public Library; Justin Pettigrew, Director, Public Relations, Turner Classic Movies; and Msgr. Francis J. Weber, Archivist, Archdiocese of Los Angeles, Mission Hills, California. On a personal note, thanks to Chris Faulkner, who helped to compile the filmography and preliminary research information; a friend, Daniel DiPlacido, who read the manuscript at an early stage and offered some helpful suggestions; my copyeditor, Virginia Clark; and, as always, my agent, Alexander Hoyt, my editor, Lisa Drew, and Lisa's assistant, Jake Klisivitch.

Introduction

Before anything else, there is the voice. Deep, rich, fluid, polished without being studied, it is a beautiful, natural instrument. Once heard, it is hard to forget and is instantly recognized. Then there is the face: a shock of black, somewhat unruly hair with a slight widow's peak over dark brows, hazel eyes, an aquiline nose, and full, sensual lips. It's a handsome face but not a vacuous one; its features suggest that its owner, Eldred Gregory Peck, is a man of character and intelligence. Which, indeed, he is. Finally, there is a rangy six-foot-two-inch frame, athletic-looking but not muscle-bound. Combined, the voice, the face, and the body are the calling cards of one of the most sought-after actors of his generation, a phenomenon who was signed to no less than four motion picture studios at the outset of his career and who was top-lined in his very first film. His friend Liza Minnelli once described him as "the ultimate movie star. You know, there's nobody more handsome or more gentle or more romantic on the screen, I think. For all ages."

He could easily have rested on his natural gifts, but he didn't. Not even close. As anyone who ever made a film with him could tell you, Greg Peck is one of the hardest-working actors in Hollywood history. "The first thing I do," he once explained, "is commit every line to memory. That's the easy part. Then I walk through the motions and read the lines. I shout the lines; I whisper them. The tilt of my head, the angle of my shoulders, my fingers, every inch of movement is rehearsed, then discarded or accepted, so that when I report to the set for work that morning, I've assembled the character to the best of my ability, and that goes on day after day when I am making a picture." For him, such preparation is a genuine labor of love. Because he considers acting a craft to be respected, not to be taken lightly—nor to be confused with the trappings of stardom. As he once said, "It's a little like being a cabinetmaker or a person who is skilled at putting things together. I enjoy the work for its own sake."

Peck would be the first to admit that he was frequently typecast. In Hollywood, the most successful movie stars carve out personas, qualities that audiences come to recognize and appreciate and want to see from picture to picture. Such movie stars become brand names, packaged like any other product. For John Wayne, it was the no-nonsense, straight-talking tough guy. For Jimmy Stewart, it was the awkward, aw-shucks boy next door. For Gregory Peck, it was the man of principle driven to almost any length to do what needed to be done. As one of his costars, Lee Remick, put it, "He represented, I guess, everything kind of strong and reliable and solid." In *Gentleman's Agreement*, for example, he was a crusading journalist out to expose anti-Semitism even at the risk of his own love life. In *Twelve O'Clock High*, he was an Air Corps general who ruined his own mental health to whip a battle-weary bomb group into combat readiness. In *Captain Horatio Hornblower*, he was the skilled naval commander willing to ignore orders to pursue his own keen battle plan. Even in *To Kill a Mockingbird*, where he was a gentler type of hero—an attorney/father in a small Depression-era Southern town—he still risked economic ruin and ostracism from his neighbors to defend the rights of a black man.

The identity of a movie star with such a clearly etched persona usually becomes confused with that of his characters. Where does the role stop and the human being start? So it is fair to ask, "Is Gregory Peck a hero in real life?" His answer is characteristically modest: "No. Sometimes I've been courageous and sometimes less so." To be sure, he is more flawed, more complex, and more human than most of the figures he has portrayed on the big screen. An associate who worked with him in the 1990s described him as "withdrawn and introverted, private and compartmentalized." To which his wife Veronique added, "He is a man of strengths and weaknesses. . . . If I had to paint Greg, I would need a whole range of colors to do a portrait because there is great variation."

But he shares with his characters a passion for the ideals in which he believes. In his case, these include civil rights, gun control, and most of the other planks in the liberal Democratic Party canon. Unlike some, he has raised his voice publicly on behalf of these issues when the occasion warranted his involvement. So much so that, in the late 1960s, when former stars Ronald Reagan and George Murphy were assuming high office on behalf of the California Republicans, Peck was often mentioned as a candidate for the Democrats. He probably could have garnered his party's nomination for governor had he wanted it. But Peck is interested in ideas and causes, not political power. Such offers were politely, but firmly, deflected.

Beyond his political activities, he is a good citizen. He has associated himself with a variety of nonpartisan issues over the years, from raising cancer awareness to helping establish a multiracial cultural center in Los Angeles to promoting the city's public library. Unlike many stars, he has not been content to simply lend his name to such philanthropic endeavors. Whenever such an activity has engaged his attention, he has worked tirelessly on its behalf—educating himself on the relevant facts and figures, logging miles and miles of travel time, and writing his own speeches.

His careers as actor and public citizen have taken him many times across the length and breadth of the United States and to countless places around the globe. Along the way he has truly become a member of the world community, a man of culture, wealth, and property, comfortable with heads of state and captains of industry, at home on the French Riviera, opening day at Ascot, and in the halls of the White House. To appraise him—with his ease of manner, his thoughtful, well-articulated utterances, his British-tailored attire—one would never guess that he is a small-town boy who had to struggle to find his place in this world. But that is, in fact, the case. The journey from where he began to where he is now is remarkable. To understand his incredible evolution, one must go back to his roots, to the tiny southern California village called La Jolla . . .

PART ONE

Eldred

CHAPTER 1

The Jewel

Today it boasts a celebrated oceanographic institute, a well-regarded regional theater, and a branch of the University of California, but the principal industry of La Jolla (pronounced "La Hoya") remains what it has always been—tourism. Blessed with a moderate climate, Mount Soledad to its rear, and a picture-perfect coastline, the centerpiece of which is a sheltered, rocky harbor called the Cove, the village more than lives up to its name—which according to popular theory, derives from "la Joya," Spanish for "the jewel."* With its sumptuous boutique-laden commercial district and million-dollar homes, it gives the impression of being a community unto itself, but it is actually the northernmost portion of California's southernmost city, San Diego.

San Diego was founded in 1789, but the area fourteen miles from downtown then known as La Jolla Park remained a pristine wilderness until the final decades of the nineteenth century. Although it offered nature lovers caves to explore, beaches for picnics and swimming, and an introduction to dolphins, seals, and other exotic marine life, getting there wasn't easy. Lacking a direct overland route, only the most intrepid travelers undertook the journey.

Then, in 1885, the Santa Fe railroad reached San Diego, kicking off a land boom. Two years later, as the boom was ending, La Jolla Park was sold in lots at a grand auction, thus opening the wilderness to development. A few dwellings were soon erected. They weren't elaborate permanent homes, but they did provide their owners with overnight accommodations, freeing them from the arduous trek back to town after a day's outing. Thus, even at its earliest stage of settlement, the character of La Jolla as a resort community was established. To give the same

*No one knows for certain the origins of the town's melodious name. Some believe it is sort of pseudo-Spanish for "the hollow," "La Hoyo." Others prefer an Indian word—spelled "Woolle," "Woole," or "Woholle"—which spoken sounds something like "Hoya." It means "hole in the mountains," a reference to the area's several caves.

opportunity to transients, construction began on a sumptuous hostelry, the La Jolla Park Hotel, in December 1887. It opened with great pomp on January 1, 1893, and burned three years later. Finally, in 1894, the San Diego Old Town and Pacific Beach Railway reached the coast, making La Jolla's charms far more accessible. To underscore the point, the railroad built a bathhouse for day visitors.

Over the next few decades, La Jolla took on the trappings of a permanent village. By the dawn of the twentieth century, it boasted about 350 residents, most of whom were white and well-educated, and more than 100 buildings.

And the boom was on. In one two-year period—encompassing 1906 and 1907—some 250 additional structures were erected, with thirty to forty more added each succeeding year until the stock market crash of 1929. "Quite a settlement has spung up here," a San Diego newspaper boasted as early as January 1901, adding, "The progress during the past year has been greater than in many other sections of the state."

Among those drawn to the bustling little resort community was a twenty-four-year-old Easterner by the name of Gregory Pearl Peck.* However, he didn't come to town as a tourist. A recent graduate of the University of Michigan with a degree in pharmacology, he wanted to establish a local drugstore.

Peck was born in upstate New York on August 3, 1886. His mother, Catherine Ashe, had arrived in America two years earlier at the age of twenty. Named for her mother, the former Katherine Prenderville, Catherine hailed from Aniscaul near Dingle in County Kerry, Ireland, where her father, John, was a farmer. The Ashes were typical black Irish. They were also patriots; a cousin of John's, Thomas Ashe, would even became a hero of the 1916 Easter Uprising, dying in a British jail.

It took great courage for a young woman to brave the rough Atlantic crossing in the 1880s, but hard times had left Catherine Ashe with little choice. So devastating was the great potato famine of 1846 that some thirty-five years later, the country still lay in economic ruin. At least Catherine had relatives with whom she could stay upon her arrival in America. Thus, she found herself in Rochester, a medium-size industrial city in the western part of New York, some 350 miles from Manhattan. There, she eventually met and married a young local of English descent by the name of Samuel Peck.

Sam died of diphtheria when son Gregory was only eleven months old, so Catherine arranged for passage—in steerage—back to the fam-

*Gregory Pearl Peck is the father of the film star.

ily farm in Ireland. Relatives met the boat in Cork and carried mother and child by horse-drawn carriage to Aniscaul. In short order, young Gregory was integrated into the local family circle, becoming a close friend to his cousins. Their favorite game was to grab hold of an iron-rimmed cartwheel as it careened down a country lane. The trick was to pull free when the wheel hit a paved road. Once Gregory failed to relinquish his hold at the opportune time, an error that cost him half a finger.

Conditions in Ireland had scarcely improved since Catherine first left for America and, after a half dozen years or so, she decided to take Gregory back to New York. By then, the lad had acquired a hint of a brogue, which he never quite lost. Once again, Catherine proved herself an intrepid woman. Enrolling young Gregory in a Catholic school, she became a traveling saleslady, selling corsets and other ladies' undergarments out West. In time, she became so successful that she was able to purchase an apartment building in San Diego. The rent from her sixteen apartments enabled her and her son to live quite comfortably in an adjoining bungalow. They even had funds to make periodic visits to the family in Ireland as well as to Hawaii and Australia, where sisters of hers had settled. Eventually, Catherine remarried, to a fellow named James Gilpin.

By 1910 Catherine was well positioned to help her son enter the promising ranks of La Jolla merchants. For a year, Gregory clerked at H. L. Setchel's Drug Store on Girard Street, the only such establishment in La Jolla at the time. A year later, he acquired the store—with funds given to him for that purpose by his mother—and the establishment became Peck's Drug Store. As with most members of his profession, Gregory was soon dubbed "Doc." A testament to the pharmacy's place in the fabric of the young community was an ad that appeared in the *La Jolla Herald* in March 1912: "Peck's Drug Store, The Store You Have Always Patronized, A Clean-up-to-date stock of Pure Drugs, Medicines and Chemicals." Toilet articles and stationery could also be found in the emporium.

Like most enterprising young merchants, Peck found it helpful to become part of the village's social scene. So he joined the town baseball team and the band. He certainly had no trouble attracting the ladies. Photos of him reveal a man of striking good looks, a tall, slender fellow with coal black hair, an aquiline nose and full mouth, and a pronounced cleft in his chin (in subsequent years he grew a mustache).

For several years, Doc was content to play the field romantically. A fun-loving companion who enjoyed pranks and a good joke, he was one of the more eligible bachelors in the village. Then, in 1914, he fell in love.

* * *

The object of Doc's affections, Bernice May Ayres, was not a local girl. She was born in St. Louis in 1894, making her eight years his junior. Her father, John Daggett Ayres, had, according to family lore, captained the sort of riverboats that traversed the Missouri and Mississippi rivers in the nineteenth century. In later years, he held a variety of jobs—game warden, clerk, secretary, and solicitor.

Unlike Doc Peck, whose mother was an immigrant, Bernice had had family in America since at least the time of the Revolutionary War. The Ayres, primarily of English and Scottish descent, had traditionally resided in New York. It was William, a farmer, who established the clan in St. Louis, in 1840. Marriage to Elizabeth Daggett tied William to one of the city's most prominent local families; she was the granddaughter of former mayor John Dickinson Daggett and was descended from one of the original *Mayflower* settlers.

Folks on Bernice's mother's side, the Forses, arrived in St. Louis twenty years after William Ayres. They hailed from Pennsylvania. In fact, family records indicate that a Thomas Forse Sr. resided in that state's Chester County as early as 1775, a year before the signing of the Declaration of Independence. He was a grocer who owned his own store.

Bernice's mother, Katherine Forse Ayres—who would play a crucial role in the movie star's life—had been born in Pittsburgh in 1853, prior to the Forse family's arrival in St. Louis. According to her great-granddaughter, Mary McKillop, Katie, as she was called, was "very round and short. She had very dark hair." Later the hair turned white and was worn pulled back in a bun. Her appearance spoke volumes about her personality. Said Mary, "She was very robust. When you see her face, you can tell there was a lot of kindness but a lot of strictness." Katie and her husband, John, were so much in love that, when he was away from her for any length of time, he sent her romantic poems. She was heartbroken when he died on February 9, 1912.

Bernice was Katie's youngest daughter. There were two other girls plus four boys. Bernice's closest sister, Myrtle, about four years her senior, had married a La Jolla resident, Charles Rannells, then an employee of Railway Express. It was on a visit to Myrtle in 1914 that Bernice, known as Bunny, met the town druggist, Doc Peck.

Unlike most of the women in her family, Bunny was quite short, but she had beautiful features, wavy hair, and was always stylishly dressed. A local paper described her as "a blonde of striking type." Photos of her and Doc suggest a woman who was as lively and fun-loving as she was pretty.

The wedding took place on June 4, 1915, at the cathedral in St. Louis; Bernice, raised an Episcopalian, had converted to her husband's religion, Catholicism. Doc arranged for a fellow pharmacist, E. E. Rutsch, to care for the store in his absence.

The couple honeymooned in San Francisco, where they took in the Panama-Pacific Exposition, a world's fair staged to mark the completion of the Panama Canal, and then returned to La Jolla. Before the journey east, Doc had purchased a home for them on Fay Street, the La-Lo-O-Mi cottage (at that time, houses in La Jolla had names rather than addresses, a quaint custom that persisted until 1918, when the post office initiated the home delivery of mail).

Although Bernice had worked as a phone company switchboard operator prior to her marriage, she now settled into a life of domesticity. As her son, the actor, later put it, "My mother was brought up in the old-fashioned way—to be a housewife and a mother and to be with and look after her man." She also had her mother to look after, for Katie came to live with the newlyweds only five days after their return from their honeymoon.

Bunny would soon have someone else to care for as well. Two months after the wedding, she discovered that she was pregnant.

The child was born in the family cottage on April 5, 1916. The fifth of April was an auspicious date for a would-be movie star, for Spencer Tracy (1900), Melvyn Douglas (1901), and Bette Davis (1908) share it with Peck. Of her only child, Bunny later said proudly, "He was a big baby. Weighed 10 pounds."

Gregory was a family name—it had been given to Doc to honor his mother's grandfather, Gregory Coke. But Bunny didn't want her son to be Gregory Peck Jr. She preferred that he have a name of his own, something that sounded distinguished. Paging through the phone book, she chose Eldred—but kept Gregory as a middle name. The choice proved an unpopular one with its owner. As soon as the child was able to make his feelings known, he told his parents that he would have preferred something more common. "You want to be a Dick or Bob or Jim," he later explained. "There's no nickname for Eldred." His relatives took to calling him Sonny, but in school the hated moniker was retained.

By the time of the child's birth, Doc no longer had his own store. He had sold it the previous November to Dr. C. C. Reed of Lincoln, Illinois. According to his son, Doc lost the business because he was "too good-natured, he trusted people and didn't ask them to pay their bills." The more practical Bunny attempted to collect the debts herself but was chastised by her husband. "How dare you go knocking on people's doors asking for money?" he asked. "We need it," she replied. "The money's ours and without it, we're in big trouble."

Doc was cavalier about more than just outstanding debts. He liked sports, hunting and fishing, and other recreational activities too much to pay sufficient attention to the running of his business—or to his accountant, who managed to abscond with his scant profits. Doc's son later maintained that his father could have obtained a bank loan and rescued the enterprise but lacked the drive for such a task. He chose instead to work for the man who bought him out. A year later, he became the night-shift pharmacist for Ferris & Ferris, a San Diego firm with which he spent the rest of his career. Doc's change in fortune forced the family to abandon their home in La Jolla and move into an apartment in town, near Ferris & Ferris. By then, the Peck marriage was in trouble.

Doc and Bunny separated when Eldred was two, forcing Mrs. Ayres to move in with her other La Jolla–based daughter, Myrtle, and Myrtle's husband, Charles Rannells. After several attempts at reconciliation, Bunny filed for divorce on February 3, 1921. In her petition to the Superior Court for the County of San Diego, Bunny accused Doc of abusive behavior. He hurled profanities at her on a daily basis, she claimed, and on two occasions struck her physically. She also asserted that, in October 1917, as she endured extreme pain due to appendicitis, he refused to send for a doctor. Finally, after two days he relented, but only after her appendix had burst. Moreover, she maintained that on at least one occasion he accused her and her sister Myrtle of going out for an evening in order to pick up men. This led to an altercation between Doc and Myrtle's husband, Charles, after which the Rannells refused to visit the Peck household. Finally, Bunny alleged that Doc was abusive to Eldred, frequently threatening to "knock the hell out of him." Her allegations were persuasive enough to lead Superior Court judge C. N. Andrews to issue a restraining order against Doc, preventing him from "interfering with the actions of" his wife, "molesting" her, or "preventing her from having free access" to their home and other jointly held property. While the legal action was proceeding, Doc repeatedly pleaded with Bunny to take him back. Finally, she relented and withdrew the petition for divorce on February 16.

Eighty years after the fact, it is difficult to know what to make of Bunny's allegations. Neither she nor Doc nor, for that matter Myrtle or Charles Rannells, are still alive to tell their stories. Eldred—that is, the film star Gregory Peck—has never acknowledged an abusive element to the marriage. He maintains that money and the difference in his parents' ages were the principal causes for their estrangement. Moreover, he has always spoken fondly of his father, with no hint that Doc was ever abusive to him. Indeed, he emphatically told this author, "Nothing like that ever happened," adding that the idea of his father physically mistreating him was "impossible. If you knew my dad, it is impossible." Of course, one must also remember that, in the 1920s, divorce was relatively uncommon, and it was far more difficult to dissolve a marriage then than it is today. It is quite possible that Doc simply allowed Bunny to charge him as she did in order to facilitate the termination of their relationship. However, the number and specificity of the allegations—and the issuance of the restraining order—are difficult to ignore.

In any event, the reconciliation didn't last long. On July 19, only five months after withdrawing her petition for divorce, Bunny left Doc again, this time for good. Once again, she sought to dissolve the union and, on July 30, the divorce was granted. Doc was ordered to pay $30 per month in alimony and $20 per month in child support.

Some fifteen months later, Bunny returned to St. Louis. Although her mother and sister Myrtle remained in La Jolla, she still had relatives in her hometown, most notably her oldest brother, Albert. For a time, Eldred stayed in San Diego with his father. As he turned six in April 1922, he even enrolled in a local school. But shortly thereafter, his parents decided that he should be with Bunny, so Doc arranged for the boy's train passage—unaccompanied by an adult—to St. Louis. "I remember my Dad tipping the Pullman porter ten dollars to look after me," Peck recalled. "It seemed a tremendous amount of money. The porter did take care of me very well, saw that I got my meals, saw that I was okay during the day, and made up my berth at night." The trip lasted two and a half days, which must have been a daunting experience for a six-year-old boy. But Peck said, "I wasn't scared. It was a big adventure, and my mother met me at the depot in St. Louis."

By then, Bunny had resumed her premarriage occupation—switchboard operator—and had rented rooms for herself and her son at 4715 A Washington, not far from her mother's former residence. More boardinghouse than apartment complex, the residence was home to a variety of shop clerks, waiters, and traveling salesmen. Presiding over this undistinguished little group was a busty redheaded landlady whom Peck later likened to Tallulah Bankhead.

Far older, larger, and more diverse demographically than any place the young Peck had previously known, St. Louis inspired his entrepreneurial skills. He and his landlady's son took to hawking newspapers at street corners, barking out the day's headlines in the time-honored tradition. They had a good location, an intersection where the trolley cars stopped, only a half block away from their home.

He augmented his wages by taking advantage of Prohibition, then in its third year. Once or twice a week, during the poker games staged by the boardinghouse residents, he would sell lemonade at a nickel a glass to soften his landlady's bathtub gin. For ten cents more, he'd also shine the shoes of the penny-ante players. It was a racy time, the "Jazz Age," but the boy enjoyed a few wholesome recreations. Occasionally, his mother would take him for an outing on Creve Coeur Lake or treat him to the movies.

Bunny didn't remain in St. Louis long. After about six months, she and Eldred traveled to San Francisco, where she had another brother, Ben. The boy attended school there for a brief period of time, but mother and son soon returned to La Jolla. There, for $25 a month, Bunny rented a bungalow for herself, Eldred, and her mother and hired on as a waitress in a tea room. She didn't care for her situation, however. She chose instead to move to Los Angeles, where she got a job as a telephone receptionist for an advertising agency.

Although Doc had cared for Eldred before the boy went to St. Louis, he was working nights and in no position to be a fulltime single parent, so Bunny left her son with her mother.

To be uprooted so frequently and finally abandoned by one's parents at such an impressionable age must have been extremely painful. But, as an adult, Peck would refuse to blame either Bunny or Doc. "My parents were good people," he asserted, "and it's not that they didn't love me, but they split up when I was very young, and they went in two different directions."

Living with Katie in a little redwood bungalow at 7453 High Avenue did have its compensations. Indeed, Peck would look back on his years with his grandmother as "the happiest time in my childhood."

For starters, she made wonderful sugar donuts. More important, she and Eldred lived right next door to Myrtle and Charles Rannells and their four kids (three girls and a boy). Thus, for the first and only time as a child, Eldred could enjoy the company of relatives close to his age in a stable family environment. He was even able to own a dog: Bud, a brown-and-black mongrel that was part Airedale. "We adopted each other one day when I was on my way home from school," he recalled. "I happened to have a leftover sandwich in my lunch pail. He looked hungry. And after I fed him he followed me home. Never did find out where he came from."

Unfortunately Bud liked to bark, which disturbed the neighbors. As a consequence, one day in 1924 Eldred returned from an outing on Santa Catalina Island to find the dog gone. Katie told him that Bud had run off, but, in fact, she had been forced to get rid of him. Peck never learned if his pal had been put to sleep or given away. It was another traumatic loss in his young life. "For the next forty years," he later said, "I always took a second look at every black-and-brown mongrel I saw."

Rather than pursue the moneymaking ventures that had engaged him in St. Louis, young Peck relaxed into the resort mentality of La Jolla. Like most kids living in an oceanside community, he grew addicted to the water, becoming a champion crab catcher and a strong swimmer and diver. But building boats was his passion. In fact, at the age of nine, he decided that, when he grew up, he wanted to design and construct watercraft for a living. In the meantime, he devoted a major portion of each summer to cobbling together a new vessel.

On one such occasion, he and a friend, Johnny Buchanan, tried their hands at constructing a boat from a professional design. They pooled their money to purchase a blueprint, and proceeded to saw, sand, nail together, and caulk their craft in Katie's backyard. The result, which they called *The Tar Baby,* did them proud on its maiden voyage. But it was moored on a beach when a fierce storm erupted unexpectedly. The boat was wrecked.

Most other summers, Eldred "designed" his boats himself. They usually lasted about as long as *The Tar Baby.* Once, he was forced to abandon ship at sea and swim to shore. Collapsing in exhaustion on the beach, he was found by a search party and taken to an elderly doctor, who treated him for exposure. Eldred was so impressed by the physician that he abandoned his plan to become a boat builder, opting to be a doctor instead.

Young Peck relished the outdoor life, including fishing, hunting, and camping. His rugged adventures were often shared with his father, who came to visit him from San Diego every Thursday, his day off. In the days when Bud was still around, the dog would join them on their outings. Once they reached open country, Eldred, convinced the dog was part greyhound, would persuade Doc to let Bud race against his automobile, a Nash. The dog usually won.

When Doc had vacation time, he would take his son on longer excursions. They went to Yosemite and Yellowstone national parks. But their favorite destination was Santa Catalina Island, a popular vacation spot a bit to the north of La Jolla. Although the island boasted a luxury hotel, the Pecks usually roughed it in tents. They'd swim and cast for fish, and sometimes Doc would play golf with his son as caddy. Occasionally, for the sake of the boy, Bunny would come down for a weekend; on those rare occasions, Eldred could pretend that he was like any other kid, living with his mother and father. But Bunny's visits, whether to Catalina or La Jolla, were relatively rare. After all, she had a job in Los Angeles, about 100 miles away, and the coastal roads in the 1920s were not very good. Consequently, time with her was to be treasured. Then, in 1926, she married a business machinery salesman named Joseph Maysuch (originally Masucci) and moved with him to San Francisco. After that, her visits with her son became even more infrequent.

When Doc was not around, Eldred often enjoyed the company of other relatives. One uncle had a ranch, where the boy learned to ride and play at cowboy. Charley Rannells, no longer with Railway Express, operated a feed and grain store out of a large barn built around 1880. "We spent a lot of time there in the summers," Peck recalled. "There was a big hayloft and it was cool and dark, a great place to hide away from everyone."

Uncle Charley was kind of a character. A silver miner in his youth, he'd once gotten into a drunken bar fight, after which he gave up liquor. He simply wouldn't allow any alcoholic beverages in his home. Often on Sunday, Eldred would accompany the Rannells clan to church—even though he was Catholic and they were Episcopalians. Afterward, Myrtle would cook a roast chicken dinner with stuffing. Charley loved her recipe. "After his second or third helping," Peck recalled, "he would always sit back and say, 'Yessir, that's the best dressing in the world. Myrt's really got a secret.' What he never found out was the secret: Aunt Myrt used to put about a pint of bourbon in her recipe."

Charley's father was a veteran of the Civil War. Every day, this elderly gentleman would establish himself on a chair under a tree in front of the feed barn. Peck remembered him as "a lean, leathery, clear-eyed old man, a solid nineteenth-century character who had had a very exciting life. He was full of wonderful stories, and almost any kid could get a yellow token from him good for a nickel's worth of candy at the sweet shop. Naturally, he was a favorite with all the youngsters. And I think he loved all of them genuinely."

Grandpa Rannells was not the only Civil War veteran in La Jolla. "There were maybe forty or fifty of them," Peck recalled, "all illustrious old characters in their seventies and eighties, the grandfathers of people who lived in the town. We knew them in everyday life. But their great day was the Fourth of July. They put on their old uniforms, both the blue and the gray, and their decorations, and they were much honored. I remember the feeling of excitement, and the tremendous pride, and the sense of romance. Now I feel very lucky to have that memory of seeing those fine old boys marching up and down the streets. At the time, it made me feel as if I were the inheritor of that great tradition. It still gives me some sense of connection with nineteenth-century America that has meant a great deal to me."

Another episode from Peck's youth also served as a reminder of the Civil War era, this one not so glorious. One night a group of young men burned a cross on Mount Soledad, then rode through the village streets wearing white sheets and yelling. "None of us youngsters knew what it was all about," he said. "But even with the sheets we could recognize some of the hot bloods of the town. They made quite an impression on us. I was told later they were trying to impress a family of colored folks who had moved into town. They were domestics, and I expect they wanted to be closer to their work. I don't know if they were frightened. But I know I was. The scene has been vivid in my memory ever since."

Such episodes were rare. For the most part, life in La Jolla in the 1920s was restful. Said Peck, "We played games like Parcheesi, or on long summer evenings we had run-sheep-run games with home base under the corner street lamp." Kids wore denim overalls and went barefoot in summer. They climbed tree houses and rolled down neighborhood streets inside old rubber tires. "We always had so much to do," he concluded, "we didn't worry about being entertained."

Besides, Eldred knew how to entertain himself, devoting himself to books almost from the moment he learned to read. "I got my first library card at age six in La Jolla," he recalled. His first reading matter was a series of tales about cavemen and cave children. Later he developed a fondness for Westerns, particularly the sagas of Zane Grey. Reading would remain a lifelong passion.

He also fell in love with the movies, a pastime shared by his grandmother. They'd take in a picture show at least once a week and sometimes more. He particularly liked cowboy stars Hoot Gibson and Tom Mix and the intrepid German shepherd Rin Tin Tin, but he was exposed to a wide variety of fare. In 1925, for example, Katie took him to see Lon Chaney in *The Phantom of the Opera.* Peck recalled, "I was positively stunned. After the picture we walked home and I held my grandmother's hand all the way. It wasn't until we got halfway home that I realized she was as frightened as I was. We were walking right down the middle of the street, terrified of the dark sidewalks." The following year, they caught Lillian Gish in *The Scarlet Letter.* Eldred didn't understand the meaning of the *A* that Gish's character had to wear across her chest, and Katie wasn't about to explain the concept of adultery to him. When Warner Bros. introduced sound with *The Jazz Singer* starring Al Jolson, Eldred and Katie became even more enthusiastic movie buffs. "We would take the trolley car downtown on Sunday," he recalled, "and try to hit two, maybe three, talkies."

Then one day he stumbled upon the actual making of a film. He and his grandmother happened to be walking along a cliff overlooking the Cove. As they gazed down, Peck could see a yacht anchored nearby and a couple of rowboats ferrying passengers to the shore. On the beach, a fellow in a yachting cap, blue blazer, and white trousers and sporting a long cigarette holder was cavorting with a bunch of bathing beauties. The fellow, Peck later learned, was Lew Cody. Nearby a camera was recording the action. Peck remembered that all of the actors had "orange paint on their faces and black lips and black eye shadow—certainly they weren't like any people I'd ever met in La Jolla." It was one of the most memorable experiences of his childhood.

Katie fostered Eldred's love of movies, but she was a major influence in more basic matters as well. A religious woman, she would read him stories from her Bible. Eldred was fascinated—"not so much with the lessons and doctrines," he later explained, "but with all the wonderful stories and tales of adventure and mayhem."

The boy loved his grandmother, the Rannells, and his other relatives, but they could not take the place of a father and a mother, living together with him, their son, under one roof. One of the things he missed out on was meeting up with his parents at mealtimes to share the events of the day. As he put it, "I never remember once sitting around a dinner table with my family and having an ordinary kind of family conversation." Rather than raging against the loss of a normal childhood, instead of acting out and becoming a discipline problem or, alternatively, the class clown, he internalized his feelings. He kept to himself, learned to hide his emotions under a pleasant but unassuming demeanor. He was something of a loner. He didn't join teams and have hoards of friends; he followed more solitary pursuits—reading, watching movies, swimming, fishing, building boats. As he later put it in a rare moment of self-revelation, "I was lonely, withdrawn, full of self-doubt."

The coping mechanisms developed in childhood often stay with an individual for life. As an adult, Gregory Peck would earn fame, wealth, love, and respect—from his peers as well as fans and critics. But a part of him would always remain shut off from others. The walls he built in La Jolla would never fully come down.

CHAPTER 2

A Lonely Boy

While living with his grandmother, Eldred attended the La Jolla Elementary School at the intersection of Gerard and Marine Streets, part of the San Diego school district. It was there that he appeared in his first play, his fifth-grade class's production of *Pandora's Box,* based on the Greek myth. "As I recall," he said, "I was resplendent in a green velvet vest. I was the one who opened the box." But he wasn't happy about the casting; he thought acting was for sissies and girls.

His attitude changed somewhat the following summer. While attending camp, he assayed the role of a traveler attacked by bandits and left for dead along a roadside. This time, he enjoyed the make-believe. Perhaps it was the more violent, earthy nature of the piece—whose name has been lost to time—that made the difference. But he still considered the theater unmanly and refused to pursue the interest further.

His other principal memory from elementary school centered on an old-fashioned pair of high-button shoes that his grandmother had given him. Knowing that she had meant to bring him pleasure, he wore the gift even though none of his classmates were similarly shod. The shoes were a source of acute embarrassment. "I suffered agonies," he recalled. "I used to hide my feet as much as possible, and the only thing I noticed about a schoolmate was his footgear." Despite his feelings, he wore the hated shoes until they wore out; to him, that seemed to take years.

It is perhaps significant that Peck's two most vivid memories from his early school days centered on an activity that he didn't enjoy and footwear that set him apart from the other kids. As an adult, he virtually never reminisced about teachers, friends, social activities, or the quality of education from this period, strongly suggesting that the experience had little impact upon him. He didn't distinguish himself academically or in sports or in any other fashion. He was simply there. School was where he was supposed to be, so he went—and got by as best he could.

Junior high was another matter.

* * *

"Maybe my mother and father decided I was having too much fun in La Jolla," Peck once said. "Or that I needed discipline." In any event, his parents decided in 1927 to send him away—to Los Angeles and St. John's Military Academy, a combination elementary school and junior high school run by an order of Catholic nuns. Fronting West Washington Boulevard in South Central L.A., the academy had started as a combination residence for working girls, orphanage, and old folks' home, all supervised by the Irish Sisters of Mercy. It was the Archbishop of Los Angeles and San Diego, John J. Cantwell, who instituted the change. Believing that young women, orphans, and the elderly were being adequately serviced elsewhere, he argued that what the community lacked was an academy for boys in need of a firm hand. So he asked the Sisters to convert the buildings to such a purpose.

The reconstituted institution opened in 1918. It featured two divisions, a lower form (elementary school) and an upper form (junior high). The nuns administered the school, taught the academic subjects, and supervised the younger boys. Retired soldiers were hired to provide military instruction and training, coach sporting activities, and supervise the older boys' dormitories.*

The students' day began with reveille at six o'clock, followed by mass three times a week. There were daily inspections and drills. Dinner was at six-thirty in the evening, with taps at nine. Peck considered it "the nearest thing to Sing-Sing that I've ever been in."

He particularly disliked the mind-numbing regimentation, recalling, "We had to shine our shoes every day like little robots getting ready for shoe inspection. We would get out of bed in the morning and have to stand at attention." After a quick shower and the rush to get dressed, he and his classmates marched to the dining room for breakfast, where, as with all meals, they ate in silence. As expressed in the school's literature, the purpose of such regimentation was to teach each cadet that he was part of a larger whole, to subordinate "his whims and desires to the needs of the group." Harsh discipline helped the more rebellious youngsters learn to fit in.

Beyond the military system, there were the demands of the church. In addition to the triweekly religious services, the students prayed before and after meals, before and after classes, and before going to sleep. As

*By 1964, the neighborhood surrounding the academy had deteriorated to the point where it seemed advisable to relocate, and a new facility was constructed in the San Fernando Valley. There, St. John's graduated its last class in 1968, after which the grounds were leased and eventually sold to the Marianist Brothers, who now operate the junior high division of Chaminade High School on that site.

Peck later joked, "From the time we woke up until the time we went to bed at night they had us hemmed in."

The academy chaplain, Father Timothy Crowley, and most of the nuns were Irish immigrants; given his own ties to the "ould sod," Eldred felt comfortable with them. At age twelve, he even became an altar boy. "I got very thoroughly indoctrinated," he recalled, "getting up at 5:30 each morning, so that I could go to the sacristy to lay out the priest's garments and to pour the sacramental wine. Then I would put on my robe and my white lace to serve the mass. I knew the whole routine, and at that time mass was still done in Latin. I knew each response by heart, when to ring the bells, when to swing the incense burner, and somehow I took to that." Perhaps, he later mused, it was the performer in him that responded to the ritual: taking his cues from the bells, knowing his lines, playing the role of acolyte, to him these represented a kind of theater.

Although the code of the military was less inspiring, Eldred had, by age thirteen, sufficiently distinguished himself on the drill field to become a cadet captain, in command of some sixty first-formers in Company D. He drove his unit unmercifully, determined that they would win the school's gold medal for excellence—which they did. "I shouted at them like Erich von Stroheim," he recalled. "God knows what I did to the psyches of those poor little kids."

By then, he had adjusted to school life; he even became editor of the monthly newspaper, the *Bugle Call.* Still, he eagerly anticipated the end of each month, when the students could leave St. John's for a weekend home. On Friday afternoon, he would take the trolley to Union Station, in downtown Los Angeles, and catch the Santa Fe train to San Diego. His father would invariably be waiting for him when he arrived.

He relished this time with his dad, but his grandmother, Catherine Peck Gilpin, had developed cancer of the uterus. As Doc and she again shared the bungalow of his youth, her illness cast a pall over Eldred's visits during his first year at St. John's. From his room, he could her moaning in agony, and the sour odor emitted by her wasted body was impossible to ignore. Still, he took time to read her the daily newspaper. She tried to be cheerful when he entered the room, but she was usually in too much pain to focus on current events. Finally, on May 19, 1928, she passed away; her grandson was back at school at the time.

After three years at St. John's, Peck graduated in spring 1930. Without question, the academy left its mark on him. As he noted, "One of the things that you didn't do there was quit anything once you'd started. You went to the finish." Such self-control would remain with him for the rest of his life, as would the sense of duty fostered at St. John's. Looking back on his military school experience, he said, "It was apparently what I needed, discipline and order," and he got it. By the time he was fourteen, many of the core elements of his adult personality had been established.

Peck left Los Angeles, but he didn't resume his pre–St. John's life in La Jolla. Perhaps, at age seventy-seven, Katie Ayres wasn't up to the task of supervising an adolescent. Instead, he moved in with his father.

During the 1920s, San Diego was enjoying a period of significant economic development. As the decade progressed, the population nearly doubled, from 74,000 to 140,000. A focal point of activity was the city's port, which was becoming a major shipping center. The navy and the marines established bases and training centers in town, and the nascent aerospace industry found a home there as well. The city had a bustling nightlife, with numerous movie theaters and clubs featuring raucous entertainment, even the occasional speakeasy.

As Ferris & Ferris was the town's only all-night pharmacy, Doc and, to some extent, Eldred encountered all manner of rough folk—sailors, merchant seamen, burlesque dancers and comics, traveling carnival barkers and roustabouts. Father and son lived not too far from the store, on the outskirts of the downtown area—in the bungalow at 2205 Broadway that Doc had inherited from his mother along with the apartment complex next door.

As Doc worked nights, he would have dinner with Eldred most evenings before leaving for the store. Returning home in the morning, he'd briefly chat with his son, then go off to sleep. Otherwise, Eldred was left to his own devices. He found this situation disconcerting, particularly after the tightly structured regimen he'd experienced at St. John's. "Little by little, though, I was learning to be on my own," he recalled. "I realized that if I didn't make things happen myself, no one else was going to."

In fall 1930, he enrolled as a sophomore at San Diego High School, an imposing ivy-covered building of masonry and gray-colored stone. It was dubbed the Gray Castle, for the Gothic-style, turreted facade that flanked the front entrance.

Eldred, one of about 450 students in the Class of 1933, never rose above the near-invisible mass. Lacking career direction and an adult to ensure that he devoted time to his studies, he was an undistinguished student. His only extracurricular activities were a small role in an all-male variety show called Boy's Hi Jinx and membership in the glee club. Even with his fellow choristers, he lacked confidence. Once, for example, a contest was held to select a new school song. Eldred worked hard on his composition. However, each author was required to perform his offering in front of his colleagues. "When my turn came," he said, "I froze. I was just too shy to get up in front of all these people and sing. Naturally, my song lost."

Although he shot up to six feet two and a half inches while in high school—growing eleven inches between the ages of fifteen and seventeen—he was skinny and gawky, adept at neither football, baseball, nor basketball. He participated in intramural sports at school, but his principal athletic outlet was crew, having joined the San Diego Rowing Club. Meanwhile, he idolized the star of the varsity football team. "I was too shy to speak to him," he recalled, "but I used to watch him, admire everything he did, and glow over his triumphs."

He also envied the fellow's way with girls, another department in which Eldred was wanting. Mostly, he found his female classmates a mystery, not surprising given his lack of sisters, infrequent contact with his mother, and his enrollment in an all-boys military academy. In the hope of feeling more comfortable with the opposite sex, he found the money for dance instruction, responding to an ad in the local paper that proclaimed, "You can dance the foxtrot . . . for ten lessons, 12 dollars." He became fairly accomplished on the ballroom floor, but the basic insecurity remained.

The irony is that girls were interested in *him.* For starters, he was a nice young man—and polite. And he was handsome; his senior year photo shows an attractive, clean-cut fellow, a younger version of the movie star he would become. A distant cousin, Helen Wetzel Wood, who was a grade behind him in high school, recalled at least two girls—both very pretty—who would have been happy to date him. But he didn't *feel* attractive; he felt clumsy and shy. Consequently, he didn't mingle well, not with girls nor with boys. "He was very much a loner," said Muriel Gutschall, who shared a commercial art class with him.

Emblematic of those years perhaps was Christmas Day, 1931. Doc came home in the morning, tired from work. He and his son exchanged gifts. Then the pharmacist went to bed. Left alone, the youngster decided to take a walk. The day was sunny, but, naturally, the streets were deserted. He strolled for miles, ending up at the athletic club where he and Doc were members. It was open, but no one else was around. With nothing else to do, he grabbed a basketball and shot hoops by himself. Later in the afternoon, he went solo to a movie. Finally, as night fell, he headed home. When his father woke up, the two of them went to a nearby café for an uninspiring dinner.

In frustration, Eldred decided to change his circumstances. The Pulitzer Prize–winning musical *Of Thee I Sing* was coming to town, and he wanted to see it. But mostly the show gave him a good excuse to approach a beautiful young woman who'd caught his eye. Screwing up his courage, he asked her to go with him, and she said yes. Ironically, what he remembered most about that night wasn't the girl or even *Of Thee I Sing.* His most vivid memory was of the time he spent with his date's father while waiting for her to appear. "I had supposed," he said, "that like my father and other men he was interested in sports, so I had boned up on all the latest scores in preparation. Turned out he didn't care at all about them. It was a dreadful wait."

Graduation came on June 16, 1933. In the 1930s, when few Americans went to college, such a milestone occasioned great ceremony. At San Diego High, the events leading up the big day included the senior play, *Oh Wilbur,* Ditch Day, the Senior Ball, and Class Day. The ceremony itself took place at an outdoor pavilion in Balboa Park.

In the fall, Peck followed several of his fellow high school grads to the San Diego State Teachers College, a commuter school founded in 1897 with an enrollment of approximately 1,400 students.* Mostly, he took the survey courses required of college freshmen everywhere. However, for an elective, he signed up for a class in public speaking, taught by Professor Paul Pfaaf. On one occasion, Pfaaf assigned Peck a passage from the play *The Emperor Jones,* by Eugene O'Neill. Without thinking about it, he acted out the selection. The startled professor encouraged the youngster to pursue acting as a career, but Peck was not particularly interested.

He did, however, take another class with Pfaaf, this one in theater. "I remember Peck's first presentation was the 'Nose Scene' from *Cyrano de Bergerac,*" said the professor, "and he did it quite well." Pfaaf liked the young man, noting, "He never made excuses for not being prepared. He did all his assignments with perception and understanding. He was always a very gracious boy." He also remembered the youngster as tall and slender with a deep tan. "He had dark, black hair that he kept perfectly combed. He wore a lot of pastel colors in those days and was quite sought after by the opposite sex."

As this comment would suggest, Peck started coming out of his shell a bit at State. He joined a fraternity, Epsilon Eta, and ran the quarter mile on the track team. Kenneth Stevenson, who knew him in high school as well as in college, recalled that on Saturday nights, he and Eldred would sometimes take in a downtown movie, then walk up to Doc's apartment. On the way, they would stop for chili and hot dogs at the Coney Island Red Hot. Stevenson also recalled going camping with Eldred at Doc's cabin in the country.

*The word "Teacher's" was dropped from the school name in 1935, while Peck was a student there. Today the institution is called San Diego State University.

In April 1934, Peck turned eighteen. Like many San Diego lads, he made the trip across the border to Tijuana. As he recalled it, the major attraction in the Mexican town was a place that showed French porn films. They were ancient but very erotic. After a screening, the aroused patrons could indulge themselves with the local bar girls if they wished.

Shortly thereafter, Eldred dropped out of school. He didn't consider the withdrawal permanent. But, lacking a firm career goal (although he still toyed with becoming a doctor), he decided to take a break and earn some money. He got a job with the Union Oil Company, beginning as a janitor or a night watchman; the accounts vary. In time, he was promoted to driver, transporting gasoline to the company's stations in the San Diego area. "Boy, that was a great moment," he said later. He loved everything about his new position, including his uniform and cap, which he insisted upon wearing at a rakish angle. He also cherished his truck, a large red vehicle with a trailer. But maneuvering it through the city streets required skill and patience, particularly since it was filled with tons of flammable liquid. Discovering that he was a good driver, he used some of his earnings—$125 a month—to purchase a vehicle of his own, a blue Model A Ford roadster with a white canvas top, a rumble seat, and wire wheels.

Peck needed the car, not just for daily transportation, but for dates. For, by then, he had fallen in love.

Exactly when he met Betty Clardy isn't clear.* According to a 1948 *Time* cover story, they were already dating when he was hired by Union Oil. In fact, he told *Time* that he took the job because he wanted to earn enough money to marry her. But, he has said elsewhere that he met Betty while working for the company. Either way, for the first time in his life, Eldred had a girl.

Betty Clardy was a lively young lady, who enjoyed picnics on the beach and playing touch football with her boyfriend as well as her two brothers, both of whom were friends of Eldred. Like Peck, Betty was Irish-American, but hers was a close-knit, loving family. Pretty soon, Eldred was spending more time at Betty's house than he was at his own. The Clardys became something of an adopted family, showering the reserved young man with meals and affection and showing him by example how a nurturing family unit behaved.

Between the Clardys and his job, Eldred was enjoying life. Then, one day, the company manager, Mr. Tilson, stopped him. Tilson complimented him on his performance, indicating that if he applied himself he might become a manager himself someday. Initially impressed, Eldred

*After he became famous, Peck referred to Betty in the media as "Kathie Moore" in order to preserve her anonymity. Now that she is deceased, he has given the author her real name.

asked his boss how much he earned. The manager replied that he made $300 a month. That was a good living in the Depression-ridden 1930s. But Peck wanted more. He also realized that a routine job in a relatively small city like San Diego was not for him. Although he was happy behind the wheel of his big red rig, he concluded that the time had come for him to consider his future—which meant going back to school and completing his education. He still didn't know what he wanted to do with his life, but at least with a degree, he might someday be in a position to choose the kind of work he would perform.

With his newfound ambition, he turned his attention toward the University of California. His grades weren't good enough for acceptance, so he reentered State, determined to qualify for a transfer. In this he had the support of the Clardys, who let him study at their home in the evenings. Betty, a good student, reviewed his assignments with him and quizzed him on the material.

Having a safe refuge with the Clardys was particularly important to Peck at this point, because things took a downturn at home. Doc had a girlfriend, Harriet Harrington, with whom Eldred didn't get along. A conservative Protestant from Denver, she was ill equipped to deal with a strapping eighteen-year-old college student. Conversely, he was annoyed by her straightlaced attitudes. They didn't quarrel; they just didn't care for one another.

Fueled by the desire to leave home, Peck studied even harder. And the work began paying off. For the first time in his life, he started earning A's and B's. With the dramatic improvement in his scholastic average came acceptance to the University of California.

Now that the boy was going off on his own, Doc proposed to Harriet, and she accepted. Marriage didn't improve the relationship between Eldred and his new stepmother. If anything, the situation was exacerbated by the arrival of her even more conservative mother, who moved in with her daughter and son-in-law. Shortly thereafter, Harriet gave birth to a child, Donald.

Despite these changes in his father's life, Eldred and Doc continued to have a warm relationship. Young Peck would also get along well with his stepbrother. But his focus was no longer on San Diego. In fall 1936, he set off for Berkeley to complete his education. He was eager to attend the prestigious university but couldn't possibly know how the experience would change his life.

CHAPTER 3

The Awakening

Founded in 1868, the University of California was comfortably ensconced in Berkeley, a community of some 82,000 located about twenty-five minutes by trolley from the business center of Oakland.

Then as now, some youngsters went to college with specific career goals in mind. But, at Cal, the professed objective was to produce men and women of culture with, to quote the *General Catalogue* for the 1935–36 academic year, "a basic knowledge of some one field of human intellectual endeavor." Character building was a second, also important, mission. In-state residents such as Peck could take a full course load for a mere $26 per semester, with the cost of books and other supplies an additional $10 or so.

Living accommodations were not included, as there was only one men's dorm, Bowles Hall, which had room for just a hundred residents or so. Everyone else lived in fraternity houses, club houses, or one of the boardinghouses approved by the university. Although Peck's mother and stepfather had an apartment in nearby San Francisco—and Eldred visited them on a regular basis—he lived in boardinghouses during his three years at Cal. Bunny would give him $10 on occasion, but he still needed to work to cover his expenses. For a time, he and his two roommates served as janitors for their boardinghouse. Their duties included emptying the garbage, sweeping the hallways, stoking the furnaces, and responding to the other tenants' complaints. Peck later admitted that he wasn't very good at his job, but it paid $40 a month, which covered his rent and netted him a bit extra.

Harkening back to his entrepreneurial youth in St. Louis, he also rented out parking spaces for two dollars apiece to visitors attending campus sporting events—without bothering to tell his customers that the lot was two miles from the stadium! "I once made eighty dollars that way," he boasted. In addition, he worked as a waiter-dishwasher at a café in the student co-op. For one hour's work, he was entitled to all the food he could eat. "I distinctly remember," he said, "sitting in the kitchen and devouring three steaks, heavy piles of mashed potatoes, and then three plates of pie and a quart of milk at a single sitting." Waiting tables at a sorority house, as he sometimes did, offered other compensations. Said Peck, "I was the fox in the hen house." He was still involved with Betty Clardy, but San Diego was six hundred miles away. There were too many temptations close at hand for the relationship to endure, and finally it ended.

Cal offered a marked contrast to San Diego State. Encompassing 530 acres, the campus was home in fall 1936 to 9,626 students, of which 7,564 were undergraduates. "Us kids, we thought of it as a kind of a factory," said one of Peck's classmates, John Brenneis. To avoid feeling like a tiny cog in a big machine, many youngsters centered their lives around one small group or another.

Eldred's group was the rowing team. In the 1930s, crew was not a major West Coast sport; it lacked the tradition and popularity it enjoyed at Harvard, Yale, Columbia, the Naval Academy, and other Eastern schools. Nevertheless, the nation's two powerhouses at that time were Cal and the University of Washington. Washington's Huskies, in fact, had represented the U.S. at the Berlin Olympics just prior to Peck's arrival in Berkeley, and Cal's Bears had taken the gold medal at the games of 1928 and 1932.

To be a good crewman, one had to be tall and muscular without carrying too much weight. Despite the Bears' impressive Olympic record, freshman coach Russ Nagler and varsity coach Ky Ebright had a difficult time attracting suitable candidates. During school registration, they would tie a string at the six-foot mark across the entranceway to the gym, where male students took the requisite physical exam. Anyone who stooped to enter the room was cornered and encouraged to sign up. Having rowed in San Diego, Peck may not have needed persuasion. Since he entered Cal as a junior, he was immediately eligible for the varsity and junior varsity squads, which together encompassed about forty-eight men.

Rowing is a grueling sport, eight guys in a boat pulling an average of twenty-eight or thirty strokes a minute. Today's races are 2,000-meter sprints, but in the 1930s, they were four miles and lasted around twelve minutes. Conditioning was paramount. As a consequence, crewmen were highly disciplined. They couldn't drink or smoke, and they had to watch what they ate. Moreover, since rowing at Cal was hardly on par with the likes of football, baseball, and basketball, it was, to quote Peck's fellow oarsman, B. H. "Buzz" Schulte, "a self-made glory."

Helping the youngsters maintain sound bodies was the responsibility of the coach, Carrol "Ky" Ebright, a short fellow with a rather prominent nose, receding chin, and rimless eyeglasses. "He didn't stand for any nonsense," Schulte recalled. He yelled, goaded, teased, whatever it took to motivate his boys. Ebright was a tough taskmaster off the water as well, insisting that his athletes excel in their studies. Perhaps as a consequence, crewmen had, according to Schulte, "the best grade record of any athletic group on the campus."

The discipline that the coach instilled in Peck reinforced his training at St. John's and the self-imposed regimen he'd employed in his final year at San Diego State. As he later put it, "Anyone who's rowed in a four-mile race knows what's expected of him. He understands . . . the agony of the last mile or half mile and the knowledge that you can't quit even if you die. That has to have some effect on his character." The desire to work hard, do his best, get things right would be hallmarks of Peck's character thereafter.

Although the team had enough crewmen to fill six boats, only two shells were entered in races against other schools, Oregon, UCLA, and Washington among them. In order to find the best eight-man combination for the varsity boat and the second best for JV, Ebright frequently shuffled his men during practice. Crew members were thus in competition with one another, even though they were teammates.

Still, the guys enjoyed a certain amount of camaraderie. Peck was liked by the other oarsmen, but his reserved nature kept him somewhat apart. "I wouldn't call him aloof or remote," said crewman Benson Rowe, "but he wasn't the kind of person you would think of as a buddy. He was just a nice, dignified, quiet, pleasant fellow that people liked but wasn't a pal."

Peck never made it past the junior varsity squad. He simply couldn't outpace crewmen as tall or taller who were also somewhat beefier. But he was a determined competitor. That quality earned him the respect of his coach and teammates—and his athletic letter.

The high point of each racing season came in June with the regatta sponsored by the Intercollegiate Rowing Association and held in Poughkeepsie, New York. Present were the two West Coast dynamos—Cal and Washington—and all of their Ivy League rivals except Harvard and Yale, which staged their own race. The Poughkeepsie regatta was a gala event, giving the youngsters from California a chance to mingle with their East Coast colleagues and to enjoy the enthusiastic crowds, some of whom followed the entirety of each event by means of a train that paralleled the racecourse on the Hudson River.

Each school sent an eight-man varsity crew to Poughkeepsie, along with an eight-man junior varsity crew, and two alternates for each boat.

Peck attended the regatta in 1938, but not as a designated crewman or alternate. He and another teammate, Frank Lawrence, stowed away in the baggage car of the train bearing the team, a common practice among Cal crewmen in those days.

Although his presence wasn't official, he was chosen to participate in an informal event at the regatta, usually composed of the teams' managers and/or alternates, and known as the "pickle boat" race. According to Peck, he and Frank Lawrence joined forces with two crewmen each from Navy, Washington, and Wisconsin, and their boat won.

No doubt Eldred enjoyed the regatta, but an even bigger thrill came when the race was over. Awarded Pullman car rides home from Ebright, he and Lawrence decided to sell their tickets and use the proceeds to visit New York City. Renting an inexpensive room at the YMCA, they did the town, visiting jazz joints in Harlem and Greenwich Village and catching a Broadway show, the musical *I Married an Angel.* The young students also walked across the Brooklyn Bridge, read Thomas Wolfe, and talked to winos on the Bowery. Eldred was entranced by all of it, particularly the Broadway show and its star, Vera Zorina.

After seeing all the major sights, the two crewmen were totally broke. On their final night, they had to move out of the Y and sleep under the stars in Central Park. Then they returned to Berkeley by train. With less than a dollar between them, they could only afford a bunch of bananas, which served as breakfast, lunch, and dinner throughout the uncomfortable four-day journey.

The Poughkeepsie regatta of June 1938 brought Peck's two-year rowing career to an end. Although he returned to Berkeley in fall 1938 for a final year of academic study, he was classified as a senior the previous year and, hence, was ineligible for a third season of crew. Later, studio publicists would maintain that he injured his back while rowing, thus mandating his withdrawal from the team, but this was not so. The back injury came several years later under far different circumstances.

Peck had entered Cal as a pre-med student, but, after struggling with calculus and chemistry, he realized that he wasn't meant to be a doctor. By contrast, he was genuinely stimulated by the literature courses he took as electives. So he decided to switch his major to English. He also took classes in political science, psychology, and anthropology and explored the graphic arts and music. Berkeley was, he later said, "a great place for me to develop." With students and faculty members from all over the United States as well as many parts of the world, Cal exposed him to new philosophies, ideologies, and lifestyles. "I was a political ignoramus until

I went to Berkeley during the Depression," he said. "There a whole tidal wave of new ideas came at me. . . . I just ate it up."

Of course, once he changed majors, his intellectual growth centered on the English department. He later said, "I was at one point so imbued with great books and literature, I thought of working for a Ph.D. and living the academic life, teaching at a place like Berkeley because I so loved the college and my time there. But that didn't last. Then I thought I wanted to be a red-hot journalist, some form of writing at any rate, and then I stumbled into the acting thing."

The "acting thing" came to him in the most innocent of ways. Strolling across campus one day early in fall 1938, he was stopped by a fellow who introduced himself as James Fitzgerald. Fitzgerald explained that he was directing scenes from *Moby Dick* for the stage and wanted to know if Peck would be interested in auditioning for the role of the first mate, Starbuck. What made Peck an attractive candidate was his height: the director wanted someone tall because his Ahab was short and stocky. "I don't know why I said yes," Peck said later. "I guess I was fearless, and it seemed like it might be fun."

At the time, Cal had no theater department; one wouldn't be established until 1941. In Peck's day, campus dramatics was in the hands of a group called the Little Theater, which mounted three major plays a semester. An organization known as the Associated Students sponsored the Little Theater along with a variety of other extracurricular activities, including the campus newspaper and the glee club. In addition to the main plays, there were numerous student-directed offerings, which were often more experimental. These were performed free of charge on Wednesday afternoons under the auspices of the Thalians, an honorary women's society.

Moby Dick, a Thalian Society production, was staged in a large lecture hall called Wheeler Auditorium on November 17. Adapted by Travis Bogart, an English professor who would later found the university's theater department, it shared the bill with an original piece, *Not That They Died.*

As things turned out, *Moby Dick* did not mark Peck's acting debut at Cal. While waiting for the Melville adaptation to be mounted, he took part nearly two months earlier—on September 29—in another Thalian Society offering. Aristophanes' *Lysistrata,* which revolves around a sex strike staged by the women of Athens in order to force their menfolk to make peace, was directed and adapted by a student named Jack Thompson. Thompson had come to know Peck in a public speaking class and was impressed by the former crewman's looks and manner. He cast his classmate as the Leader of Old Men.

As was the custom with all Thalian Society shows, a critique session followed the performance of *Lysistrata.* At least one student actor, Kenneth Tobey, was less than impressed by Eldred's debut. The beefy redhead, who would later become a close friend, rose and said forcefully, "I don't know why we have to watch people who don't know how to speak or act. I refer, of course, to Mr. Peck." Looking back, Grace Fretter, the production's assistant director, conceded that the newcomer was "kind of awkward on stage." She also noted that, "when he spoke he had a very sibilant *s,*" meaning that he hit the consonant too hard, producing a hissing sound.

Peck acknowledged his shortcomings as a fledgling actor, saying, "I was terrible at first—awkward and stiff and self-conscious." For someone as shy and reserved as he, the idea of getting up in front of people and performing was, to use his word, "agonizing." At the same time, acting offered an escape from his inhibitions. In an unusually revealing comment, he later said, "I suppose part of my fondness for it was that I could be someone else. My real personality had always been held back. Who knows why? I didn't have a very warm childhood, I guess. My real name was Eldred Peck. That's fairly repressing right there." In addition, the company offered a more prosaic attraction for the handsome, muscular newcomer—it was a good way to meet girls.

Peck soon graduated from short experimental plays to a major Little Theater production, *Rain from Heaven.* Performed on October 28 and 29, 1938, it was the second offering of the fall season following T. S. Eliot's *Murder in the Cathedral.* Written by S. N. Behrman, the play centered around a charming, sophisticated British society woman, Lady Violet Wyngate, who is romantically torn between two men—a Jewish music critic forced to flee his native Germany by the Nazis, and a dashing American explorer, Rand Eldridge, who turns out to be an anti-Semite. The drama had opened on Broadway four years earlier for a moderately successful run. The Cal production brought an unusual number of newcomers to the Little Theater stage, including freshman Betty Beaumont as Lady Wyngate and Peck as Rand Eldridge.

As with the Thalian Society productions, the Little Theater's major offerings were performed in Wheeler Auditorium. Far from a legitimate theater, the lecture hall featured a platform so shallow that extensions had to be added for most productions. It had no flies from which to hang scenery, so flats had to be wheeled in from the wings. Follow spots, when needed, could be placed at the rear of the auditorium, but otherwise the productions relied on fairly primitive overhead lights controlled by a portable dimmer board that remained in full view of the audience. Because the space was an active lecture hall, the actors had to rehearse elsewhere. They had access to the auditorium for only a couple of evenings prior to opening night and, even then, everything on the stage—sets, props, and so forth—had to be stored in a nearby classroom so that the daytime lectures could proceed undisturbed.

Despite the primitive conditions, the Little Theater productions generally drew large, enthusiastic audiences. They also attracted a devoted core of student actors, designers, technicians, and administrators. As one of Peck's classmates, Bill Musladin, put it, "Little Theater at Berkeley was populated by a very dedicated and intense group of people, who worked an incredible schedule and produced some outstanding work." Grace Fretter shared this viewpoint, noting, "Many of them, I think, were quite gifted. And they had wonderful minds. They had read and were very broadly interested in the world. And, when they worked, they worked with great integrity."

Much of the group's success was due to its director, Edwin Duerr, the only adult involved. Duerr had graduated from Cal in 1926 and went on to earn an M.A. in drama from Cornell. He took charge of the campus drama program in fall 1931. Only about ten years older than the students, Duerr was a man of tremendous energy and enthusiasm, with a pixie-like sense of humor. "But," recalled Grace Fretter, "when he was working, he was dead serious and right on and very concentrated."

Duerr was on sabbatical during the first semester of the 1938–39 academic year. Thus, *Rain from Heaven* was directed by Everett Glass, who was known to the Associated Students through his work with a Berkeley community theater. Glass was also the husband of a popular Cal physical education instructor. According to Elizabeth Berryhill, who was in the cast, Glass' directorial style was rather different from that of Duerr. "Duerr hit hard," she said. "If he didn't like what you were doing, boy, he really talked to you. He was very honest and very direct and pulled no punches. Everett Glass was a very elegant and gentlemanly sort of person, who directed in a more elegantly and gentlemanly fashion."

Perhaps Glass' softer touch made the newcomers in *Rain from Heaven,* including Peck, feel more at ease. For there is no question that at this early juncture, Eldred was uncomfortable in his new vocation. In fact, one time, during rehearsal, he shook so hard that the teacup and saucer he was holding emitted a disturbing clatter. To Peck's great embarrassment, Glass stopped the action until the source of the disruption was located.

Although Glass was gentle, Peck might have benefited from Duerr's stronger hand. "Kind of wooden" is the way fellow thespian John Brenneis described the newcomer's performance in *Rain from Heaven.* Elizabeth Berryhill pointed out that, eager and nice as he was, Eldred was "way out of his depth" in the role of the explorer. He was particularly awkward, she recalled, in the moment when Rand reveals his anti-Semitism by calling the music critic a "dirty Jew." No doubt, the epithet made Peck uncomfortable personally, and he lacked the experience to invest his character with convictions he didn't share.

Raw though he was, Eldred nevertheless radiated something that spilled across the Wheeler Auditorium footlights—sex appeal. "You could hear an audible gasp go through the women in the audience," recalled John Brenneis, "when he walked on stage." Peck was not oblivious to the stir nor to the fact that his technique lagged behind his appearance. Brenneis remembered that after the opening night of *Rain from Heaven,* the novice said wryly, "I think I could make a living out of this if I could learn to act."

Peck sat out the last play of the fall season, *S. S. Tenacity,* and the spring opener, *The Devil's Disciple,* by G. B. Shaw. However, in January 1939, he appeared in another Thalian Society production, *Invitation to Murder.* Written by Rufus King, this mystery melodrama about a California family whose wealth came from piracy had debuted in New York in May 1934 for a mere thirty-seven performances. Unlike most Thalian Society productions that were given one afternoon outing, *Invitation to Murder* ran for two evenings, January 27 and 28. It was staged to benefit the Mousetrap Theatre, a summer program in acting and stagecraft established in 1938 by the Little Theater troupers. Duerr, back from his sabbatical, supervised the production, although it was directed by James Fitzgerald, with whom Peck had worked on *Moby Dick.* Eldred had a minor role as one of two undertakers.

Six weeks later, on March 17 and 18, he was back on the Wheeler Auditorium stage, this time in a major role in a major Little Theater production, *Anna Christie.* Winner of the Pulitzer Prize, Eugene O'Neill's poignant 1921 drama is the story of a prostitute, Anna, who falls for a dashing sailor, Matt Burke, whom she and her father rescue from drowning. Peck played Matt, with Robert Goldstein as the old man and Peck's *Rain from Heaven* costar, Elizabeth Beaumont, in the title role. Naturally, Duerr was the director.

Apparently, Peck hadn't grown much as an actor since *Rain from Heaven* five months earlier. At one point during rehearsals, he tried to follow—literally—a stage direction that called for Matt to turn "purple with rage." Facing upstage just before the crucial moment, he held his breath for as long as he could. Exasperated, Duerr said to him, "What the hell do you think you're doing, Peck? How can you turn your back on the audience in this big scene?" When Eldred explained that he was trying to get his face to turn purple, the director told him to forget about the stage directions and worry about what the character was feeling.

The university yearbook, *The Blue & Gold,* named *Anna Christie* the outstanding Little Theater production of the year. Such was the demand for tickets that both performances were sold out, with patrons clamoring for additional play dates. Unfortunately, however, Wheeler Auditorium wasn't available. Once again, Peck's handsome face and muscular frame created a buzz among the female theatergoers, all the more so in this play because he appeared naked to the waist for part of the performance. Before the opening, the stage manager, Richard Barthel, attempted to pencil in stomach muscles to augment Peck's own, but the former crewman stopped him. Even as a green newcomer, he wanted to present himself in an authentic fashion.

The Blue & Gold praised the performances of all three of the principals. However, the school newspaper, *The Daily Californian,* adopted a different perspective with regard to Peck, arguing that he "almost endangered the success of the production with his exhibition of inexperienced acting technique." Technique could be learned; Grace Fretter credited him with having something better, a "kind of touching quality underneath the surface role" of Matt.

After opening night, Peck joined some of his colleagues at Spangers, a seafood restaurant in lower Berkeley where the students could order beer (the places closer to campus were restricted to nonalcoholic beverages). "That was the first time that I ever remember that Greg went along with the group," said Elizabeth Berryhill. "It was also clear that beer was not his usual drink, and I was the one who held his head in the alley on the way home."

As Berryhill noted, Peck didn't readily socialize with the other Little Theater troupers outside of rehearsals. Thespians like Bill Musladin found him pleasant but reserved. "He kind of walked alone," recalled actress Mindy McCorkle. Even so, he felt that he was among kindred spirits. Many of them, like actors everywhere, were also insecure. They, too, craved applause and approval and welcomed the chance to walk in someone else's shoes, even if only for a little while. More than the hearty, beefy oarsmen on crew, these were people with whom he could identify.

Nevertheless, his lack of experience set him apart from the best of the Little Theater players. Said Berryhill, "If he'd been more effective as an actor—it seems so snooty—I think he would have been regarded more as an insider. But for those of us who did everything [in the productions] and whose life really was the theater (and academics was something you did cause you had to), he was more of an outsider." She cited, by way of contrast, the vastly more experienced Ken Tobey, who was truly one of the gang.

Anna Christie marked the end of Peck's acting career at Cal. But the production had made a profound impression upon him, as did its four predecessors. In acting, he had finally found something that he wanted to do for the rest of his life.

But how? He knew that he lacked the experience to go out and launch a professional career. Then he encountered a Cal grad named Crahan Denton, who paid a visit to the campus. During his years as a student, Denton had been in numerous Little Theater productions and was something of a hero to the other thespians in the group. When he told them that he was studying acting at the Neighborhood Playhouse in Manhattan, Peck was intrigued. He wanted to go east and study there as well.*

Bunny and her husband, having seen Eldred's performances at Berkeley, encouraged him to try his hand in New York. His father, however, was appalled at the idea of the boy becoming an actor. "You'll be broke by the time you're thirty-five," he warned. Peck later explained that all his father knew "of show business were the people who came into the all-night drugstore where he worked at that time. Burlesque dancers and musicians from third-rate night clubs would go there for a cup of coffee at two or three in the morning. He didn't want me to suffer or waste my life."

But Eldred's mind was made up. He was determined to pursue his dream.

That spring, he completed his studies at Cal, although he wouldn't be awarded his B.A. until 1941. He explained the delay thus: "I had a D in Geometry left over from high school. I was to make it up but never did. . . . I think maybe they were annoyed by that little item on the books." Apparently, he added, "they grew tired of holding that D in Geometry against me and [eventually] sent me my diploma."

Nevertheless, his time in Berkeley had a profound impact upon his life. He had arrived three years earlier, a somewhat raw twenty-year-old with a rather narrow worldview and a vague idea of becoming a doctor. Over the ensuing years, his body was honed to a fine edge through a grueling sport, which had also reinforced his sense of discipline. He had opened himself to new ideas about politics, race, and social relations,

*Denton became a professional actor. He can be seen in *To Kill a Mockingbird*, portraying Walter Cunningham, the proud but indigent client of the attorney played by Peck.

marking the start of his lifelong support of liberal ideas and the Democratic party. And above all, he had found a career he wanted to pursue. As he later put it, "Berkeley was in every way an awakening for me."

Now the time had come to leave. He was so eager to reach New York that he grabbed a train as soon as he finished his last final exam. Instead of purchasing a sleeping berth, he decided to save money by sitting up the entire way. Gazing out the window on the long ride across the country, he realized that he was about to embark on a new life in a new city. It seemed fitting that he should take on a new identity as well. Thus, he decided to drop the hated "Eldred." From now on, he would be known by his middle name—Gregory.

Part Two

Becoming Gregory Peck

CHAPTER 4

The Playhouse

As Europe inched toward war during the summer of 1939, New York remained a bastion of international goodwill, thanks to the World's Fair, which was inaugurated on April 30. There was no more exciting place to be than the fairgrounds in Flushing Meadows, Queens, and, at age twenty-three, Peck found himself working right in the heart of it!

Arriving at Penn Station one morning in late May, he wasted little time getting settled. For six dollars a week, he rented a small room on West 114th Street, not far from Columbia University. "I didn't know anyone in New York," he said later, "and since I was used to the college atmosphere at Berkeley I thought I might meet someone up there at the university." Then he took a subway to the fairgrounds. In his pocket, he carried a letter of introduction from his stepfather, Joseph Maysuch, to J. W. Shillam, an Englishman who had an attraction at the fair called the Meteor Speedway. Shillam took one look at the strapping lad with the booming voice and hired him as a barker—at $25 a week. "It was the closest I could get to show business," Peck later joked.

Symbolized by the 200-foot Perisphere and 100-foot Trylon, the Fair covered 1,216½ acres with exhibition halls organized into thematic areas. The Transportation Zone included GM's Futurama pavilion, which featured a massive model of the future American city. In the Communications Zone, visitors could gawk at RCA's latest wonder, television, while the Government Zone showcased the cultural, agricultural, and technological achievements of thirty-three states and sixty-one nations.

Peck's meal ticket was located in the Amusements Zone. The Meteor Speedway consisted of a steel arm that carried a revolving coach around a steep-sided bowl. The coach, outfitted with a powerful motor complete with an ear-splitting roar, could carry up to fourteen screaming passengers at a time. Sporting white coveralls, a helmet, and goggles, Greg stood outside the entranceway and spouted an endless stream of patter, enticing likely prospects to spend fifty cents for the thrill ride.

He worked a twelve-hour shift, between noon and midnight. For each half hour of work, he got a half hour's rest. Despite the breaks, his throat was raw after only a month. If he wanted to have any voice left, he realized that he needed to find another line of work.

Preserving his voice was particularly important, for on July 24, he learned that the Neighborhood Playhouse had accepted him as a first-year student. The education director, Rita Wallach Morgenthau, and the secretary, Rebekah Dallas, had interviewed him for a place in the fall class the previous month. According to Peck's Little Theater colleague, Elizabeth Berryhill, Ed Duerr had paved the way for Greg and Ken Tobey by asking Cra Denton, the Cal grad who had gone on to study at the Playhouse, to look after the aspiring young thespians. Denton complied, taking them to the school and introducing them to its administrators.

Both made favorable impressions. Rita Wallach Morganthau noted on Greg's application that he was "Fine looking, tall, wishes to enter next year, can maintain self outside, eager for techniques—acting, speech; most attractive, intelligent." Because he applied for a scholarship, Greg was called back for a subsequent interview with the director of the acting department, Sanford Meisner. "Looks like very good material for the school and commercially" was Meisner's opinion. Peck received the scholarship.

As classes wouldn't begin until October 3, the young man looked for another job. Once again, he ended up on the fringes of show business, this time as a tour guide for Rockefeller Center.

Designed by a team of architects headed by Henry Hofmeister, H. W. Corbett, and Raymond Hood, the fourteen-building complex extended between Forty-seventh and Fifty-first streets, and Fifth and Sixth avenues. It incorporated a unique combination of high-rise office buildings, shops, gardens, restaurants, and a world-famous movie palace, Radio City Music Hall—all punctuated by massive outdoor sculptures, lobby murals, art deco motifs, and other noteworthy decorative elements.

To shepherd tourists around the twelve-acre complex, Peck traded in his overalls, goggles, and helmet for a blue blazer, gray slacks, and a cap. Each tour lasted an hour, for which Greg received $1.50. Some days he conducted as many as eight tours, with an average weekly take of $54, more than double his salary at the fair.

Steering wide-eyed tourists around the vast complex hour after hour was lucrative but tiring. On one occasion, Peck took a group into the Music Hall for what was supposed to be a ten-minute peek at the show. Settling himself into one of the comfortable padded seats while his party gawked at the stage, he promptly fell asleep and didn't wake up until the auditorium lights came on. His customers were thrilled; they had gotten to see the entire program for free, but the nap cost Peck several tours. The biggest pitfall of the job, as far as Greg was concerned, was his lack of familiarity with New York, a city he'd only lived in for a few months. Once, for example, when he took a group to the observation roof atop the RCA Building, a woman asked him where Brooklyn was. "Over there, madam," he replied, pointing with élan—toward New Jersey.

After about two months, Greg turned in his blazer and cap. It was time to do what he'd come to New York for—learn to act.

The Neighborhood Playhouse began not as a training school but as a producing organization. Founded by Irene and Alice Lewisohn, well-educated upper-class liberals who wanted to bring culture, education, and social training to members of the lower class, it was initially affiliated with the Henry Street Settlement House on the Lower East Side of Manhattan. Then, in 1915, the Playhouse became a separate entity operating out of a theater on nearby Grand Street. After several years of amateur offerings, the company turned professional, launching productions that were often experimental in content or method of presentation or both. Finally, after the 1926–27 theatrical season, financial pressures, the limitations of the Grand Street Theater, and other problems brought an end to the venture.

As part of its mission, the Neighborhood Playhouse had offered training in movement and speech and the specialized forms of drama that underscored its productions. That objective survived the demise of the performing organization. Thus, in 1928, the Neighborhood Playhouse School of the Theater opened at 16 West Forty-sixth Street in midtown Manhattan.* Offering an extensive two-year program, which included courses in movement, speech, stagecraft, theater history, and acting, the Playhouse became one of only three major professional training schools in the United States at the time. The other two were the far older and more conservative American Academy of Dramatic Arts, also in New York, and the Pasadena Playhouse in California. The enrollment for the new venture suggested why there weren't more such institutions; its initial class encompassed a mere nine members. However, by 1939, when Peck enrolled, things had picked up; there were about sixty first-year and thirty second-year students.

Alice Lewisohn was no longer involved with the organization, but Irene was the school's senior administrator. Her education director was

*Today the Neighborhood Playhouse is located at 340 East Fifty-fourth Street.

Rita Wallach Morgenthau, a sister of Henry M. Morgenthau, FDR's Secretary of the Treasury. Not only had Rita taught classes at the Henry Street Settlement, she had also been active in establishing vocational guidance and protective legislation for young people. Members of the school's ten-person faculty included the celebrated modern dancer Martha Graham and composer-choreographer Louis Horst. In 1935, a new acting teacher, Sanford Meisner, came on board; in future years his name would become synonymous with that of the Playhouse.

Born in Brooklyn in 1905, the son of Hungarian Jews, Meisner was initially a musician. He had even studied piano for a year at the Damrosch Institute of Music before talking his way into a job as an extra in a Theatre Guild production. After that, acting became his first love. In the early 1930s, he joined the Group Theatre, where he participated in the first significant attempts by an American producing company to simulate on stage the lives of ordinary people, notably through the dramas of the Group's resident playwright, Clifford Odets. Led by Harold Clurman, Lee Strasberg, and Cheryl Crawford, the Group took as its inspiration the teachings of Konstantin Stanislavski, whose Moscow Art Theatre had electrified them when it performed in New York in 1923. Stanislavski's acting technique forms the basis of what has become known as "the Method." Meisner brought what he had learned of the Method with him to the Playhouse.

In earlier eras, eloquent diction, fluidity of movement, and a commanding stage presence were the hallmarks of a good actor. Instead of focusing on such external qualities, Stanislavski urged actors to look inward, to find ways to understand and identify with the feelings of their characters and to project those emotions on the stage.

Since the 1950s, Stanislavski's method has come to be associated with self-indulgent actors who mumble, scratch themselves, turn their backs on their audiences, and live lives of outrageous nonconformity. This impression is due largely to Lee Strasberg and the Actors Studio, which was founded in 1947. Although many of his ideas were valid, Strasberg interpreted Stanislavski's approach as rooted in "affective memory." As such, the actor's task was to find something in his own past that could be used to simulate the emotional state of his character. If, for example, one had to confront the death of one's mother on stage, he would try to simulate how he felt when his own mother died—or, if she were still alive, his sorrow when he'd lost someone else to whom he was close.

Meisner didn't believe in using "affective memory." According to the Playhouse's current director, Harold Baldridge, who studied with both Meisner and Strasberg, "Meisner always felt it was healthier for an actor to use his imagination. Whereas Strasberg would want you to remember the day your little dog died and dwell on that, Sandy felt it was more healthy to think about *what if* your little dog died." He added, "Sandy never lost sight of the fact that someday you were going to be doing it on the stage or in front of the camera. And in Strasberg's classes, I felt it was sometimes getting a little close to the couch in the psychiatrist's office." Hence, the indulgence.

By the time Peck began working with Meisner, the acting teacher had begun developing the system of exercises for which he would become famous. At the beginning of the first year of training, he would start at a very elementary level. Dividing the students into pairs, he would ask each to examine the other and report what they had observed. He'd ask them to listen to the sounds in the air, isolate them and identify them. As he put it, "The foundation of acting is the reality of doing," and sensory exercises such as these put students in touch with the basic elements of reality, the observable phenomena around them. Some exercises were also designed to free students of their inhibitions; a self-conscious actor can't be a good actor.

As the first year progressed, he would advance to improvisations. In each of these exercises, a student or sometimes a pair of students would be placed in a specific situation and given a task to perform. For example, a student would be asked to enter a room occupied by another student and told to steal a specific object without getting caught. The purpose of these exercises was to help the young actors isolate and play specific intentions with the utmost veracity. In all of these instances, they were themselves; they were not portraying characters.

Like the best of students when exposed to something totally new, Peck gave himself earnestly to Meisner's teachings during his first year at the Playhouse, although he remained somewhat inhibited. As he confessed to secretary Rebekah Dallas the following summer, he felt that he had lacked "emotional freedom" because he was "afraid all last year to do things the 'wrong way,' or not strictly according to technique."

Despite his reserve, he made a favorable impression. "The thing I remember most about Peck at this time," said David Pressman, then Meisner's assistant, "is that there was nothing phony about him—in his personality or when he acted. You know, some actors come with a whole fixed notion of what they want the world to see and sometimes it takes on a very phony—what you might call actor-y—layer, and you have to tear that away. Peck didn't have that. Whatever he did was honest and sincere. We could tell that he had the capacity to be very truthful on stage or on screen." Eli Wallach, a year ahead of Peck at the Playhouse, formed a somewhat similar impression. "I found him not so stuffy," he said, "but concerned about his work. And sincere and dedicated."

* * *

If Meisner was passionate about emotional truth, he cared little about the technical demands of acting. Fortunately for Peck and his classmates, instructors like Martha Graham and Laura Elliot, who taught speech, were there to fill the void. According to Eli Wallach, what the students learned from Graham was that movement was the "synthesis of thought and the body and the brain. . . . She instilled in the actors the sense that one simple little movement can indicate a great deal" about a character's emotional state.

It was in Graham's class that Peck did permanent injury to his back. One day, as the students exercised on the floor, the dancer called for them to sit up straight, extend their legs, and bend their torsos until their heads touched their knees. She didn't feel Peck was bending far enough. Saying "Come along, Gregory, you can do better than that," she put one knee against his back and pushed. There was a loud pop. The pain wasn't excruciating, so Peck continued with the class and followed his regular routine for the rest of the day. However, the next morning he could barely move. A doctor was summoned to his room and, after examining the young student, he announced that Greg had a ruptured disk and a displaced vertebra.

The injury had one beneficial side effect: a few months later, Congress, as a measure of military preparedness, passed the Selective Training and Service Act, which required men between the ages of twenty-one and thirty-six to register for the draft. Because of his back problem, Peck was classified 4-F. Unquestionably, the exemption helped jump-start his career. Still, the injury was serious and painful, requiring him to wear a canvas brace for years. Finally he underwent an operation that alleviated the condition.

Aside from this crisis, Peck's biggest worry at the time was money. The Playhouse had awarded him a scholarship, so he didn't have to pay tuition. And he'd found a room—at 42 West Fifty-fourth Street—which was within walking distance of the Playhouse and cost no more than the six dollars he'd paid uptown. But coming up with even this meager rent wasn't easy. Nor was finding the money for food, clothes, and other necessities. Greg knew that he could count on Mrs. Morgenthau and Mrs. Lewisohn for an occasional loan. In time, they even set up a weekly ten-dollar stipend for him. But even that wasn't enough. Then the Arthur Manning Agency signed him, and he began to get work as a photographer's model—at twenty-five dollars a day. He was in particular demand for catalog work, gracing many a page in Montgomery Ward's hefty mail-order offerings—dressed in suits, outerwear, casual wear, even tennis outfits. "When I'd get to the photographer's studio," he recalled, "there would be a rack of clothes a block long waiting for me. A tailor stood by with clips to make them fit me." He did other print work as well. On one occasion, he donned formal wear for a Palmolive soap ad (the woman who appeared with him was the user of the advertiser's product). At the opposite social extreme, a brochure for the New Jersey Lighting Corporation found him in hard hat and coveralls, smiling atop a tall pole.

But his studies gave him only so much time to freelance. To economize on food, he frequently dined at the automat, a now-vanished New York institution where one chose from a variety of dishes displayed behind glass windows. "For twenty cents," Peck recalled, "you could get three vegetables and spaghetti, a very decent meal."

That his sacrifice was paying off became evident at the end of his first year at the Playhouse. It was then that he auditioned for a scholarship that would entitle two actors—one male, one female—to apprentice for the summer at the Barter Theatre in Abingdon, Virginia. Two hundred applicants were expected to audition; five hundred showed up. With each candidate limited to a one-minute monologue, Peck earned one of the coveted berths, performing a speech from *Saturday's Children* by Maxwell Anderson. Each year, the awards were designed to honor an American actor or actress. The 1940 honoree was Dorothy Stickney, then starring in *Life with Father* on Broadway. Although Stickney made the final selection, her legendary colleague Laurette Taylor played a role in the decision-making. Apparently Taylor was impressed with Peck, for later that summer Ed Duerr wrote to Greg, saying, "To have such a great artist . . . see you in a crowd, find you, speak for you and your values, is something indeed. A spur. An impetus."

Located about 350 miles southwest of Washington, D.C., the Barter Theatre had been founded in 1933 by a young Broadway actor from Virginia named Robert Porterfield. Peck later described him as "a Will Rogers in his way. Never lost his country color but it's genuine." With the Depression at its zenith, 1933 was not an opportune moment for the establishment of such an enterprise, but Porterfield felt that audiences outside of the major metropolitan areas needed legitimate theater and, of course, his fellow actors needed work. He hit upon the rather unique idea that players could come to Abingdon, where they were guaranteed lodging, three meals a day, and a percentage of the take, but no salary, and theatergoers lacking the price of a forty-cent ticket could pay for their admission with the equivalent in food—poultry, dairy products, canned goods, and the like. A pig was worth a season's pass! Of course, these items were used to feed the company. In addition to its season in Abingdon, the Barter would send its offerings on a series of one-night stands around the small towns and villages of Virginia. Said Peck, "We played one place, Big Stone Gap, hadn't had a legit show in forty-two years."

Of the nine plays in the Barter's 1940 season, Peck appeared in five, including *On Earth As It Is,* an original drama by Leslie MacLeod, a member of the acting company; *Davy Crockett,* from an anonymous source; and *Edward III,* an Elizabethan piece often attributed wholly or in part to William Shakespeare, in which Greg had the title role. One of his best roles came in *Family Portrait* by Lenore Coffee and William Joyce Cowen, which transferred the story of Jesus and Mary to a rural American setting—with Peck as Judas (he let his hair grow long for his part). And, in *The Lees of Virginia* by Edward Bobykin, he was double cast, as John Brown and Stonewall Jackson. "It was in this play," explained Robert Porterfield, "that Peck had to use the old cross-over beard technique. He would come off the stage as John Brown, jerk off bandages, hang a beard over his ears and a cape over his shoulders and walk unobtrusively across the back of the stage in full view of the audience. On the other side of the stage he quickly donned General Jackson's uniform and came in playing a scene with General Lee."

Greg would later ask Arnold Sundgaard, a friend who worked with him at the Barter, to critique his work that summer, and Sundgaard's written reply offers an instructive assessment of Peck's strengths and weaknesses at this early stage of his professional training. After praising his friend's beautiful vocal timber and "splendid physical equipment," Sundgaard noted, "First, I sometimes felt a certain monotony in the melody pattern of your voice. Before a speech was given, let us say, I could tell what the pattern was going to be. . . . [Y]ou probably are so intent on learning how the character thinks that you don't listen to him talk."

Sundgaard also felt that Peck's body language was stilted. He cited, by way of example, the moment in *Family Portrait* when Peck as Judas rose to his feet after learning that Mary was Jesus' mother. "Well, there was something very awkward about that movement," wrote Sundgaard, "that was apparent, to a lesser extent, in other movement. I don't know what it was but it didn't flow, it failed to tell anything. It didn't describe surprise or pleasure or awe or anything. It just made [me] think here was an actor with a chair and a table in his way."

In addition to performing, Peck, like all members of the Barter acting company, had backstage duties—loading and unloading scenery between engagements, rigging lights, and so forth. Given his experience with Union Oil, he was also tapped to drive a truck loaded with sets and other equipment from one venue to another. As if these duties weren't enough, Porterfield asked him to perform one more. Recognizing that Peck was somewhat stiff and shy, the producer ordered the actor to "come to me each day and tell me a story: a clean story, a dirty story, a funny story or otherwise. Over a period of several months he became one of the best story tellers I know."

On one occasion, Peck needed all the storytelling skills he could muster, for the star of a comedy called *Button, Button*—one of the troupe's productions in which Peck was not cast—got sick, and Greg had to step into the role, that of an old man. He had only twenty-four hours to memorize 102 pages of dialogue. During that time, he also had to drive eighty miles from Abingdon to the town where the performance was to take place and help mount the set and the lights. By curtain time, he had learned only a small portion of his lines. And, as stage fright set in, most of those flew out of his head. Fortunately, his friend Ken Tobey, also a member of the Barter company, offered to feed Greg his lines from the wings. Even with Tobey's help, however, the performance was a shambles.

On June 30, while at the Barter, Greg learned that he had been accepted for a second and final year of study at the Neighborhood Playhouse—no mean feat since only about half of the first-year students were asked to return—and that his scholarship had been renewed. A month later, he replied to the school's secretary, Rebekah Dallas, glowing with youthful enthusiasm over his summer of professional experience. "I have had a very valuable season at Barter so far," he wrote. "Plenty of practical application of my Playhouse training, excellent parts, trouping the near-by towns with our shows, some good and some bad direction, infinite gain in stage assurance, etc. Most important, the proof that our ideas about acting at the Playhouse are right, so right. Whether or not we are finished actors, the approach that Tobey and I have to acting, and the results that we have been able to get, have created a great deal of interest in the N.P."

He also corresponded with Ed Duerr that summer. His former director continued to be a source of inspiration and encouragement. On July 3, for example, Duerr wrote Peck a lengthy letter, suggesting, in part, that he trust his instincts more: "I know you to be a gent of tremendous will-power. I have the notion that you are the sort who sets his mind at something, and then come weal come woe achieves it. . . . But that isn't all . . . You are sensitive, very much so. To nuances, to people, to reactions, to color, etc. I know that. It is your art-saving quality. But I want you to know it."

Peck spent eight weeks in Virginia. Later, he would look back on his work with the Barter as "the most valuable experience" he'd ever had. "Getting those shows on and trucking the scenery around and setting up the lights—you were part of real theater for the summer. It was good groundwork and good training."

In the second year, Meisner moved from exercises and improvisations to scene study, helping the students add character development to the believable behavior of the first year. "Here simply being honest is not enough," explained journalist Arthur Seidelman. "The actor must develop the ability to make the most interesting choices on how to do each thing he must do; to have a character concept and work it out decision by decision. Does Hamlet say, 'To be or not to be' whimsically, petulantly, like a frightened child or a brave warrior? The example is rather simplified, but the process is that by which a character is constructed."

This part of the training particularly resonated for Peck. He would later credit Meisner with helping him learn to feed "out the story to the audience bit by bit with my mental and emotional processes going on underneath the words. What's underneath the words is more important than the words themselves because what's underneath produces the external effect."

Among the scenes that Greg worked on was "Christmas Eve" from a Schnitzler play called *The Affairs of Anatol.* "It's raining [in the scene]," explained Meisner's then-assistant David Pressman, "and he meets this young lady waiting for a cab, and it turns out they were ex-lovers. It's a charming, lovely scene." The actress who played the girl was Jane Rennie. "Sandy [Meisner] liked it very much," Pressman added. "Greg was very elegant, very debonair in it."

Such was Peck's development that members of the small New York theater community began hearing about the tall, handsome young student with the glorious voice. Early in his second year at the Playhouse, he was offered a role in a Group Theatre production, most likely *Retreat to Pleasure* by Irwin Shaw, which opened at the Belasco Theatre on December 17, 1940. Greg seriously considered doing it, but that would have meant dropping out of the Playhouse. Although the decision was difficult, he opted to finish his studies. As it happened, the play was not a hit. In fact, it turned out to be the Group's final production.

Also, during Peck's second year, independent film mogul David O. Selznick, producer of the epic Oscar-winning film *Gone With the Wind,* gave him a screen test. It was Mildred Webber, an agent with the William Morris Talent Agency, who brought Greg to the attention of Selznick's East Coast representative, Katherine Brown. Even though Peck thought of himself as a stage actor and was not interested in a film career, he agreed to make the test. On the appointed day, he arrived at the Fox Studios on Tenth Avenue and Fifty-seventh Street. The test director showed him where he wanted him to stand and told him not to move. The scene he was given to read came from *This Above All,* which was later filmed with Tyrone Power. Playing an RAF officer in London during the Blitz, Peck was to tell his girl—played in the test by Augusta Dabney—that he couldn't face going back to war. He then did another scene, from *The Young in Heart,* which had already been shot with Douglas Fairbanks Jr. At the end of the test, the director said, "Gee, that's great."

Selznick, however, was not impressed. "I am sorry to say that I don't see what we could do with Gregory Peck," the producer wrote Katherine Brown on March 11, 1941. "Maybe a big studio could use him, but we would have great difficulty in either using him ourselves or getting other studios to use him that didn't have him under contract. He photographs like Abe Lincoln, but if he has great personality, I don't think it comes through in these tests. He must be a fine legitimate actor, judging by your great interest in him, and while his performance in the scene from *This Above All* is satisfactory, considering how much work was done in a day, and considering the circumstances under which it was made, it is nothing to get excited about. As for his performance in *The Young in Heart,* my respect for Doug Fairbanks, Jr., goes up after seeing Peck play this scene."

As was the custom at the time, Peck had signed a contract with Selznick prior to the test—without reading the document. He thought it was simply a release. "Afterward," he said, "I discovered I had signed a seven-year screen contract at a starting salary of $75 a week and rising to the munificent sum of $350 a week at the end of seven years. I was a very happy man, believe me, when Selznick informed me that I had not tested well and he was canceling his contract."

Despite his bright prospects and considerable growth as an actor, Peck remained reserved and somewhat inhibited. A friend cautioned him at the time, "You cannot learn about people from an ivory tower or by looking through a curtained window at the passing train. If you expect people to give of themselves to you, you must give of yourself to them—and not just what you want to give either, but also what they need of you—individually and collectively." Duerr offered him somewhat similar advice, writing, "Never run from people; run to them in order to know them, in order (best of all) to be a person yourself. Artists inhabit the lonely places often enough, meeting only themselves; they must, for change, for ammunition, for release, go out among people, too."

It was customary each spring for the Playhouse to introduce its second-year students to the trade by means of a final production, to which all of the leading agents, producers, and theatrical managers in New York were invited. Staged at the Heckscher Theatre at Ninety-fifth Street and Fifth Avenue, the principal requirement of these so-called "demonstration plays" was that they feature a large cast, so that each of the graduating actors could be showcased.

For the class of 1941, the demonstration play was Nicholas Evreinoff's *The Chief Thing,* a Russian comedy-drama in three acts that had debuted in New York in 1926 for a brief run. Set in the early twentieth century, the fable-like play centered around the unhappy inhabitants of a boardinghouse who are given comfort by a troupe of actors. Peck played a debonair con man with gray in his hair, a mustache, and a long thin cigarette.

Duerr, who by then had left Cal for Cleveland's Western Reserve, came to New York to see the production and reported back to the kids in Little Theater, "The lads have progressed. The readings were often true and the people were real. But somehow or another the whole play didn't come off. It was all too crucial. Crucial, working too hard, too tense—their first public performance after two years of schooling. And then I felt that Stanislavski is not the right system for *The Chief Thing.*"

As was the custom, the students gathered around the reception desk at the Playhouse the morning after the performance, hoping that a producer, agent, or manager would phone with an offer. Shortly after Greg arrived at the Playhouse, a call came in for him! Taking the receiver from the school's receptionist, he discovered to his amazement that the party on the other end was Guthrie McClintic, the husband of actress Katharine Cornell and one of Broadway's most important producer-directors. McClintic told Peck that he wished to see him that very morning. Greg knew where the impresario's office was: he'd stopped by numerous times to leave his photo and résumé. Handing the receiver to the receptionist, without even saying good-bye to McClintic, he dashed to the intersection of Forty-sixth Street and Sixth Avenue, went up four blocks to Fiftieth Street, entered the RCA Building, and grabbed an elevator to the eighth floor. When he entered McClintic's office, the Broadway luminary was still talking to the receptionist! He took one look at Peck and started laughing so hard that he literally fell off his chair.

Finally, when he composed himself, McClintic told Greg that he was interested in him for a small role in Cornell's touring production of *The Doctor's Dilemma* by G. B. Shaw. Looking at the panting, sweating actor before him, there was little question of his eagerness for the job. Still laughing, McClintic told Peck the part was his.

Greg's student days were now behind him; he was ready to enter his profession. But he took with him from the Playhouse the fundamentals

Sanford Meisner had taught—how to listen, how to play intentions, how to build a character, in short, the essence of the Method passed down from Stanislavski. These would serve as his guides for the entirety of his career.

CHAPTER 5

The Apprentice

The Doctor's Dilemma wasn't scheduled to go into rehearsal until late August. So Peck was free to accept an acting job with Sanford Meisner's summer stock company, the County Playhouse in Suffern, New York. Meisner comanaged the troupe with actress Jean Muir.

Greg was cast as "Nutsey" Miller, a college football player, in *The Male Animal,* the hit 1940 comedy by James Thurber and Elliot Nugent about the trials and tribulations of a college professor at a midwestern university. Greg's role was small; the spotlight was on José Ferrer as the professor and Uta Hagen as his wife.

As was typical of stock companies, *The Male Animal* rehearsed for a week and ran for a week—leaving Peck plenty of time to accept an offer from another stock company, the Ridgeway Theatre in White Plains, New York. This time the production was a musical comedy, *Captain Jinks of the Horse Marines,* a 1925 adaptation of a 1901 play. The stars of the White Plains production were Diana Barrymore, daughter of matinee idol John Barrymore, and Winston O'Keefe.

As with *The Male Animal, Captain Jinks* ran for only a week—starting on August 4, 1941—but among those who caught the brief engagement was talent agent Maynard Morris. An associate of Leland Hayward, whose power-packed client list ranged from Greta Garbo, Fred Astaire, and James Stewart to Ernest Hemingway and Lillian Hellman, Morris was impressed by Peck and signed him to the agency.

Between rehearsals and performances, *The Male Animal* and *Captain Jinx* lasted only a month. During the rest of the summer, Greg did the best he could to make ends meet. He wasn't much of a saver. When he was flush, he was fully capable of blowing a substantial sum on one good meal and then subsisting on sandwiches and milk until the rest of the money ran out. Once, he and Ken Tobey emptied their pockets and discovered that they had a mere eleven cents between them. As Ken had a box of pancake mix in his cupboard, he and Greg used their capital to purchase a quart of milk. Then they whipped up an enormous pile of flapjacks; they had neither butter nor syrup, but at least they didn't starve.

Greg had long since left his digs on West Fifty-fourth Street, but he found other midtown lodgings for the same amount of money—six dollars a week. When he lacked the rent, he would take his one valuable possession, a Ronson black enamel cigarette case with a built-in lighter, to a pawn shop at the corner of Forty-sixth Street and Sixth Avenue. The owner would give him six dollars and a pawn ticket. When he managed to pick up some cash, he would return with the ticket and get the cigarette case out of hock. He later figured that he went through this routine about twenty times.

When even the cigarette case failed to do the trick, he stored his belongings in a locker at Grand Central Station and slept out in Central Park. He didn't mind. Most of the other aspiring actors he knew were as broke as he. Such things just seemed part of getting a start in the theater.

Given his financial condition and the liberal atmosphere he'd enjoyed at Berkeley, it isn't surprising that Peck was drawn to New York's political left. For a time, he lived in the city's hotbed of radical thought, Greenwich Village. He even attended a few rallies of the American Communist Party at Madison Square Garden. "Communism was in the air at that time," he recalled, "there is no doubt, and the girl I was going with at the time was pretty far to the left. Incidentally, she was a damned good-looking Bolshevik! She was an American girl working as a researcher for Time-Life." In addition to attending rallies, he enjoyed reading an ultra-liberal periodical, *The New Masses,* but, in his words, it "never occurred to me to become an actual communist."

Finally, the summer ended, and Peck started work on *The Doctor's Dilemma.*

Debuting in London in 1906 and premiering in the United States ten years later, the drama offered the spirited intellectual debates and high wit for which its author, George Bernard Shaw, was already celebrated. The title derives from the choice facing the central character, Dr. Colenso Ridgeon, who has developed a cure for tuberculosis. He must either save a charming, ne'er-do-well artist named Louis Dubedat or a physician who tends to the indigent.

The Guthrie McClintic production of *The Doctor's Dilemma* had opened at the Shubert Theatre on Broadway on March 11, 1941. It was a triumph for its star, Katharine Cornell, setting a record for the Shaw play in New York with 121 performances. Curiously, Cornell's role, that of Jennifer Dubedat, is not the play's principal focus. But, as her biographer, Tad Mosel, explained, "in one way it is an actress's dream." For, before Jennifer appears on stage, a stream of sophisticated men talk so enthusiastically about the character that, by the time she makes her entrance, "the audience is in a fever of impatience to see her."

McClintic surrounded his wife with, to quote Mosel, "a stalwart honor guard of leading men," including Bramwell Fletcher as her dying artist husband and Raymond Massey as the surgeon with the power to save his life. All of the principal actors would join her for the tour. This was most unusual, for in the 1940s, traveling productions of Broadway hits were typically recast with lesser luminaries. Cornell and McClintic, however, favored actors who were willing to re-create their performances on the road. In fact, only Peck and actress Gina Malo were new to the large *Doctor's Dilemma* company.

Greg was to play Mr. Danby, the curator of an art gallery posthumously displaying Louis Dubedat's work. The small role, played on Broadway by David Orrick, consisted of a total of eight speeches in the fifth and final act (he is on stage at the top of the act, goes off in search of exhibition catalogues, and returns just before the play's final curtain). For his work, Peck was to receive $50 a week.

Before rehearsals began, Ed Duerr advised Greg, "The chance is one to be grabbed, treasured, fully utilized, but not idealized too highly." The director praised McClintic and Cornell, concluding "[Y]ou should learn much, as well as attain much confidence, in the association."

Indeed, the actress and her husband stood at the apex of the American theater of the time. At forty-nine, Kit, as Cornell's friends called her, had been a star for more than two decades, having vaulted to prominence as the lead in *Bill of Divorcement* by Clement Dane. Since then, she had scored triumphs in Shaw's *Candida,* as Elizabeth Barrett Browning in *The Barretts of Wimpole Street,* and as Juliet in *Romeo and Juliet,* which she toured for two years.

McClintic, six months Kit's junior, was a graduate of the American Academy of Dramatic Arts. After a modest acting career, he produced and directed his first play, A. A. Milne's *The Dover Road,* in 1921, the same year in which he married Cornell. Four years later, he directed her for the first time, in *The Green Hat* by Michael Arlen. Although he would compile a distinguished record on his own, including the Broadway productions of *Yellow Jack* by Sidney Howard, Maxwell Anderson's *Winterset,* and John Gielgud's *Hamlet,* McClintic became best known for his collaborations with his wife.

McClintic was a demanding craftsman. Instead of sitting in the center orchestra during rehearsals for *The Doctor's Dilemma,* the favored spot for most directors, he would climb to the last row of the balcony. When he couldn't hear an actor to his satisfaction, he would interrupt the scene, shouting, "Can't understand you! They pay to get in up here, too, you know." Greg quickly learned to project. As he put it, "You didn't want him yelling at you all the time."

The tour kicked off at the Forest Theatre in Philadelphia on September 8. At it happened, opening night coincided with the McClintics' twenty-fifth wedding anniversary, and some of their New York friends, including actress Helen Hayes and the husband-wife team Alfred Lunt and Lynn Fontanne, came to the theater to help them celebrate. In an effort to combat first-night jitters, Cornell had imbibed more than her share of champagne before the play began. By the time she reached act 5, she was feeling the effects of the alcohol. As the curtain rose—with just her and Peck on stage—she opened her mouth to speak but nothing came out. She couldn't remember her lines. Showing the aplomb of a far more experienced trouper, Peck turned his face upstage, whispered her first line to her, and she recovered. Later, backstage she said, "Gregory, you've saved my life. I completely dried up. I didn't have a clue what I was going to say." Later, she told the Lunts and Helen Hayes about the wonderful young man who had rescued her performance.

Word of Peck's quick thinking soon reached New York. Within days, Sanford Meisner fired off a typed letter to his former student, saying, "Dear Greg, I hear you saved Miss C from ignominy. Keep it up; this is only the beginning. You have a lot of work to do." He added in pen, "I have faith you'll do it. Yours, Sandy M." One of Peck's friends, Mike Strong, hired shortly thereafter for another McClintic project, told Greg, "When McClintic first spoke to me about my job, he told me so many wonderful things about you that I was proud to be your friend. He described in detail the opening—how tired Miss Cornell was on her anniversary and how you stuck by her when she almost 'dried up.' I honestly feel that the good work you've done will make it easier for Playhouse graduates as far as Mr. McClintic is concerned." It didn't hurt Peck either. McClintic would later play a major role in launching him to stardom.

Peck was thrilled to be working with such a prestigious company. He was particularly eager to watch the great Cornell in action but was surprised to discover that she was shy and suffered from stage fright. "I used to see her backstage," he said years later, "before her entrances, keyed up and trembling, and then sweep on stage and take command, projecting self-assurance, grace, nobility." He added, "Since then I have observed many great actors constantly struggle with stage fright, even after years of success. It seems true that courage is not so much the absence of fear as the ability to overcome it, and to do what has to be done. Courage, intelligence, and personal detachment are the qualities I most admire in an actor."

The Doctor's Dilemma offered Peck a wonderful learning experience, but most of the cast members were considerably older than he. They were also British and vastly more experienced. Socially, he was in a different—lesser—league. Of course, his own reserve stood in the way of forming friendships as well. So he didn't have many pals within the cast.

Soon, however, Greg caught the eye of one of the few members of the company who was close to his own age and social status, a perky young blonde by the name of Greta Konen. She was Cornell's hairdresser.

Greg had first noticed her while standing on a station platform in Philadelphia, waiting with the rest of the company for a train. Although he didn't speak to her, Greta was aware of his presence as well. Having caught sight of him backstage at the Forest Theatre, she checked him out on the company callboard and learned that his name was Gregory Peck. She thought it was a stage name, which, in a way, it was, but, as she said later, "somehow it seemed to fit him."

In Boston, he asked her out, and they went to a nightspot called the Merry-Go-Round. She soon discovered that, when he was in a comfortable setting, he could be as talkative as the next guy and that he possessed a wry sense of humor. In fact, on that first date, he told her that he was a full-blooded Indian. She didn't find out that he was joking until months later when she met his parents. He also told her he could read palms, a rather obvious line that gave him an opportunity to hold her hand. He was pleased with the ploy, but Greta said years later, "I've always hated to spoil his illusions, but who do you suppose *started* the conversation about palm reading?"

In time Peck learned that Greta was born in Helsinki, Finland, in 1911, making her five years older than he, and that she was the youngest of four children, two boys and two girls. The family emigrated to America when she was two, settling in Jersey City. There, they shortened their name from Kukkonen to Konen. Greta's father commuted to Manhattan each day; he was a jeweler and watchmaker at Tiffany's on Fifth Avenue. Upon graduation from Jersey City's Lincoln High School, Greta studied art at a private academy in New York. By the time she met Greg, her five-year marriage to a man named Charles Rice had ended in divorce. Tiny, especially compared with the six-foot-two-inch actor, she looked Scandinavian, with blond hair swept back from her face, a broad forehead, and a button nose. She had a kewpie-doll countenance, more pert than pretty. But she was vivacious and cheerful, full of life—and a good cook as well.

Greg began spending more and more time with Greta. "We were on the road six months in all," he recalled, "and you get pretty damned tired of sightseeing and having all your meals out." As they had little in common with most of the company members, they formed what Greg called "a proletarian club." The third member of their little group was a comedian by the name of Lester Ampolsk. He sold souvenir programs of *The Doctor's Dilemma* during the production's bookings. Unlike the older company members, Greg, Greta, and Lester could only afford the venues' lesser-priced hotels—Greta's weekly salary was $60 ($10 more than Peck's) and Lester only earned $35. "Our entertainment after a performance," Greg recalled, "was to chip in on a bottle and go back to one of the rooms and play rummy."

Occasionally, the struggling actor found a bit of cash to spend on his girl. She later remembered that the first gift he gave her was "just a gadget, a little gold-plated angel for my lapel. I loved it so I nearly cried myself sick when I lost it in a movie theater one night. We waited until after the last show and went down on our knees looking under almost every seat in the house."

In love and working with a first-rate company, Peck was enjoying life. Duerr commented on the rise in Greg's fortunes in a letter dated October 18, 1941, noting "a happy feeling all around you, a new slant on things, money in the pocket and food a-plenty in the belly, plenty of time to think things out, a place to try out acting, to discover theatre inside. All of that. All on the credit side. All things you've won and richly deserved."

In December, the company reached the Curran Theatre in San Francisco, where the Cal graduate was treated as the hometown boy made good. The local paper, the *Chronicle,* which had covered Peck's Little Theater performances, even noted the change of his first name in its review of the play. But December 1941 was not a propitious time for theatrical entertainment. On December 7, at the end of the company's first week in San Francisco, the Japanese bombed Pearl Harbor, and America was suddenly at war. The following evening, the city experienced a blackout. In the days that followed, as San Franciscans adjusted to the frightening realities of wartime, ticket sales for *The Doctor's Dilemma* plummeted, and the play closed.

Greg was not out of a job, however. Cornell and McClintic decided to stay in the Bay area and rehearse her next vehicle, an original play entitled *Rose Burke.* Greg wasn't in the cast, but he served as assistant stage manager. "Which wasn't much," he said later. "But I'd have come on as a caterpillar, just for the chance of working with and learning from Katharine Cornell."

Rose Burke was written by a French playwright named Henri Bernstein who had fallen in love with Cornell after seeing her in *The Barretts of Wimpole Street.* A refuge from his Nazi-occupied homeland, he fulfilled his pledge to write a play for her one day, creating the role of a glamorous sculptress with a tempestuous love life. It was his first drama in English.

In addition to his duties backstage, Peck understudied two roles in *Rose Burke,* one played by a fifty-year-old actor named Philip Merivale, the other by twenty-nine-year-old Jean Pierre Aumont, a rising French star making his English-language debut in the drama. As an understudy, Greg was able to rehearse with Cornell and was, of course, directed by McClintic. He even devised his own makeup for the Merivale role, which included a silver-gray mustache. For Aumont's part, that of the sculptress' lover, he had to develop a French accent, at which he was decidedly unsuccessful.

He knew that he was ill-equipped to step into Aumont's shoes if the French actor took sick. One night in Detroit, however, it looked like he would have to do just that, for, as curtain time neared, Jean-Pierre was nowhere to be found. Peck tried phoning his hotel room at the Brook Cadillac but got no reply. Not knowing what else to do, he dashed over to the hotel, only a few blocks from the theater. Hearing a frenzied pounding from the hallway, Aumont opened his door, yawning. Sheepishly, he explained that he had fallen asleep and had forgotten to request a wake-up call. Peck quickly helped the actor dress and dash to the theater. En route, Aumont slipped on a patch of ice. But Peck, determined not to make a fool of himself on stage, helped the actor to his feet and guided him firmly to the theater. They arrived promptly at 8:30, just enough time to get Jean-Pierre into his costume and makeup, and point him toward the wings. No one was happier to see his entrance than Peck.

The plan was to tour *Rose Burke* in an easterly direction, then open the play in New York. Ticket sales in Portland, Seattle, and Detroit were good, but clearly the play wasn't working. After about eight weeks, while performing at their fourth venue—Toronto—Cornell and McClintic decided to close the show. It was only the second time that one of Kit's productions failed to reach Broadway.

Cornell immediately launched a New York revival of one of her biggest successes, *Candida.* No doubt McClintic could have found a spot for Peck with the company, but he had something else in mind for the young man: the juvenile lead in a new comedy that he was to produce and direct, *Punch and Julia.*

Written by George Batson, *Punch and Julia* revolves around a romantic triangle: Phil Powell, a publishing tycoon; Julia, a book reviewer and radio commentator; and Leo Christy, a radical writer whose latest book includes an attack on Powell. With the beautiful, talented Jane Cowl as Julia and Arthur Margetson as Phil, Peck was third-billed as Leo, the largest role of his very young professional career.

Unfortunately, *Punch and Julia* had no punch—and neither did Peck. One critic described the newcomer as "a little lost as how best to approximate the high proficiency of bewitching the ladies with whom he fell in love."

The show's entire run lasted a mere two weeks in May 1942, spread out over three cities: Wilmington, Delaware; Washington, D.C.; and Baltimore, Maryland. So tepid was the response that one matinee in Baltimore drew only twenty-four patrons to a 1,600-seat house. Arthur Margetson didn't want to go on, but Cowl said, "Arthur, we're going to give them the show of their lives. Take the curtain up. Everyone give of their best." Peck was impressed by her professionalism, but admitted that doing a comedy for such a small audience was difficult.

Fortunately for Greg, by the time the closing notice for *Punch and Julia* was posted, summer was close at hand. He managed to spend the whole of July 1942 doing four plays in succession at the Cape Playhouse in Dennis, Massachusetts.

Founded in 1927, the Cape Playhouse is generally regarded as the first company to feature major Broadway stars in a nonurban setting for one-week summer engagements. Typically, one or two stars would topline each offering with young unknowns rounding out the cast. Bette Davis, Humphrey Bogart, and Henry Fonda were just a few of the youngsters to get a start there. The theater was a charming refurbished nineteenth-century Unitarian Meeting House, moved from its original location to pastureland on Cape Cod. By 1942, Richard Aldrich was the Playhouse's producer. But he was in the Navy, so his wife, the celebrated actress Gertrude Lawrence, was managing the company in his absence. At the end of the season, she would close the theater for the duration of World War II.

Peck's first role on the Cape was that of Teddie Luton in *The Circle,* which opened on July 6. The sophisticated 1921 comedy by Somerset Maugham starred Fritzi Scheff as a world-weary English countess.

In addition to his supporting role, Peck was an assistant stage manager for the production. His primary duty was to make the rounds of the actors' dressing rooms before the curtain went up, keeping them informed of the time. In most cases, the actors responded cheerfully to these reminders, but on opening night, Peck got no acknowledgment when he gave Scheff the half-hour warning. Nor did he hear a response for his subsequent announcements. Finally, he pounded on the door and shouted, "Curtain going up, Miss Scheff." After a moment, the actress, who specialized in Viennese light operas and was known as the "Kiss Me Again Girl," came to the door. She appraised Peck coolly and said, "Young man, I'll tell *you* when the curtain's going up." Her regal manner was a bit daunting, but he was mostly relieved that she wasn't dead.

While *The Circle* was in performance at night, Peck spent his days rehearsing the following week's offering, *The Rebound,* a comedy by Donald Ogden Stewart that had enjoyed a very successful run in New York in 1930. Greg was given a fairly substantial supporting role, that of a jilted suitor named Johnny Coles. The star of the play was Ruth Chatterton. One of the Boston critics singled out Greg in his review of the production, calling him "the complete actor. Inside and out he gives an electrifying performance."

Peck's third appearance at the Playhouse was in *You Can't Take It with You,* the Pulitzer Prize–winning Kaufman and Hart hit of 1938 about a large family of eccentrics. Greg relished his casting as ballet master Boris Kolenkhov, for the lively character part differed from the typical, and often thankless, juvenile role that usually came his way. The laughs he received from the audience convinced him that his future lay in comedy.

His fourth and final role that summer came in *The Duenna,* a musical version of Richard Brinsley Sheridan's restoration comedy that was first performed at London's Covent Garden in 1775. Although the principal character is Donna Louisa, a young woman betrothed to a man she doesn't love, the star of the Playhouse production was Jimmy Savo, a popular vaudevillian who specialized in pantomime routines. As Don Ferdinand, the brother of Donna Louisa, Peck had to dance and sing in six numbers. "God knows how," he said later, "because I can't sing. In those days, I did anything they told me to do." *The Duenna* opened at the Playhouse on July 27.

Singing and dancing without the requisite skill, taking on otherwise unlikely character roles, even performing an assistant stage manager's duties, such are the benefits of summer stock. They give promising newcomers the chance to stretch themselves, explore the depths of their talent, and, at the same time, work alongside and learn from experienced veterans. Peck soaked up all he could. He was also able to enjoy the splendor of Cape Cod, one of the nation's premier summer vacation spots. The romantic setting may even have inspired him to propose to Greta on one of her visits to Dennis. Although she accepted, they decided that they were too poor to marry and would wait until their fortunes improved.

The hoped-for change came sooner than expected.

CHAPTER 6

Broadway and a Bride

While working on the Cape, Greg received a telegram from Guthrie McClintic. The producer-director had a home on nearby Martha's Vineyard and asked his young protégé to pay him a visit. When Peck arrived, McClintic gave him a play entitled *The Morning Star* by Emlyn Williams, the Welsh playwright and actor who had written two major dramas, *Night Must Fall* and *The Corn Is Green.* Williams was then starring in the London production of *The Morning Star,* which had opened the previous December and was a smash hit (it would eventually run for 474 performances in the West End).

McClintic told Greg that he intended to bring the show to New York that fall and that he wanted Peck to make his Broadway debut in the drama. Not in a small role, like the one he'd played in *The Doctor's Dilemma,* but in the part that the author himself was portraying in London, the central role! Peck was stunned. His first decision when he recovered was to upgrade his living arrangements. For fourteen dollars a week, he rented a one-bedroom apartment on the top floor of a house on East Thirty-ninth Street near Lexington Avenue. He shared a kitchen with a young woman who lived across the hall.

The Morning Star was set in London in 1940. Peck's role was that of Cliff Parrilow, a medical researcher who abandons his promising career to write a cheap best-selling novel. He also cheats on his wife with an unsavory, money-loving blonde. During the blitz, as squadrons of German Luftwaffe planes make nightly bombing raids on the British capital, he comes to his senses, reuniting with his wife and developing an important new technique for heart surgery.

McClintic surrounded Peck with a first-rate cast headed by Gladys Cooper as Cliff's mother. A star of the London stage for twenty years, she had made her American debut with Raymond Massey in *The Shining Hour.* She had also appeared in such films as *Rebecca, That Hamilton*

Woman, and *Now, Voyager* (which had yet to be released when the play opened).

Rehearsals for *The Morning Star* began in August 1942. Cooper told friends back in England that she thought the play was quite good and that McClintic was "an exciting director." She was less impressed with Peck, however, noting, "I don't think he'll ever get it right, although I may be wrong."

The play tried out for a week at the Walnut Theatre in Philadelphia starting on September 7. The local critic for *Variety* was cautiously optimistic about the production's chances in New York. He also prophesied, "There is going to be plenty of talk about Gregory Peck," whom he likened to Philip Merivale, the actor Greg had understudied in *Rose Burke*.

A week later, on September 14, the play opened at Manhattan's Morosco Theatre. The previous day, Peck received an encouraging letter from Sanford Meisner, who wrote, "Before to-morrow night—which is, after all, going to be only one of many first-nights for you—I want you to know how really confident of you I am. In that long line of actors yearly passing out of my clutches—there are too few in whom one senses an integrity of purpose and the ability to work it through that you have. And now at the beginning of what will be, I know, a distinguished career I offer you all my best wishes and whatever help you might at any time think I can contribute."

Meisner's words were of little comfort, however, when the big moment arrived. "I was scared to death the first time I went out there," Peck said years later. But he recalled how Kit Cornell had risen above her stage fright and was determined to do the same thing. The first act was an hour long, and he was on stage the entire time. After five minutes of butterflies in the stomach, he lost himself in the demands of the role.

And acquitted himself quite well, as the critics noted the following morning. "Especially praise must go to Gregory Peck, a remarkable young actor," enthused John Mason Brown in his review for the *New York World-Telegram*. John Anderson of the *New York Journal-American* noted that Peck did "a superlative job with sensitiveness and fine restraint," while Brooks Atkinson of the *New York Times* wrote, "Gregory Peck plays with considerable skill . . . avoiding in his acting the romantic tosh of the writing." The critics were less enamored of the play, however. Most found it too long, too melodramatic, and too contrived.

For Peck, only twenty-five years old and about sixteen months out of acting school, it was enough to have survived the ordeal. The mere fact of having opened on Broadway was a major milestone, and he knew it. As he later said, "To walk out in front of all the critics, and get away with it, that changes your insides around. You're no longer one of thousands of hopefuls. . . . When you make the leap from obscurity to Broadway, you're crossing a much greater chasm than when you move from Broadway to Hollywood, because, once you believe in yourself, you're no longer making leaps. You're taking incremental steps."

Although Maynard Morris had not played a significant role in Greg's Broadway debut, the actor nevertheless showed his gratitude toward his agent, sending him a silver letter opener as a gift. "It may not seem much to you," Morris said years later, "but I assure you that in my business I am not used to any such acknowledgement." This sort of kindness and generosity would characterize Peck's professional associations for the rest of his career.

Although *The Morning Star* wasn't a hit, the critical response and audience reaction to its young star drew several Hollywood notables to the Morosco Theatre. The motion picture industry had been looking to Broadway as a source of new talent since the advent of the talkies. Humphrey Bogart, Spencer Tracy, Katharine Hepburn, Henry Fonda, and James Stewart were just a few of the Hollywood stars who had jump-started their film careers on the New York stage.

Among those who took a keen interest in Peck was Samuel Goldwyn. But when the celebrated independent producer called Leland Hayward about casting the actor in a film, the agent, who was based in Los Angeles at the time, had no idea who Gregory Peck was! Stalling, he said, "I'll call you right back, Sam." Then he turned to his secretary and asked, "Do we have somebody by the name of Peck?" She said, "We might have in our New York office. He might be in a play." Ascertaining that this was so, Hayward called Goldwyn back and said, "Sam, I'll give him to you for five thousand a week for ten weeks." That was an outrageous sum for an unknown in 1942 and Goldwyn exploded, saying, "What the hell are you trying to do, hold a gun to my head? Nobody's ever heard of this kid. We don't know if he's photogenic, or what he looks like. Forget about it."

Also interested were screenwriter Casey Robinson, then under contract to Warner Bros. but looking to become an independent producer, and Warners' production chief, Hal Wallis. In New York to work on a project, Robinson and Wallis saw *The Morning Star* together.

As Robinson's boss, Wallis had the right to bid on Peck's services first. Hal summoned Greg to his hotel room at the Waldorf-Astoria and, after a pleasant meeting, phoned Jack Warner about the actor. Apparently Hayward's asking price was different for a standard studio contract—or perhaps Goldwyn's reaction had created a strategic reassessment—for Wallis told Warner that they could get the kid for a thousand dollars a week. The price was still steep, but Wallis thought it could pay off, because they could use Peck in as many pictures a year as they wished. With the war seriously impacting the availability of leading men in Hollywood, Warners, like every other studio, needed to take advantage of a tall, handsome prospect who was exempt from the draft.

What Wallis had in mind was the typical arrangement between studio and actor at the time. A player was signed to a contract that gave his employer the exclusive right to his or her services. With annual options for renewal (by the studio, not the actor), the standard term of the arrangement was seven years. If another studio wanted to use that actor in one of its films, it had to negotiate a loanout with the parent company, and any salary it offered over and above the contract player's earnings went to the studio rather than the actor. Moreover, a contract player had to accept whatever roles and whatever films the studio offered. Those who turned down unwanted assignments were placed on suspension, and the weeks or months when they sat idle were added to the total term of the contract. Thus, a seven-year contract could actually run far longer. Of course, it was in the studios' interests to keep their leading players as happy as possible, but the system was a form of benevolent servitude.

Although Wallis' interest in Peck made sense, Jack Warner, like Samuel Goldwyn before him, balked at Hayward's asking price. Unable to sign the youngster himself, Wallis then gave Casey Robinson his blessings to talk with Greg.

Robinson approached Peck with a different kind of proposal. He told the actor that he had no interest in an exclusive relationship. Rather, he would hire Greg for a specified number of pictures, leaving him time to pursue any other opportunities that came his way. Moreover, he wouldn't follow the typical pattern, casting the kid in small roles and letting him gradually work his way up; he'd start him out as a star.

Many actors would have found Robinson's offer enormously appealing, but Peck, having just reached Broadway for the first time, wasn't eager to become a movie star. He believed that his future lay in the theater. In fact, as Robinson noted, "he kind of looked down his nose at Hollywood, as was popular in those days for people of the stage to do; and he said he had no desire to go to Hollywood and acquire a swimming pool." Still, the two men developed a warm personal rapport. "If I ever do come to Hollywood," Peck told the screenwriter, "I will come to you."

On October 3, after twenty-four performances, *The Morning Star* closed. Not only had it drawn mixed reviews, it had been preceded by two other plays about the blitz—*The Wookey* by Frederick Hazlitt Brennan and *Heart of a City* by Lesley Storm. With the United States now at war, the

Battle of Britain was simply too removed in time to interest most American theatergoers.

Peck was out of a job, but, having seen his name on a Broadway marquee and knowing that the likes of Samuel Goldwyn and Hal Wallis were vying for his services, he felt confident enough about his future to finally marry Greta.

On October 4, the day after *The Morning Star* closed, they and some friends journeyed to the Bronx for the fourth game of the World Series between the New York Yankees and the St. Louis Cardinals (the Cardinals won). On the way back to Manhattan, at about 5:30 in the afternoon, they went to the Methodist Church on Sixty-first Street and Park Avenue, where a minister performed the ceremony in a lounge normally used by the congregation's men's club. "We wanted it informal, not in the church," said Peck. "The minister was one of those regular guys—didn't wear his collar backwards or anything." As Greta was a Protestant and a divorcée, there was no question of their marrying in a Catholic church.

After the ceremony, the newlyweds and their friends—including a few actors and Greta's brother Paul—celebrated with a steak dinner at a nearby hotel. "There was no honeymoon," Peck recalled, "I was broke. Greta and I moved into my flat on East Thirty-ninth Street. It just meant carrying a suitcase across from her brother's apartment."

Getting married was an important step for Greg. At the age of twenty-six, he was still something of a loner, and he yearned for the sort of stable family environment that he had lacked as a child. Moreover, he was trying to establish himself in a profession where the unemployment rate was about 90 percent. Even with one Broadway show to his credit, the process of making the rounds of producers' and casting directors' offices was a lonely and painful way to spend one's days, as was auditioning for shows and being rejected. Occasionally he met someone who gave him a bit of encouragement. Such an instance came with his audition for the musical *Lady in the Dark*, written by Kurt Weill and Moss Hart. He was too young for the role, but Hart, who was also directing, told him, "Go out and learn your business, and we'll work together someday."*

Such kind words were few, however. Like every other young actor, Greg frequently wondered if he would ever get another role again. From time to time, he even thought about quitting the profession. "And when it wasn't on my mind," he said years later, "my father was writing to me, reminding me that I was on a fool's errand, at best, and that I should go back and take a graduate degree—go to law school, go to medical school.

*Hart was right. He wrote the screenplay for Peck's 1947 film, *Gentleman's Agreement.*

. . . All of those things seemed eminently more respectable to my dad and to offer more promise for a future for his son than what I did." To keep his spirits up, Greg even bought a book called *Willpower: the Dynamo's Secret.* But, with Greta beside him, the struggle was less awesome. She was a nurturing soul, and she believed in him. She bolstered his confidence when he felt depressed.

Peck's dry spell lasted less than two months. By the end of November, he was hard at work on his next Broadway play, *The Willow and I* by John Patrick.

Directed by Donald Blackwell (who also coproduced), *The Willow and I* starred Martha Scott—Emily in both the stage and screen versions of *Our Town*—and Joanna Roos as Southern sisters at the turn of the century who fall in love with the same man, a doctor named Robin Todd. Peck played the physician in act 1. He returned in acts 2 and 3, which took place many years later, as the deceased doctor's son, Kirkland.

The Willow and I tried out in Boston and Philadelphia. Following the show's stint in the City of Brotherly Love, Barbara O'Neill replaced Joanna Roos as the more willful of the two sisters, after which *The Willow and I* opened at the Windsor Theatre in New York on December 10, 1942. As with *The Morning Star,* the critics considered the play itself the evening's chief disappointment, finding it overly dramatic, repetitious, and with an unsatisfactory resolution. By contrast, they found the production and the leading players superb. Howard Barnes of the *New York Herald-Tribune* called Martha Scott "both radiant and terrible" and Barbara O'Neill "excellent." He added, "Given more explicit dramatic material, and they would have made it something of a theatrical event."

But the critics were at their most rapturous when discussing Peck. Wilella Wardorf of the *New York Post* called him "enormously ingratiating," and Burns Mantle of the *Daily News* praised his "poise," "good looks," "splendid voice," and "compelling sympathy." Robert Coleman of the *Daily Mirror* went so far as to cite a conversation between two women that he had overheard after the final curtain. One woman indicated that she wanted to see the play "again and again because of that handsome Gregory Peck. He's a darling. He's really something." Which led Coleman to conclude that "it looks like a majority of the girls are going to go for *The Willow and I* and its Mr. Peck." The second half of Coleman's prediction was right. After the play's opening, folks in the know began thinking of Greg as Broadway's next matinee idol. As actor-director Norman Lloyd put it, "I knew about Greg and it was a given—people talked about him—this is the next big star."

Indicative of Peck's growing reputation was the interest of another medium, radio. In the 1930s and 1940s, the airwaves were filled with all sorts of anthology series. Usually thirty minutes in length and underwritten by a single sponsor whose name was often attached to the series' titles, these programs drew freely from novels, plays, and films as well as original scripts. Several aired in Hollywood and featured some of the best known movie stars of the era; others originated in New York, utilizing the city's large pool of stage actors. With his beautiful, rich speaking voice, Peck was a natural for the medium.

The program that introduced him to a national listening audience was an original drama called *That They Might Live* by Frederick Gilsdorf, which aired on NBC on January 24, 1943. Sponsored by the American Red Cross, the drama featured Peck's *Willow* costar, Martha Scott, as a nurse torn between staying in her hospital job and joining the army, where nurses were badly needed. Peck played her fiancé, an army officer. Unfortunately, by the time the drama aired, *The Willow and I* was history. Attendance had been insufficient to keep the show afloat for more than twenty-eight performances, only four more than *The Morning Star.*

In the wake of his second Broadway disappointment, Greg was persuaded by his agents, Maynard Morris and Leland Hayward, to take a trip to Hollywood to meet some of the studio executives who were interested in him for pictures. Peck saw the trip as exploratory; "[j]ust to talk," as he said later.

With the powerful, debonair Hayward as his guide, Peck visited with David O. Selznick, Samuel Goldwyn, and 20th Century–Fox's Darryl F. Zanuck. "I had a lot of fun," the actor recalled. "I remember going on a set at Paramount. I was thrilled to stand there and watch those people work."

But the mogul who made the biggest impression on him was Louis B. Mayer, the head of the largest and most powerful studio in the world, Metro-Goldwyn-Mayer.

Dangling a seven-year contract before Greg, Mayer cited MGM's roster of male stars, including Clark Gable, Spencer Tracy, Robert Taylor, and James Stewart, detailing his pivotal role in the success of each one and promising to make Peck a star as well. It was evident that Mayer thought of the studio as a family, with himself as the benevolent but dictatorial father. When he finished, he asked Peck what he thought. "Sorry, Mr. Mayer," Greg replied. "I'm a stage actor. I want to continue to be one. I'm determined not to sign an exclusive contract for anyone."

Convinced that Peck was simply angling for a better deal, Mayer said, "Please, Gregory, understand what I am offering you." The mogul then launched into another tribute to his own skills and the glories of his studio. As he spoke, tears began rolling down his checks. Finally he had to remove his spectacles to wipe his eyes. When he finished, he again asked Peck to sign with him and once more Peck declined. Mayer looked dumbfounded. As Greg and Hayward left the mogul's presence, the actor turned to his agent and said, "God, Alfred Lunt couldn't have given a better performance." Hayward blithely replied, "Oh, he does that every day."

While in Hollywood, Peck also met with Casey Robinson, the Warners screenwriter who had talked to him about a contract after seeing him in *The Morning Star.* Once again, Greg found himself relaxing with the aspiring producer, whom he later described as a very "quiet, very sincere fellow," only thirteen years his senior. As in New York, Casey stressed that what he had in mind for Peck was a nonexclusive arrangement—two pictures a year for four years—which would leave Greg plenty of time to pursue other opportunities. He also described his vision of a company that would be small and intimate, unlike the typical Hollywood dream factory. To Greg, it sounded "kind of like an art venture," more in keeping with the stage productions that he was used to.

Robinson was even willing to sign Greg without a screen test. As much a part of studio practice as the seven-year contract, such tests gave motion picture executives the opportunity to determine how a prospective contract player registered on film before investing in him or her. But Casey told Greg, "I love your voice; I love your stature. I can see you on the screen. I don't have to put a camera on you to see you on the screen."

However, what truly piqued Peck's interest was not Robinson's appealing character or the relative freedom he offered or the small scale of his enterprise. It was the money he was willing to pay—$1,000 a week for ten weeks' work, compared to the $250 the actor had earned per week for *The Willow and I.* By this point, Greg and Greta had moved to a larger one-bedroom apartment on Lexington Avenue—not far from their previous home—to accommodate their expanding household, which included a snow-white police dog named Perry and a Persian cat called Widgie. The new apartment was nice, but Greg was having a hard time meeting the rent. At $200 a month, it was far more than anything he had paid previously. Moreover, he had needed extensive work on his teeth, for which he owed his dentist, Julius Y. Pokress, $1,400. Pokress, said Peck, "was famous for being a softy with actors. He'd allow you to run up a big dental bill and not press you for payment." Still, Greg wanted to retire this financial obligation, and signing with Robinson would allow him to do so.

The contract was dated February 25, 1942. As it turned out, Robinson didn't act with complete independence; he was partnered with RKO, and the studio insisted upon being able to use Greg in pictures of its own.

Thus, Robinson could only retain half of his eight-film commitment; the studio claimed the remainder. Two pictures were specified in the contract: the first was to be one of Robinson's, then called *This Is Russia*; the second was to be a studio property, either *The Prodigal Women*, in which Joan Fontaine was to star, or *Thieves Like Us*, which Dudley Nichols was slated to direct.* For the second picture, Greg's salary would rise to $1,200 a week. The remaining six pictures would be determined later, assuming, of course, that the annual option for his services was exercised.

Greg was given a $5,000 bonus upon signing the contract. "When I got back to Greta with the check," he recalled, "we danced a jig all over our small apartment." After paying off the dentist, they had a considerable sum left and decided to splurge on a honeymoon. Poring over possible choices, they selected the Camel Back Inn in Phoenix, where for three weeks, they swam, rode horses, square-danced, picnicked in the desert, and, as Peck put it, "romped like a couple of kids."

Tanned and rested, they returned to New York. Before Greg could start work on his first film, he had to fulfill a prior commitment. As he had explained to Robinson before signing the contract, he had a verbal agreement to appear in a Broadway play entitled *Sons and Soldiers*. "Hayward thought I was nuts to do it," Peck recalled; the agent feared that if Greg bombed in the play, RKO might cancel his contract. But Greg remained certain that his future lay on the stage and insisted upon doing the show.

Peck would receive $400 a week for *Sons and Soldiers*, an impressive increase over his earnings for *The Willow and I* but significantly less than his salary with Casey Robinson. Money, however, was not his prime reason for doing the play; he wanted to work with its director, Max Reinhardt.

Born in Austria in 1873, Reinhardt was a towering figure in the German theater during the first third of the century. He also directed a few silent films in his adopted homeland, as well as Warner Bros.' 1935 version of *A Midsummer Night's Dream*. Not only had he had worked with many actors who would become movie stars, including Luise Rainer, Emil Jannings, Marlene Dietrich, and Joseph Schildkraut, but his expressionist style influenced directors like F. W. Murnau, Ernst Lubitsch, Otto Preminger, and William Dieterle, all of whom had assisted him or acted for him or both (Dieterle even codirected his *Midsummer Night's Dream*).

Sons and Soldiers needed the skill of a Max Reinhardt, for the play was

*As it turned out, Peck did neither *The Prodigal Women* nor *Thieves Like Us*.

rather unconventional for its time. Set in a small American town in 1916, the principal character, Rebecca Tadlock, faces a terrible decision: she is pregnant but is told by her doctor that she will probably not survive childbirth. As she decides whether or not to abort the fetus, she imagines what her child's life might be like. These visions occupy the greater part of the play. Its author, Irwin Shaw, had penned two previous dramas, *Bury the Dead* and *The Gentle People,* as well as numerous short stories, but he would gain subsequent fame as a novelist, notably as the author of *The Young Lions* and *Rich Man, Poor Man.*

Unfortunately, by 1943, Reinhardt's best days were behind him. Seventy years old, a refugee from Nazi Germany, and uncomfortable with English, he was reduced to living in a modest hotel in a foreign country. But, despite the diminution of the director's skill and stature, there were, in Peck's opinion, "some embers still glowing there and I got the impression of a very big creative talent, of a warm and loving disposition, of a man who is used to a lot of power but who had adjusted to no longer having it."

Reinhardt summoned up some of his legendary prowess to help the young actor through a difficult rehearsal period. Peck, cast as the woman's imagined son, Andrew Tadlock, had one scene that built to an argument between his character and the boy's parents. The scene required that he laugh, cry, and experience a wide range of emotions. Peck, who would remain a relatively controlled actor throughout his career, had such difficulty letting go that whenever he had to rehearse the climactic scene, he would feel his chest muscles tighten. The more self-conscious he became, the worse the scene played. Finally, his poor performance started to impact the work of the other actors.

Reinhardt, who liked to watch rehearsals from the back of the orchestra section, usually sent his assistant, Lili Darvas, to convey directions to the actors; he was in no condition to repeatedly trek back and forth to the stage. But such was Peck's difficulty with the scene that Reinhardt decided to make an exception. As he made his way down the aisle and took Greg off to a corner, the actor was distinctly nervous. What would the great man say to him? At a mere five feet four inches, Reinhardt barely reached Peck's chest. Getting as close as he could to his young player, he said in a heavily accented whisper, "Gregory, see the great advantage of being a play actor. We do not stop being children when we grow up. Play act, play act—it's all performance and imagination. It's nothing to be afraid of. It's only playing."

For Peck, the words were inspiring. As he put it, they "helped me throw off my self-consciousness," and allowed him to risk making a fool of himself. At least, he did the best he could. But Greg, a man who retains a tight control over his emotions, would never be as willing as some to simply explode, to give full vent to his character's feelings, whether on the stage or on the screen.

In addition to Peck, *Sons and Soldiers* featured several other cast members with notable futures ahead: the distinguished film actors Karl Malden and Millard Mitchell; one of America's foremost acting teachers, Stella Adler; and the comic character actor, Jesse White. Top-billed as Peck's mother was Dublin-born Geraldine Fitzgerald, returning to Broadway after four years in Hollywood where she had appeared in *Dark Victory*, *Wuthering Heights*, and *Watch on the Rhine*, among other films.

Given its talented cast, *Sons and Soldiers* might have settled into a long run at the Morosco Theatre, where it opened on May 3, 1943, were it not for the play. Despite "sharply observant scenes, good incidental comedy and moments of soaring dialogue," to quote the review of the *New York Sun*'s Ward Morehouse, the drama needed considerable pruning and shaping. Unfortunately, Shaw was a private in the army, serving in Africa while the play was in production. As his contract prevented the producers from altering or cutting even a single line, *Sons and Soldiers* couldn't be trimmed or shaped in the usual fashion. This constraint proved to be a major source of frustration for all involved. Peck later said, "Several of us felt, and still do, that we might have had a hit if we could have cut twenty-five minutes from the play."

As with Peck's previous Broadway productions, the show's director and cast were well received. His personal notices echoed the sentiments expressed for his work in *The Morning Star* and *The Willow and I.* But *Sons and Soldiers* never found its audience. It closed on May 22, after twenty-two performances.

Although Peck had seen three dramas open and close in New York in about twenty months, he remained determined to succeed on Broadway. It wasn't an idle ambition. The productions had failed, but he had emerged as one of the theater's most promising new talents. As soon as he finished his film assignment with Robinson, he fully intended to return home and pick up the major thrust of his career. After all, he reasoned, movies were just a sideline, a way of earning decent money.

CHAPTER 7

"The Phantom Star"

Greg and Greta arrived in Los Angeles in late August or early September 1943. The twenty-seven-year-old actor's coming was hardly trumpeted in the press or anywhere else. Outside of a few studio executives, no one knew who he was. After all, the combined total of his Broadway output had not equaled one three-month run.

Indicative of his status was his difficulty in finding a place to live. Thanks to the war, which had brought the construction of new homes to a virtual halt, Los Angeles was experiencing a severe housing shortage. The Pecks were forced to stay at the Monterey Motel on Sunset Boulevard while Greg worked on his first film.

Casey Robinson, whose screenplays for Warners included *Captain Blood,* several Bette Davis vehicles, and *This Is the Army,* chose a rather odd property with which to launch his new star. *This Is Russia* (originally called *Revenge* and ultimately titled *Days of Glory*) was a humanistic and timely but decidedly subdued depiction of the resistance mounted by ordinary Soviet citizens to the Nazi invasion of their homeland.

Peck was cast as Vladimir, the leader of a group of guerrillas. For his love interest, Nina, a dancer who joins the rebel band, Robinson chose the Russian-born ballerina Tamara Toumanova, with whom he was having an affair and whom he would later marry. A star of the Monte Carlo Ballet Russe, Toumanova was far better known in the world of dance than Peck was in the theater. But when it came to film, she was as much a novice as he.*

Having selected two newcomers for his leads, Robinson decided to "go the whole hog and cast the whole picture with unknowns." It was a daring experiment. As Thornton Delehanty noted in the *New York Her-*

*Today Tamara Toumanova is best remembered by film buffs as the prima donna ballerina in Alfred Hitchcock's 1966 thriller *Torn Curtain,* starring Paul Newman and Julie Andrews.

ald-Tribune in October 1943, while the picture was in production, it was "the first time in the memory of the film capital a Grade A picture is being filmed with a cast of which all the members are new to the picture business, most of them never having appeared on the screen before." Supervising Robinson's newcomers was an RKO contract director named Jacques Tourneur. The thirty-nine-year old Paris-born filmmaker had recently garnered widespread acclaim for two low-budget horror-suspense films, *Cat People* and *I Walked With a Zombie.*

During principal photography, Peck had some difficulty adjusting to the requirements of the new medium, a common problem for stage actors. Performing for a live audience is quite different from acting before a camera. The process of creating a role is the same, but, in the theater, an actor primarily concentrates on filling the house, making sure that he or she can be heard, and that the character's emotions register, even in the balcony. He must also learn to re-create his performance eight times a week, sometimes for months or years, so that the show remains fresh for each new audience.

In film, the tasks are quite different. Movies are often shot out of sequence. Two related events might be filmed weeks or even months apart, so an actor must learn to tap into the emotional life of his character without having necessarily experienced the steps leading up to the moment at hand. A film actor must also exercise much greater control over his movements. It is not at all uncommon for a technician to take a tape measure to an actor's nose or finger in order to determine an optimal lighting effect or camera angle. Because of the requisite precision, an actor's stopping points are taped on the floor, and he must learn to watch for these "marks" without appearing to do so. Naturally the size of the screen, which blows up an actor's features to many times life size, requires a subtly of expression that is exactly the opposite of how one emotes on stage. A film actor quickly learns that the slightest lift of an eyebrow or the barest hint of a smile can speak volumes about what he is thinking or feeling.

Peck later described how filming initially impacted him: "You feel like a bug under a microscope, and then to move freely and to speak freely and concentrate and forget all of that equipment, it takes a bit of practice, you know. It's a trade that has to be learned. And you get kind of frozen; most newcomers do."

He had particular difficulty with his diction. It was too crisp and clear for ordinary speech, and he had a tendency to project too loudly. After a take, Jacques Tourneur would call "Cut," then pull Peck aside and say, "Greg, can't you common it up a bit?" At first, the actor didn't know what he meant, then, finally, as he put it, "I got the idea that by 'commoning it up' he meant not to speak for the gallery, but to speak for the microphone which was sometimes two feet over my nose."

His adjustment may have been eased by the fact that he didn't take the business of filmmaking all that seriously. Associated Press reporter Rosalind Shaffer, who visited the set during filming, wrote that he exhibited a "devil-may-care casualness, the confidential twinkle in his eyes that seemed to say: 'You and I know this is a bunch of nonsense, but it's a way to make a living, and it's fun.'"

He also struck reporters as being different from the typical Hollywood actor. A journalist for the *Boston Post* was impressed by the fact that Greg, while "always agreeable," was "not one to talk about himself unless prodded. The truth is that Peck's interests are more outside of himself than those of most actors. What concerns him most is the sad state of the world at present."

Like Greg, Toumanova was rather nonplussed by the process of moviemaking; to her, *Days of Glory* was a lark, a break from the rigors of the ballet. She enjoyed visiting the studio even when she wasn't on call, as did Peck. "This is the craziest picture I've ever seen," Robinson said at the time. "You can't keep the actors away from it even on their days off." The ballerina also had a problem with her voice, but it was just the opposite of Peck's: never having learned to project as a dancer, she spoke in a whisper; Tourneur was constantly asking her to speak up.

The picture wrapped in late October or early November. About seven months later, on June 16, 1944—ten days after the Allied invasion of Normandy—it premiered at the Palace Theatre in New York.

As American boys were slugging it out against the Germans and the Japanese in real life, Hollywood was refighting the war on the silver screen, with considerable support from the public. Half the top-ten box-office hits of 1944 were related to the worldwide conflict, from the historically based *Thirty Seconds Over Tokyo* to a story of pilots in training called *Winged Victory* to *Since You Went Away,* a heartwarming drama of the home front. *Days of Glory* was less commercial than these pictures. Aside from a cast of unknowns, it featured Chekhovian-like character vignettes rather than blood-pounding combat sequences, plus mood lighting, a leisurely pace, and a script with literary pretensions.

And, of course, all of the principal characters were Russian. To help American audiences keep the guerrillas straight, they were introduced through voice-over narration at the outset of the film. As the stars, Peck and Toumanova were identified by their real names as well as those of their characters. To Greg's embarrassment, he was described as a "distinguished star of the New York stage," which was laying it on a bit thick in light of his three short-lived Broadway shows. Toumanova was introduced in equally glowing terms but, as a celebrated ballerina, she had greater claim to the accolade.

Some of the critics admired *Days of Glory*'s artsy ambitions. Leo Mishkin of the New York *Morning Telegraph* even called it a "*succès d'estime.*" But most saw the picture for what it was, "a slow, talky drama with too little action," to quote *Variety*. It also featured some truly terrible dialogue. Moreover, in depicting the Nazis as virtually subhuman and the Russian guerrillas as a mix of lovable peasants, idealistic youths, and noble men and women, *Days of Glory* came very close to propaganda, a salute from America to its Soviet comrades-in-arms.

Despite their reservations about the film, the critics offered near universal acclaim for Toumanova and Peck, whom the *New York Post*'s Archer Winsten called "two new faces of considerable impressiveness." Several of Winsten's colleagues likened Greg to Gary Cooper, and Kate Cameron of the New York *Daily News* predicted that he was "destined for stardom," providing the quality of his pictures improved.

To be sure, Peck was relatively raw in his first film outing. Sporting a shock of unruly hair with his clothes hanging loosely on his frame, he appeared so thin at times that he looked almost emaciated, more like an earnest graduate student than a guerrilla firebrand. And he was unable to completely solve his vocal problems. In the end, he compensated for his tendency to overproject by speaking almost as softly as Toumanova, often in a near monotone. And either by his own volition or under direction from Tourneur, he turned away from the camera on several significant lines rather than waiting until their conclusion, thereby undercutting their impact.

There were occasions, however, when he rose above his own inexperience and the pretentiousness of the material—as in a moment early in the film, when Vladimir looks up at the ballerina, practically a stranger to him at that point. Listening to her recite a love poem, his face takes on a sweet, soulful quality. As Greg's face shines forth from the shadowy light, his high cheekbones and full lips in sharp relief, his physical beauty is impressive indeed.

Even more memorable is a forest scene in which Nina asks Vladimir if he enjoys fighting and killing. He tells her he was an engineer before the war and that he loved to build useful things, a great dam in particular. Then he adds, "And when the Germans came, I helped to destroy it. . . . Sometimes when I destroy something that's been built, I could weep." There is a simple honesty to Peck's delivery here, underscoring the decency and integrity with which he endows his character. Indeed, in this scene, he offers viewers—without knowing it himself—a first glimpse at the great hallmark of his screen persona, the intelligent, thoughtful man of principle. A moment later the ballerina is in his arms, asking him to promise that he will never send her away, and in his tender response one can catch the arrival of a potent new screen lover. As John T. McManus observed in his review of the film for *P.M.,* Peck looked "like a sure heart-throb for the postwar world."

But *Days of Glory* would not establish Peck as a rival to Gable or Cooper or Tyrone Power. Lacking big names to attract an audience, the picture needed glowing reviews to succeed at the box office. Failing to win the necessary acclaim, it quickly disappeared from the nation's movie houses. Thus, Gregory Peck's film debut came and went with barely a ripple of public notice.

Filmgoers may not have been aware of Peck, but while *Days of Glory* was in production, interest in him continued to escalate within the motion picture community. As his contract with Robinson allowed him considerable time for freelancing, Leland Hayward cleverly fanned the flames at other studios, offering the actor on outrageous terms—a high starting salary, only leading roles, project approval, top or near-top billing. It was, according to one journalist, "a classic demonstration of how to whip callous producers into a buying frenzy over an unknown quantity."

Soon the agent's efforts were paying off. Wrote gossip columnist Louella O. Parsons, "You couldn't go to a party without hearing the buzz about this wonder man's rugged handsomeness, his thin height, his magical speaking voice." As a result of the hype, Peck was signed to three more contracts by March 30, 1944, two and a half months before *Days of Glory* opened. No one in the motion picture industry—or its observers—could recall such a fury over a single, untested actor. Parson's principal rival, Hedda Hopper, called Peck "the hottest thing in town." Because he had been signed to four multi-picture deals yet the public hadn't a clue who he was, an astonished media dubbed him the "Phantom Star."

Among his new employers was MGM. With contract players Clark Gable, James Stewart, and Robert Taylor serving in the military, L. B. Mayer abandoned his insistence on a seven-year contract and settled for a three-picture deal. Greg was also picked up by David O. Selznick, the producer who had rejected Peck after viewing his 1941 screen test. Offering Greg a seven-year contract, which the actor refused, Selznick went to RKO, where he had once been in charge of production, and acquired the studio's entire percentage of the Casey Robinson deal and half of Robinson's, or a total of six pictures.

But the first to fall in line had been 20th Century–Fox.

* * *

Fox's interest in Peck stemmed from a problem confronting the studio's production chief, Darryl F. Zanuck. Zanuck was sitting on a hot property in a 1941 best-selling novel by A. J. Cronin called *The Keys of the Kingdom,* for which he had paid a significant sum, $102,000. The book's central character, a dedicated Roman Catholic priest who becomes a missionary in China, was a plum role but difficult to cast. Father Francis Chisholm had to be seen as thoughtful, intelligent, and sensitive but capable of taking a principled stand when circumstances warranted. Moreover, the actor who took the role would have to be credible as both an idealistic seminarian and a senior citizen, as the Scottish priest's story covered six decades. Zanuck had several stars who might have played the part, including Tyrone Power and Henry Fonda. But they, along with several other Fox players—Victor Mature, Richard Greene, and John Payne—were off serving the Allied cause.

During a nine-month search for the right actor for Father Chisholm, Zanuck considered most of Hollywood's remaining leading men, including Spencer Tracy and Franchot Tone. He also tested dozens of unknowns without success. Then, while *Days of Glory* was in production, he viewed some of the rushes featuring Peck and knew that he had finally found his man. He was so certain that he offered Greg the role without even testing him for it. "That is unusual," Peck said a few months later, "but it is grand for the actor. It gives you great confidence, makes you feel that the part is really yours, that you belong to it."

The opportunity didn't come without strings. Zanuck knew that *The Keys of the Kingdom* had the potential to make Peck a star, and, if it did, he wanted to share in the actor's success. Thus, before the mogul would cast Greg as Father Chisholm, the young man had to agree to do three more films for Fox. Confident that he would still have time to return to the theater, Peck agreed. Thereafter, he and Greta redoubled their efforts to find a house. They finally located something suitable, a small gray-and-white stucco structure atop Mulholland Drive, overlooking the San Fernando Valley. The home had once belonged to Boris Karloff.

Peck's contract with Fox, dated November 2, 1943, called for him to play Father Chisholm for $1,500 a week with a ten-week guarantee. That was $500 a week more than he'd earned for *Days of Glory* and $200 more than his second Robinson picture specified, but far below what established actors could command for such a major role. Assuming the studio picked up its option for the three other pictures, he would earn $2,500, $3,500, and $4,500 per week, respectively.

Before principal photography for *The Keys of the Kingdom* commenced on November 15, 1943, numerous supporting roles had to be cast. Peck appeared in many of the tests for these parts. He also shot about thirty-five makeup tests to ensure that he would look believable as his character aged. Because of all this preproduction work, Greg joked that "by the time we were ready to do the picture, I was so completely at home in the part . . . the portrayal was like simply being myself."

With a budget of $3 million—more than triple the cost of *Days of Glory*—*The Keys of the Kingdom* was a first-class production, involving some seventy sets. In addition to using the Fox lot, the company shot in Malibu (substituting for Scotland) and at Laguna in Orange County. Adding to the complexity of the shoot was the fact that many of the Chinese extras spoke no English. A representative from Central Casting was engaged to translate the instructions of the director, John M. Stahl, into Cantonese.

In total, principal photography took six months, more than double the length of the average shooting schedule at the time. Peck was on call for all but five days, during which the scenes involving his character as a boy were shot. He didn't mind the hard work. He truly enjoyed acting, and he loved the role of Father Chisholm. It had, in his words, "such range and variety. Some of the scenes were on a note of comedy, others were tragic." He also felt that the priest offered "a delightful mixture of traits, especially his rebelliousness and idealism."

In establishing Father Chisholm's character, he began to develop an approach to film acting that would reflect the hallmarks of his screen persona—his use of a slow, emphatic manner of speaking; a comfort with stillness; a strategic application of pauses, within his own lines and when another actor finishes speaking; a way of looking down as he takes in someone's words, his mouth slightly open, and then lifting his head with his eyebrows raised. Watching him, one can almost *see* the character thinking. Compare his manner in *The Keys of the Kingdom* with many of the other male stars of the day, including Clark Gable, Spencer Tracy, and Humphrey Bogart, and the differences are striking. In his naturalism, he paved the way for the postwar generation of leading men, including Montgomery Clift and Marlon Brando.

But he was still a novice, and there were moments in *Keys* that gave him difficulty. One was a scene near the film's conclusion when Father Chisholm bids farewell to his Chinese congregation and missionary friends. "I did it very ineptly," Peck confessed. Director John M. Stahl, a former actor who had previously directed Clark Gable in *Parnell,* Robert Taylor in *Magnificent Obsession,* and Henry Fonda in *Immortal Sergeant,* took him aside and talked to him about the story, emphasizing what the priest was feeling at that moment. Finally, he told his leading man, "Now do it again, and don't act—just feel it." Said Peck, "I did a much better job on the next try."

As the rough cut of the picture ran about three hours and twenty minutes, several scenes were eliminated in postproduction and, by the time *The Keys of the Kingdom* opened at New York's Rivoli Theatre on December 28, 1944, its length had been trimmed by slightly more than an hour. Still, at 137 minutes, it was longer than the average film of its day, and a few critics, including *Variety*'s Abel, thought that it dragged. The *New Yorker* even called it "interminable." But the general critical consensus, articulated by *Time* magazine, found the film "human, dramatic and moving."

There was universal praise for Peck's performance, and it was well deserved. It wasn't so much that he exercised a major departure from his portrayal of Vladimir in *Days of Glory,* but rather that he built upon the simple, honest delivery he had attempted in his film debut with far better material to support him. Moreover, in contrast to the guerrilla leader, Father Chisholm, a gentle but vigorous soul keenly aware of his minor imperfections, including his rebellious streak, was perfect for his clean, uncluttered style. Peck had no fiery sermons to deliver and only one or two angry moments—which were modulated by the priest's wish to control his temper. Arguably the role's biggest challenge was Chisholm's progression from youth to old man, but, generally, Peck left that to the makeup. What remained were mostly a series of one-on-one scenes between the priest and the individuals he encounters, including a non-Christian Mandarin (Leonard Strong), the pompous bishop Chisholm's known since boyhood (Vincent Price), and an arrogant Mother Superior (Rosa Stradner). And most of these encounters emphasized the priest's humility and compassion.

Peck would later argue that he could have given the character more dimension if he'd had more experience as an actor and in life. "All I could do [at the time]," he said, "was invest all the sincerity that I could in it, which I did." The portrayal *is* arguably a bit one-dimensional, but, as the critical response suggests, it is very effective on a moment-to-moment basis.

The Keys of the Kingdom performed well at the box office but failed to return Fox's $3 million investment. For Peck, it was more rewarding. To begin with, Darryl Zanuck gave him a $25,000 bonus for his long, untiring work on the picture. In addition, his performance earned him an Academy Award nomination for Best Actor. The Oscar went to Ray Milland for *The Lost Weekend,* but the recognition Peck received from his peers for only his second film outing was an extraordinary accomplishment.

Moreover, his nomination catapulted him to the top of the Hollywood pecking order. By the time of the Oscar ceremony on March 7, 1946, he was hobnobbing with some of the biggest stars in town, including Bogart, Tracy, and Cagney. "I met everybody," he said years later. Perhaps the one who impressed him most was the fellow with whom he was frequently compared, Gary Cooper. When they were introduced, Coop, with dozens of films to his credit, asked the newcomer how many pictures he'd done. "Two," Greg replied. "How were they?" Coop inquired. "One good, one bad," Peck admitted. The veteran mused. "You're ahead of the game right now. Don't be worried if you get a few flops. An actor is lucky if he has two good movies out of every five he makes."

Peck was more than ahead of the game. *The Keys of the Kingdom* had established him not just as a star, but as a phenomenon. As the *New York Times* observed shortly after the film's release, "Not since Clark Gable crashed upon the screen over a dozen years ago has the arrival of a young leading man created as much commotion as did that of Gregory Peck as the saintly and human Father Chisholm."

Suddenly, at age twenty-nine, he was a celebrity. When he visited a store or he and Greta dined out, people stared and asked for his autograph. Said Peck, "It was a novelty, I must say, to suddenly be recognized more and more as I went about, to feel myself losing my anonymity." Many people thrust into the limelight so quickly are changed by the adulation, usually not for the better. Greg, however, remained anchored. He attributed his years of stage training and work in the theater for this. He was, and would remain, more interested in doing quality work than in being famous. But famous he was. No one could call him the "Phantom Star" anymore.

CHAPTER 8

The Hottest Guy Since Gable

The Keys of the Kingdom represented traditional Hollywood storytelling, but Peck's next project, *Spellbound,* was ultra-modern, utilizing psychotherapy as a major element in its plot. The film's producer, David O. Selznick, who had been in analysis himself, went to great lengths to convey at least one of the principal components of Freud's methodology, the interpretation of dreams, hiring the renowned surrealistic painter Salvador Dalí to design a sequence in which subconscious fantasies were portrayed.

The film was based on *The House of Doctor Edwardes,* a 1927 novel by Francis Beeding, which was initially acquired by Alfred Hitchcock. The British director, who was under contract to Selznick, then sold the rights to his boss for $40,000. Although the novel had psychiatric underpinnings, it wasn't exactly a medical treatise. Set high in the Alps, it focused on a maniac named Geoffrey Godstone, who imprisons the chief of a mental home and then takes over the management of the facility himself. One of the staff psychiatrists, Constance Sedgwick, discovers who Godstone really is but is powerless to stop him. Finally, the owner of the hospital, a distinguished psychiatrist named Dr. Edwardes, arrives and sets matters to right.

Hitchcock planned on retaining the Godstone character, hoping to use Joseph Cotten in the role. The previous year, the Selznick contract player had ably portrayed a psychopath in the director's *Shadow of a Doubt.* But as work on the project progressed, the story shifted: instead of a maniac taking over the asylum, Hitch and his collaborator, Angus McPhail, created a character with amnesia who *thinks* he's Edwardes. The staff and patients accept him as such. Constance, the female doctor, even falls in love with him. Then, upon discovering his amnesia, she uses psychoanalysis to cure him. She also unmasks the killer of the real Edwardes.

To write the script, Selznick engaged Ben Hecht, the author of some two dozen screenplays, including *Gunga Din* and *Wuthering Heights*, and coauthor (with Charles MacArthur) of two popular stage plays, *The Front Page* and *Twentieth Century.* Hecht had a lifelong interest in psychology and, like Selznick, had been in analysis. By the time Hecht finished, the screenplay bore little resemblance to the original novel.

Initially, Selznick considered Jennifer Jones for the psychiatrist, who was eventually called Constance Peterson. Hitchcock was not happy with the idea, for Selznick, although married to a daughter of L. B. Mayer, was in love with his contract player. Hitch was afraid that if Jones were used, the producer would be hanging around the set throughout filming. He wisely said nothing, and eventually Selznick decided that the role was better suited to another of his leading ladies, Ingrid Bergman.

Even though the central male character had gone from homicidal maniac to troubled amnesiac, Hitchcock still wanted to cast Joseph Cotten. But Selznick needed his contract player in another feature, *I'll Be Seeing You,* which was already in production. According to Leonard Leff, author of a significant book on the Hitchcock-Selznick collaboration, the producer turned to Peck after reviewing an as-yet-unreleased print of *The Keys of the Kingdom.* It was a major break for Greg. Hitchcock was a very successful director and Bergman was among the most popular actresses in the world.

Working for Selznick was different from employment at the major studios. To one extent or another, the latter used an assembly-line approach to filmmaking, churning out roughly a picture a week through operations that were tightly disciplined and well organized. Selznick, by contrast, released few films and took every one personally, lavishing considerable attention on each detail, from the script, which he would endlessly rewrite himself, to the leading lady's hairstyle. Because everything depended upon one brilliant but erratic man, chaos often reigned.

During the filming of *The House of Edwardes,* however, Selznick was preoccupied with the release of another picture, *Since You Went Away.* He wasn't even in Hollywood during much of the summer of 1944, when the thriller was shot. Moreover, according to Bergman, on the few occasions when Selznick did visit the set, Hitchcock would announce that there was a mechanical problem with the camera and stop filming. "I think Hitchcock was the only director who was independent of Selznick," the actress asserted.

Forty-five years old in the summer of 1944, the rotund Londoner had immigrated to America in 1939. Through films like *The Man Who Knew Too Much* and *The Thirty-nine Steps* in his native Britain, and *Foreign Correspondent, Suspicion,* and *Saboteur* in the United States, he'd become

Gregory Peck's birthplace, La Jolla, California, looks like a self-contained village but it is, in fact, part of San Diego. This photo was taken around 1924, when the future actor was eight years old. (San Diego Historical Society)

Eldred Gregory Peck was born on April 5, 1916. His mother was twenty-one at the time. (Archive Photos)

A lonely, introverted boy, Eldred's closest companion for a time was Bud, a stray dog who followed him home from school one day. Eventually his grandmother had to get rid of the pet, because his barking disturbed the neighbors. (The Gregory Peck Collection)

Eldred's father, Gregory Pearl Peck, was a pharmacist, first in La Jolla and then in San Diego. He is seen here with his second wife, the former Harriet Harringon, whom he married when his son was in college. (Archive Photos)

Peck began to blossom as an undergraduate at the University of California, Berkeley, where he spent two years as an oarsman on the junior varsity rowing crew. In his final year, he became involved in campus dramatics. (The John and Meghan Collins Collection)

In October 1939, Peck, now known by his middle name Gregory, enrolled in the two-year acting program at the Neighborhood Playhouse in New York. One of his more successful scene study projects was from Schnitzler's *The Affairs of Anatol.* His partner was Jane Rennie. (The Neighborhood Playhouse Collection)

In October 1942, Greg married a perky hairdresser named Greta Konen. This photo was taken several years later. He could have hardly afforded a fur coat at the time of their wedding. (Archive Photos)

In *Days of Glory,* Greg's first feature, he and ballerina Tamara Toumanova played Soviets resisting the German invasion of their country during World War II. The RKO-Casey Robinson production, released in June 1944, was not a hit. (RKO/The Kobal Collection)

The Keys of the Kingdom, Peck's second feature, found him playing a gentle but headstrong Scottish priest. The role made him an instant star, brought him his first Oscar nomination, and launched his long-term relationship with 20th Century–Fox. (20th Century–Fox/The Gregory Peck Collection)

Peck earned his second Oscar nomination for his portrayal of Penny Baxter, the good-natured, fun-loving Florida scrub farmer in MGM's 1946 hit, *The Yearling.* Ten-year-old Claude Jarman, Jr., portrayed his son. (MGM/The Gregory Peck Collection)

(Below) For a change of pace, Greg played a n'er-do-well rancher in David O. Selznick's lavish 1947 Western *Duel in the Sun.* He was paired with Jennifer Jones, whose wanton half-breed was an equal departure from type. (Vanguard/The Kobal Collection)

(Above left) In 1947, Peck joined with two other Selznick contract players, Mel Ferrer and Dorothy McGuire, to launch a summer theater company housed in his hometown's high school auditorium. He coproduced the La Jolla Playhouse for five seasons and starred in several productions as well. (John Swope/The La Jolla Playhouse)

(Above right) Gentleman's Agreement, an exposé of American anti-Semitism based on the bestselling novel by Laura Z. Hobson, brought Peck his third Oscar nomination. He lost, but the film was named Best Picture of 1947. Fellow nominee Dorothy McGuire played his fiancée, Kathy. (20th Century–Fox/The Gregory Peck Collection)

During the 1940s, Peck lent his rich baritone to a wide variety of radio dramas. He is seen here with Ed Begley, emoting for an episode of *Suspense* entitled "Hitch-hike Poker." It aired on CBS on September 16, 1948. (Steve Hannagan Associates/Archive Photos)

Another Oscar nomination—Peck's fourth in five years—was accorded his moving portrayal of a World War II bomb squadron leader who cracks under the stress of combat command. 1950's *Twelve O'Clock High* was based on the real-life story of Col. Frank A. Armstrong, Jr. (20th Century–Fox/The Kobal Collection)

Although *The Gunfighter,* released in June 1950, was one of the best Westerns ever made, it was a box-office disappointment. "Gregory, you cost me a million dollars with that goddamn mustache," Fox president Spyros Skouras told its star. Karl Malden played a saloonkeeper who basks in the gunman's celebrity. (20th Century–Fox/The Gregory Peck Collection)

(Above) In 1951, Peck portrayed a dashing British naval hero during the Napoleonic Wars. Based on three novels by C. S. Forester, *Captain Horatio Hornblower* was a rousing sea-and-sword adventure saga. Robert Beatty played his first officer. (Warner Bros./The Gregory Peck Collection)

(Right) Returning home from England, where *Hornblower* was filmed, the Pecks—including sons Jonathan, age five (*second from bottom*), Stephen, three (*bottom*), and baby Carey (*not shown*)—were the picture of a happy all-American family. But, in fact, Greg's marriage was in deep trouble. (Bettman/CORBIS)

(Left) One of Peck's biggest hits of the fifties was *The Snows of Kilimanjaro,* released in September 1952. It marked the second of three pairings with his friend, Ava Gardner. (20th Century–Fox/The Gregory Peck Collection)

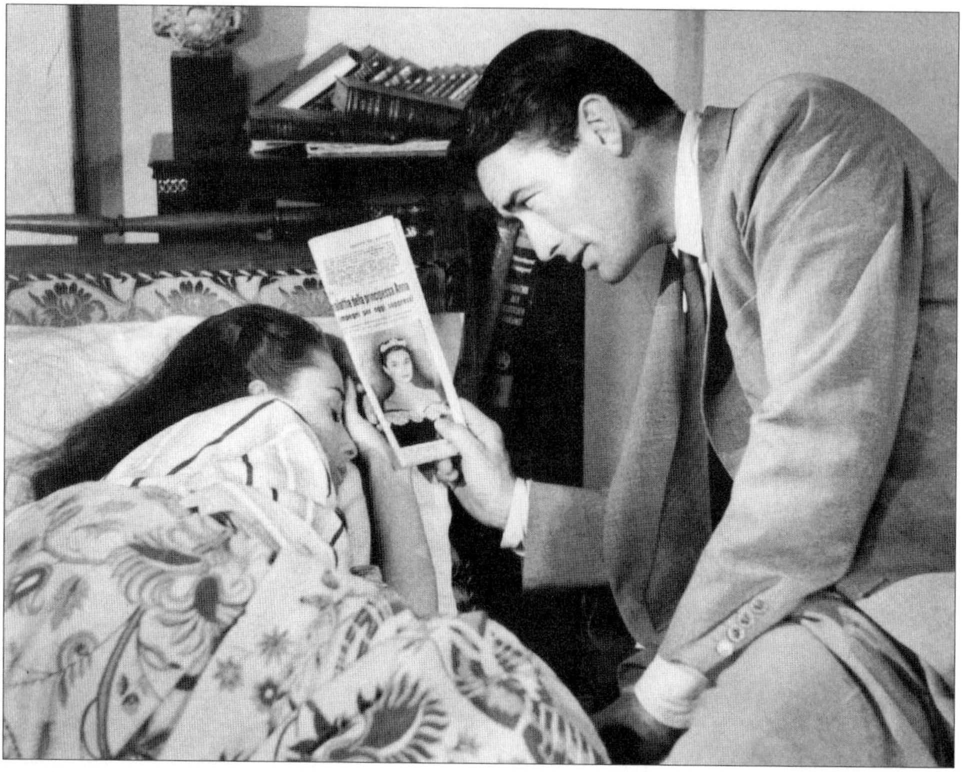

Filmed on location, 1953's *Roman Holiday* paired Peck with Audrey Hepburn, a young Belgian dancer in her first major film role. The result was an entrancing, bittersweet romantic comedy. (Paramount/The Gregory Peck Collection)

On December 31, 1955, one day after his divorce from Greta became final, Greg married a young French journalist, Veronique Passani, whom he'd been seeing for several years. (The Gregory Peck Collection)

Released on July 4, 1956, John Huston's noble but troubled *Moby Dick* starred Peck as the obsessed sea captain, Ahab. The actor nearly lost his life filming this climactic confrontation with a rubber whale. (Warner Bros./The Gregory Peck Collection)

By the end of the 1950s, Peck had joined the swelling ranks of actors and directors with their own production companies. The second feature developed by his Melville Productions was 1962's *Cape Fear*, in which he played an attorney terrorized by ex-con Robert Mitchum. (Universal-International/The Kobal Collection)

Peck played another member of the bar in his next release, *To Kill a Mockingbird,* based on the Pulitzer Prize–winning novel by Harper Lee. Atticus Finch, a loving father with strong moral convictions, became his most celebrated role. (Universal/The Gregory Peck Collection)

(*Left*) After four losses, Greg finally captured an Academy Award in 1963 for his performance in *To Kill a Mockingbird.* He later posed with (*left to right*) Joan Crawford, who accepted the Best Actress award for Anne Bancroft; Best Supporting Actress Patty Duke; and Best Supporting Actor Ed Begley. (Archive Photos)

(Above) Blending intrigue, romance, humor, and glamour, 1966's *Arabesque* featured Peck, Sophia Loren, and assorted bad guys in pursuit of an ancient Egyptian hieroglyph. It was a triumph of style over substance. (Universal/The Gregory Peck Collection)

From the mid-sixties on, Peck devoted himself to numerous political, cultural, civic, and health-related causes. His roles included a seat on the brand-new National Council on the Arts, to which he was appointed by Lyndon B. Johnson. The president became a personal friend. (The Gregory Peck Collection)

By the late sixties, movies were becoming more violent and sexually explicit and featured antiheroic leading men. Suddenly, Peck's films, including the $10 million science fiction epic *Marooned,* seemed old-fashioned. (Columbia/The Kobal Collection)

When he wasn't working, Greg enjoyed traveling with Veronique and a few close friends. These included in later years Cary Grant and Frank Sinatra and their wives. (The Gregory Peck Collection)

The Omen, a supernatural thriller released during the summer of 1976, was a blockbuster hit, restoring Peck to the top ranks of Hollywood stars. (20th Century–Fox/The Kobal Collection)

For Greg, playing the brilliant but egomaniacal Douglas MacArthur in 1977's *MacArthur* became a genuine labor of love. The film's lack of critical and commercial success was a bitter blow. (Universal/The Gregory Peck Collection)

While filming *MacArthur*, Greg and Veronique found their "dream house," a five-bedroom Norman-style home in the Holmby Hills section of Los Angeles. (The Gregory Peck Collection)

The virulent Nazi doctor, Josef Mengele—known as the "Angel of Death"—was the only genuine villain of Peck's career. He primarily accepted the role in 1978's *The Boys from Brazil* in order to work with his old friend, Laurence Olivier. (20th Century–Fox/The Gregory Peck Collection)

(Above left) An avid Civil War buff, Peck had long wanted to play his hero, Abraham Lincoln. He finally got the opportunity in the CBS miniseries, *The Blue and the Gray,* which aired in November 1982. (CBS/The Gregory Peck Collection)

(Above right) In his last leading role in a feature film, Peck portrayed an old-fashioned businessman trying to avoid a corporate takeover. A framed portrait of Greg's relative, the Irish patriot Thomas Ashe, suggested the founder of the company. *Other People's Money* was released in 1991. (Warner Bros./The Gregory Peck Collection)

Greg, Veronique, and their two children, Cecilia and Anthony, were all on hand on November 8, 2000, for a gala marking the fifth anniversary of the Gregory Peck Reading Series on behalf of the Los Angeles Public Library. (Alex Berliner/Library Foundation of Los Angeles)

known as a master of suspense. He wasn't yet a cultural icon, but he was extremely well regarded, particularly for his meticulous preparation. Storyboarding every shot before filming began, he found the making of a movie anticlimactic. He'd already completed the picture in his head.

A skilled storyteller, Hitchcock had little regard for the craft of acting. To him, actors were somewhat like the sets, costumes, camera, and music, that is, another element at his command. He cared about a performer's movements and facial expressions, the external elements that contributed to his own scenic compositions, but he had no interest in how an actor justified his behavior. "It's only a movie," he would often reply to questions about attitudes or motivations.

Though initially puzzled by the director's breezy disdain, Ingrid Bergman accepted the dismissals and went about her business. But she'd been acting in films for a decade, first in her native Sweden and then in Hollywood. Peck, with only two pictures behind him, had a more difficult time. Trying to employ what he'd learned from Sanford Meisner, he approached his role from the inside out: first, he determined what his character was feeling, and then he posited the emotions in behavior. From the behavior came the character's movements and facial expressions, the elements of concern to Hitch. The director didn't have much patience for Peck's way of working. As Greg put it, "[I]t took me more time to try to arrive at the exterior that he had visualized." Of course, if his search led to something other than what Hitchcock envisioned, there could be trouble; as Peck said, the director didn't "like to readjust his thinking in that sense." Conversely, when Hitch did give Peck guidance, it had little meaning for the actor. At one point, for example, he asked Greg to let his face drain of expression. That told him nothing about what to feel; only how to look. It was too technical for him.

Frustrated and a bit intimidated by Hitch's methodology, Peck faltered, making mistakes on the set that caused unnecessary retakes. According to Leonard Leff, Greg was responsible for at least some of the sixteen versions of an easy dolly shot that showed him and Bergman walking toward a train. A simple moment in which the amnesiac awakens from a drug-induced sleep required three hours to get in the can.

To his credit, Hitchcock never lost patience with his star. Indeed, Peck recalled that the director was always "gracious and friendly." Adopting a somewhat paternalistic attitude, Hitch even took Peck's personal wardrobe in hand, steering him away from the brown suits he favored toward more conservative grays, navys, and blacks. To help Greg learn about wine, the director sent him a case of twelve assorted bottles, fine vintages such as Montrachet and Lafite-Rothschild. He attached a handwritten label to each bottle indicating how it should be served: "This is best with roast beef," "This is a dessert wine," and so forth. Looking back, Peck called this gift "a very wonderful, generous" gesture.

Although working with Hitch could be frustrating for an actor, Peck found Bergman a joy. "I think you fall in love a little bit with a woman like Ingrid Bergman," he told journalist Gregory Speck, "and I don't think there's any way to avoid it, for she was incredibly beautiful, and a very sweet person. . . . Her lovely skin kind of took your breath away, and her whole radiance was something to behold."

Peck didn't talk that way in public about many women. In fact, over the years, there have been persistent rumors of an affair between the costars. In his biography of Bergman, Laurence Leamer quoted an unnamed colleague who recalled a day during filming in which "Ingrid and Peck came in late, all disheveled." Their arrival, in the costar's words, gave rise to "a lot of speculation" about the twosome within the company. In an interview for his book, Leamer questioned Peck about the rumors, but the star replied, "That is not the kind of thing I talk about." However, in 1987, when Brad Darrach of *People* magazine asked Greg about his favorite leading ladies, he did allude to a deeper relationship with Bergman, noting, "All I can say is I had a real love for her, and I think that's where I ought to stop. . . . I was young. She was young. We were involved for weeks in close and intense work." Darrach added, "Ever gallant, he declines to confide more intimate matters"—implying, of course, that there *were* more intimate matters to confide.

The House of Edwardes wrapped on October 13, three months after filming began. About two weeks later, on October 30, Peck was reunited with Bergman for a thirty-minute CBS radio dramatization of Tolstoy's *Anna Karenina,* his first assignment for the airwaves since coming to California. The drama aired on the *Lady Esther Screen Guild Players*; the show was named for its sponsor, a cosmetics manufacturer.

During an unusually long postproduction period, *The House of Edwardes* was renamed *Spellbound,* although Hitchcock favored the original title. It was screened several times for preview audiences. After one showing, Selznick reported the response to Peck in a memo to Neil Agnew, the vice president of Selznick's then-new production company, Vanguard Films: "We could not keep the audience quiet from the time his name first came on the screen until we had shushed the audience through three or four sequences and stopped all the dames from 'ohing' and 'ahing' and gurgling."

Finally, on November 1, 1945—more than a year after principal photography ended—*Spellbound* opened at the Astor Theatre in New York. Although Selznick gave his director the unusual distinction of attaching his name to the title—thus it became Alfred Hitchcock's *Spellbound*—he played up the film's stars in the posters and newspaper ads, emphasizing the picture's romantic elements. Given the hottest new male star in Hollywood and the current Oscar-winning actress (for another thriller, *Gaslight*), he made a wise decision. The picture grossed $7 million, making it far and away Hitchcock's biggest hit to date.

Spellbound was a critical success as well. Howard Barnes of the *New York Herald-Tribune* called it a "fascinating chase through the labyrinth of a man's tortured mind," while the *New York Times*' Bosley Crowther pronounced it "the most mature of the many melodramas Mr. Hitchcock has made." Accolades also went to Bergman, Peck, and several of the supporting players, notably Leo G. Carroll as the head of the mental institution and Michael Chekhov as Constance's mentor. The latter earned an Oscar nomination, as did the film, Hitchcock, the cinematography, the special effects, and Miklos Rozsa's musical score. Only Rozsa won.

In later years, Peck would acknowledge *Spellbound*'s merits, saying, "I respect it. It did exactly what it set out to do." He was less fulsome about his own performance, calling it "spotty" and inconsistent. He's not entirely wrong. He appears unduly uncomfortable and restrained when his character becomes agitated by his inability to remember his past. Fortunately, the amnesiac faints each time he becomes upset, cutting short the demands placed on Peck's ability to let go. But he is fine otherwise, portraying a confused but decent, congenial man. His love scenes with Bergman are very credible.

Unlike Hitchcock, who resented Selznick's control, Peck enjoyed working for the independent producer. In time, he came to consider David a friend as well as his employer.

He liked and respected Darryl Zanuck as well. A former screenwriter, Zanuck had a keen sense of storytelling. His memos analyzing a book or play or the flaws in a script were masterful. Moreover, Greg felt at home at Zanuck's studio, 20th Century–Fox. In his opinion, the producers there "did things properly, they spent money where it had to be spent." Fox was more stable than RKO, which was always beset with financial problems.

But neither Fox nor RKO was quite in the league of MGM.

Metro was the ultimate dream factory. Not only did it boast "more stars than there were in the heavens," it reeked of elegance. But it was elegance combined with the old-fashioned family values that L. B. Mayer held sacred.

Peck felt less comfortable amid such grandeur, but MGM paid better than Fox or RKO. He earned $45,000 for his first studio project, more than twice his guaranteed salary for *The Keys of the Kingdom.* For his subsequent MGM films, he would receive $55,000 and $65,000, respectively.

His first assignment at Metro was a classic example of the studio's style. Like *The Keys of the Kingdom, The Valley of Decision* was based on a best-selling novel, in this case by Marcia Davenport. When MGM purchased the book—for the impressive sum of $76,000—few readers could imagine how the 792-page multigenerational saga could be turned into a conventional-length feature. What screenwriters John Meehan and Sonya Levien did was focus on only one twelve-year segment of the story, that which was set in Pittsburgh in the 1880s and featured Mary Rafferty, the plucky daughter of an embittered former steelworker. Against her father's wishes, Mary becomes a servant in the home of the wealthy owner of the steel mill and falls in love with his dashing older son, Paul. The ill-fated romance between Mary and Paul serves as the film's centerpiece. It wasn't very realistic, offering a highly romanticized view of interclass relationships, but with a substantial budget—$2.16 million—and the usual MGM gloss, it became, to quote *Life* magazine at the time of the picture's release, "first rate heart-throb entertainment."

Peck, of course, was Paul, replacing an actual Pittsburgh native, John Hodiak, whose casting had been announced the previous August. For Mary, Mayer turned to the studio's reigning queen, Greer Garson. The Irish actress, seven and a half years Peck's senior, had made her film debut in the studio's 1939 hit, *Goodbye, Mr. Chips,* and had won an Oscar three years later as the title character in *Mrs. Miniver.* Leland Hayward, for one, was delighted with the pairing. "Greer's audience would be a good thing for you," he told Greg.

Garson was, in Peck's words, "L. B. Mayer's pride and joy." Not only was she talented, she represented his idealized notion of womanhood—classically beautiful, noble, feminine, and self-sacrificing. Mayer ensured that she was photographed to emphasize her aristocratic mien, with shadows beneath her cheekbones and a glow around her flowing red locks. This job was usually assigned to Joe Ruttenberg. Ruttenberg paid less attention to her costars. "When it came to viewing the rushes," Peck said, "I saw that every time I was in a scene with her, her face was a lovely luminous moon floating in the center of the screen and I was the rather dim figure beside her in semi-shadow." He compared notes with another Garson costar, Adolphe Menjou, who told him, "I know exactly what you mean. I made a picture with her and every time we were in a two-shot, I thought I'd freeze to death."

The role of Mary Rafferty gave Garson plenty of opportunity to feature the noble, self-sacrificing side of womanhood, but the character was lively and fun-filled as well. Peck, who called his costar Big Red, found that Mary's lighter side was more akin to the actress' true nature. He thought Greer had a wonderful sense of humor.

The duo worked well together—as noted by Jessica Tandy, who was cast as Peck's shrewish wife. In particular, she recalled a scene in which Mary and Paul are sitting at a kitchen table, drinking cocoa and chatting. As she watched Greg and Greer on the soundstage, Tandy, primarily a stage actress at that point, thought that the scene was too "small and quiet." Then she watched the rushes. "And," she said, "of course, it was perfection. Both of them had the ability to be absolutely true with the greatest economy. And I said, 'Ah, that's the way screen acting is done.'"

As Tandy's recollection suggests, Peck was quickly learning the demands of the new medium. The film's director, Tay Garnett, was impressed. Years later, he would say, "Peck had everything it takes to make a star. He had the looks, the personality, the poise, and the control, and a magnificent voice. He was very serious about his work."

When *The Valley of Decision* opened in New York on May 3, 1945, roughly five months after *The Keys of the Kingdom* and six months before *Spellbound,* Bosley Crowther of the *New York Times* cautioned readers of the novel "not [to] expect to find . . . anything like the monumental scope and pageant of human destinies that distinguished the memorable book." But, he added, the "movie audience should find the screen version to its taste, for the picture . . . has many elements of dramatic appeal."

Most of Crowther's colleagues were even more enthusiastic, with several, including *Variety* and the *New York Herald-Tribune,* predicting that the film would be, in the words of the latter, "a thumping box-office success." It was. With earnings of $4.5 million, *The Valley of Decision* became the third-biggest hit of the year, preceded only by two other MGM films, an Esther Williams aquatic spectacle, *Thrill of a Romance,* and the Gene Kelly–Frank Sinatra–Kathryn Grayson musical, *Anchors Aweigh.*

The picture earned Garson a well-deserved Oscar nomination. But it was an important vehicle for Peck as well. Although she was top-billed and the principal focus of attention, he had a chance for the first time since coming to Hollywood to play an affable, decent, idealistic young man, one who grows dignified and admirable as the story progresses. It was a far more traditional leading role than anything he'd been given to date, and Peck seemed quite comfortable with the job. Moreover, in the romantic scenes with Garson, he proved an even more effective screen lover than he had been in *Days of Glory* or in the still unreleased *Spellbound. Cue* called it "his best film performance to date."

After *The Valley of Decision* wrapped in early December 1944, Greg finally got a few months off, his first real break since coming to Hollywood. This respite gave him an opportunity to spend some quality time with the latest member of his family, his first child, who was born on July 20, while *Spellbound* was in production.

Greta had been pregnant once before and miscarried. Thus, when Greg learned that she was expecting again, he was understandably concerned. According to one friend, he even mapped out five different ways of getting her to the hospital at the appropriate moment. When she went into labor, he paced the waiting room, his thoughts taking him back to his own childhood. Now, as he started a family of his own, he had a chance to create the kind of stable home life that he had lacked in his youth. He was determined to give his child a normal upbringing, with two loving parents for support. Finally, he heard his name called over the hospital's public address system. Then the speaker added, "Mr. Peck, your son wants to talk to you," prompting Greg to whoop with glee. He and his wife named the boy Jonathan.

Peck enjoyed his vacation. He told Louella Parsons shortly thereafter, "I did nothing but lie around and I filled out a lot, which I needed for I'm still only 185 pounds for my 6 feet 3." In fact, he gained about twenty pounds during his layoff. But, as the weeks stretched into months, he grew restless and by the end of the eighth week, he was, in his words, "nearly nuts."

Finally, on March 1, 1945, he went back to work—on his first Western.

Based on a novel by Niven Busch, *Duel in the Sun* is the story of a sensuous half-breed named Pearl Chavez and the two sons of a wealthy Texas rancher who fall for her. After the book's publication in January 1944, Busch took the property to RKO. But eventually he withdrew from the project, and RKO put it up for sale. It was purchased by David O. Selznick.

RKO had budgeted *Duel* for a modest $1 million, and Selznick saw no reason to up the ante. He assigned the property to screenwriter Oliver H. P. Garrett and director King Vidor, saying, "I want this to be an artistic little Western. You take it over and if you need any help, let me know. But it's your baby."

But the producer was unable to remain on the sidelines after casting his amour, Jennifer Jones, as Pearl. Selecting the virginal Oscar-winning star of *The Song of Bernadette* to play an unbridled sexpot was a bold choice, but he hoped that *Duel in the Sun* would do for her what *Gone With the Wind* had done for Vivien Leigh. He even hired Josef von Sternberg to ensure that she received the same sort of glamour treatment in her scenes that the German director had orchestrated for Marlene Dietrich in *The Blue Angel* and *Shanghai Express.*

Selznick compounded the unusual casting by selecting Peck not for the decent brother, Jesse McCanles—that went to Joseph Cotten—but for the part of the villainous younger brother, Lewt. Greg later said that Selznick "liked the idea . . . of taking me from *The Keys of the Kingdom* where I had played a priest, and making me a rapist, a forger, a killer, a liar, a thoroughly rotten no-good but with a certain likability."

As Selznick exercised more and more control over *Duel in the Sun,* the intimate little Western grew increasingly sumptuous. He wanted the picture to be important so that Jones would benefit from her association with it. But he was also obsessed with topping his greatest success, *Gone With the Wind.* When asked why, he said, "I know that when I die, the stories will read, 'David O. Selznick, producer of *Gone With the Wind,* died today.' I'm determined to leave them something else to write about."

Thus, *Duel*'s production values became monumental. What began as a Texas ranch house evolved into a palatial prairie mansion. A typical cowtown saloon because a gigantic cantina and gambling hall. And the screenplay was expanded as well. As King Vidor recalled in his autobiography, *A Tree Is a Tree,* "Everything that had ever happened west of the Rocky Mountains was considered for the script." By the start of production, the screenplay had reached a whopping 170 pages and would soon grow to 200.

Selznick's largesse extended to the casting as well. In addition to Jones, Cotten, and Peck (billed in that order), he selected Lionel Barrymore and Lillian Gish as the brothers' parents, Walter Huston as a lay preacher, Herbert Marshall as Pearl's father, Charles Bickford as an elderly cowpuncher, and Harry Carey as a railroad attorney. Except for the senior McCanleses, none of these roles required name actors. But that was of little concern to Selznick. In the case of Huston, he was even willing to pay the actor's asking price, $40,000 per picture, for what amounted to four days of work. And then he had to pay overtime—because he was unable to release him after the *ten weeks* specified in his contract.

Aside from the leads, the script involved dozens of small speaking parts and thousands of extras. There was also a 150-person crew and experts on hand to authenticate the sets, props, and costumes. According to the Associated Press' Bob Thomas, Selznick even hired a bartender to ensure that in saloon scenes the drinks were poured correctly and that the bottles of colored water had the right hues.

During the nine months of filming, the company would utilize six locations. They began in the desert about forty miles from Tucson. There, a two-story prefabricated ranch house was constructed to serve as the McCanles home, along with two barns and a windmill. And tracks were laid for an 1880s-style train that was hauled to the site.

Calling the Arizona shoot rough was a vast understatement. During filming, the early March temperatures reached as low as twenty-five degrees; high winds made the company feel even colder. To make matters worse, Selznick, who ultimately received sole credit for the screenplay, frequently rewrote scenes at night that had already been filmed to Vidor's satisfaction. Although the changes were often minor, the producer demanded that the scenes be reshot. He also insisted on being called before each scene was filmed so that he could check the lighting, set decoration, actors' makeup, and so forth. On one occasion, he asked that Peck's hat not rest so far down on his head. He feared that people would think they were using a double instead of the star.

The sixty-one-year-old Vidor, who had been directing features since 1919, with such classics as *The Big Parade, The Champ,* and *Stella Dallas* among his credits, didn't care for Selznick's heavy-handed supervision but held his temper. He understood that the film was David's baby and that the producer's own money was at stake.

Peck had a better time than his director. For starters, he liked working with Jennifer Jones. They had a lot of common. They were both intense about their craft and eager to succeed. They each came from a relatively small town (she was from Tulsa) and had been struggling actors in New York at roughly the same time. Peck recalled that during breaks between setups, they "compared notes on who was the hungriest, and who was more broke than the other one, while we were on Broadway."

Greg also relished the chance to play a rogue for a change. He told Hedda Hopper shortly thereafter, "I never enjoyed a role better than the one I did in *Duel in the Sun.*" He based the character in part on a La Jolla cousin, Warren Rannells, known to friends as Stretch. Stretch "took great pride in being a small-town Lothario," Greg recalled, "who went from job to job; was married about four times." A further inspiration, according to King Vidor, was Sportin' Life, the snakelike tempter in *Porgy and Bess.*

Greg and Vidor liked working with one another. The director found his young star "as flexible and pliable as any actor with whom I have worked." And Greg found Vidor "the kind of man that I work best for," one who was skilled at "storytelling and character development" without being an auteur. He also enjoyed talking with the well-rounded older man about a variety of subjects, including books, paintings, and music.

Ever the showman, Selznick invited numerous members of the press to the watch the film in production. On one occasion, a *Life* magazine photographer asked Peck to ride a horse into the dining room of the hotel in Tucson where the company was staying. Greg had ridden a bit in his youth, but, in preparation for *Duel,* he'd trained for weeks in the San Fernando Valley with Ralph McCutcheon, a rancher who furnished horses and livestock for Hollywood films. "He taught me not only to be a good rider," the actor recalled, "but to do a number of tricks, such as the running dismount, the vault into the saddle, etc." So Greg complied with the *Life* photographer's request. "I was having dinner with Selznick," Vidor recalled, adding, "The floor was slippery, and David nearly fainted when he saw his star riding in on that horse. . . . It sure made a great photograph."

Peck had less luck with the animal that carried him in the film. A show horse selected by Selznick for its appearance, it was unaccustomed to the rugged Arizona terrain and to performing in front of a motion picture camera. One day, as Greg was leading the horse into some scrub, it panicked and took off. Crashing into a barbed-wire fence, it tossed the actor twenty feet in the air. Greg was just shaken, but the horse became entangled in the barbed wire. The camera crew freed it with wire cutters and its lacerations were sutured by a vet, but it was scarred for life. Another mount had to be found for the picture, and all the scenes of Greg on the first horse were reshot.

On April 18, about six weeks into principal photography, a union strike affecting the entire motion picture industry forced the production to shut down. Vidor used the break to lobby for a new cinematographer, replacing Hal Rosson, whom he found difficult, with Lee Garmes. Meanwhile, Selznick continued to rework the script, adding among other things a sequence in which Peck's character engineers a train wreck and then breaks into a chorus of "I've Been Workin' on the Railroad." Vidor felt that the scene would destroy what little sympathy the audience might feel for the cowboy, but Selznick insisted it be shot. "I want to make Lewt the worst son of a bitch that's ever been seen on a motion picture screen," he told the director, "and I believe the train wreck scene will prove my point."

On June 24, the strike was settled and filming resumed. By then, *Duel in the Sun* was seventy-five days behind schedule and the original $1 million budget had reached nearly $3.5 million and was still climbing.

About six weeks later, on August 10, King Vidor walked off the picture. At the time, the company was filming at the Lasky Mesa—named for film pioneer Jesse Lasky—in the San Fernando Valley. Accounts vary as to the cause of King's departure. According to Selznick, the director called for a complicated tracking shot, one that would have taken hours to set up, after the producer had approved another camera position; when he countermanded the director's order, Vidor quit. According to Vidor, he resigned not because of Selznick's interference but because the producer berated him in front of the cast and crew. Peck maintained that Vidor blew because Selznick called for a retake of a scene between Jones and Cotten that the director considered unnecessary.

Regardless of how it happened, the result was the same: Vidor was off the picture. With about 30 to 40 percent of the screenplay left to be shot, Selznick halted production for several days while he considered his options. Finally, he brought in William Dieterle to finish up. He had, in fact, thought about using the German-born director before hiring Vidor, on the strength of Dieterle's prior direction of Jennifer Jones in *Love Letters.* He had chosen Vidor because of his greater experience with action sequences.

"In a bizarre way," noted Selznick biographer David Thomson, "the picture began again" with the new director at the helm. Peck, who described Dieterle as "a colorful Germanic type who always wore white cotton gloves, and was always well dressed," maintained that the new director shot all of the film's interiors, the massive barbecue/dance scene, the train wreck sequence, and the final scene for which the picture is named. Despite Dieterle's contributions, however, the Directors Guild decided that Vidor was entitled to sole credit for *Duel in the Sun.*

By the time the company finally wrapped in late November, the tab for Selznick's "artistic little Western" had climbed to $6 million. It was the most expensive movie ever made to that point, according to *Time* magazine, exceeding the cost of *Gone With the Wind* by $1 million.

Never one to rush a project to completion, Selznick would spend a full year cutting, shaping, previewing, and recutting *Duel in the Sun.* Outcries from religious leaders—both Catholic and Protestant—forced deletions in the numerous romantic scenes. Eventually, the Catholic Legion of Decency gave the picture a "B" rating, meaning that it was considered "morally objectionable in part for all" members of the faith. The film was banned in Memphis and several other cities.

To qualify for Academy Award consideration, the picture was launched on December 30, 1946, with a two-week, reserved-seat showing at the Egyptian Theatre in Los Angeles. It did earn two Oscar nominations, for Best Actress (Jones) and Best Supporting Actress (Gish), but neither won.

The rest of the country had to wait five more months to see the epic. During that interval, Selznick lavishly promoted the picture, which he distributed himself under the newly formed Selznick Releasing Organization. He ran frequent ads in the newspapers of major markets and staged outrageous publicity stunts—such as dropping thousands of war-surplus parachutes bearing information about the film on spectators at sporting events. In total, he spent $2 million on promotion, roughly the equivalent of Fox's publicity budget for an entire year.

He took one more gamble. Instead of following the usual practice of premiering a major movie in a few exclusive venues and expanding the distribution over time, he blitzed the country with a widespread release in 300 theaters starting on May 7, 1947. Some industry insiders argued that he hoped to cash in on the public's appetite for the Western—whipped to a frenzy by that point—before negative critical reaction could sink in. If so, he was prescient, for, indeed, the reviews were mostly hostile. Howard Barnes of the *New York Herald-Tribune* spoke for the majority of his colleagues in calling the picture "a munificent muddle" while acknowledging that it contained images that were photographically "stunning." Jesse Zunser of *Cue* went even further, dubbing *Duel* the "biggest and emptiest thing since the Grand Canyon."

Good or not, the public wanted to see the outrageously excessive Western, particularly the steamy sex scenes that had led pundits to the dub it "Lust in the Dust." As a consequence, *Duel in the Sun* yielded $17 million in its initial release, making it one of the most successful motion pictures of all time. It wouldn't eclipse *Gone With the Wind* as far as Selznick's epitaph was concerned, but it gave people plenty to talk about.

For Peck, the Western represented something of a milestone, though not artistically. Given his tall, lanky frame and ease with horses, he made a credible enough cowboy and one could readily see why he appealed to Pearl, but he never really achieved the sinister charm that the role suggests. In the hands of a Robert Mitchum or a Richard Widmark, Lewt's evil deeds might have had more impact. In later years, as Peck's screen persona took root, the notion of him even playing such a villain would seem incredible.

Rather, while working on the picture, he achieved a kind of breakthrough in the *craft* of film acting. In his earlier pictures, he'd been uncomfortable with the process; he couldn't relax and concentrate before the camera. "I thought I finally got ahold of it in *Duel in the Sun*," he maintained. No doubt, the four preceding films had helped; not to mention a badly needed vacation after an intense period of work. Certainly, he looked better; the weight he gained during his time off added a bit of bulk to his face and frame. And perhaps playing an affable bad guy gave him the emotional freedom he needed. Watching the film today, there is little doubt that he had fun doing it. Soon, however, he could apply his newfound comfort to a project more worthy of his skill.

CHAPTER 9

Literary Properties

The Yearling, Marjorie Kinnan Rawlings' 1938 Pulitzer Prize–winning novel, is the coming-of-age story of Jody Baxter, a twelve-year-old boy living in Florida's inland scrub country in the late nineteenth century. He learns a bitter lesson about life when his pet, an orphaned fawn, grows into a destructive yearling. His father, Ezra "Penny" Baxter, is a warm-hearted, fun-loving small-time farmer and hunter, but his mother, Ora, embittered by the death of several children and the harsh living conditions, has buried her loving nature under a crusty shell.

Under the aegis of producer Sidney Franklin, MGM began filming *The Yearling* in 1941 with Spencer Tracy, Anne Revere, and Gene Eckman, a thirteen-year-old boy from Georgia. Victor Fleming was the director. Although location filming was unusual at the time, the studio decided to shoot *The Yearling* in Ocala, Florida, as close to the setting of the novel as possible.

From the outset, the production was beset with problems. The studio was unhappy with Eckman's acting. Tracy and Fleming didn't get along. There were delays due to rain and excessive heat. And an infestation of insects aggravated everyone. Finally, after three weeks, MGM called the company back to Hollywood, where, despite a $500,000 outlay, the project was shelved indefinitely.

Then, in 1944, Franklin decided to try again, with a new director, Clarence Brown. One of MGM's most dependable filmmakers, the Tennessean had a keen sense of Americana—an important component of Rawlings' tale—as he had demonstrated with *Ah, Wilderness!,* from the comedy by Eugene O'Neill, and *Of Human Hearts,* a saga of pioneer life.

Although Peck was twelve years younger than Spencer Tracy when Tracy was cast as Penny Baxter, Brown and Sidney Franklin decided to give Greg the role. This would mark the second of his three contractual obligations to Metro. Having chosen a more youthful Pa, the studio needed a younger Ma, as Anne Revere was thirteen years older than Greg.* At least at the outset, Brown and Franklin went with a blond contract player by the name of Jacqueline White. White's credits included a Laurel and Hardy picture called *Air Raid Wardens,* Robert Taylor's *Song of Russia,* and the Spencer Tracy hit *Thirty Seconds Over Tokyo.* But she hadn't tackled anything like Ma Baxter. For the crucial role of Jody, Clarence Brown cast ten-year-old Claude Jarman Jr. The son of a Nashville railroad accountant, Jarman had not acted outside of school and community theater productions.

Filming began in Ocala on May 14, 1945, while *Duel in the Sun* was in production. As the Western contained numerous scenes without Lewt, Greg was able to travel to Florida with the MGM company.

Again, the location proved difficult, with rain, heat, humidity, and bugs conspiring against the filmmakers. Moreover, the livestock made life difficult. The fawn cast as Jody's pet, Flag, couldn't grow as fast as Clarence Brown needed, so the director arranged for a dozen backups at slightly different ages. By the time the production wrapped in January 1946, thirty different deer appeared in the role.

After about a month, the company returned to Hollywood, where MGM replaced Jacqueline White with one of Warner Bros. leading ladies, Jane Wyman.† Primarily known as a light comedienne, Wyman had recently demonstrated considerable dramatic skill in *The Lost Weekend,* a moving film about alcohol addiction. Some of the moments featuring White were reshot. In a few scenes, however, long shots of the MGM contract player were retained with close-ups of Wyman inserted.

Back in L.A., Peck resumed work on *Duel in the Sun,* alternating his portrayal of the unredeemable Lewt with that of the tender, loving Baxter. He didn't mind doing double duty. "Oh, I thought it was fun," he said. Occasionally, he joked, he may have confused the cowpoke with the cracker, but he was "a bear for work in those days."

In addition to filming on the MGM lot, the *Yearling* company traveled to Lake Arrowhead, where the town sequences were shot on a set constructed on the site. A resort area east of San Bernardino, Lake Arrowhead provided the stars with pleasant off-hour diversions. "We all had our own houses [on the lake]," recalled Jane Wyman. "I had a house and a boat on one side and Greg and his wife had a house on the other side.

*But Revere could look old enough to be Peck's mother, as she would demonstrate in the upcoming *Gentleman's Agreement.*

†This author has discussed White's involvement in *The Yearling* with Peck, Claude Jarman Jr., and Jane Wyman. It is difficult to state with certainty if the contract player had been cast for the role and replaced or merely served as a stand-in until a suitable star could be found. In this author's opinion, the latter is a likely prospect.

And my husband [then-actor Ronald Reagan] liked to barbecue so we . . . would barbecue the steaks and light the fire and just congregate." Speedboats took them to and from the set.

For the first time in his career, Greg had to work with a child in a major role, something all actors are warned against. But he was good with kids. "I thought Peck was wonderful," Claude Jarman Jr. recalled. "I mean, he was very patient, just very easy to get along with, made things very easy for me." Greg enjoyed a warm relationship with Wyman as well. "He was one of my favorite actors," she said. "Peck is so easy to work with. He's a gentleman, number one. And number two, he takes his career very seriously. . . . No matter how many takes, it didn't matter to him. As long we kept going and doing it right."

The scenes involving Flag required particular perseverance, because the fawns were untrainable. The cast simply had to keep doing scenes over and over until the deer performed as needed. This put considerable pressure on the actors; no one wanted to ruin a take in which the animal cooperated. Peck recalled that one such scene, which ran two and three-quarter pages, required an incredible seventy-two takes and three days to get in the can. That he and his costars managed to keep their irritation from registering on film during this ordeal was, in his view, "probably the best acting we did in the picture."

Arguably, Peck did his best acting thus far, period—deer or no deer. Transferring from *Duel in the Sun* his newfound ease before the camera, he gave a wonderfully modulated performance. He wasn't exactly credible as a Florida cracker, having imbued his character with more dignity and nobility than a nineteenth-century scrub farmer would have possessed in real life, but he made audiences believe in and care about the *man,* a fellow earnestly doing his best to give his wife and son a decent life. Particularly affecting was the breadth of the Pa-Jody relationship. As Bosley Crowther noted in the *New York Times* upon the film's release, "It isn't very often that there is realized upon the screen the . . . anxiety that a father feels for his boy. These are human emotions which are a little too sensitive and fine for easy comprehension in the usually artificial terms of films. But we've got to hand it to Metro and to everyone who helped to visualize *The Yearling* . . . they have caught these rare sentiments . . . in this picture."

Crowther and most of his colleagues raved about Jarman, Wyman, and the film as well. The only recurring complaint—albeit a relatively minor one—was the film's sentimentality, epitomized in the final scene that depicts Jody drifting off to sleep, dreaming that he and Flag are once more romping on a lush Florida hillside. Peck himself shared this criticism. He told *Time* magazine a few years later, "I would have liked the picture better with its Walt Disney aspects pushed into the background."

Although *The Yearling*'s New York premiere was held at Radio City Music Hall on January 23, 1947, some three months before the release of *Duel in the Sun,* MGM debuted the film in Los Angeles at the end of 1946 in order to qualify it for that year's Academy Awards. It was a wise decision, for the film garnered seven nominations, including those for best picture, director, editing, color cinematography, and color art direction–interior direction. It won in the latter two categories. In addition, Jarman received a special Oscar as the year's "outstanding child actor." As a Best Actress nominee, Wyman was pitted again Peck's other leading lady, *Duel*'s Jennifer Jones, but they both lost to Olivia de Havilland for *To Each His Own.* Greg, having earned a nomination two years in a row, was bested this time by Fredric March for *The Best Years of Our Lives.* The Samuel Goldwyn–William Wyler drama beat *The Yearling* in several other categories, including Best Picture and Best Director. It also outperformed *The Yearling* at the box office—as did *Duel in the Sun.* Still, the MGM release did quite well, becoming the ninth most popular film of the year, with grosses of $5.25 million.

Because *Duel in the Sun* and *The Yearling* were only shown in Los Angeles in 1946, fans around the country went thirteen months without a Gregory Peck picture, a very long time in the forties when contract players often made three or more films a year. But they could *hear* Greg; he guest-starred in no fewer than ten radio broadcasts during 1946, beginning on New Year's Day. Twice during the year he re-created his own movie roles—in *The Valley of Decision,* which aired in January on CBS's *Lux Radio Theatre* and in *The Keys of the Kingdom,* heard on CBS's *Academy Award Theater* in August. In February, he costarred with Bette Davis in the *Lux Radio Theatre*'s re-creation of the actress' most popular tear-jerker, *Now, Voyager.* Davis recalled the experience years later, saying, "What a nightmare! We always had audiences in the studio for these performances. Peck was madly worshipped by his fans—especially his female fans. Every time he read a line, they squealed with joy. I felt sorry for Peck. There was nothing he could do about it. It certainly made our radio performance . . . anything but ideal."

Between stints before the mike, he squeezed in another feature film drawn from literature, this time from a short story by Ernest Hemingway.

After the disappointing reaction to *Days of Glory,* Casey Robinson and RKO disbanded their partnership. As part of the settlement agreement, the producer-screenwriter retained his contractual right to one more film with Peck.

A free agent, Robinson paid $75,000 to acquire a short story by Hemingway entitled "The Short Happy Life of Francis Macomber." Published in 1936, it is the tale of a rich, cowardly American—the title character—who goes on safari in Africa with his haughty wife, a fading beauty named Margaret. Caught between them is the big game hunter they hire, a Brit named Robert Wilson. Although Macomber disgraces himself while stalking a lion, he redeems himself the following day in pursuit of buffalo. Just as he has found his courage, his wife shoots him in the back. The story's ending is open to interpretation, but it is likely that Margaret murdered him and will get away with the deed.

"I happened to love the story," Peck recalled. Conveying his interest to Robinson, he suggested that they take the project to Zoltan Korda, the Hungarian-born director who had done several pictures—*Elephant Boy, The Four Feathers,* and *Jungle Book*—that were rife with action sequences and exotic locales. Independent producer Benedict Bogeaus, whose credits included *The Bridge of San Luis Rey* and *Captain Kidd,* came on board as coproducer, and the package was picked up by United Artists, reflecting the studio's burgeoning interest in independent ventures. Peck's involvement in the developmental stage of this project was a first for the actor who, until this point, had functioned like any studio contract player—he did the pictures assigned to him. This time, he was, in his words, "kind of an uncredited coproducer on the picture."

Hollywood has a way of dismissing serious literary works, freely adapting them to suit popular taste. But Peck and Robinson were determined to be as faithful to Hemingway's short story as possible. To flesh out the taut narrative, the screenwriter set the entire tale in the form of a flashback, and added a sequence showing the arrival of the Macombers in Nairobi.

It was a commendable adaptation, but the ending presented a serious problem. At the time, the Production Code of the Motion Picture Producers and Distributors of America (MPPDA) set the standard of "good taste" in American films, part of an industry-wide self-censorship established in 1934 to stem possible government regulation. According to the practices of the day, a film simply couldn't show a man or woman going unpunished for murder. Robinson attempted to get Hemingway's thoughts on an alternative ending, but Papa failed to respond to their entreaties for help. Left to their own devices, the filmmakers created a final scene showing the wife about to testify before an inquest into the murder. Tortured and repentant, she tells Wilson that she isn't sure if she shot her husband accidentally or on purpose. What she knows is that she wanted him dead. While her fate isn't depicted, it appears that she will go to prison.

Filming began in April 1946, with Peck as the game hunter—changed from a Brit to an American—plus Joan Bennett as Margaret and Robert Preston as Macomber. In the fifties, Preston would leap to stardom in the smash Broadway musical *The Music Man,* but in 1946, he was simply a reliable second lead who'd been mostly stuck in B films.

Although the final cut, shot in black-and-white, would have an authentic feel to it, the company never left the Americas. A second unit, dispatched to Africa two months before principal photography began, was responsible for the footage of the veldt and the wild animals that inhabit it. When the unit returned to Hollywood, Korda and Bogeaus searched for a nearby location that could match what had been shot abroad. They scouted sites in California, Arizona, New Mexico, and Texas without success. Then someone recalled that *Trader Horn,* a film with a similar background, had been filmed near Tecate, Mexico, and that proved acceptable. The studio leased land outside the small town from the government of Mexico for two months.

The nearest hotel to Tecate was in Rosarita Beach, forty-five miles away. The conditions were so primitive that the company had to build a road to transport the cast and crew to the location. A fleet of eighteen yellow taxicabs were hired to make the journey, which took about an hour and a half and often longer due to tire blowouts.

According to Peck, shooting for six weeks with about eighty men and only two women, Bennett and her hairdresser, was a monotonous business. The ladies typically went to sleep around eight-thirty each evening, so, to quote the star, "there was just a big stag party every night." To the strains of a local marimba band, the men drank tequila, played poker, shot pool, and just gabbed. Occasionally, the more adventuresome members of the company made the eighty-mile trek to Tijuana, but the road between the towns was so terrible it was called "Dead Man's Highway."

Korda was a demanding director, with something of a temper. Peck recalled one time during the making of the picture when Benedict Bogeaus incurred Korda's wrath. They were filming a scene in which Preston was supposed to shoot a buffalo, which would then fall at his feet while Peck looked on. For the scene, a buffalo head was attached to an elaborate mechanical contraption created out of rubber and fur. At the moment Bogeaus appeared on the set, filming wasn't going too well. Oblivious to the tense atmosphere, the producer waved at the director. "I finally figured out what we should call the picture," he shouted, everyone having agreed that the title of the short story was too long. Korda stared at Bogeaus, and then said, "Well, what the hell is it, Benedict?" The producer raised his arms, a look of triumph on his face, and shouted, "*Congo! Congo!*" After a pause, the director took out a pocketknife, unfolded it, walked over to Bogeaus, and stuck the point against the producer's chest. "You stupid son-of-a-beech!" he shouted. "You get off my set and if you ever come back here again, I cut your leever out!" Peck said they never saw Bogeaus again.

The Macomber Affair, as the picture was finally called, opened at the Globe Theatre in New York on April 20, 1947. *Time* called it "a brilliantly good job—the best yet—of bringing Hemingway to the screen." The magazine, like many reviewers, objected to the conclusion, but that hadn't satisfied the filmmakers either. As Peck put it years later, it was "the best and least compromising ending we could think of."

The warmest praise was reserved for Preston in the flashiest role, but Peck acquitted himself well. As Alton Cook of the *New York World-Telegram* pointed out, he wasn't the "ruthlessly lustful guide" of Hemingway's story, but he offered up an acceptable alternative in the form of a dashing man's man. After his roles as a troubled amnesiac, a bad-seed cowboy, and a Florida cracker, Greg's return to the ranks of traditional leading man made a refreshing change—that is, for the relatively few who caught the film. Shortly after the picture's opening, *Duel in the Sun* blasted its way into theaters, all but engulfing the small black-and-white adventure tale.

With no film work scheduled for the summer of 1946, Peck returned to his roots, the theater, assaying the role of Christopher Mahon in John Millington Synge's *The Playboy of the Western World.* The Irish comedy was part of the summer season of the Cape Playhouse in Dennis, Massachusetts, where Peck had done four shows in 1942. How much had changed since then! Four years ago Greg had been a complete unknown, trying to establish himself in his profession, and the world had been at war. Now, at age thirty, he was a famous movie star, and America was enjoying the first summer of peace since 1941.

Peck rehearsed for a week while the season's opener, Shaw's *Pygmalion,* was in performance. The presence of the handsome movie star caused quite a stir in the resort community. As *Screen Guild* reported a few months later, "What he said, what he wore, what he ate for breakfast were leading topics in local conversation."

Peck tried to ignore the tumult, focusing on the difficult role of the mild Irish lad who becomes a braggart and rake. Having to master a brogue and cope with Synge's poetic language wasn't easy. His director, Arthur Sircom, who had helmed Greg's previous shows with the company, was impressed with his efforts, saying, "Greg has great sincerity, real strength. I don't think he has realized all that he has. His amazing reticence and modesty hold him back." Sircom also felt that *Playboy* was a good choice for Peck, "because it gave him a chance to bring out uninhibited emotions."

When the play opened on July 8, the critics were less than awed, however. The *Boston Herald*, for example, found Peck "on the stolid rather than imaginative side." The actor was philosophical about the reaction, saying, "I stuck my neck out and that's what happened."

No doubt, he would have preferred raves, but he had long since ceased to think of himself as a serious stage actor. For starters, his multiple-picture contracts mitigated against a concerted theater career. More importantly, he had become fascinated by the craft of screen acting. In his opinion, the intimacy of the camera demanded "greater honesty" than did performing on the stage. So he viewed *Playboy of the Western World* as a lark, a chance to do, in his words, "something I hadn't done before." On that level, the experience was valid. He felt that he would "go back to Hollywood and do better work because of it."

Greta didn't accompany Greg to the Cape, because she was pregnant again. On August 16, about a month after he returned to Los Angeles, she gave birth to their second son, whom they called Stephen.

By this point, the Pecks had been in California for about three years. Then, as now, Los Angeles is a company town; socializing with others in the business is part of the business. Greg, still introverted and shy, avoided the Hollywood scene whenever possible. "I'm afraid of a lot of people," he told reporter Gladys Hall. "I think I am more at ease on a stage or before a camera than at a cocktail party." He disliked nightclubs as well. He felt more comfortable having a few friends over to his home for dinner or an occasional game of poker. He and Greta held an informal open house on Sunday afternoons, with Greg serving up beef stew. A few drinks and some interesting conversation suited him just fine. In comfortable surroundings, he could hold his own. "He has a great Irish charm," noted Associated Press reporter Rosalind Shaffer, "mixed of good humor, quick wit, a native courtesy and a pleasant warmth that comes out at you."

Shaffer, like many others who came to know Peck, was struck by the fact that he not only conducted himself with more grace and dignity than many actors, but that his intellect was wider ranging. She described him as "a philosopher" and noted his concern "with the woes of the world." He remained the avid reader he'd been as a boy. His taste ran to serious literature, history, and biography. The Civil War and Abraham Lincoln were areas of particular interest. In time, he would own some one thousand books on the sixteenth president and the War Between the States.

Of course, working long hours six days a week on a film, with frequent radio performances plus the other demands on a star—sitting for photographs, meeting with studio publicists and reporters, attending premieres—left him little free time. One journalist noted that about the only opportunity he had for physical exercise came on Sundays when he mowed the lawn, puttered around in his garden, washed his car, or hiked across the summit of Coldwater Canyon.

While working on a role, he used his free time to pore over his script, making extensive notes about his character's motivations, behavior, and personality traits. Looking at these jottings, one is struck by their sheer number and frequency. They often consist of no more than a couple of words or a phrase, but they are everywhere.

Meanwhile, Greta tended house. Columnist Sidney Skolsky described their home as "neatly furnished," with paintings on the wall that Greg had selected. But there were always a few dogs and cats about the place to create some disarray—especially after Perry, the white German shepherd, sired a litter of puppies. And Greg made his own contribution to the clutter. According to Greta, "He never wants to comb his hair, and he has a bad habit of leaving his clothes around until you pick them up in self-defense."

Greg and Greta were beginning to realize that theirs was not a match made in heaven. Both had quick tempers and neither liked to admit to being wrong. Sometimes they would find themselves in the midst of a heated argument without even realizing that a quarrel had begun. Typically it would end quickly—"usually whoever feels the guiltiest does the making up," Greta claimed. But she recalled one time when they went for several days without speaking to one another. After forty-eight hours of silence, she went up to her room, and there she found a new camelhair coat draped over a chair, a scarf in her favorite colors hanging out of a pocket, and a large bottle of perfume nearby. She said, "I ran to him—crying—asking myself, 'How can you be mad at a man like that?'"

For the moment, peace was restored to the Peck household. But it wouldn't last.

For years, David O. Selznick had been trying to film *The Paradine Case*, Robert Hichens' 1933 novel of a beautiful woman of dubious morals on trial in London's Old Bailey for the murder of her husband. At various points during his tenure as vice president and producer at MGM, Selznick had hoped to cast Diana Wynyard, Greta Garbo, or Hedy Lamarr as the defendant, Mrs. Paradine, and John Barrymore, Lionel

Barrymore, Leslie Howard, or Ronald Colman as one or another of her attorneys. But the project failed to materialize. Finally, in 1946, when casting about for a project for Hitchcock, to whom he was paying $5,000 a week for doing nothing, he remembered the property, purchased it from MGM, and put it into the works immediately.

Selznick again tried to enlist Garbo for the role of Mrs. Paradine, and once more she declined. Ingrid Bergman also refused the assignment. Finally, David cast an Italian actress. Alida Valli—billed simply as "Valli"—was popular in her home country but was completely unknown in the United States. The film introduced another actor to American audiences, Frenchman Louis Jourdan, cast as the dead Mr. Paradine's butler.

Had Garbo or Bergman accepted Selznick's offer, Mrs. Paradine would no doubt have become the film's central character. With Valli, however, the emphasis shifted to Anthony Keane, the successful middle-aged barrister who falls in love with her, then jeopardizes his marriage and career in the hope of securing her acquittal.

Most Hitchcock biographers argue that the director wanted either Laurence Olivier or Ronald Colman, and that Selznick insisted on Peck. But Leonard Leff, author of *Hitchcock & Selznick,* maintained that the opposite was the case: Selznick wanted Olivier and, as a second choice, Maurice Evans, and Hitch, impressed by the grosses of *Spellbound,* suggested Peck. To be sure, Greg was far more popular than the British actors under consideration, but he was too young for the role and an American, drawbacks that worried him. According to Leff, Selznick shared those concerns, but Hitchcock eventually brought Peck and the producer around.

Once cast, Greg's first thought was to work on a credible British accent, but Hitchcock told him not to bother. The director figured that a mustache would sufficiently Anglicize the star. Then he found out that barristers were always clean-shaven. So he decided to simply add a bit of gray to Peck's hair. That wouldn't make him look British, but it brought him closer to the character's age.

When filming began on December 19, neither Hitchcock nor Selznick was up to the challenge. The director, at the end of his seven-year contract with the producer, was eager to be on his own. He had, in fact, already formed an independent production company with producer Sidney Bernstein. *The Paradine Case* was a mopping-up operation. Peck could tell that Hitch was "really bored" during filming. After most takes, the director was found sleeping—or pretending to sleep—in his chair.

Selznick, meanwhile, was in the midst of a personal crisis. His marriage had collapsed, taking his relationship with Jennifer Jones into new and somewhat rocky territory. Moreover, he had sunk a fortune into *Duel in the Sun* and was throwing more money into the pot every day, but the Western's general release—and a potential return on his investment—still lay some five months away. Worse, he was not only producing *The Paradine Case,* he was rewriting the script that had been drafted by the Scottish dramatist James Bridie and partially reworked by Ben Hecht (eventually, he would receive sole credit for the screenplay). David was in such distress that, about two weeks before the start of principal photography, Selznick told his closest associate, Daniel O'Shea, "I am on the verge of collapse and not thinking very clearly and am having under these conditions to try to patch up and rewrite the Hitchcock script (Hecht leaves us tomorrow, with an enormous amount of work remaining to be done); and the business problems are mounting daily." He added, "It is clear that even though I continue to work eighteen hours and twenty hours daily, *Paradine Case* will not be what it should be, and may even be dangerous at its cost, which I predict right now will be between $3,200,000 and $3,300,000, with only one star of importance, Peck. Clearly I have neither the time nor the energy nor the clarity of mind to improve the situation, and to straighten out its problems."

The cameras started to turn on December 19, 1946. Within a week, the company was three days behind schedule, a condition for which Selznick blamed Hitchcock. Hitch, in turn, put the onus on Selznick's antiquated equipment, which was, in fact, below par.

As the project progressed, the director and the producer clashed over the look of the film. Hitch opted for a gritty realism while Selznick, still driven to outdo *Gone With the Wind,* wanted glamour and gloss. Selznick won. But the biggest problem between the two men stemmed from Selznick's never-ending rewrites. It was not uncommon for the actors to arrive at the studio in the morning and be given pages of new dialogue to memorize. "So very often," Peck recalled, "we didn't shoot anything until eleven o'clock or twelve o'clock or even until after lunch." As with *Duel in the Sun,* the new dialogue didn't improve upon the original. "David was not a good writer," said Peck. "If there was anything subtle, he would manage to take it out and spell it all out in an obvious way." Hitchcock maintained his composure on the set, but he was infuriated by Selznick's meddling. "What am I to do?" the director asked an old friend. "I can't take it anymore—he comes down every day, he rewrites the scene, I can't shoot it. It's so bad."

Working under such conditions wasn't pleasant for anyone. The only aspect of the shoot that Peck truly enjoyed stemmed from the trial scenes. These were filmed on an elaborate courtroom set at RKO, a painstaking re-creation of the Old Bailey drawn from photographs.

Hitchcock utilized four camera units during these scenes, each trained on a different actor or group of actors and running simultaneously during every take. This method allowed the director to shoot for ten minutes at a stretch, the maximum length of a reel of film in 1946, rather than filming in the traditional snippets—for long shots, medium shots, and close-ups. "Well, it was like the theater," said Peck, "and it was great fun from that point of view to play."

Greg was at his most effective in the courtroom scenes, forcefully and theatrically challenging witnesses and Leo J. Carroll as the prosecutor, and wryly bantering with Charles Laughton's reptilian judge. In the rest of the picture, however, he was somewhat stolid. Despite Hitch's blithe indiffierence, Peck studied speeches by prime minister Anthony Eden in an effort to blend his accent with those of his real English costars, but he just couldn't master the dialect. Worse, he couldn't effect the character's transformation from confident professional dedicated to his wife to someone totally infatuated with his client. Naturally, Hitchcock was of no help as Greg negotiated this difficult transition. Neither was Valli. She was attractive, but her performance was glacial and stolid, her face mask-like most of the time. Moreover, the screenplay failed to provide early scenes that lay the foundation for the attorney's evolving passion. By contrast, the sequences with Keane's wife effectively traced her growing suspicions about her husband's infatuation and her refusal to give him up. Ann Todd brought such conviction to the wife that it further unbalanced the love triangle.

Principal photography mercifully ended on March 13, 1947, ninety-two days after it began, a record length for a Hitchcock shoot. The following month, Hitch presented Selznick with a rough cut that ran three hours and then washed his hands of the editing. By summer, the producer had trimmed the film by nearly an hour. He then called for a few retakes, which Hitch agreed to shoot for $1,000 a day. Eventually, the picture was cut to 132 minutes.

Although a couple of previews produced a lukewarm response, Selznick had learned from *Duel in the Sun* the benefits of an aggressive promotional campaign. Accordingly, he spent even more money to publicize *The Paradine Case* than he had on the Western.

Lightning failed to strike twice, however. Upon its opening at Radio City Music Hall on January 8, 1948, the picture garnered lukewarm praise from the *New York Times*' Bosley Crowther and the *New York Herald-Tribune*'s Howard Barnes, but audiences found it slow-moving, talky, and confusing. Prior to the film's general release, Selznick went back to the editing room and made further cuts, shortening the trial sequences, reducing the footage of Valli, who was not registering with audiences, and playing up Louis Jourdan, whom people seemed to like. "I have goosed around this film a dozen different ways," he wrote in early 1948, "and got a lot of values out of it that aren't in the original film."

But to no avail. The picture came nowhere near to recouping the $4 million that it ultimately cost, making it the biggest financial failure of Selznick's career. It didn't help Peck either. Although Bosley Crowther called him "impressively impassioned," *Time* magazine came much closer to the truth in asserting "Gregory Peck turns in the first performance that may trouble his well-wishers. Although he has worked exceedingly hard to become an Englishman . . . he remains unmistakably American in appearance and bearing. A tremendously cagey and accomplished actor might conceivably have made a convincing character out of this attorney, in spite of the inadequacies of the script. Peck is not yet cagey or accomplished enough."

Some years later, a Spanish reporter asked Greg which of his pictures he would like to burn. He replied, *The Paradine Case.*

As he slogged his way through the last of the Selznick-Hitchcock collaborations, Peck continued to make numerous radio appearances. On January 6, he, Jane Wyman, and Claude Jarman Jr. gave the listeners of the *Lady Esther Screen Guild Players* a thirty-minute preview of *The Yearling,* which would open in New York on the twenty-third. The day before *The Yearling*'s debut, Greg joined his *Duel in the Sun* costars Jennifer Jones, Lionel Barrymore, and Joseph Cotten in an adaptation of Edward Everett Hale's *The Man Without a Country.* The thirty-minute program on NBC was sponsored by the March of Dimes, but the publicity didn't hurt the Selznick picture, still months away from release. On February 4, Peck returned to NBC as a guest on *The Bob Hope Show.* During the broadcast, he received the *Look* Magazine Achievement Award for the "Outstanding Actor of 1946." Finally, on May 5, he could be heard in an episode of NBC's *Cavalcade of America.* Thereafter, his radio work for the year ended. While making *The Paradine Case,* he had found a new venture to occupy his free time. He decided to start a summer stock company with several other Selznick contract players, notably Mel Ferrer and Dorothy McGuire.

Like Peck, Mel Ferrer came from the New York theater. One year younger than Greg, the New Jersey–born actor had also worked at the Cape Playhouse. In addition, he was a radio producer and director, and his credits as a stage director included a successful Broadway revival of *Cyrano de Bergerac* with José Ferrer in the title role.

Upon his arrival in Hollywood, Ferrer told Selznick that he didn't want to completely abandon the theater for film. The producer was surprisingly sympathetic. However, there weren't many opportunities to do plays in the Los Angeles area. If Mel wanted to act on the stage in southern California, he would have to create an outlet for himself. He decided to establish a summer stock company.

Selznick suggested that the newcomer speak with Peck, saying, "He is as crazy about the theater as you are." Since Greg was working on *The Paradine Case* at the time, David sent Mel to the appropriate soundstage. As the two young men strolled the RKO lot, Greg picked up Mel's enthusiasm for a theater-related venture. At first, Ferrer thought Peck wanted to limit his involvement to appearing in the occasional play, but that wasn't so. He wanted to help set up the company. "We'll do it together," Greg said. "We'll be coproducers."

They found support from several other Selznick contract players who came from the stage: Joseph Cotten, Jennifer Jones, and Dorothy McGuire, who would be teamed with Peck for his next feature, *Gentleman's Agreement.* Although all five would ultimately be listed as the venture's producers, Greg's *Duel in the Sun* costars never played an active role in the company's management. Said Peck, "[I]t was the three of us—Dorothy, Mel, and I—who ran the Playhouse."

Initially, they considered locating their company in Santa Barbara, which boasted a well-established road show house called the Lobero Theater. Then Peck mentioned that his birthplace, La Jolla, was a wealthy resort community not unlike the Cape Playhouse's Dennis, Massachusetts. It might be a good spot for a stock company, he argued. The aspiring producers decided to visit the village, talk to some local merchants, and see if anyone had an interest in such a venture.

Greg's local relatives directed him to Frank Harman, a La Jolla car dealer who was civic minded and able to get things done. Immediately enthusiastic, Harmon approached the Chamber of Commerce about the company. The Chamber wasn't interested, but the Kiwanis Club agreed to support the venture, providing that Harmon head the sponsoring committee, which he agreed to do. The car dealer then persuaded the San Diego school board to make the La Jolla High School auditorium available for performances. It was nowhere near the caliber of the Lobero Theater. In fact, it was, in Ferrer's words, "sort of a rectangular box with wooden chairs." The acoustics weren't good and the seats would have to be cushioned, for their target audience, affluent tourists and townsfolk, weren't likely to sit through three-act plays on hard, uncomfortable furniture. But the would-be producers were undaunted. They dubbed the auditorium the La Jolla Playhouse and went about their business.

Now all they needed was the capital to finance their productions.

Despite his own money problems, Selznick generously agreed to loan his contract players $10,000 (or $15,000, the number varies in different accounts). By way of thanks, Ferrer, McGuire, and Peck dubbed themselves the Selznick Actors' Company (this name was soon shortened to the Actors' Company and then dropped altogether—after which they simply used the name given the auditorium, the La Jolla Playhouse).

With financing in hand, a theater in which to perform, and a base from which to build community support, the trio set about reading plays and talking to other stars about appearing in their productions. But, as they labored away on their exciting new venture during the spring of 1947, frequently visiting La Jolla to meet with local boosters, they had to tend to their bread-and-butter jobs. For Peck and McGuire that meant reporting to Fox at the end of May to start work on *Gentleman's Agreement.*

One day in the mid-forties, Laura Z. Hobson came across an article in *Time* magazine that reported Mississippi Congressman John Rankin's anti-Semitic remarks on the floor of the House of Representatives. The Jewish novelist and short story writer wasn't surprised by Rankin's statements—he was a known bigot—but by the fact that none of his colleagues protested the use of "kike," "Jew boy," and other slurs in their august chamber. She decided to write a novel exploring the extent to which anti-Semitism was passively accepted in polite society. Her protagonist, a writer named Phil Green, isn't himself a Jew, but rather a Christian assigned to write a series of magazine articles on the subject. Green decides that the only way to get to the heart of the story is to tell people that he is Jewish. He then discovers prejudice in people and places that he never suspected, even in the well-bred WASP he's come to love, Kathy Lacey.

Hobson called her novel *Gentleman's Agreement.* Published by Simon & Schuster in February 1947, it became a whopping best-seller. Darryl F. Zanuck had snapped up the film rights for $75,000 when the book was still in galleys; with escalators tied to sales, the purchase price eventually reached $150,000.

To direct the picture, Zanuck hired Elia Kazan, who had previously directed Fox's 1945 production of *A Tree Grows in Brooklyn,* based on another best-selling novel, and 1947's *Boomerang,* about a New York City murder trial with political overtones. Although Gadge, as Kazan was known to friends, was relatively new to features, he was a towering figure on the New York stage, having directed some of the most important American dramas of the twentieth century—*The Skin of Our Teeth* by Thornton Wilder, *A Streetcar Named Desire* by Tennessee Williams, and *All My Sons* and *Death of a Salesman* by Arthur Miller.

To adapt Hobson's novel for the screen, Zanuck turned to Moss Hart, the celebrated coauthor (with George S. Kaufman) of such sharply etched comedies as *You Can't Take It with You* and *The Man Who Came to Dinner.* Although Hart eliminated some of the novel's secondary characters, including the reporter's bigoted sister, and streamlined the plot, he hewed closely to Hobson's basic storyline and theme.

Gentleman's Agreement was part of a wave of hard-hitting films tackled by Hollywood in the late 1940s. To be sure, lavish MGM musicals like *Easter Parade* and the nonsensical Bob Hope–Bing Crosby "road" comedies remained enormously popular, but Americans, tempered by a long, costly war, also embraced *The Lost Weekend, The Best Years of Our Lives,* and the soon-to-be released *Snake Pit* and *Pinky.* These films dealt respectively with alcoholism, the problems of returning veterans, mental illness, and race relations.

Features like 1945's *House on 92nd Street* and 1947's *13 Rue Madeleine* and *Kiss of Death* placed Zanuck at the forefront of the movement toward greater film realism. He championed location shooting, crisp dialogue, and sharp black-and-white photography. But none of his pictures dealt with as sensitive a subject as American anti-Semitism. The issue struck a particularly sore note with film moguls Samuel Goldwyn and Louis B. Mayer, both of whom were Jewish. Not wishing to "rock the boat," they pleaded with Zanuck, the only gentile studio head in Hollywood, to shelve *Gentleman's Agreement.* But Zanuck would not be dissuaded. He was certain that the time had come for a frank consideration of the problem.

Kazan and Hart shared Zanuck's enthusiasm—as did Peck, the obvious choice for Phil Green, particularly since he owed Fox three pictures. But not everyone was eager to see Greg tackle the role of a writer out to expose prejudice. Some fans wrote him letters, saying they couldn't understand why he would want to play a Jew (actually he was playing a gentile who pretended to be Jewish, but that was a fine point). Also mystified was Ron Myers, one of the agents at MCA who had inherited Peck from Leland Hayward.* He encouraged Greg to refuse the part. But Greg wouldn't be dissuaded.

Still, neither he nor anyone else involved in the picture was out to make a polemic. As with the novel, the message was couched within the context of a human drama, which involved Phil's developing romance with Kathy (Dorothy McGuire) and his concern over the health of his mother (Anne

*Eager to become a Broadway producer, Leland Hayward decided to retire from the talent agency business in 1944. He sold his client list to the Music Corporation of America. Some of his former colleagues, including Maynard Morris, also joined MCA.

Revere). Also important were his relationships with his young son (Dean Stockwell), his best friend, a returning vet named Dave Golden (John Garfield), and several colleagues at the magazine, including a sharp but lonely fashion editor named Anne Detrie (Celeste Holm). As Peck put it, "We had a very good story to tell, with a set of good characters, and at the same time were able to get in a few good licks against bigotry, prejudice and hatred, all the things we think of as being anti-American."

With a $2 million budget, the picture was shot in a brisk sixty days. Peck was on call for all but one. Although the majority of the work took place at the studio, Greg made two trips to New York, where filming occurred at Radio City Music Hall and along Park Avenue and in the nearby Connecticut communities of Darien and Stamford.

If Hitchcock was the antithesis of an actor's director, Kazan was an actor's dream. Indeed, he had been an actor himself, a member of the same Group Theatre that had molded Sanford Meisner. "Not only does he rehearse more than most directors," Peck said shortly after the picture wrapped, "but we'd get together in his trailer to break down and analyze the script ahead of time, just like in the theater. And the man is fairly loaded with ideas."

Greg and Gadge got along in a professional manner, but they didn't really mesh. The director found his star "very closed off and rigid. . . . He didn't have an artist's nature. He had his own way, and that was always correct. He was logical and listened. He was cooperative. But it was hard to light a fire in a guy like that." Kazan admitted that he also got a bit irked by Peck's occasional preoccupation with the La Jolla Playhouse. As the director put it, "[W]hen I looked for him to give him a note or to rehearse, he was often on long distance."

Peck attributed some of the lack of chemistry to their backgrounds and temperaments—he was small-town California, Kazan was born in Constantinople and grew up in New York. Where the director was "aggressive, dynamic," he was "more easygoing." Given their differences, the actor concluded, it "was hard for him to understand my way of doing things. And I, on the other hand, couldn't make myself an Elia Kazan—an aggressive, taut, highly strung product of an entirely different background."

The company wrapped in July. Thereafter, Zanuck worked rapidly to ready the picture for release. It opened at New York's Mayfair Theatre on November 11—two months before *The Paradine Case*—to near-universal raves. Jesse Zunser of *Cue* called it an "an extraordinary achievement. One of the finest films of this or any other year, it is a mature, honest and well-balanced drama." And *Variety* dubbed it "brilliant and powerful . . . one of the most vital and stirring and impressive [films] in Hollywood history."

Despite Kazan's criticisms of Peck, it is difficult to imagine a better match between actor and role. He brings a tender understanding to Phil's relationship with his son, and an easy warmth and concern to the writer's relationship with his mother. He is suitably charming and romantic as he courts Dorothy McGuire's Kathy. And he is passionate and uncompromising, without becoming strident, in his pursuit of his story. All of the hallmarks of the emerging Peck persona are present and fully developed for the first time in this drama. And he demonstrated that no one was his equal when it came portraying an intelligent, principled yet sensitive modern man. *Variety* called it "unquestionably the finest performance of his career to date," and this is a fair assessment.

For an impressive third year in a row, Greg received an Oscar nomination for Best Actor, but he lost once again, this time to Ronald Colman for *A Double Life*. *Gentleman's Agreement* garnered seven other nominations—for Best Picture, Director, Actress, Supporting Actress (Celeste Holm, Anne Revere), Editing, and Screenplay. Kazan and Holm won. So did the film, which, by a strange coincidence, was up against an RKO picture called *Crossfire,* which also had an anti-Semitic element in its storyline. *Gentleman's Agreement* became Fox's top-grossing picture of the year, with receipts of $3.9 million.

Today, it is fashionable to look upon *Gentleman's Agreement* as safe and outmoded. Even Kazan has distanced himself from the picture, calling it "the perfect example of that day's 'liberal' films" and labeling it "patronizing." This is a valid criticism. But, considering that ten years earlier, when Warner Bros. released *The Life of Emile Zola,* the word "Jew" wasn't even spoken, the makers of *Gentleman's Agreement* pushed the envelope as far anyone could have expected at the time. Moreover, in accepting his Best Picture Oscar, Zanuck said, "I would like to emphasize that *Gentleman's Agreement* was primarily planned for entertainment rather than for any social message. I believe this is the chief reason for the success of the film." As human drama, it still works.

By the time *Gentleman's Agreement* wrapped, the Actors' Company's inaugural season at the La Jolla Playhouse was under way.

What Greg and his associates settled on was an eight-week season of typical stock, that is, primarily light fare—a mix of recent comedies and mysteries—with an occasional classic to liven things up. Each production, which featured at least one name actor, rehearsed for a week and ran for a week. Openings were on Tuesdays, closings were on Sundays, and there were matinees on Wednesdays and Saturdays. Rehearsals were held in a small room at the high school. Each Monday, the previous show's set would be struck and the new set mounted. That evening, the actors would get the stage for a dress rehearsal. Last-minute polishing took place on Tuesday, before the opening that night.

The principals were housed at the Valencia Hotel near the high school. The hotel's owner, Dick Irwin, was one of the company's most ardent supporters, and soon the Valencia became something of a home-away-from-home for Peck and his colleagues. "It had two dining rooms," said Ferrer, "and we just spent all of our free time and ate most of our meals at the Valencia."

McGuire had informed Greg and Mel early on that she wasn't good at organizing things. Although she submitted scripts, made casting suggestions, and starred in plays herself, she left the rest of the producing chores to her two colleagues, who shared the duties. To assist them, they hired a general manager, a press representative, two box-office treasurers, two staff secretaries, and a casting director, Ruth Burch, who also worked for Selznick. In time, they rented a year-round office on Canon Drive in Beverly Hills. It was near MCA, the talent agency that represented both of them. The proximity turned out to be beneficial. "They were very helpful in getting us some of their clients to do shows," Ferrer recalled.

Although Mel would occasionally take the helm of a production, James Neilson was the company's principal director. He and Peck had come to know one another when Neilson was a stage manager for Katharine Cornell and Guthrie McClintic. "His devotion to a production and his meticulous attention to detail had won him the respect of everyone in the theater," Greg recalled. Harry Carey Jr., who would act in several La Jolla Playhouse productions, called Neilson "terrific."

The pros derived considerable help from La Jolla volunteers. In addition to the men on the Kiwanis Club's Sponsoring Committee, dozens of socially prominent women from the San Diego area served on the Women's Committee, headed by Mrs. Walter M. Trevor and later by Marian Longstreth, who became the company's foremost advocate. "The actors and actresses took care of the plays," noted San Diego reporter William Sullivan years later, "but the committee handled all the details, such as selling tickets, publicity, selling Coca-Cola and acquiring properties and costumes." Some locals even took small roles in the productions.

The volunteers worked particularly hard in the first year to sell subscription tickets to all eight plays. "We sold out I think it was about 80 percent of our first season on subscription," Ferrer recalled. This feat was all the more remarkable because they had been unable to announce far in advance what shows or stars would be featured, as the casting and play selection depended upon the availability of talent on hiatus from film work.

Illustrative of such uncertainty was Greg's own situation that summer. He had hoped to star in the inaugural show, choosing a 1929 mystery called *Rope's End* by Patrick Hamilton, which Hitchcock would film the following year as *Rope.* Once it became apparent that Fox wouldn't be able to release Peck in time to rehearse the play for an early July opening, he, Ferrer, and McGuire replaced it with Emlyn Williams' *Night Must Fall.* Dame May Whitney starred, re-creating her role from the 1937 film version, for which she had received an Oscar nomination.

The season's other productions were *Dear Ruth* with Diana Lynn, Guy Madison, and Fred Clark; *The Hasty Heart* with Richard Basehart, Beatrice Pearson, and Henry Morgan; *The Guardsman* with Ruth Hussey and Kent Smith; *Biography* with Eve Arden and Barry Sullivan; *Tonight at 8:30* with McGuire, Heather Angel, and Una O'Connor; and *The Shining Hour* with Robert Walker, Beatrice Pearson, and Karen Morley.

Peck closed the season, costarring with Laraine Day in *Angel Street,* another thriller by Patrick Hamilton. The drama about a fiendish husband who tries to drive his wife insane had opened on Broadway in 1941 with Vincent Price and Judith Evelyn and ran for an astonishing 1,295 performances. The 1944 film version, released as *Gaslight,* had starred Charles Boyer and Ingrid Bergman. Peck wasn't suited to the role of the villainous Mr. Manningham, but part of the fun of doing stock was in tackling characters that one wouldn't otherwise get to do. Greg even grew a mustache and beard for the part. Helping him and Day, who was also rather miscast, was the original Broadway director, Shepherd Traube.

The company ended the season about $5,000 in debt. To earn money for a second season, the producers formed a partnership with Shepherd Traube and toured their production of *Angel Street* along the West Coast, starting at San Francisco's Geary Theater on October 21.

"The eight-week run of the play was a great success financially," Peck wrote his agent, Maynard Morris, that December. "We averaged around $19,000 a week and had a couple of really big $25,000 weeks up north. The notices in L.A. were not so hot. In fact, they were poor, but they loved us in Sacramento, and all in all, I am very glad that we did it and feel that the experience will be invaluable to me. It was a tough part for me and I didn't do it very well, but I feel that the stage experience is something that will stand by me and make it much easier for me when I go back in a part that is closer to me."

After expenses and Traube's share of the profits, the Actors' Company had a nice little nest egg for the future.

CHAPTER 10

The End of a Momentous Decade

After the *Angel Street* tour ended, Peck devoted several months to reading plays and otherwise helping plan the La Jolla Playhouse's second season. He also resumed his radio career, undertaking two broadcasts in January 1948, one of which was another dramatization of *The Yearling*, this time a sixty-minute version for the *Lux Radio Theatre.*

That same month, on January 12, *Time* magazine, one of the most influential and widely read publications in the nation, featured him on its cover. In the accompanying article, Greg was described as an average guy—"luckier, better looking and more gifted than" most people but not that different from the folks who bought tickets for his movies. The magazine also detailed his earnings, noting that equivalent stars were commanding $200,000 or more per film while his multi-picture deals kept him at around $50,000 to $65,000. "By Hollywood standards," *Time* concluded, "Peck is shamefully underpaid."

Time also reported that Greg and Greta had purchased a new home—for $50,000—which they occupied during Greg's eleven-month hiatus after *Gentleman's Agreement* wrapped. Located at 1700 San Remo Drive in the high-toned suburb of Pacific Palisades, the onetime residence of Nobel Prize–winning author Thomas Mann was a long, low, one-story ranch house designed in the late 1930s by Cliff May. Situated on four acres and perched on the side of a hill, the house featured large glass windows that afforded twenty-mile views in all directions. It also included a swimming pool, which the Pecks' previous home had lacked and which Greg used to ease his chronic back ailment.

In keeping with her heritage, Greta furnished much of the home in the blond woods and clean lines of the Scandinavian modern style. Bold colors in the upholstery, draperies, and rugs provided cheerful accents. The den, which was Greg's turf, reflected his taste. It included a dark green, deep leather sofa; a glass-topped bar also upholstered in green leather with matching stools; an upright piano; a fireplace; and bookshelves with bound plays and stacks of records—mostly classical and jazz—plus a turntable. Before moving in, the Pecks constructed a high wall around the property to protect their sons and pets from accidents on the adjacent hillside.

While they enjoyed their new home and the recognition by *Time*, the Pecks endured several mishaps during the early months of 1948. On March 6, while relaxing in Florida, they chartered a boat with mystery writer Leslie Charteris and his wife. Caught in a bad storm with forty-six-mile-per-hour winds, they were unable to reach their destination, the town of Craig in the Florida Keys. A radio alert brought the Coast Guard, which carried them to shore. They were lucky; the storm caused the disappearance of two other boats carrying six people.

Less than a month later, on April 2, Greg was horseback riding to get in shape for his next picture, a Fox Western called *Yellow Sky*. In the wake of *Duel in the Sun*, he decided to choose his own mount. After trying three horses at the ranch owned by Ralph McCutcheon, he spied another interesting prospect and climbed on board. The horse moved into a gallop, which Greg accommodated. Then it went into a turn, lost its footing, and plummeted to the ground. Unable to remove his left foot from the stirrup, Peck fell with the horse, which landed on his left leg. The animal, totally unhurt, picked itself up and galloped away. Greg, however, remained in the dirt, quickly going into shock. A wrangler ran to the McCutcheon's house to summon an ambulance, which arrived a few moments later. Taken in great pain to Cedars of Lebanon Hospital, Greg learned that the leg had been fractured in three places. It was reset and placed in a cast, and he was sent home on April 5, having been told to remain in bed as much as possible.

While Greg was laid up, Greta was party to a hit-and-run automobile accident on April 21. Returning home from Birmingham Hospital in Van Nuys where she was a Red Cross volunteer, she reached the intersection of Sunset Boulevard and Sepulveda and rammed into the rear of a car owned by a forty-five-year-old man named Max Usland. Instead of stopping, she drove away at a high speed. Usland chased her for two miles, then gave up and went to a police station. Eventually two officers located Greta at home. In a state of hysteria, she told them that she had only bumped Usland but had been afraid to stop because of the heavy traffic on Sunset and the lateness of the hour. Once home, she explained, she took a couple of drinks in an effort to calm herself.

On May 6, Assistant City Attorney Donald M. Redwine conducted a hearing into the accident. After visiting the crash site, he determined that there was insufficient evidence to issue a hit-and-run complaint against Greta. Meanwhile, Mrs. Usland, a passenger in the car at the time of the accident, filed a civil suit against the Pecks in Los Angeles Superior Court, claiming that she had experienced internal bleeding, contusions, and abrasions as a result of the crash.

There is, of course, no way of knowing what really happened that night; L. M. Long, one of the police officers assigned to the case, testified at the hearing that Mrs. Peck told him she had been drinking prior to the accident, a charge she denied. But several of her acquaintances would tell this author that she had a problem with alcohol. The drinks she took at home might have been designed to mask her inebriation while driving.

Of the unfortunate events that spring, the most enduring in impact for Greg was the leg injury. Fox, eager to begin work on *Yellow Sky,* put considerable pressure on his physician to free him for filming. Bowing to studio pressure, the doctor okayed Greg's return to work. Consequently, the leg failed to heal properly. Ever since, the actor has suffered from a weak left ankle. Whenever he's been required to do something strenuous involving his legs, he's had to support the left limb and wear heavy-soled rubber shoes.

Far more conventional than the overblown, operatic *Duel in the Sun, Yellow Sky* was something of a cross between an old-fashioned shoot-'em-up and a morality tale à la *Treasure of the Sierra Madre,* John Huston's paean to greed in the contemporary West. Peck played Stretch, the leader of an 1870s outlaw gang that stumbles upon a desert ghost town, Yellow Sky, Arizona, inhabited only by an old prospector and his attractive but tomboy-like granddaughter, Mike. The outlaws decide to steal the old man's gold but, as Stretch falls in love with Mike, he comes to side with her and the old man. That, of course, leads to a showdown between him and his former comrades, notably the troublemaking Dude, played by Richard Widmark. The Minnesota-born actor had made his film debut the previous year as the sadistic killer in *Kiss of Death.*

Based on a story by W. R. Burnett (better known for his crime novels *Little Caesar, High Sierra,* and *The Asphalt Jungle*), *Yellow Sky* reunited Zanuck with producer-screenwriter Lamar Trotti and director William Wellman, who had worked together on the 1943 adaptation of Walter Van Tilburg Clark's *The Ox-Bow Incident.* Zanuck was enthusiastic about the project, believing that it had the potential to be another *Stagecoach,* the 1939 John Ford classic that the mogul revered. He urged Trotti to keep deepening the characters. "The payoff is not in the plot," he noted, "it is in the people."

For Peck, who had pored over the novels of Zane Grey as a child, the opportunity to work in a traditional Western was "like a small boy's dream true." Anne Baxter, cast as the tomboyish Mike, was somewhat less enchanted. During filming she joked that "someone got me mixed up with somebody else. I'm a homebody, not a female wrestler." The granddaughter of architect Frank Lloyd Wright was seven years younger than Peck but had appeared in more than double the films since her debut in *Twenty-Mule Team* in 1940. One of them, *The Razor's Edge,* had earned her a Best Supporting Actress Oscar in 1946.

Baxter's reference to "female wrestler" pertained to a scene early in the film in which Mike rebuffs Stretch's romantic advances by tussling him to the ground. Wellman would later tell interviewer Frank T. Thompson that Baxter didn't like Peck—the director didn't explain why, and both he and the actress are now deceased—and that this scene gave her a chance to vent her feelings. Wellman warned Greg, "[W]hen you start that fight, you better look out for yourself and wear something over your balls, because she'll destroy you."

The fifty-two-year-old director, known as Wild Bill, was a rugged character who had served in the French Foreign Legion and the Lafayette Escadrille during World War I. A former stunt pilot, he directed the silent classic *Wings,* winner of the first Academy Award for Best Picture, as well as *The Public Enemy, A Star Is Born, Beau Geste,* and numerous other well-regarded pictures. The man lived up to his nickname during the making of *Yellow Sky.* Said Peck, "He yelled and he swore and chewed tobacco, and he was tougher than any of the actors. He just kind of rallied the whole crew and cast to make a film in his way, his style, to reflect his feeling about the story and the characters."

Yellow Sky was shot in part in Death Valley and in the desert around Lone Pine, California, where the ghost town set was constructed. The company endured sandstorms, temperatures in excess of 120 degrees, and even scorpions and tarantulas, but Wild Bill remained undisturbed. He got the realism he was after for the picture.

While the Western was in production, Peck continued to read plays, explore casting options, and otherwise help ready the La Jolla Playhouse for its second season, which opened in early July. Once again, the fare reflected the popular stock repertoire of the day; for a bit of balance, Tennessee Williams' *The Glass Menagerie* was featured that season as well. Peck, Ferrer, and McGuire again attracted an array of distinguished film actors, including Richard Basehart, Ann Harding, Eve Arden, Wendell Corey, June Lockhart, and Leon Ames. But problems did arise. For starters, Van Heflin, who had been booked to star in *Berkeley Square,* had to bow out at the last minute because MGM placed him on call for a film—even though he'd already memorized his lines for the play and his costumes had been constructed. *Berkeley Square* was replaced by *Rope,* starring Roland Culver, Hurd Hatfield, and John Ireland.

And Selznick created difficulties. After agreeing to Jennifer Jones' appearance in a play called *Serena Blandish,* he insisted that she be surrounded by a first-rate supporting cast, including Louis Jourdan, Constance Collier, Mildred Natwick, and Reginald Owen. Because Collier and Owen were not Americans and the stage actor's union, Actors' Equity, didn't allow aliens to appear in summer stock productions, *Serena Blandish* had to be upgraded to a higher production level, which doubled the cost of salaries. Selznick also had Jones' wardrobe designed by celebrated couturiers Charles James, Mainbocher, and Christian Dior.

Peck had to contend with such problems from afar, as *Yellow Sky* remained in production throughout the summer. But he journeyed to La Jolla twice a week for the opening and closing of each show. In late August, he got time off from the Western to rehearse and perform in the ninth production of the year and the season closer, *The Male Animal,* by James Thurber and Elliott Nugent, the comedy that he had done in stock in 1941. This time he had the lead, Thomas Turner, the university professor whose marriage and job are thrown into jeopardy during a football weekend. The general consensus was that he acquitted himself better than he had as the psychotic husband in *Angel Street.* The production was so popular, its run was extended for an extra four performances.

After ending in the red the previous season, the La Jolla Playhouse closed its second year of operation with a slight profit, about $2,000, according to Mel Ferrer. On average, the company operated at 89.5 percent capacity, selling a total of 30,552 tickets for seventy performances, about 40 percent of which were purchased on a subscription basis. These were impressive statistics for a two-year-old venture.

Back in Los Angeles, Peck resumed work on *Yellow Sky,* which wrapped in September. He also managed to squeeze in two more radio appearances. The second, an adaptation of *Gentleman's Agreement* for the *Lux Radio Theatre,* featured his costar in the Western, Anne Baxter.

Yellow Sky debuted at New York's Roxy Theatre on February 1, 1949. Bosley Crowther spoke for the majority of his colleagues, writing "It doesn't take too much experience at spotting the points in Western films to see that you're in on a good one at the start of the Roxy's *Yellow Sky* . . . the guns blaze, fists fly and passions tangle in the best realistic Western style." Peck was acceptable as the outlaw leader, but the role was better suited to the talents of Alan Ladd or even Humphrey Bogart. The picture didn't eclipse *Stagecoach,* but it grossed a very satisfactory $2.8 million at the box office.

By the time *Yellow Sky* debuted, Peck had completed his third film for MGM. Arguably, the principal distinguishing feature of *The Great Sinner* is that it marked the first of three pairings between Peck and Ava Gardner. The beautiful North Carolina–born brunette, five and a half years younger than Greg, had made her film debut two years earlier than he but didn't become a star until 1946, when she was teamed with newcomer Burt Lancaster in *The Killers,* a noirish adaptation of the short story by Ernest Hemingway. She had since played a goddess come to life in *One Touch of Venus.* In *The Great Sinner,* she would portray Pauline Ostrovsky, the cool but vulnerable daughter of a Russian general who unwittingly lures Fedja, the earnest young writer played by Peck, into a ruinous addiction to gambling. The picture was set in a popular health resort, Wiesbaden, Germany, in the 1860s.

Unacknowledged in the screen credits, *The Great Sinner* was based, in part, on a short 1886 novel by Fyodor Dostoyevsky called *The Gambler.* Elements were borrowed as well from the author's *Crime and Punishment,* also published in 1886, and from Dostoyevsky's own life. As "The Gambler" was unavailable for use as a title—it had been registered by another studio—MGM drew inspiration from something Dostoyevsky once said. In the late 1880s, he conceived a multinovel cycle based on his own youthful experiences, which he called "the life of a great sinner." Despite its literary origins, Peck wasn't fond of the title. He considered it "pompous."

To direct the project, L. B. Mayer borrowed Robert Siodmak from Universal. The son of a Leipzig banker, Siodmak was born in Tennessee but grew up in Germany, the setting of *The Great Sinner.* More important, he had recently distinguished himself with several dark psychological dramas, including *The Killers.*

From the outset, Siodmak wasn't happy with the script for *The Great Sinner,* which was far too long. If shot entirely, he warned the film's producer Gottfried Reinhardt before principal photography began, the result would run six hours. Reinhardt, son of Peck's old Broadway director Max Reinhardt, insisted that Siodmak shoot every scene. The weight of the material, compounded by the director's meticulous attention to period detail, added up to a tedious shoot.

Siodmak's personality didn't help matters. "He was a hyperthyroid type in the first place," Peck recalled, "jittery and nervous and now he had the responsibility for this very 'heavy' picture on his shoulders."

When the pressure got too much for him, the director positioned himself on a camera crane and ordered the operator to take him up. High above the set, he gathered his thoughts, while down below, Peck and Ava Gardner looked at one another, grinned, and said, "There he goes again!"

As filming progressed, a friendship ripened between the two stars. Not only did they share somewhat similar backgrounds, coming from small, middle-class communities where everyone knew everyone else, Greg admired Ava's independent, unspoiled personality. As the film's cinematographer, George Folsey, put it, she "behaved like the farm girl she was, without any pretense."

Where the stars differed was in their ambition. Greg took his profession seriously and worked hard at it, studying each role and relevant research material at home in the evenings. Ava, who was signed by MGM with no acting training whatsoever, treated her career diffidently, with little regard for her own talent. Peck tried to give her confidence, saying, "Come on, for Christ's sake. You can act as well as anybody out here. You just have to let go, and stop talking in that breathy little voice!" He even coached her a bit behind Siodmak's back. "I wanted her to be good," he said, "to be her best."

Peck also enjoyed two of the film's supporting actors. Ethel Barrymore, with whom he'd worked in *The Paradine Case,* played Ava's grandmother. She and Greg typically spent their time comparing notes about baseball and boxing. Walter Huston played her son in the film. Peck had shared virtually no scenes with him in *Duel in the Sun,* so *The Great Sinner* gave him a chance to get to know the star of *Dodsworth,* one of his favorite pictures. He found Huston to be a warm, lovable character but also an unrepentant ham who was not above gently steering him by the arm during their two-shots in order to "hog" the camera. Once Peck asked Huston, a little sheepishly, the secret of being a great actor. He never forgot the old man's reply: "Son, always give 'em a good show and travel first class."

With a $2 million budget—at the time, a lavish sum for a black-and-white picture—*The Great Sinner* was definitely "first class." It boasted an outstanding cast which, in addition to Peck, Gardner, Barrymore, and Huston, included Melvyn Douglas, Frank Morgan, and Agnes Morehead. And its extravagant sets and costumes offered a wonderful evocation of a posh nineteenth-century European spa.

But was it "a good show?" When principal photography concluded in December, that remained to be seen. The first cut was eight hours long! Eventually it was reduced to three hours and then to 130 minutes. Peck viewed the result on January 28, 1949, and offered Reinhardt a detailed reaction, first in a meeting held immediately after the screening and then in a five-page typed letter the following day. His criticisms show how far he'd extended his grasp of filmmaking since his arrival in Hollywood five years earlier as well as his impressive ability to articulate his ideas.

For starters, he told Reinhardt that the function of Fedja's voice-over narration, used throughout the story, had changed significantly from screenplay to rough cut. What had once been useful, he felt, had now "taken on the flavor of a lecture tour by a sightseeing guide." He cited by way of example the fact that Fedja describes in voice-over people and places that are shown on the screen. The result, he asserted, might bore the audience. "I do not think," he wrote, "that we can win them by over-simplification and over-clarification in the typical MGM manner."

He then addressed a few specific cuts and the use of shots in the gambling sequences. Finally, he noted that the picture as a whole was confusing, adding, "It had a certain excitement and color but no dramatic focus."

Dory Schary, MGM's new production chief, agreed. In an effort to bolster the love story, he called for reshoots that Siodmak refused to undertake. The director would later assert that Mervyn LeRoy replaced him, but according to Deborah Lazaroff Alpi, author of a study of Siodmak's career, a studio contract director, probably Jack Conway, was given the assignment.

A preview of the picture was held in Santa Monica at the beginning of April. Afterward, Peck wrote Reinhardt a letter noting the differences between the plot of the shooting script and that of the movie he had just seen. He asserted, "I think that the film is so far from being right now and so sick that the only way you will save it is to go back to scratch and cut it exactly according to the script with all of the sequences in and all in their proper place." Eventually, Schary ordered that some of Peck's suggested cuts and changes be made over Reinhardt's opposition—an amazing testament to the actor's tenacity or box-office clout or both.

The picture was again previewed, this time in Pasadena. Although Reinhardt was unhappy with the alterations and wanted to tinker further, Greg felt better about the result, as did Schary, and no additional changes were made.

However, nothing could have truly saved *The Great Sinner.* When it opened at the Loew's State Theatre in New York three days after Peck's final letter to Reinhardt, Bosley Crowther of the *New York Times* called it a "dreary picture," to which *Newsweek* added, "Despite its impressive cast . . . this long and ponderous tale is too drearily artificial in concept to meet any of its pretensions of being either entertainment or moral drama." The supporting players drew generally praiseworthy notices, but Peck and Gardner were less well received. Although Greg looked dashing and he and Ava were well matched, he was unable to genuinely portray the writer's terrible addiction to gambling. This reflected his inability to let go in deeply emotional moments.

The Great Sinner performed moderately well at the box office, as MGM's costume dramas usually did, but it was a disappointment to the studio, then celebrating its silver anniversary. Having used up its three-picture commitment from Peck, Metro parted company with the actor.

The Great Sinner wrapped shortly before Christmas 1948. As Peck's next picture, Fox's *Twelve O'Clock High,* wouldn't start until the spring, he was free at the outset of the new year to take a small role in a touring production of *What Price Glory?* Written by Maxwell Anderson and Laurence Stallings, the 1924 play focused on a group of marines during World War I. The organizing force behind the tour was director John Ford, who earmarked the profits for one of his pet projects, the Purple Heart Recreation Center. Although Ford cast the play, he wasn't a theater director. He hired Ralph Murphy to stage the production.

The principal roles were played by Ward Bond, one of Ford's favorite actors, and Pat O'Brien. Maureen O'Hara, John Wayne, and Harry Carey Jr., all members of the director's stock company, were also involved, as was Oliver Hardy of Laurel and Hardy, and Albert Morin, a member of the original Broadway cast. According to Carey, Peck signed up even though his role was small "out of his respect for John Ford."

It is interesting to imagine the shy, somewhat introverted, and politically liberal Peck on tour with John Wayne, his virtual opposite in every respect. "Well, they got along fine," Carey recalled. "I don't think they became close friends or anything, because they were so far apart politically. I know they laughed and joked together and would have a drink together when we were out on the road." Peck and Carey did become friends. "I found him to be a great companion," the character actor recalled. "We used to love to drink together."

The company played Los Angeles, Long Beach, Pasadena, San Jose, Oakland, and San Francisco. According to Carey, the tour was a success, but none of the money reached its intended, charitable goal. The company manager stole all the proceeds.

Ironically, while Peck was touring with political conservatives John Wayne and Ward Bond, liberals, including him, were coming under fire back home. In September 1947, the House Un-American Activities Committee (HUAC) announced its plan to hold hearings to determine the extent to which the motion picture industry had been infiltrated by Communists and Communist sympathizers. To protest, liberal members of the Hollywood community, including Peck, formed an organization called the Committee for the First Amendment. Founding members included actors Humphrey Bogart, Lauren Bacall, and Danny Kaye, directors John Huston and William Wyler, and screenwriter Philip Dunne. During the course of HUAC's hearings, which opened in October, eleven subpoenaed witnesses refused to divulge their political affiliations and were cited for contempt of Congress. One of the eleven, German playwright Bertolt Brecht, fled the country; the others, known as the Hollywood Ten, were tried and convicted in spring 1948.*

These events formed the cornerstones of one of the motion picture industry's darkest periods, as hundreds of actors, writers, and directors identified as Communists or Communist sympathizers—often without proof—found themselves unable to work anywhere in the U.S. entertainment industry. Those who were named were forced to name others, compounding the list of blacklisted personnel and casting an aura of paranoia over Hollywood.

For the most part stars of Peck's stature were exempt from persecution; they were too valuable to the studio powerbrokers to lose their livelihoods. But the *threat* of such an eventuality was ever present—as Greg discovered. His problems started in 1948, with the publication of a book called *Treason in Hollywood,* in which the author, Myron C. Fagin, named him as a Communist sympathizer. Fagin also cited Fredric March, March's wife, Florence Eldridge, Eddie Cantor, and Edward G. Robinson.

A few days after the book's publication, Peck publicly denied the allegations, saying that he didn't believe in Communism and that he had never been a member of the Communist Party. He also warned, "There is more than one way to lose your liberty. It can be torn out of your hands by a tyrant—but it can also slip away day by day while you're too busy to notice and too confused or too scared."

Despite the denials, he was investigated by the California legislature's equivalent to HUAC, the Joint Fact-Finding Committee on Un-American Activities. The committee determined that he had been associated with six Communist front organizations, including the Progressive Citizens of America, the Actors' Laboratory Theatre, and the China Conference Arrangements Committee.

Preparatory to subpoenaing Greg before the committee, its chairman, State Senator Hugh Burns, invited the actor to meet with him informally

*The Hollywood Ten were Alvah Bessie, Herbert Biberman, Lester Cole, Edward Dmytryk, Ring Lardner Jr., John Howard Lawson, Albert Maltz, Samuel Ornitz, Adrian Scott, and Dalton Trumbo.

at the committee's offices in downtown Los Angeles, and Peck accepted. During the meeting, the actor strongly asserted that he had never been a Communist and that his involvement with the cited organizations had been for "idealistic or humanitarian or theatrical purposes and ideals."

Burns accepted Peck's explanation. "I was not dragged on the carpet," the actor recalled. "I was not put under oath, I was not accused of anything, I was not asked to name any of the other people. Because as a matter of fact, it would have been pointless anyway because they were all on the letterheads of these groups." He did so well, in fact, that in its next bulletin, the committee praised him for his cooperation.

He'd managed to escape a potential disaster, and in April 1948, he eagerly returned to work.

Of Peck's first eleven features, only the first, *Days of Glory*, hadn't begun as a novel or short story, an indication of the extent to which Hollywood drew from previously published material in the forties. His twelfth film continued the tradition.

Published by Harper & Brothers in April 1948, *Twelve O'Clock High* told in fictional terms the story of Colonel Frank A. Armstrong Jr. In January 1943, after leading several precision bombing missions over Nazi-occupied Europe, Armstrong, then a major general, was ordered to take command of another bomb group, the 306th, which badly needed shaping up. He did an exemplary job but drove himself so hard in the process he suffered a nervous breakdown. Sy Bartlett, a major in the U.S. Army Air Corps during World War II and a friend of Armstrong, wrote the novel with Beirne Lay Jr., who'd also been a bomb group commander during the war. The title derived from the tendency of the German fighter planes to attack American bombers where they were most vulnerable—head-on or "twelve o'clock high" in Air Corps parlance.

At the urging of producer Louis D. "Bud" Lighton, Fox purchased the screen rights to the novel for $100,000. Lighton then hired Bartlett and Lay to write the screenplay. It didn't come easily. After three drafts, the story still hadn't jelled—as Zanuck discovered when he submitted the project to six major directors and several actors, including Peck, and they all turned it down. The principal problem, they said, was the subject's familiarity. In particular, it was likened to a hit Broadway play, *Command Decision,* which MGM had turned into a successful 1948 film starring Clark Gable, Walter Pidgeon, and Van Johnson.

For nine months, *Twelve O'Clock High* sat on the shelves. Then Zanuck took the drafts with him on a vacation to Sun Valley. Poring over the material, he realized that the deterioration of the Armstrong character called Frank Savage was getting lost in a more generalized story of an

American bomb group. Thereafter, Lay and Bartlett cut out extraneous scenes and characters, including the only female, Savage's love interest, and a fresh, human drama emerged.

Eventually, Zanuck fired Lighton and took over the project himself.* He then offered it to one of his favorite contract directors, Henry King. The Virginia-born former actor, then sixty-one years old and celebrating his thirty-fourth anniversary as a director, had done dozens of features, including *Stanley and Livingstone, A Yank in the R.A.F., The Song of Bernadette,* and Zanuck's personal favorite, *Wilson.* King felt a particular kinship with a story about aerial combat. He'd been an aviator with his own plane since 1918 and was also a licensed commercial pilot.

Peck liked the revised script, but he was concerned about his ability to portray an Air Corps officer. King reassured him on that score. Said the director, "You'll be so surrounded by military people who'll be giving us advice that you'll find yourself thinking like a military man." Peck agreed to play the role.

The "military people" to whom King alluded came as part of the assistance that Zanuck secured from the Pentagon. In fact, two of the picture's technical advisors, Colonel John H. de Russy and Major Johnny McKee, had been members of Frank Armstrong's bomb group. Furthermore, Air Force Chief of Staff Hoyt Vandenberg helped locate a dozen then-outmoded B-17 bombers for use in the filming.

But King and Zanuck needed to find an airfield that could pass for a World War II installation in Britain. After scouting various alternatives, the director determined that Fort Walton, Florida, the home of Elgin Air Force Base, could reasonably serve, as long as cinematographer Leon Shamroy avoided the local pine trees. Ozark Field, an inactive army air base near Dothan, Alabama, about ninety-five miles from Elgin, was ideal for the film's opening and closing sequences, set in 1949 when the base lay in ruins. Vandenberg granted permission for the use of these facilities.

In return for his cooperation, Fox had to agree to several changes in the script. The most significant was the depiction of Savage's mental breakdown. Instead of an hysterical outburst, as written, Vandenberg wanted a much more subdued approach. Zanuck aquiesced. In the new version, Savage would simply be overwhelmed by fatigue.

Of the nine weeks of principal photography, roughly four were spent

*As studio chief, Zanuck was, of course, the ultimate decision-maker on all of Fox's films, but he served as the producer on relatively few; the remainder were assigned to other producers on the lot. For example, *The Keys of the Kingdom* and *Yellow Sky* were produced by Joseph L. Mankiewicz and Lamar Trotti, respectively.

at Elgin, where the production company constructed Nissen and Quonset huts as well as a hospital, briefing room, and interrogation room. The topography of Fort Walton may have allowed it to pass for England, but the weather was in no way comparable. Despite the tropical climate, Peck and his fellow actors were decked out in heavy flying suits with fur-lined boots and jackets. Sweating under the hot Florida sun may have caused Peck to develop an eye infection. In any event, he had to be hospitalized upon his return to Los Angeles. Since he was in almost every scene in the picture, filming was held up for five days while he recovered.

As principal photography progressed, Peck and Henry King developed a high regard for one another. The director came to admire the hard work and preparation that Greg lavished on his role. He also found the actor a "very pleasant person to be with."

For his part, Peck considered making a picture with Henry "great fun" because the director was so enthusiastic about his work. Moreover, he felt they meshed. "Once in a while," the actor explained, King "would have an idea I did not agree with, about interpretation, movement, or business, and I would suggest a change. We would talk it over, and he would very often give me my way without any rancor or any sense of my being a meddlesome actor. The other side of the coin is that very often he would contribute things that had never occurred to me, valuable observations, insights into character or behavior. So it was give and take, and it always worked."

In time, they became extremely close. Said Peck, "We were somewhere between father and son, big brother and little brother. We never seemed to run out of things to talk about."

Over the next decade, they would collaborate on five additional films, more than Peck would undertake with any other director. None turned out better than *Twelve O'Clock High*, which premiered on January 26, 1950, at the Roxy Theatre in New York.

When the film began its regular run the next day, every facet of the production drew applause from virtually every quarter. "20th Century–Fox has made one of the great and heroic dramas of the war," raved *Cue*. The *New York Times'* Bosley Crowther wrote that no Hollywood Air Force movie could compare with *Twelve O'Clock High*'s "rugged realism and punch." And *Variety* dubbed it a "a topflight drama, polished and performed to the nth degree."

Several supporting players, notably Dean Jagger as Savage's adjutant and Gary Merrill as the general's predecessor, drew raves. But no one received stronger notices than Peck, who deserved them. In his depiction of the spit-and-polish officer who grows dangerously attached to his men, he built upon his work as Phil Green in *Gentleman's Agreement*, rendering the clearest evocation yet of an intelligent, methodical man of principle willing to go to virtually any length for a cause in which he believes.

A month after the premiere, on February 20, Peck graced the cover of *Life* magazine, sporting his airman's outfit from the film. Subsequently, he was named Best Actor by the New York Film Critics and Best Foreign Actor at the Paris Film Festival. And he earned yet another Academy Award nomination, his fourth in five years. Unlike with the previous occasions, he thought that this time he might win.

The picture was also nominated but lost to *All the King's Men*, a fictionalized account of the rise and fall of Louisiana politician Huey Long. The star of that film, Broderick Crawford, also took home the statuette for Best Actor. However, Dean Jagger won for Supporting Actor and Fox earned the award for Sound Recording.

Despite competition from a string of World War II films, including *Battleground, The Sands of Iwo Jima,* and *Command Decision, Twelve O'Clock High* performed well at the box office, ending the year as the tenth-highest-grossing film, with revenues of $3.2 million.

Twelve O'Clock High wrapped in late June, just in time for the start of the La Jolla Playhouse's third season. Although some of the plays—*Here Today, Art and Mrs. Bottle*—remained as forgettable by modern standards as those of the previous years, the company also included more classics, notably Oscar Wilde's *The Importance of Being Earnest,* which starred Dorothy McGuire, Jane Wyatt, Mildred Natwick, Hurd Hatfield, and Mel Ferrer; Richard Basehart in Shaw's *Arms and the Man*; and the season opener, Noël Coward's *Blithe Spirit,* with Natwick, Tamara Geva, Jacqueline de Wit, and John Emery, a replacement for Randolph Scott, who had to bow out. In late July, Peck starred with Jean Parker and Benjay Venuto in Moss Hart's *Light Up the Sky.* The saga of a theater company's pre-Broadway tryout in Boston, the comedy was brand-new, having opened in New York the previous November. Peck as the play's writer, Peter Sloan, assumed the role created on Broadway by a fellow Cal Little Theater alumnus, Barry Nelson.

Inspired perhaps by *Twelve O'Clock High,* the company closed the season with *Command Decision* by William Wister Haines. Although the producers and their stars took the productions seriously, this was, after all, stock, and occasionally a bit of sophomoric humor got the better of them. On the final night of *Command Decision,* Peck and Ferrer decided to take the roles of a couple of flyers who appear at the end of the final act. Instead of donning Air Corps uniforms, however, Mel decked himself out in a polar bear costume and Greg chose a gorilla suit. "Everybody broke up and forgot their lines," Ferrer recalled. "The audience became hysterical."

Such was the continuing success of the La Jolla Playhouse that, after the 1949 season, Peck, Ferrer, and McGuire began looking for ways to expand their horizons. They produced Kaufman and Hart's urbane comedy *The Man Who Came to Dinner* as a one-hour radio drama for CBS. Airing on Christmas Day, it was hosted by Henry Fonda and John Garfield and starred Jack Benny as Sheridan Whiteside, with Charles Boyer, Gene Kelly, and Rosalind Russell in featured roles. Peck was Burt Jefferson, the earnest reporter who falls in love with Whiteside's secretary, Maggie, played by Dorothy McGuire. It marked his sixth radio drama of 1949.

That fall, Greg, Dorothy, and Mel also staged a production in Los Angeles of Jean Anouilh's *Eurydice,* with a new translation by Ferrer. Although the production was not a success, the producers were determined to create a permanent Los Angeles version of their La Jolla company. Virtually all of the participants in *The Man Who Came to Dinner* were part of the new venture, which was appropriately dubbed the Actors' Company. Having elicited financial support from the heads of several film studios, they formed a partnership with architect William Periera and several real estate people to construct a home of their own, one that would include a movie house as well as a legitimate theater.

Producing plays wasn't the limit of their ambitions. They also planned to air more radio dramas and explored with RCA the creation of spoken-word record albums. The first was to feature company members reading love letters by famous historical figures. With the rising popularity of television, they investigated the creation of an anthology drama series, and movie producer Jerry Wald even tried to launch a feature film venture between the Actors' Company and RKO.

None of these grand notions came to fruition. In fact, by 1951, the company had produced nothing beyond *The Man Who Came to Dinner.* Finally, the three producers realized that the original impetus, staging plays in their own backyard, was not going to work. Far from a wealthy summer resort community like La Jolla, Los Angeles was a notoriously bad theater town. The audience to support what they had in mind simply wasn't there. Around 1951, they gave up.

By the fall of 1949, Peck's contract with Fox had expired, the studio having been unable to schedule a fourth film with him during the specified time frame. Thus, when Zanuck found a Western to follow *Yellow Sky,* he arranged to borrow Greg from Selznick.

Curiously, *The Gunfighter,* one of the best Westerns of all time, was inspired by a boxer. One evening, writer William Bowers was dining at Jack Dempsey's restaurant in New York when the former heavyweight champ mentioned that men were always trying to pick a fight with him simply because of his success in the ring. With the help of director and sometime writer André De Toth, Bowers turned Dempsey's remark into a story about a gunslinger whose reputation made him the target of a local braggart in every town he visited. Bowers and William Sellers then turned the story into a ninety-four-page screenplay called *The Big Gun.*

Bowers initially took the screenplay to John Wayne, who turned it down. He then showed it to Fox screenwriter-producer Nunnally Johnson, who convinced Zanuck to buy it. Johnson, who would produce the film, worked with the writers—without credit—to flesh out the screenplay, as ninety-four pages was too short for a feature. The result was a near-flawless character study of a once-cocky quick-draw artist who has grown weary of his notoriety. Loosely based on a real Texas desperado, Jimmy Ringo yearns to settle down with his wife, who has carved out a life on her own with their young son. The gunfighter's poignant story is played out against a West that's grown civilized, where there's little room for a man who attracts trouble despite himself.

The first time Peck read the screenplay, he knew that it had the makings of a fine picture, providing that Henry King directed.

All hands set out to make a distinctive Western. Instead of the usual genre actors, they sought fresh faces for the supporting roles, two of which went to Peck's old *Sons and Soldiers* costars, Karl Malden (as the bartender) and Millard Mitchell (as the sheriff).* Helen Westcott was cast as Ringo's wife and Richard Jaeckel as a punk kid who challenges the gunfighter at the outset of the picture.

After looking at old photos of gunfighters and lawmen, King encouraged Peck to grow a mustache and have his hair cut as if an amateur had trimmed it using a soup bowl. And he dressed the star simply—in a hat with a short brim and low crown, a plain cloth jacket, and tall boots with his baggy pants tucked in the tops. He and Peck also gave Ringo a distinctive way of reaching for his gun: Greg used his left hand and a cross-over draw.

About two weeks into filming, Fox president Spyros Skouras saw the first rushes for the Western and became apoplectic at the star's down-home appearance. He demanded to know how much it would cost to reshoot all of Peck's scenes with the actor clean-shaven. The actual price was $150,000, but Peck and King convinced the company manager to

*Mitchell had also portrayed Peck's c.o. in *Twelve O'Clock High.*

double that figure. Skouras had no choice but to allow the shoot to proceed. But he never let Peck forget the error. Every time he saw the star, he would say, "Gregory, you cost me a million dollars with that goddam mustache."

As filmmaking goes, *The Gunfighter* was smooth and uneventful. "We just worked away at it for about ten or eleven or twelve weeks," Peck recalled, "and it all came out on the screen just about the way it was on paper—airtight."

The critics recognized the Western's distinctive quality immediately. When it opened at the Roxy Theatre in New York on June 23, 1950, adjectives like "extremely convincing," "arresting and quite exciting," and "relentless . . . and intense" permeated the reviews. But the public failed to respond to the picture. It made a profit, thanks primarily to die-hard fans of the genre, but it didn't equal the earnings of *Yellow Sky.* Its mediocre performance was generally blamed on the film's downbeat ending and Peck's deglamorized appearance.

Still, the star was so believable in the title role, he could have spent the rest of career making shoot-'em-ups had he wanted to. His agent even said to him, "You've found the archetype. Stay with it and you'll be another John Wayne." But Greg wanted variety, so he refused most of the offers that followed. Among them was *High Noon,* which would earn an Oscar for Gary Cooper in 1952. Greg conceded that he might have made a mistake with that one.

The Gunfighter was the last feature that Peck completed during the 1940s. It had been a remarkable decade for Hollywood. During the war years, millions of Americans—two-thirds of the population, according to some estimates—went to the movies every week to escape, albeit briefly, the hardships and tribulations of daily life. In 1946, the first full year of peace, box-office receipts reached an all-time high.

But, as the decade waned, a series of events combined to signal the beginning of the end of the studio system. For starters, movie attendance dropped dramatically as veterans returned to their spouses or married. The baby boom, the dramatic rise in new home construction, the increased enrollments in colleges and vocational training programs, thanks to the GI Bill, all signaled that Americans were intent upon improving their daily lives, not escaping from them. The advent of television, still in its infancy at the end of the forties, would soon give families another reason to stay home.

Changes within the industry were occurring as well. Still reeling from the strike of 1945 and the blacklist, the moguls learned in 1948 that they would need to sell either their studios or their chains of movie theaters, as the Supreme Court had determined that ownership of both constituted restraint of trade. This was a bitter blow; MGM, Warners, Paramount, and others drew about 70 percent of their annual revenues from their own theater chains, which served as ready outlets for their pictures, good or bad.

Moreover, creative personnel—directors, writers, actors—were becoming less inclined to toil under long-term contracts. Many were following the likes of Casey Robinson and Alfred Hitchcock, forming their own production companies, developing their own properties, and establishing alliances with studios to bring those projects to fruition. Within a decade, 68 percent of all Hollywood movies would be made by these independents, including Gregory Peck.

Profit participation was another new option. At the end of the decade, agent Lew Wasserman pioneered this concept when Universal wanted James Stewart for a Western, *Winchester 73,* but couldn't afford the star's usual asking price. Wasserman arranged for Stewart to do the picture for no salary in exchange for 50 percent of the profits, a deal that made the actor rich.

Given their declining revenues, studio executives opted to downsize their operations, programs, and expenditures. The number of films in annual production dropped appreciably at decade's end. Employment fell by about 25 percent. Conversely, reliance on original screenplays rose, because the cost of purchasing hit plays and novels accounted for hefty up-front expenditures.

As films got leaner and more cost-efficient, a new breed of stars emerged. Burt Lancaster, Kirk Douglas, Richard Widmark, and Robert Mitchum, all products of the immediate postwar years, were more rugged than their handsome, refined predecessors—Errol Flynn, Tyrone Power, Robert Taylor among them—and tended to play characters with greater flaws and imperfections. The new stars were roughly the same age as Peck; Lancaster was three years older. But Greg fell somewhere in between the two generations; in looks and temperament, he was a throwback to the gentlemen of the thirties and early forties; in the naturalism of his acting, he came closer to the young Turks.

But he was one of the most popular movie stars in the world when Burt, Kirk, and the others were just starting out. Talent accounted for some of his success. But he'd also enjoyed the red carpet treatment from his arrival in Hollywood. As he was not under contract to any one studio, he was never taken for granted. One could even argue that L. B. Mayer, David O. Selznick, and Darryl F. Zanuck vied with one other to see who could make the best use of his craftsmanship and physical attributes. Consequently, of the thirteen features he completed during the forties, there were three Academy Award nominees and one winner, *Gentleman's Agreement.* Many of his films boasted unusually lavish budgets, were based on huge best-sellers, involved important directors, and featured celebrated supporting actors. He was paired with some of the most popular leading ladies of the day: Greer Garson, Ingrid Bergman, Jennifer Jones, Jane Wyman, Dorothy McGuire, Ava Gardner, and Anne Baxter, most of whom were also gifted actresses (Garson, Bergman, and Baxter had already won Oscars by the time they worked with Peck; Wyman, Jones, and McGuire, as well as Garson, would earn nominations for the pictures they made with him.)

Little wonder that he became so popular.

Of course, he had disappointments as well. Though it earned a fortune, *Duel in the Sun* wasn't well regarded. And *The Paradine Case* and *The Great Sinner* were neither commercial nor critical hits. But Peck felt these projects contributed to his growth, saying, "I've learned more from my failures than I have from any successful films I've made. Only failure can bring an actor down to earth and show him his limitations."

If one views Peck's forties features back-to-back, one sees a thoughtful, meticulous actor working through each role and each scene to arrive at a truthful portrayal. He struggles with moments where his characters lose emotional control, as in *Spellbound* and *The Great Sinner.* Otherwise, however, the performances always have the ring of truth; the way he looks, listens, and responds to others is credible and natural. But he also exhibits a tendency to turn these extremely diverse characters into *Peck* characters, or as close to Peck characters as their natures would allow. Pa Baxter in *The Yearling,* for example, is too dignified for a typical Florida cracker. Despite Selznick's wishes, Lewt McCanles in *Duel in the Sun* isn't really a bad guy, he just engages in inexplicable behavior, like blowing up trains.

Hollywood has a term for actors who do this; they're called personality actors. A personality actor is one who, consciously or not, invests each role with a range of general qualities: a way of moving, speaking, looking, and behaving. This approach contrasts with that of other actors, such as Alec Guinness, who disappear into each character they play. To be a personality actor isn't a bad thing, not if the persona created has broad audience appeal. That recognizable, desirable essence is, in fact, what elevates most actors to the level of movie stars. Humphrey Bogart, Marilyn Monroe, James Dean, Cary Grant, Katharine Hepburn, skilled craftspeople all, are personality actors.

In some cases, the nexus between the actor's screen persona and his or her real nature is wide. Marilyn Monroe was far from a dumb blonde. Humphrey Bogart played streetwise toughs but was, in reality, the prep school–educated son of a wealthy Manhattan doctor. Cary Grant is quoted as saying that he, too, wished he could be like Cary Grant. In other cases, the actor sticks closer to himself. Jimmy Stewart's folksy, slow-talking boy-next-door was more or less an exaggeration of the man in real life. Katharine Hepburn *is* headstrong and opinionated yet feminine.

In Peck's case, it is fair to say that he started with the tools closest at hand, his intelligence, innate dignity, and sensitivity. His zeal to get the story right in *Gentleman's Agreement* and his determination to make his men combat ready in *Twelve O'Clock High* ring true, because those qualities have equivalents in his unwillingness to give less than his best in every performance. As screenwriter Sy Bartlett put it, "Greg is a driven man. Perfection is his goal in almost all things, and he's in torment when he can't find a key to what he wants."

When given men of lesser character to play, he endowed them with greater nobility, decency, and/or affability, because he felt more comfortable operating on an elevated plane. A director friend once told a reporter, "Greg wants to be loved." Acknowledging the truth of this statement, Peck conceded that "that desire to be loved may have led in the direction of playing heroes, of people who wanted to make the world a better place." When he wasn't given a hero to play, he turned the character he was given into the closest possible facsimile.

While Peck drew from himself as he grappled with his early roles, he also borrowed elements of what radiated on the screen and made them his own. In his early years in Hollywood, it was not uncommon for peers to perceive him as colorless. Alfred Hitchcock once described him as "the most anecdoteless man in Hollywood." He was never that. As Nunnally Johnson pointed out, "Greg is not a gag or joke man. His outstanding traits are integrity, honesty and conscientiousness. While these are not the most lovable or quotable characteristics, they are extremely admirable." But, with fame, money, recognition as an actor, and the adoration of fans, notably women, he gained in self-confidence and poise. He even gave greater vent to his wry sense of humor. In time, he became comfortable in his own skin. As he said many years later, "Yes, I believe I have found an identity gradually through the years. I think I'm a whole man today. But I certainly wouldn't deny that at the beginning I was searching for myself and that role playing in some way compensated for the lack of roots, the lack of a whole personality formed in youth theoretically from a stable family life."

The small-town fellow with scars from a painful childhood would never completely disappear. "Sometimes I sense a hint of insecurity," said his son Stephen, "a fear of being revealed as the person he was before he became a star. But I like that person. I see not only a man who dreamt what he wanted to be and became it, but also a man less imposing and more vulnerable than his thirty-foot image on the screen."

While Greg would always carry Eldred inside him, he would continue to develop and grow in the decade ahead, ultimately becoming in reality a cultured, sophisticated, well-traveled gentleman with a keen social conscience. Also, in the coming years, as the essence of what he projected best on the screen became more evident, the range of roles offered to him narrowed. No longer would he be considered for villains or laborers or people in serious emotional distress. Well-educated, well-bred, highly motivated professionals became his stock in trade. Thus, the man and his roles were on twin paths. They finally converged around the mid-1950s, by which point it was difficult to separate Peck from the characters he portrayed.

If Hollywood shaped Greg, it impacted Greta as well. To begin with, he was frequently away from home, filming, meeting with the press, doing photo shoots, producing the La Jolla Playhouse, making radio appearances, and so forth. He also had business investments requiring his attention. These included running his own cattle on grazing land he rented near Modesto and Santa Barbara. Moreover, when he *was* home, he spent hours alone, studying, researching, and preparing his performances, driven to better himself as an actor and to stay on top in his profession. He had little time left over for his wife.

Greta, more so than Greg, was drawn to the L.A. social scene. She liked rubbing shoulders with celebrities, being the wife of a celebrity herself. As the Pecks accumulated a bit of money, she tried to fit in, to dress the part. But she was never really accepted by the elite members of the rather clannish motion picture community. As one of Greg's friends put it, "They always considered her a hairdresser." As her husband tended to seek out the community's more talented, accomplished members, Greta was left somewhat behind. Although she was hardly stupid, she was less educated and well read than they. Uncomfortable expressing her opinions in such company, she developed her own circle of friends. Thus, husband and wife drifted further apart.

Then there was the liquor. Alcohol had always been part of the Pecks' lifestyle. They traveled in a hard-drinking crowd. Predinner cocktails, wine with the meal, and after-dinner aperitifs helped foster scintillating conversation, games, songfests, and good old-fashioned storytelling. Greg was able to keep the liquor under control; Greta wasn't.

By 1949, indications of a troubled marriage started surfacing in the press. At the outset of the year, on January 21, Louella Parsons reported,

"For some days the rumor has been current in Hollywood that Gregory and Greta Peck have reached the breaking point." Parsons' announcement had been prompted by her discovery that Greg had left home several days earlier and that Greta hadn't heard from him since. Some months later, Peck explained that he and his wife had gotten into an argument, and he decided the best thing to do was just go off by himself for a bit; he wound up fishing with a friend. "Then I came back home," he told Hedda Hopper, "and things have been fine ever since."

Whether they believed him or not, Hopper and Parsons reported that the Pecks were back together. As Parsons told readers, "They had a misunderstanding—the kind that happens in the best regulated of familes." She also announced that the Pecks were expecting a baby. On June 17, Greta gave birth to another son, named Carey, for Peck's *Duel in the Sun* costar, Harry Carey.

Thus, as the forties came to an end, Greg, age thirty-three, had weathered the threat of the blacklist and was riding the crest of almost unprecedented popularity and respect. Hollywood was changing, but, as he'd never been tied to any one studio, there was little reason to think his momentum would be slowed. As for his private life, he and Greta papered over their differences and celebrated the arrival of their new child. On the day after Christmas, the whole brood set sail for England, where Greg was to start another film. As they left the New York dock, they were the picture of a happy family. But it was an illusion.

PART THREE

Playing the Hero

CHAPTER 11

World Film Favorite

Born in Cairo in 1899, Cecil Scott Forester wrote adventure novels like *The African Queen* and true-life chronicles such as *Sink the Bismarck!,* but he is best known as the creator of Horatio Hornblower, an officer in the British navy during the Napoleonic Wars. Forester traced his intrepid character's career from midshipman to admiral in eleven novels. The first, *Beat to Quarters* (known as *The Happy Return* in the United Kingdom), was published in the United States in 1937. The last, *Hornblower and the Crisis,* was published in 1967, a year after Forester's death.

Warner Bros. had been interested in bringing the naval hero to the screen since at least 1940—initially as a vehicle for its in-house swashbuckler, Errol Flynn, and later as a project for then-husband and wife Laurence Olivier and Vivien Leigh. At various points, William Dieterle and John Huston had been involved, as director and screenwriter respectively. But, when the project finally jelled at the end of the decade, Raoul Walsh was at the helm of a screenplay by Ivan Goff, Ben Roberts, and Aeneas MacKenzie. The adaptation by Forester himself drew from the first three novels in the series. In addition to *Beat to Quarters,* these included *Ship of the Line* and *Flying Colors.*

Instead of an Australian like Flynn or an Englishman like Olivier, Warners made the somewhat controversial decision to go with an American, Gregory Peck. David Selznick, harder hit than most by Hollywood's changing economics, agreed to loan out the actor for a second film in a row. For this, he received $150,000, well in excess of the $60,000 he had to pay Peck. Using British earnings that could only be spent in the United Kingdom, Warners shot the picture, which it called *Captain Horatio Hornblower,* in England, making it Greg's first overseas venture.

As usual, the star thoroughly researched his role. Not only did he read all of the Hornblower novels published to that point, he consulted accounts of nineteenth-century naval warfare and treatises on ships, navigation, and sailing. Upon his arrival in London, after settling his family in a house in Gloucester Square, he continued his studies, notably at the Royal Naval College and the adjacent National Maritime Museum. He also took fencing lessons and worked on his English accent, although he and Walsh ultimately decided against using it.

Principal photography began on January 23, 1950, and continued through May 9, exceeding by several weeks the term of the Warners-Selznick loanout agreement (requiring the studio to pay the producer an additional $15,833.34 for Peck's services). Raoul Walsh, an old pro like William Wellman and Henry King, would call the film the toughest he'd ever made, thanks to its many shipboard sequences. Because of the confines of space, the camera, sound equipment, and lighting fixtures had to be hoisted from position to position by crane, a time-consuming and tedious procedure. Moreover, a setup often allowed just enough room for the actors, forcing Walsh to direct the action from the rigging. "Every day of shooting," he concluded, "meant . . . a good physical workout for everyone involved."

A total of five ships were used in the production. For the *Lydia,* Hornblower's ship, Warners chose the *France,* a three-masted scooner that had been launched in 1914. Set decorators used the model of a 1785 frigate, the *Ariel,* housed in London's Imperial Science Museum, as a guide for transforming the *France* into a royal warship.

Whenever possible, Walsh filmed not on the *France,* but on a full-size reconstruction. Weighing more than fifty tons and outfitted with hydraulic machines to simulate the roll of a ship at sea, the reconstruction was an awesome sight, 140 feet long, approximately thirty feet wide in the beam, and with masts that reached to the rafters. Only one studio in the area—located in Denham—was large enough to accommodate the massive set, and it was closed. Warners had to pay a significant sum for it to be reopened. The Elstree Studios in London were used for the other interiors. The company also filmed on location, in Portsmith and in the South of France.

Like Henry King, Walsh had started as an actor. In fact, he had portrayed John Wilkes Booth in D. W. Griffith's silent classic, *The Birth of a Nation.* In 1929, with dozens of silent features bearing his directorial stamp, he lost an eye in an automobile accident, after which he wore a rather dashing patch. But the disability didn't stop him. Hits such as *High Sierra, They Died with Their Boots On, Objective, Burma!,* and *White Heat* followed, reflecting his particular mastery of the high adventure drama. Peck, who liked Walsh enormously, called him, "One of the saltiest, toughest, funniest old men I ever met."

Perhaps because of his silent film origins, Walsh wasn't terribly interested in dialogue. Peck recalled that sometimes during the shooting of a particularly talky scene, the director would sit in his chair, reading a newspaper. At the conclusion, he would say, "Print." When Peck pointed out that he'd forgotten a line or garbled a word, Raoul would reply, "Did you, kid, what was that?" If the gaffe seemed significant or if Peck wanted a retake, Walsh would do the scene over. "But," said Peck, "if he thought it didn't matter or the audience's attention would be somewhere else, he'd say, 'Kid, it's fine, let's go, let's keep moving.'"

Although the focus was on action, and plenty of it, there was also a subdued but engaging romance between the married Hornblower and an aristocrat, Lady Barbara Wellesley, in the person of Virginia Mayo. Although Mayo was also an American and excelled at modern brassy blondes—as in her portrayal of the self-centered wife in *The Best Years of Our Lives*—she brought a saucy but decidedly aristocratic air to her performance. She enjoyed working with Peck, whom she called "a beautiful, sensitive man: what he gives you as an actor, he gives with gentility and kindness." She was also impressed by his dedication, noting that "he studies each role so thoroughly that it is little wonder that his performances are so great."

Peck's portrayal of Hornblower *was* impressive, even to the English, who had been skeptical about his casting. As *Britain To-Day* put it, "Mr. Peck not only gets under the skin of the character, but wears the uniform—a very rare thing in actors—as though he had lived in it, and created it to his body, and sweated in it, and shivered in it, through a long career of active service."

Called upon for the first time to play an old-fashioned, larger-than-life hero, Greg invested his portrayal with just the right blend of daring, gallantry, youthful impetuousness, and military skill. But everything was rendered with kind of a twinkle in the eye. When, for example, an enemy Spanish vessel approaches, his officers are nervous, but he calmly plays whist. And, whenever the highly proper captain becomes embarrassed or agitated, Peck emits a peculiar harumphing sound, which is both funny and endearing.

Opening at New York's Radio City Music Hall on September 13, 1951 (following its world premiere in London in April), *Captain Horatio Hornblower* was embraced by the public and by enthusiastic critics. The picture ended up in fourteenth place among the top-grossing films of 1951, with earnings of $3 million.

Peck himself was pleased with the result. Years later, he even tried to develop a sequel. In conjunction with his son Stephen, he put together a treatment that combined a couple of Forester's later sagas, when Hornblower was an older man. But no studio was interested. The film would have been too expensive for a genre that was, by then, passé.

On June 6, after more than five months abroad, Peck and his family returned home just in time for the start of another season of the La Jolla Playhouse. It was an exceptionally good year for the company. The lineup of plays featured *Born Yesterday, Summer and Smoke, Arsenic and Old Lace, The Front Page,* and *Our Town,* and the roster of stars included Robert Ryan, Pat O'Brien, Ann Blyth, Millard Mitchell, Beulah Bondi, José Ferrer, and Teresa Wright. During the fall, *Summer and Smoke,* which paired Dorothy McGuire and John Ireland, toured the West Coast and later Texas and Colorado. At year's end, the producers showed a profit of $22,769.22, with a total bank balance of $42,973.71.

Peck's involvement during the summer was restricted to visits on the productions' opening and closing nights, for on July 27, he had to travel to Gallup, New Mexico, for the start of a new film, a Western entitled *Only the Valiant.* Once again, Selznick had loaned him out.

Despite his fondness for *The Gunfighter,* Peck was weary of Westerns. Cowpokes rarely dealt in complex ideas, so he found the dialogue in most shoot-'em-ups a bore. He also considered the work primarily physical, requiring an archetypal way of looking and moving. As he put it, "You lend yourself to . . . a kind of a harkening back to the old West in visual terms."

The genre aside, he thought *Only the Valiant* lacked the quality of his prior projects. For starters, the screenwriters Edmund H. North and Harry Brown had produced an extremely conventional potboiler that pitted a by-the-book cavalry officer, Captain Richard Lance, against the sorry group of misfits under his command. As they battle one another, they must also hold their desert outpost against a band of marauding Apaches. The script was based on a novel by Charles Marquis Warren.

Apart from the screenplay, the Western was being produced on a modest budget by actor James Cagney and his brother William under a long-term independent contract with Warner Bros. Moreover, the director, Gordon Douglas, lacked the prestige of the filmmakers with whom Greg had previously worked, and his designated costar, Barbara Payton, was a former model who possessed neither the cachet nor talent of most of his other leading ladies.

Peck, who derived so much of his personal identity from his career, was distraught by the idea of working on such pedestrian fare. He even asked Selznick to release him from the commitment. But the producer had to agree to the loan-out, which would net him $90,000 over and above

Peck's $60,000 salary. Selznick needed the money, thanks to the losses suffered by *The Paradine Case* and a subsequent release, *Portrait of Jennie.* As his empire crumbled, he made similar deals for other contract players, including Jennifer Jones, Joseph Cotten, and Shirley Temple.

As if to confirm Peck's negative attitude toward *Only the Valiant,* Warners assigned him a costume that had been worn in another Western by actor Rod Cameron. That angered him even more. But there was no getting out of the project, so Greg kept his resentment to himself and did his best. Indeed, Michael Ansara, who costarred as the Apache leader Tuscos, was amazed at how hard the star worked during filming. "He's meticulous," Ansara noted. "He'd do a scene over and over again until he got it the way he wanted it. A very professional actor."

Principal photography consumed around five weeks. Aside from shooting in Gallup, New Mexico, the company worked mostly on the Warners lot. Peck was right in his assessment of the project—in terms of budget and the professional standing of its director and leading lady it wasn't on par with most of his previous features, but it wasn't a slipshod mess. As Jeff Corey, who costarred as the troupe's scout, pointed out, "It had a good cast, a good crew." Aside from Corey and Ansara, Greg's costars included Gig Young, Ward Bond, Neville Brand, and Lon Chaney Jr. Moreover, Gordon Douglas may not have been the equal of Hitchcock, Kazan, or Henry King, but he was, in Corey's opinion, "a damn good director" who "knew the camera well" and "was well organized." Testament to the latter was that, despite the exceedingly tight schedule, Douglas wrapped the picture—on September 2—on time and on budget.

Only the Valiant was released on April 13, 1951—five months to the day before *Captain Horatio Hornblower.* Although it placed only forty-third among the year's top-grossing films, some critics found it fresh and exciting. *Cue*'s Jesse Zunser, for example, noted its "effort to dig beneath the surface heroism and cowardice of the eight chief characters."* There were those who felt that Peck's character was too much the clichéd military martinet, less interesting than but akin to *Twelve O'Clock High*'s General Savage, but virtually no one faulted the actor's performance. Dorothy Manners of the *Los Angeles Examiner* spoke for the majority in writing, "The starring role does not exactly call for an actor of Peck's stature. But he is a conscientious performer and gives it his best."

Although his performance may not have suffered, Peck wasn't in good shape physically or emotionally during the making of *Only the Valiant.* He was having difficulty sleeping—for which he began taking a powerful

*It should be noted that the film treats one character's problem, alcoholism, as a humorous indulgence; it is an embarrassing depiction by modern standards.

tranquilizer, Seconal—and he was drinking too much. He also drifted into an affair with his costar, Barbara Payton. According to N. E. Benson of *Confidential* magazine—admittedly a somewhat dubious source—Payton, a playful buxom blonde of Scandinavian descent, invited Greg to her home one evening after work, and the two wound up in bed together. Thereafter, the stars met regularly in the actress' trailer.

By then, Benson asserted, Warner executives were concerned that the stars' fling might delay the production; they also feared that the press would learn of the affair. "So," Benson noted, "down came the order to Barbara that she was to stay in her dressing room or get off the set, except when she was due to appear in a scene. The edict did little good, though. Barbara dutifully kept to her dressing room—but Greg was there, too, every chance he got." Finally, the journalist noted, filming ended and so did the affair.

At this point, there is no way of ascertaining the story's veracity with absolute certainty; Peck doesn't comment on such matters and Payton died in 1967. But the relationship was confirmed by two people interviewed for this book.

If, indeed, the affair took place, it says less about Peck's tendency toward infidelity or Ms. Payton's physical charms than it does about Greg's state of mind at the time. Neither the birth of his third child nor the family trip to England for the making of *Captain Horatio Hornblower* had repaired the holes in his marriage. They were, in fact, irreparable. The star found this heartbreaking reality a source of major stress. As he later put it, "I felt like my head was going to go off, so I was turning to the booze and the drugs just to cool me down." In October 1950, a month after *Only the Valiant* wrapped, he suffered a physical collapse.

The first symptoms appeared the previous summer. One night when he was in La Jolla he awoke with heart spasms and paralysis in his left arm. Thinking he was experiencing a heart attack, he checked into a hospital, but the doctors could find no physical explanation for his condition, which, in fact, quickly subsided. Then, in October, while undergoing costume fittings at Fox for his next film, *David and Bathsheba,* he had another attack; his chest became tight, his left arm went numb, sweat began to pour off of his forehead, and he was convinced that he was about to die. He was dispatched by the studio doctor to Cedars of Lebanon where an electrocardiogram revealed that he had not, in fact, experienced a coronary. Physicians determined that he was suffering from nervous anxiety and advised him to consider a long rest.

Shortly thereafter, another fight with Greta ensued, and Greg took his doctors' advice. He rented a bungalow at a resort in the Mojave Desert, an isolated spot frequented by writers and artists. The cabin featured an open wood-burning fireplace, a Navajo rug on the hard floor, and a private patio. There, Greg spent weeks in solitude, reading long, leisurely novels by the likes of Anthony Trollope and Jane Austen, sunbathing on the patio, and dining alone in his cabin. Later he took to horseback riding and simply walking through the desert, relishing the hot sun on his back. He didn't allow himself to think about work or his marriage nor did he take a drop of alcohol. Sleep came more readily, and he awakened feeling wonderful.

After a month, his equilibrium restored, he was ready to return home. Instead of escaping into booze and pills, he was finally prepared to deal with reality: his marriage wasn't going to last. He wasn't prepared to end it just yet. He needed to stick it out awhile longer for the sake of his children, but now he felt strong enough to do so.

With *Only the Valiant,* Peck worked off his final obligation to David O. Selznick, thereby concluding the last of his original multi-picture deals. Clearly there was no reason to continue with the producer, who was on a downward spiral. Peck's two films with Casey Robinson hadn't been box-office hits. He'd never felt comfortable at MGM. But the pictures with Fox—*The Keys of the Kingdom, Yellow Sky,* and *Twelve O'Clock High*—had served him well. Consequently, even before he started work on *The Gunfighter,* Greg signed another three-picture contract with the studio.

Under the new agreement, which took effect on September 21, 1950, his earnings went from $45,000 per picture, the cap on his first contract, to $100,000, a figure more in keeping with his box-office stature. The revised association commenced with *David and Bathsheba,* which went into production on November 27.

In 1947, Darryl Zanuck had acquired the film rights to a short-lived Broadway play entitled *Bathsheba.* It recounted the story in the Old Testament's Second Book of Samuel about the beautiful wife of a soldier, Uriah the Hittite, who entrances David, ruler of Israel. The play wasn't very good, but it whetted Zanuck's appetite for a film about the shepherd boy who became king; the mogul asked screenwriter Philip Dunne to research the project.

Dunne, who had adapted numerous works of fiction for the screen, including *The Count of Monte Cristo, The Last of the Mohicans, The Late George Apley,* and *Forever Amber,* lacked Zanuck's enthusiasm for the biblical story. But as he learned more about David, he discovered that the man was extremely complex and multifaceted; at once a fearless warrior; a scheming politician who united his people by marrying the daughter of King Saul and then discarding her; a concerned ruler; a doting father; an adulterer; the writer of beautiful psalms; and a murderer. "You could call him a mirror of mankind," said Dunne, "the difference being that David actually did what most of us merely think about doing."

While focusing on the romance between the king and Bathsheba, and their affair's impact on the people of Israel, he wove references to other elements of David's life into his screenplay, including a flashback to his celebrated battle with Goliath and a recitation of his most famous work, the Twenty-third Psalm.

Dunne suggested Laurence Olivier and Vivien Leigh for the leading roles, but Zanuck wanted Peck. "He has a biblical face," the mogul asserted. The star, however, wasn't interested. He expected the project to become a lavish, emotionally over-the-top spectacle like those produced and directed by Cecil B. DeMille. Then Zanuck told him that he wanted to do a character study of a leader with both good and bad qualities, and Peck changed his mind. Thereafter, Greg became the project's ardent champion. As Zanuck told Henry King, to whom he assigned the project, he had never heard the actor "as completely enthusiastic about any story as he is about this one."

Because the filmmakers eschewed the usual emphasis on spectacle, most of the story would play out in a handful of interiors that could be shot on the Fox lot, but a hilly desert setting was needed for a few exteriors. In Nogales, Arizona, near the border with Mexico, a $250,000 re-creation of the ancient city of Jerusalem was erected. Of the fifty-one days of filming, roughly eleven were spent on location.

Among the sequences shot in Nogales was the one in which Peck's David climbs Mount Gilboa, site of a pivotal battle in his youth. After several tests, King and cinematographer Leon Shamroy determined that at six o'clock in the morning the sun was in a perfect position to provide a silhouette of Peck against the rocky precipice. In order for Greg to be in makeup and costume and on his marks at the right time, he had to get up at around four o'clock. King was impressed by his star's willingness to make the sacrifice. As the director later explained, "There are many people who say, 'I wouldn't get up that early. I wouldn't do that.' But Peck just wants the picture to be good, and he'll give everything he had for it to be good."

Back at the studio, the heart of the story, the relationship between David and Bathsheba, took precedence. Tapped for the role of the king's lover was Susan Hayward, the husky-voiced, Brooklyn-born redhead, two years Peck's junior. Having earned an Oscar nomination three years earlier for *Smash-Up: The Story of a Woman* and on the brink of becoming Fox's most popular leading lady, Hayward was less than thrilled with her casting. She felt that the title of the film said it all: just as Bathsheba's name came second, so her role was subordinate to that of the king. But, as a contract player, she had little choice about the assignment.

The demure actress, fair and soft, with a pert nose and luxurious auburn locks, offered a striking physical contrast to the tall, angularly featured Peck, whose coal black hair was cut much longer than usual. The difference made for good chemistry, although the relatively tame love scenes between Greg and Susan reflected the Production Code's continuing regulation of film sex. David's initial discovery of Bathsheba, for example, as she takes her celebrated milk bath revealed absolutely nothing of Hayward's form. (Arguably, the most erotic scene in the picture featured a belly dance by an unknown performer named Gwyneth Verdon; she would soon gain fame on Broadway as Gwen Verdon.)

Off-camera, there was little camaraderie between the stars. One coworker described Hayward as shy and insecure and cold to everyone. Someone reserved like Peck would have been hard-pressed to get her to open up. Jayne Meadows, playing David's wife, Michal, said, "I never saw the two of them on the set even talking!" One day Meadows watched the costars film a love scene. When it was over, Hayward didn't say a word to Peck. She quickly turned away from him and asked her dresser for a cup of coffee. Said Jayne, "It was like, 'Listen, brother, the scene is over, and you mean nothing to me.'"

Hayward's unhappiness over her role was understandable. She had little to do in the film but look alluring, and from time to time ask the king a rather insipid question about his past, like "David, did you really kill Goliath? Was he has big as they say?" Meanwhile, Peck's David experienced myriad emotions. His biggest challenge came in the film's last segment, when Bathsheba stands accused of adultery, a crime punishable by public stoning. A drought has fallen on the land and the king is told that only by adherence to the law can the people of Israel be saved from ruin. Torn between duty and love, he goes to the Ark of the Covenant and prays to the Lord for guidance. This extended sequence is the heart of the film.

Peck played the sequence with an appropriate mixture of dignity, anger, love, ambivalence, and, finally, reverence. Years later, director Martin Scorsese would say, "In the last fifteen minutes of the picture, from the moments starting with his recitation of the Twenty-third Psalm to his supplication before the Ark of the Covenant, we experienced his truly remarkable ability to convey the darkest struggles of the human soul."

When the picture opened in New York on August 14, 1951, a month before *Captain Horatio Hornblower,* many critics also praised Peck's work. The *New York Times'* Andrew Weiler called it "an authoritative performance," one that kept from the film from being "merely a two-hour dissertation."

Not surprisingly, Hayward drew less favorable notices. As for the film itself, the reviewers were split between those who considered it a failed attempt to rise to the level of a DeMille epic and those who recognized the effort to achieve a richer human drama. Regardless of what the critics thought, the public simply loved the biblical story. Taking in $7 million at the box office in its initial release, *David and Bathsheba* became the biggest hit of the year, eclipsing three MGM musicals, including *An American in Paris*; several comedies, among them *Born Yesterday* and *Father's Little Dividend;* and the acclaimed dramas *A Streetcar Named Desire* and *A Place in the Sun.* It also earned five Academy Award nominations—for best story and screenplay, color cinematography, color art direction–set decoration, color costuming, and score (drama or comedy). It lost to that year's Best Picture winner, *An American in Paris,* in four of the five categories.

David and Bathsheba wrapped on January 25, 1951. That same month, Peck won the World Film Favorite Award, based on a poll of more than one million moviegoers from fifty countries. A few months later, in May, he received the Silver Spur Award as the outstanding Western star of 1950. He won for his performance in *The Gunfighter,* which was also named best film.

In July, Greg was on hand for the start of the La Jolla Playhouse's fifth season. As with the previous year, he, Ferrer, and McGuire opted for more durable fare, including *Ring Around the Moon; The Voice of the Turtle; Come Back, Little Sheba; Room Service; The Cocktail Party*; and *The Petrified Forest.* Among the star performers were Joan Bennett, Barry Sullivan, Patricia Neal, Vincent Price, Charlton Heston, and Victor Moore.

Notably absent from the roster was Peck himself—although Greg had a totally free summer for the first time since the Playhouse opened. But he didn't feel up to tackling a major stage role that year. In fact, he had reluctantly concluded that he needed to resign from the company's management in order to avoid the stress that had contributed to his health problems the previous summer. He announced his decision at the end of the season.

In the wake of Greg's departure, Ferrer managed the La Jolla Playhouse solo for a year or two, after which he turned the company over to Dorothy McGuire's husband, John Swope. The Playhouse continued to operate through 1964. The 116th and final production was the Noël Coward comedy that had opened the third season, *Blithe Spirit.* This time Zsa Zsa Gabor was the star.

Although Greg's direct involvement with the Playhouse was at an end, he would retain an active interest in La Jolla's cultural affairs. In the mid-1950s, he became a board member of the Theatre and Arts Foundation of San Diego County, whose primary mission was to build a modern performing arts complex.

Finally, in 1980, after several disappointing false starts, the groundbreaking ceremonies were held for the long-hoped-for center. Peck was unable to attend, but he was present three years later, in June 1983, when the new company, under the auspices of artistic director Des McAnuff, premiered its first production, *The Visions of Simone Machard* by Bertolt Brecht. Greg even spoke at the inaugural gala. In the years since, he has demonstrated his support, both through personal contributions and by a willingness to lend his name to fund-raising efforts.

The new venture, a nonprofit resident theater company focusing on classics and original plays, bears little resemblance to the stock company created by three movie stars thirty-six years earlier, but in its memory, the new facility is called the La Jolla Playhouse.

With only a film-a-year commitment to Fox, Peck was essentially a free agent for the first time since coming to Hollywood. In 1951, he took advantage of his new status by forming the same sort of relationship with Universal that James Stewart had established several years earlier with *Winchester 73*, that is, Peck would forgo a large up-front salary for a substantial share of the profits. The project that he and the studio selected was *The World in His Arms*, a lively adventure tale set in the 1850s and based on a novel by Rex Beach.

The central figure of the screenplay by the author of *Winchester 73*, Borden Chase, was an exuberant, two-fisted, high-living sea captain named Jonathan Clark, better known as the "Boston Man" for his Salem, Massachusetts, roots. Based in San Francisco, Clark has come up with an outrageous scheme—to purchase Alaska from Russia for $10 million. But he abandons the notion in order to rescue a kidnapped Russian countess with whom he has fallen in love.

Peck, of course, was the Boston Man. A Universal contract player, Ann Blyth, remembered primarily for her subsequent musicals at MGM, was cast as the countess. And, for the role of Clark's oft-time nemesis, a boorish Portuguese sea captain known as Portuge, the studio engaged Anthony Quinn. The Mexican-born actor, a year older than Peck, had been playing bit and supporting roles since the mid-1930s, but his career had recently taken a major leap forward when he was cast as Eufemio Zapata in Elia Kazan's *Viva Zapata!* Quinn would soon receive a Best Supporting Actor Oscar for that performance.

After the success of *Captain Horatio Hornblower*, the job of directing another seafaring tale with Peck naturally fell to Raoul Walsh. During filming, which took place entirely on the Universal lot between September 15 and October 31, 1951, the star and director frequently shared a lunch consisting of a thick steak accompanied by a couple of healthy shots of bourbon. Occasionally, during the afternoon's filming, the star's eyelids would start to droop, and Walsh would shout, "Wake up, Greg. Give it all your energy, kid. Keep running 'til you drop, like a thoroughbred."

One thing Walsh didn't have to do was energize Anthony Quinn. Indeed, it is hard to imagine two more different actors than he and Gregory Peck. Where the latter comes across as dignified, intelligent, and well-bred, with a relatively tight rein on his feelings, the former is full of emotions and earthy in looks and manner. The contrast made for good screen chemistry. Greg later described their relationship as a "[f]riendly rivalry," adding, "[T]here's always room for two on the screen. He does everything he can think of to attract attention to himself. I don't mind that. He's a good, salty actor, one of the best." Peck and Quinn would costar in two subsequent features.

In *The World in His Arms*, the rivalry between the two climaxes in a winner-take-all sea race, with Clark and Portuge leading their crews from San Francisco to their favorite hunting ground for seals, the Pribilof Islands off Alaska. With a budget of only $1.5 million, Walsh couldn't engage in the sort of extensive shipboard principal photography that he had used in *Captain Horatio Hornblower*, but Universal did the next best thing. It hired forty-five seamen from Lunenburg, Nova Scotia, to race two fishing schooners chartered for the picture and outfitted to look like mid-nineteenth-century vessels. A second-unit crew headed by James Havens, a specialist in maritime action sequences, spent fifty days in Canada filming the race. When Havens was finished, Walsh shot close-ups of Peck, Quinn, and their crews back at the studio, with the sea footage running behind them. These process shots were later intercut with Havens' race footage.

Appropriately, the world premiere of *The World in His Arms* took place in Anchorage, Alaska, on June 18, 1952, seven and a half months after the picture wrapped. It was the first time that a Hollywood-style opening had been staged in Alaska, then a U.S. territory. When the picture finally made its way to New York on October 9, the critics saw it for what it was, a bright, colorful adventure story, what would be called a "popcorn movie" today. Peck himself likened the film to "a boy's adventure tale, done with a lot of gusto and a lot of fun, and a lot of humor."

Borden Chase later conceded that he wrote the screenplay with John

Wayne in mind, and the result bears testament to that effort. The role of Jonathan Clark clearly demanded Duke's outsized temperament as well as his physical presence. While Peck, a much more restrained actor, tried commendably, he was never totally credible as the boisterous sea captain. By contrast, Quinn was so unceasingly exuberant, he was over the top.

The World in His Arms did quite well at the box office, earning $3 million in its initial release. Its success was all the more remarkable, because at the time Peck was competing with himself for the moviegoers' dollars, having opened in another, and arguably more significant, picture a mere three weeks earlier.

Like "The Short Happy Life of Francis Macomber," Hemingway's 1938 story, "The Snows of Kilimanjaro," was set in Africa. A writer named Harry (no last name given) lies on a cot in his safari encampment overlooking an African plain. Having squandered his talent through drink, indolence, and meaningless relationships with wealthy women, he has returned to a place where he was once happy to seek rejuvenation. Instead, he faces death, the result of a gangrenous leg infection.

In 1948, Darryl F. Zanuck purchased the screen rights to the story for $75,000, the same amount that Casey Robinson had paid for "Macomber." He then hired Robinson to turn the tale into a screenplay.

"Kilimanjaro" proved a more difficult assignment. To begin with, it was shorter than "Macomber," running only seventeen pages in book form. Secondly, the story lacked a strong romantic element, which both Robinson and Zanuck felt it needed. Thirdly, the writer dies at the end, a resolution that Fox president Spyros Skouras refused to echo on film.

It took three years and eleven drafts for Robinson to solve the problems to everyone's satisfaction. In the end, he adhered to the framework of the story, which alternates between Harry's death throes in Africa, in the company of his unhappy wife, Helen, and Harry's memories of the past. Robinson expanded the campsite scenes but remained faithful to their source. Harry's memories, however, were too fleeting and fragmentary to make for compelling drama. So the screenwriter created new flashback sequences centered around three women: the girl Harry falls in love with at seventeen; his first wife, Cynthia, a member of the "lost generation" who fears trapping her husband in unwanted domesticity; and Liz, a cool artistocrat who treats the writer as a plaything. These interludes played out against typical Hemingway locales, the Midwest of his youth, Paris in the twenties, and Spain of the bullfights and flamenco dancers and a devastating civil war.

Arguably, the biggest difference between the story and the screenplay

lay in their resolutions. Where the writer dies at the end of the story, the screenplay has a rescue party arrive at the encampment just as his fever breaks. The concept jelled when Robinson and Zanuck decided to link Harry's redemption to a new appreciation for his wife.

Henry King, who directed the picture, later called the screenplay "one of the best pieces of writing I ever saw in my life. . . . You could never tell where Hemingway stopped and Robinson started." Papa was somewhat less fulsome. After seeing the film, he felt that the screenwriter had borrowed a little too liberally from his other writings. As he told Zanuck, "When I sold you 'The Snows of Kilimanjaro,' I didn't sell you my entire work."

Ironically, Robinson, the screenwriter who had launched Peck's career, didn't want him for *The Snows of Kilimanjaro.* He thought that Greg's style was too ponderous and that he lacked the character's worldview. Humphrey Bogart would have been perfect, he felt, but Bogie was too old for it. He considered Burt Lancaster the next best alternative.

Zanuck, however, wanted Peck, who was proving to be a major box-office draw for Fox and with whom he had two remaining film commitments. Henry King was also in favor of casting Greg.

But the actor needed persuading. *The Great Sinner* had used the flashback technique, albeit more sparingly than *Kilimanjaro,* and that film's failure turned him off to the format. Nevertheless, he agreed to meet with King to discuss the project. At the end of the conference, his attitude was unchanged. King told him how sorry he was. Flattered but still disinterested, Peck left. Then, a moment later, he returned, telling the director that he'd changed his mind. The reason, he conceded, was that he was afraid King would make a good picture without him. "I considered that the greatest compliment I'd ever had from anybody," the director concluded.

Once Greg was on board, Zanuck cast Susan Hayward as Helen, hoping for the same box-office magic as *David and Bathsheba.* For the ill-fated Cynthia, Robinson wanted Ava Gardner; he'd created the character with her in mind. But she would do the picture only if she could keep a promise to her husband, Frank Sinatra, namely that she would be present for his upcoming nightclub engagement in New York. That meant that all of her scenes in the film would have to be shot in a ten-day period. King agreed to this condition; thus, Peck would be reteamed with one of his favorite leading ladies. The role of the icy Liz went to a Fox contract player, the German-born star of *Decision Before Dawn* and *Diplomatic Courier,* Hildegard Neff.

Where *The Macomber Affair* had been shot in black-and-white, on a tight budget, with only three main characters and one locale, and ran a tidy eighty-nine minutes, *Kilimanjaro* operated on a grand scale. It was budgeted at a comfortable $3 million, shot in Technicolor, spanned the globe with a large cast, and came in at just under two hours.

But the principals never left the Fox lot. As with *The Macomber Affair*, a second unit was dispatched to Africa to obtain authentic footage of the landscape and wildlife. Background material was also shot in Madrid and Paris and on the French Riviera.

The second-unit filming took six months. Then, in early 1952, principal photography commenced. For Harry's safari encampment, Fox erected a huge set on Stage 8, backed by a 350-foot-by-40-foot cyclorama that duplicated the bush country around Mount Kilimanjaro, as well as the snow-capped peak itself.

Peck wasn't particularly comfortable acting on a set with location footage screened behind him; it seemed so artificial. He recalled during the making of *Kilimanjaro* that he had to stand on a soundstage amid a field of scruffy brush, aiming his rifle at a screen on which the second-unit footage of a rhino was running. When a red light flashed off-camera, he knew the rhino was about to fall down; that was his signal to raise his gun and fire.

To add to his difficulties, on April 7, he and Ava were filming her character's death scene on the Fox backlot. He was supposed to pull her from beneath an overturned ambulance, as she lay like dead weight in his arms. When he crouched down to lift her up, he felt a sharp pain in his left leg, the same one that had been injured by the falling horse in 1948. This time, he tore a ligament. Filming had to be suspended while he recovered.

Zanuck debuted *The Snows of Kilimanjaro* on September 18, 1952, at the Rivoli Theatre in New York—where it met with decidedly mixed reviews. To Bosley Crowther of the *New York Times* it was "a handsome and generally absorbing film." Conversely, Hollis Alpert of the *Saturday Review* found it "a dull, long and pretentious movie."

The most noteworthy performance came from third-billed Ava Gardner. Peck thought so as well. "She did things in *Kilimanjaro*," he said, "that she could not have done three years earlier in *The Great Sinner*." Even Ava was pleased with her acting. "Of all the parts I've played," she wrote in her 1990 autobiography, "Cynthia was probably the first one I understood and felt comfortable with, the first role I truly wanted to play." Five years later, King and Zanuck would cast her as another Hemingway heroine, Lady Brett Ashley, in *The Sun Also Rises*.

Despite its flaws, *The Snows of Kilimanjaro* scored with the public, becoming the fourth-biggest hit of 1952, with earnings of $6.5 million. It was surpassed only by the Cecil B. DeMille circus spectacle, *The Greatest Show on Earth*, and two MGM costume dramas, *Quo Vadis?* (in which

Peck was originally cast but had to withdraw due to an eye infection) and *Ivanhoe.*

The back-to-back mega-successes of *David and Bathsheba* and *The Snows of Kilimanjaro* represented the commercial high-water mark for Peck during the 1950s. Not until the start of the next decade would he have a top-ten box-office hit in two successive years.

While Greg's career was peaking, his personal life remained at a low ebb. According to Casey Robinson, he had been difficult during the making of *The Snows of Kilimanjaro.* As the screenwriter put it, "He was picky. He was going through a very bad personal period in his life." Greg was no longer using Seconals or drinking to excess, but the gulf between him and Greta remained. They would argue frequently. After a fierce fight, he would do as he did in 1949, pack a bag and go off by himself. Eventually, he would return home for another uneasy truce. Then the next battle would erupt, and the cycle would begin anew.

Given his profound unhappiness, it is not surprising that he sought temporary comfort with other women—or so the myriad rumors would have it. According to one reporter, Vincent Rogers, "[I]t was constantly rumored that Gregory's phenomenal realism in his pictures was inspired by the fact that his leading ladies often meant more to him than a cue in the script." Even Casey Robinson asserted years later that Greg "was experimenting with all kinds of dames on the set" of *Kilimanjaro.* One of the "dames" may have been Hildegard Neff, with whom his name was frequently linked at the time.

If the rumors were true, any sexual infidelities were a symptom, not the root cause, of the Pecks' marital problem. What kept husband and wife together were their children. Greg tried to be with the kids as much as possible, organizing picnics, outings on horseback, and camping trips to Lake Arrowhead and other nearby resorts. Sometimes his father joined them on their adventures. Occasionally, Greg also took the boys to San Francisco, so they could get to know his mother. During the summers when he was managing the La Jolla Playhouse, he rented a beach house—his film schedule permitting—so that his family could enjoy the pleasures of the resort community. Even when he was on location for a picture, as with *Captain Horatio Hornblower* in 1950, he wanted his kids with him. He thought that being together as a family was all that mattered. Greta felt it important that the boys' lives be rooted in their Pacific Palisades home.

They did agree on one thing: that Jonnie, Steve, and Carey should live normal lives, or as normal as possible. Thus, Greg refused to feature them in photo layouts and publicity shots. But there was no avoiding the attention the Pecks drew when they went out in public.

It was in the spirit of family togetherness that, when Peck's next film called for him to be in Rome during the summer of 1952, he decided to rent a villa about twenty-five miles outside of town. He went over first. Greta and the boys would join him as soon as their living quarters were ready.

En route, he stopped in Paris where, at the request of Paramount, the studio producing his new film, he agreed to an interview with the leading French daily newspaper, *France Soir.* The reporter assigned to the story was a young beauty by the name of Veronique Passani. The two hit it off. "She struck me immediately," Peck recalled, "as a very attractive, very bright, very smart girl." He was particularly impressed by the fact that she didn't ask him specific questions for the interview; they just talked. For her part, Passani found Greg a delightful conversationalist. She also liked his modesty.

The interview concluded, they parted. But not for long.

CHAPTER 12

Working Abroad

Like *The Yearling, The Paradine Case,* and *The Snows of Kilimanjaro, Roman Holiday* was a long time reaching the big screen. As far back as 1948, Dalton Trumbo, one of the Hollywood Ten, wrote a scenario about two people from disparate backgrounds who meet and fall in love in the Eternal City. One was a princess named Anne, who runs away from her stultifying ceremonial duties to experience ordinary life; the other was Joe Bradley, a freelance reporter who accompanies her on her escapade in order to sell her story to the highest bidder.

Fronting for the blacklisted Trumbo, Ian McLellan Hunter sold the story to director Frank Capra, who had formed his own independent production company, Liberty Films, with a business associate, Sam Briskin, and two other celebrated directors, George Stevens and William Wyler. Capra hoped to make *Roman Holiday* with Elizabeth Taylor and Cary Grant. Then, the assets of the financially plagued Liberty Films were sold to Paramount. According to the terms of the acquisition, Capra, Stevens, and Wyler were to make five pictures apiece for the studio, with no project costing more than $1.5 million.

Given this restriction, Capra chose not to make *Roman Holiday.* The project languished on Paramount's shelves until William Wyler agreed to take it on, but only if it could be filmed on location. Paramount studio chief Frank Y. Freeman acquiesced, principally because Paramount, like Warners, had European financial assets that were frozen, meaning they could only be used abroad. In order to free these lire for *Roman Holiday,* Wyler had to secure script approval from the Italian government, which he was able to do.

Born in 1902 in Alsace, then part of Germany, William Wyler had come to America in 1922 at the behest of Carl Laemmle, a distant cousin who was head of Universal Pictures. After a stint at the head office in New York, Wyler went to Hollywood, where he performed a variety of jobs before taking the helm of his first feature, *Crook Busters,* in 1925. Over the next quarter century, he became one of the highest-regarded filmmakers in the industry. Not only had he earned eight Academy Award nominations for Best Director by this point, winning for *Mrs. Miniver* and *The Best Years of Our Lives,* his films brought more actors Oscar nominations than those of any other director in Hollywood.

Peck was eager to work with him, and he yearned to do something lighter, as he hadn't yet made a single comedy. But, according to Wyler, Greg wasn't sure about *Roman Holiday:* he thought the role of the princess was stronger than that of the reporter. When he raised this objection, Wyler claimed to have replied, "You surprise me. If you didn't like the story, okay, but because somebody else's part is a little better than yours, well, that's no reason to turn down a film. I didn't think you were the kind of actor who measures the size of the roles." The argument worked.

Peck disputed this story. "I have no recollection of hesitating [over *Roman Holiday*] at all," he told Wyler's biographer Jan Herman. "As far as I'm concerned that's apocryphal." But Peck did ask for, and got, approval of his costar as well as solo billing over the film's title.

Capra's original choice for Princess Anne, Elizabeth Taylor, wasn't available. Neither was Jean Simmons, a strong alternative. So Wyler decided to cast an unknown. "I wanted a girl without an American accent," he said, "to play the princess, someone you could *believe* was brought up as a princess." He found what he was looking for in a gamin-like, Belgian-born twenty-three-year-old named Audrey Hepburn. Primarily a dancer, Hepburn had played a couple of small roles in British films, notably *Laughter in Paradise* and *The Lavender Hill Mob,* and was about to star on Broadway in Anita Loos' adaptation of Colette's *Gigi.* After testing her, Wyler was so impressed that he agreed to postpone filming until after the run of the play. But *Gigi* was a hit, and eventually Paramount had to pay the play's producers $50,000 for Hepburn's release. After filming, she would return to New York for the road tour of the production.

While Wyler waited for the outcome of Audrey's Broadway debut, work proceeded on the script. The original draft was by Hunter. The project went through several other hands as well, but Wyler was still dissatisfied with it when he sailed for Europe to scout locations. He labored on the screenplay en route, but when he reached England it was still wanting. So he hired John Dighton; the British author's adaptation of a romance called *Saraband for Dead Lovers* also revolved around a royal figure's conflict between love and duty. Dighton agreed to go to Rome and work on the script during filming. "He was writing new scenes, new lines, whatever it took," recalled the movie's editor, Robert Swink. "The picture was kind of put together as it went along." Dighton and Hunter shared credit for the screenplay.

Principal photography commenced in June 1952. Although some interiors were shot at the Cinecittà Studios, Rome's largest film center, Wyler took advantage of the opportunity to shoot on location. He staged scenes at the Forum; the Pantheon; several piazzas and churches; the artists' colony in Via Margutta; and three palaces. For the embassy ball sequence at the outset of the picture, shot at the Palazzo Brancaccio, he enticed Princess Virginia Ruspoli, queen of Italian society, to appear as an extra. She persuaded forty-two of her titled friends to join her, with all of their salaries going to charity. Likewise, for Princess Anne's press conference at the end of the film, thirty-eight working reporters and photographers from fourteen nations played themselves. Many used the breaks during shooting to get photos and interviews with Wyler and the stars.

Although the locations were picturesque, filming in Rome that summer had its drawbacks. The heat and humidity were stifling. And Italy was in a state of political unrest; there were frequent demonstrations and street battles between the ruling Christian Democrats and the opposing Communists and fascists. Moreover, large, enthusiastic crowds turned out everywhere the company went. In a few years, U.S. production companies would be so prevalent that pundits would dub Rome "Hollywood on the Tiber." But in 1952, American filmmakers were still a novelty, so much so that approximately 10,000 people came out to watch one of the first scenes between Peck and Hepburn. "The police couldn't stop them from whistling and heckling," Greg recalled. "For Audrey and me, it was like acting in a huge amphitheater before a packed house of rowdies. I asked her if she didn't find it very intimidating. Ah no, not at all. She believed her role. She took it as calmly and serenely as a real princess would have."

As this comment suggests, Peck was impressed by his inexperienced costar. Although she lacked formal acting training, she had wonderful instincts. And, as a dancer, she had the grace and bearing the role demanded. Beyond those qualities, she was lively, disingenuous, good-hearted, and fun. Peck later described her as "wonderful. An amazing girl, really. She can do anything, without effort."

He was so taken with her performance that, shortly after filming began, he phoned George Chasin, by then his principal agent at MCA, and told him that Hepburn's name should also appear above the title. Chasin answered, "You can't do that. You've worked for years to get top billing." To which, Peck replied, "Oh yes I can. And if I don't, I'm going to make a fool out of myself because this girl is going to win the Oscar in her very first performance." Audrey's name appeared above the title.

While Peck was impressed by Hepburn's instincts and spontaneity, he was awed by Wyler's unrelenting perfectionism. Not being an actor himself, the director didn't know how to tell his stars what he wanted, but he knew when a scene was right. He thought nothing of calling for retake after retake until he got a satisfactory performance. His methodology drove some stars crazy, but Peck admired him for it. "I don't really see the point in settling for two takes, or three takes, if you can get it better on the thirty-second," the actor explained. "It's a small consideration, if you're trying for perfection. And that was always his reason."

Although Wyler prepared meticulously, he was open to suggestions from his actors. Such an instance occurred in one of the most memorable scenes in *Roman Holiday,* that in which Joe and the princess encounter a wall bearing an ancient sculpted face with an open mouth. The reporter dares her to stick her hand in the opening, warning her that, according to legend, the creature will bite off the hand of anyone who is lying. Since neither she nor he has been completely honest with the other, the prospect is intimidating. Afraid to take the risk, she dares him to go first. The script called for Peck to comply, then, with his hand inside the mouth, act as if it were being chewed off. Before filming, Peck suggested to Wyler that he keep the gag going by pulling his arm out with his hand hidden in the sleeve of his suit jacket. Wyler liked the idea but told him not to tell it to Audrey. "Keeping her in the dark is what made the scene work, of course," Peck said. "Her startled look of surprise leaps off the screen. She screams then dissolves into laughter. It is one of the most candid and indelible moments of *Roman Holiday.*"

For the scene in which the lovers part, Wyler needed a harsher approach to get what he wanted. "I was supposed to cry," said Hepburn. "It was late at night, and I was tired from working all day. I played the first part of the scene very nicely, but tears didn't come and I didn't know how to turn them on." After numerous unsatisfactory takes, Wyler came over to her and yelled, "We can't stay here all night. Can't you cry, for God's sake!" He'd never spoken roughly to her before, and she began to sob, at which point he called "Action." Afterward, he apologized to the actress, saying, "I'm sorry, but I had to get you to do it somehow."

Peck worked so hard during filming that, as he told a reporter at the time, "I've lost sixteen pounds, worked every day, from dawn to long after dark, grabbed a sandwich on the run, and been so exhausted I couldn't sleep, but every second has been worth it. In Hollywood you get ingrown. Here, working in the natural settings with live audiences, has been wonderful." Indeed, between the enthusiastic crowds, the invigorating locations, the entrancing film story, and the joy of working with Wyler and Hepburn, that summer—despite the continuing deterioration of his marriage—became one of the happiest of his life.

When he did manage to find a bit of free time, he took his sons sightseeing, usually dragging along his own movie camera. As he put it, "Filmmaking is my hobby as well as my job, and I shot thousands of feet of film when I was in Rome for showing back home on my private screen." Greta, less enamored of the experience, took off about halfway through the summer to visit family members in Finland. She returned in September, shortly before the picture wrapped.

Nearly a year passed before *Roman Holiday* debuted. But when it opened at Radio City Music Hall on August 27, 1953, it more than met the expectations of those associated with it. Paul V. Beckley of the *New York Herald-Tribune* captured the general consensus of his colleagues, calling it "a rather remarkable film. There is absolutely nothing uncommon about the plot . . . yet, with this scanty material, a capable director and a remarkable young actress have made one of the better pictures of the year, certainly one of the brightest comedies." Curiously, no one lamented that *Roman Holiday* wasn't filmed in color, which was Wyler's principal regret. Hollywood legend has it that he realized his mistake after seeing the first week's rushes, but, according to his biographer, Jan Herman, he had hoped to make the picture in color from the outset. But Paramount refused to increase the budget accordingly.

Peck's performance was generally deemed acceptable, if not laudable. Hollis Alpert of *Saturday Review*, for example, called him "smooth and competent enough to get by." In truth, he was better than that. He brought a breezy confidence and charm to the reporter, finding the right balance between the calculating opportunist and the soft-hearted romantic—all of which neatly counterbalanced Hepburn's royal reserve and sense of wonder. His running banter with his editor is fun, as are the occasions when he tortures his photographer friend—nicely played by Eddie Albert—spilling drinks on him and knocking him down to keep him from revealing things to the princess and to Joe's editor at inopportune moments. Most important, he shared a wonderful screen rapport with Hepburn. His face simply fills with delight whenever he looks at her. Still, the princess *was* the flashier role, and Hepburn dominated the reviews. *Life* magazine was hardly alone in calling her "the most gifted star hired by Hollywood in years." Moreover, Peck's prediction during filming turned out to be accurate: Hepburn won the Oscar for her first Hollywood venture.

Roman Holiday was also nominated for Best Picture, making it the first Peck film since *Twelve O'Clock High* five years earlier to be so recognized; it lost to *From Here to Eternity.* In addition to Best Actress and Picture, it secured eight other nominations—for supporting actor (Eddie Albert), director, motion picture story, screenplay, black-and-white cinematography, black-and-white art decoration–set decoration, black-and-white costume design, and editing. Edith Head and Ian McLellan Hunter won for their costumes and story, respectively. In 1993, a posthumous Oscar was given to the real author of the story, Dalton Trumbo.

In 1951, a change in the U.S. tax code exempted any American who lived abroad for at least seventeen out of eighteen months from paying income tax during that interval. MCA encouraged its clients to take advantage of this tremendous savings by working in Europe. Peck was among those who heeded the call, contracting for several features to be filmed in England, Germany, and other parts of the world. Consequently, he stayed abroad for nearly three and a half years, commencing with his sojourn in Rome in June 1952.

After *Roman Holiday* wrapped, he went to Paris with his family. As he had nearly eight months until the start of his next project, he rented sight unseen a Norman-style villa in a small town west of the city. He was disappointed to find it cold and rather dreary, but it symbolized the stultifying state of his relationship with his wife.

At some point during this interval, Peck remembered the attractive young French reporter, Veronique Passani, who had interviewed him on his way to Rome, and decided that he wanted to see her again. Exactly when that occurred isn't clear. It is possible that the relationship started when Greg was making *Roman Holiday.* Verónique told Maggie Savoy of the *Los Angeles Times* in 1967 that *France Soir* had sent her to Rome that summer, and she acknowledged seeing Peck in the Eternal City. "Greg was there. I interviewed him again," is the way she put it. Furthermore, Axel Madsen, author of an authorized biography of William Wyler, asserted that Peck and Passani fell in love that summer—something the director told him—adding, "Since he was still married, it had to be kept halfway secret and elaborate plots were hatched. Once, the lovers and the Wylers had lunch on an island in the middle of a lake outside Rome. They had been told they would be alone, but paparazzi photographers soon came out of the bushes." Peck placed this episode some months later, when Wyler recalled him to Rome for dubbing.

According to Greg, it was after *Roman Holiday* wrapped and he was back in Paris that the relationship with Veronique developed. As he recalled its origins, he phoned her newspaper, only to learn that she was now working for another publication, *Paris Presse.* When he called her there, the operator asked his name and then paged Passani over the loudspeaker system. Thus, all of her colleagues knew that the famous American film star was on hold for her. When she came to the phone, he invited her to join him for the races at Auteuil that afternoon. She seemed reluctant to reply, which unnerved the actor until he realized that she was probably surrounded by all of her colleagues, eager to know what he wanted. Undaunted he said, "Well, last chance. Will you go to the races with me?" Finally she agreed to meet him. Unknown to Peck at the time, Veronique had to interview Albert Schweitzer that afternoon. At the appointed time, she went to the home of Jean-Paul Sartre, where the doctor was staying. But Schweitzer was running late. As the hour approached for her date with Peck, she had to decide whether to stay and get the interview or leave to meet Greg. She met Greg.

They had an idyllic afternoon; en route to Auteuil in Peck's Jaguar, Passani, later described by reporter Lyn Tornabene as "an enchanting, petite Parisian with great, almond-shaped eyes set in a delicate oval face," chatted gaily with the much taller, more reserved American. After the races, they had dinner; then Peck dropped her off at the apartment that she shared with her mother and grandfather. Thereafter, they began seeing one another on a regular basis.

In time, Peck learned that Veronique was twenty years old—sixteen years his junior. Her mother was a White Russian whose parents had owned a paper manufacturing company. Forced to leave their homeland after the Russian Civil War, they settled first in Berlin and then Paris, the Russian nobility's city of choice. Her father was French, an aristocratic, somewhat uptight architect. Although her parents were divorced, Veronique's dad lived nearby and paid frequent visits to his ex-wife and daughter. During World War II, her mother had remarried, to an American colonel; the union lasted only two years but produced a son, Cornelius, whom Veronique's father subsequently adopted.

Educated at Marymount, a private school in Paris, Veronique decided at eighteen to become a journalist. Although there were few women reporters in France at the time, she pursued the editor of *France Soir* until he hired her. Starting as a cub reporter—called a pup reporter in France—she covered minor crimes and human-interest stories, eventually graduating to profiles of such celebrities as Samuel Goldwyn, Senator Estes Kefauver, and Melina Mercouri. Despite her success, Passani wasn't career driven. She later said, "I was not a very good reporter. Giving up writing was no loss to either the magazine or myself."

If, in fact, Greg began seeing Veronique in Paris, the question still remains when. Contrary to plans, Greta decided in January 1953, roughly four months after moving into the villa, to leave France and return with the children to Los Angeles. Greg would suggest that he started seeing Veronique thereafter, but it is possible that the burgeoning relationship began while Greta was still in France and that this accounted for her decision to leave. One tabloid published at this time gives credence to this theory. It cited an argument between the Pecks during a housewarming party at their villa, in which another woman was at the center of the controversy. That woman would most likely have been Veronique. The tabloid described this event as the "blow-up that sent Greta rushing home to Hollywood."

Whether or not Veronique was the root cause, Greta left. She and Greg maintained publicly that the reason for her departure had to do with the boys' education, that it was, as she put it, "just too difficult trying to raise them abroad under Greg's schedule." They insisted that their marriage was fine and denied the rumors of an impending divorce.

But, between themselves, they acknowledged that it was time to stop torturing one another; they were doing neither themselves nor their children any good. When Greta left for America, it was clear to both her and Greg that the separation was permanent, and that divorce proceedings would be instituted when practical.

The decision having been made, husband and wife parted on friendly terms. Greg even accompanied Greta and the boys to Le Havre, where they boarded the *Île-de-France* for home. Although he knew this moment was coming for a long time, he was wracked with sorrow now that it had finally arrived. As he left the docks, he recalled the faces of his tearful sons and the look of resigned defeat on his wife, and the images cut deeply. He wondered as he drove back to Paris if he was condemning the boys to the same kind of loneliness that he'd experienced in his own childhood—and vowed to do everything he could to ensure against that eventuality. Later, looking back on the long, solo drive, he described it the lowest moment of his life thus far.

Shortly thereafter, Mel Ferrer arrived in Paris en route to Africa where he was to start work on a film. He and Greg enjoyed a two-week motor trip, which gave Peck a badly needed respite from his anguish. Finally, in April 1953, it was time to go to work, the best remedy of all as far as Greg was concerned.

By the early fifties, television had become the biggest threat the motion picture industry had ever known. Never before could people sit in the comfort of their own homes and watch comedies, dramas, quiz shows, variety acts, and news—all for free. Hollywood, looking for ways to entice audiences into theaters, began producing what TV could not—

large-scale, Technicolor features with huge casts and extravagant production values. Gimmicks like 3-D and wide-screen formats like CinemaScope were also developed to contrast with the imagery of the small black-and-white tube.

In the forties, Peck's pictures were far grander in terms of budget, running time, and scope than most of the assembly-line products churned out by the studios. Ironically, now, when the fare became epic, he undertook three innocuous and not very memorable programmers, *The Man with a Million,** *Night People,* and *The Purple Plain.*

The Man with a Million and *The Purple Plain* were produced by a British film company, the Rank Organisation, which paid Peck a reported $350,000 per picture. The former, a comedy based on an 1884 story by Mark Twain, cast Greg as Henry Adams, a penniless American ship builder stranded in London. As an experiment, two eccentric but extremely wealthy brothers give him a million-pound note, which he parlays into sumptuous lodgings, an extensive wardrobe, an introduction to British society, and finally wealth, without ever spending a farthing. Along the way, he also falls in love with a pretty society girl.

Shot in color in and around London with lavish sets and costumes, *The Man with a Million* was lovely to look at but, as the *New York Times*' Bosley Crowther noted upon the film's American debut on June 28, 1954, it "doesn't spark with humor, it doesn't glow with warmth and charm and, particularly, it doesn't flash with the satire on money-madness that is lodged in the yarn. It simply ambles along very nicely." It made a resounding thud at the box office.

Night People and *The Purple Plain* were more conventional Gregory Peck vehicles. The former, a Fox feature written, produced, and directed by Nunnally Johnson (marking Johnson's debut as a director), placed Peck in the middle of the Cold War. As Colonel Steve Van Dyke, the U.S. provost martial in Berlin, he attempts to retrieve an American soldier kidnapped by the Russians. Peck liked Van Dyke because the colonel was, in his words, "sort of tough and crisp and full of wisecracks, and a little bit more aggressive than some of the characters" he'd portrayed.

Shot over five weeks in Berlin and Munich during the summer of 1953, at a cost of only $800,000, this espionage drama opened in New York on March 12, 1954, three and a half months before *The Man with a Million.* It drew respectable reviews, but the public failed to respond. Even though it was shot in color in the new wide-format CinemaScope, *Night People* seemed like a throwback to the small-scale, documentary-like pictures championed by Zanuck in the mid- to late-1940s, films like

*The film is known as *The Million Pound Note* in the United Kingdom.

13 Rue Madeleine and *Call Northside 777*. The Cold War thriller placed only fifty-second among the year's box-office hits.

The Purple Plain kept Peck in uniform, this time that of a World War II Canadian Air Force pilot. His character, a man named Forrester, is stationed in Burma during the waning days of the war. Haunted by the death of his wife during the London blitz, he is reckless in combat and rude to his fellow officers. When he meets a beautiful Burmese woman named Anna, he finds a new reason to live, then ironically faces near-certain death when his plane crashes in the jungle behind enemy lines.

As in *The Man with a Million,* Peck was the only international star in the cast. It was shot on location in Ceylon (now Sri Lanka) between January and April 1954 under the auspices of an American director, former child actor and editor Robert Parrish.

Although Greg created another of his flawed but heroic martinets, prompting William K. Zinsser of the *New York Herald-Tribune* to describe him as "his old competent self," his performance wasn't enough to compensate for *The Purple Plain*'s rather plodding story line, slow pace, and absence of costars recognizable to American moviegoers. It, too, failed to resonate at the box office.

During the making of *The Man with a Million, Night People,* and *The Purple Plain,* two incidents occurred that reveal noteworthy facets of Peck's character.

The first occurred as the *Night People* company assembled in Munich to film interiors at the Geiselgasteig Studio. When Greg arrived, he learned that one of the film industry's principal trade newspapers, the *Hollywood Reporter,* had just run a front-page article reporting that he was objecting to everything Nunnally Johnson wanted to do, and, as a consequence, the production was falling way behind schedule. He was chastised in an editorial by publisher Billy Wilkerson, also on the front page. "Today's picture-making is too tough and expensive," Wilkerson asserted, "to stand off such delays as Peck is reported to be causing in Munich and right or wrong news of this type will add little to the Peck lustre. He now becomes a dangerous investment, one that major producers might shy from because regardless of Peck's star value, the loss of production time with antics he's now being accused of makes things too hazardous."

In point of fact, Peck and Johnson were getting along fine. Peck recognized that Johnson wasn't an actor's director like William Wyler or Henry King. "I don't think Nunnally was greatly gifted in that way," he said. "But in every other way he was an ideal director, patient, wise, he kept a good mood on the set, never blew his top, always dealt with things in terms of humor." For his part, Johnson considered Peck "a genuinely nice man." He acknowledged that the actor could be "stubborn" and "opinionated," and "has to be convinced of the necessity of doing something before he'll do it," which Nunnally found time-consuming, but he also noted that Peck "helped me on *Night People* in so many ways. He would make suggestions, but never try to impose his ideas."

Johnson later attributed the *Hollywood Reporter* story to Darryl Zanuck. Unbeknownst to the director at the time, the mogul wanted to visit a girlfriend in Paris. He hoped that he could go to Germany, mediate the "feud," and then make a side trip to France for purposes of his own.

As it turned out, Zanuck's ploy failed, and he stayed in Hollywood. But Peck was so infuriated by the unwarranted attack on his character that he was seething on the set the following day—which turned out to be a good thing. The schedule called for him to do a scene with his costar, Broderick Crawford, cast as the powerful father of the kidnapped soldier. When the industrialist comes to Berlin to get his son back, he incurs the anger of Peck's provost marshal. The sequence in which the two men butt heads ran about ten pages and was budgeted for two days' shooting. As the camera started to roll, Peck turned his full fury on Crawford. As a result, the sequence was finished in one take. The whole thing lasted about two hours including rehearsals and setup time. Since the next set wasn't finished, the company had the rest of the day off. (Anyone who watches *Night People* can see that this story is not apocryphal. Peck, full of righteous indignation, runs right over the blustery Crawford.)*

The second incident took place during the making of *The Purple Plain*. The cast and crew spent part of the shoot living in pitched tents. The director, Robert Parrish, shared his accommodations with Greg. "Most nights," Parrish recalled, "he would crawl onto his mosquito-netted cot, turn on his flashlight, and read. Some nights he would lie there on his back, starring at the ceiling of the tent. I would usually flop on my cot, say, 'See you tomorrow,' and sink into a dreamless sleep. From time to time, I would wake up at some odd hour and look over at Greg. He was always reading or staring. I never caught him sleeping."

One morning, at about 2 A.M., Parrish was awakened by, in his words, "an ungodly scream." He saw Peck jump out of his cot, knock down the center tent pole, and race through the front entrance, his mosquito netting in a tangle behind him. Still screaming, he headed barefoot for the

*Remembering this incident years later, Peck attributed his ire and the basis of the *Hollywood Reporter* story to two Germans on the production staff, Otto Lang and Gerd Oswald. Tensions between these producers and the star started in London before filming began, over the tailoring of Peck's uniform for the picture. But the trade paper attributed the problem on the set to a Peck-Johnson conflict, not one among Peck, Lang, and Oswald.

jungle. Parrish managed to tackle him at the edge of the compound. He asked the actor if he was all right, but Peck just stared at him. Then, Greg put his hands over his face, gasping for air. After several minutes, he recovered and quietly told Parrish he was okay. They returned to the tent, where Peck managed to get a few hours sleep. When he awoke around 5 A.M., the director asked him how he felt. "Fine. Why?" came the reply. At first, Parrish thought Peck had forgotten the earlier episode, but sheepishly Greg acknowledged what had happened. Parrish used the experience to create a new opening for the picture. As the director quipped, "We got it all in one take. I guess that's because Greg and I had rehearsed it so well."

It is difficult to know what to make of Parrish's story. There is nothing to suggest that insomnia and nightmares plagued Peck at other moments in life. The most likely explanation is that, although he had settled nicely into a relationship with Veronique, he was still haunted by the demise of his marriage. In any event, the image of the controlled, dignified movie star in a state of uncontrolled terror is daunting indeed.

In addition to the money he earned from his trio of European films and the tax benefits of remaining abroad, Peck got to visit some interesting places—Berlin, Munich, Ceylon. Veronique spent at least part of each shoot with him. He also took the journalist to the South of France, soon to become their favorite vacation spot, after *The Man with a Million* wrapped. And, following his work on *Night People,* they enjoyed a holiday in Switzerland, with Greg's oldest son, Jonathan. Throughout their courtship, they tried to stay out of the public eye and, for the most part, their efforts were successful. By spring 1954, however, the couple had been together for close to two years, and the press was beginning to catch on. As one photographer put it, "No girl can go around with Gregory Peck and hide behind sunglasses forever!"

Confronted with this reality and its potential impact upon his image, Peck flew home to meet with Greta on June 13, about six weeks after *The Purple Plain* wrapped, marking his return to Los Angeles for the first time since he left for Rome in June 1952. His wife and kids were on hand to great him, as were his father, stepbrother, and Louella Parsons. The following day, Parsons told her readers, "Gregory has been in Europe for two years, and there has been much talk he and his wife were estranged. . . . but everything seemed all right last night."

Of course, things weren't all right, and on July 3 Greta and Greg made it official—they announced their decision to divorce. Shortly thereafter, Greg flew to London to start work on his next project, *Moby Dick.*

* * *

Peck later called it the "most dangerous film I ever made." It was also one of the most arduous. Scheduled for six months, the shoot took nine—and ran more than a million dollars over budget, an enormous sum in the 1950s.

The project started with the best of intentions. The Oscar-winning screenwriter-director-actor John Huston had long wanted to bring *Moby Dick* to the screen. Herman Melville's novel had been filmed twice before—as a silent feature, *The Sea Beast,* in 1926, and as a talkie under its original name four years later. Both versions starred John Barrymore as Ahab, a New England sea captain obsessed with the giant white whale that took his leg. Neither version was very faithful to its source.

Huston, whose impressive directing credits included *The Maltese Falcon, The Treasure of the Sierra Madre, The Asphalt Jungle, The Red Badge of Courage,* and *The African Queen*—all of which he also wrote or cowrote—seemed the perfect man to give life to what is arguably the great American novel. To be sure, his goal was a faithful rendering. As he explained upon the film's release, "We had decided at the outset that our picture was going to be as close to the original novel as we could possibly make it." He went through several screenwriters before settling upon Ray Bradbury. A rather curious choice, Bradbury was best known for his science fiction, but, according to Lawrence Grobel, author of *The Hustons,* John "saw something of Melville's elusive quality in his work."

Bradbury labored for months on the project. When he finished, Huston rewrote and added scenes himself. He also invoked the aid of two other writers, Roald Dahl and John Godey. In the end, Huston and Bradbury would share credit for the screenplay.

Initially, the director had hoped to star his father, Walter, as Ahab. After the actor's death in 1950, Orson Welles and Fredric March were considered. Bradbury favored a third candidate, Laurence Olivier. But Warner Bros., for whom Huston was producing the picture, wanted Peck. When John first mentioned the project to Greg, the actor thought he was being asked to portray the first mate, Starbuck, the role that he had played years earlier at Cal. When Huston said he wanted him for Ahab, Peck was stunned; he really couldn't see himself in the role. But the director could very persuasive when he wanted to be. "John wove his spell," Greg later said, "and convinced me I'd be the ticket as Ahab."

The director then amassed a talented group of costars, including Richard Basehart as Ishmael, Leo Genn as Starbuck, Harry Andrews as Stubb, and Orson Welles as Father Mapple. The most unusual bit of casting was that of a friend, Austrian aristocrat Friedrich Ledebur, for the tattooed harpooner Queequeg. Huston later said that a Rockwell Kent drawing in a limited edition of the novel reminded him of his pal.

Of course, the toughest part to fill was that of the title character. Ultimately, the Associated British Studios and a Midlands rubber plant created what was then a state-of-the art mechanical whale. It was ninety feet long and weighed thirty tons, with a steel frame covered in a rubber-plastic substance called vermiculite. Costing $30,000 and operated by remote control, it could dive, surface, move its tail, and spout water.

While the problem of the whale was being considered, Huston conducted an extensive search for a ship to serve as Ahab's *Pequod.* He finally found what he was looking for, the *Rylands,* a 104-foot wood-hulled, three-masted vessel, in Scarborough on the Yorkshire coast of England. After purchasing the ship, which was serving as an aquarium and tourist attraction, Warners outfitted it to look like a mid-nineteenth-century whaler. The model for this makeover was the *Charles W. Morgan,* an authentic whaler berthed at Mystic Seaport, Connecticut's living history museum. Engines and generators were also placed on board to support the production company's lights, cameras, and other equipment.

Before filming could begin, one other technical problem had to be solved. Although the picture would be shot in Technicolor, Huston wanted it to echo the quality of a nineteenth-century lithograph. After considerable trial and error, cinematographer Oswald Morris came up with the idea of desaturating the color and adding a gray image to it, in what he described as "a marriage of color and black and white." This solved the problem to Huston's satisfaction.

With the director present, a second unit under Freddie Francis began filming whales and whalers off of Madeira, Portugal, in April 1954. The location was perfect, because, as Huston noted, "Portuguese whalers still hunt from open longboats just as they did generations ago." Meanwhile, Peck readied himself for the challenge of playing the obsessed sea captain.

As usual, Greg littered his script with notes about the character's behavior and attitudes. Adjectives such as "stark" and "possessed" were common. At one point, he reminded himself, "Every scene does not have to be a tirade," and at another juncture, he wrote, "Moby is never a fish to Ahab. Something between God and Ahab. Especially when you fight him, this will always help."

He also worked with the Warners makeup department to devise a look for the character, which involved growing his hair long and adding a Lincoln-like beard—with touches of white in both—plus a scar along his cheek. And he learned to use Ahab's peg leg. For several weeks before filming began, he practiced at home with the whalebone prosthetic, his own leg strapped to his upper thigh and buttocks. In time, he could endure the discomfort for about half an hour without getting a cramp.

Principal photography began in July in Youghal (pronounced "Yawl"), Ireland, which stood in for Ahab's home port, New Bedford, Massachusetts. Although Youghal was a picturesque old sea town, most of the homes and shops were constructed of stone. New Bedford's buildings were primarily clapboard. Thus, dozens of structures along Youghal's waterfront had to be covered in wood—at a cost of $50,000.

Huston would later accuse Warners of being penny wise and pound foolish, by not dredging Youghal's harbor deep enough to adequately accommodate the *Rylands* except at high tide. As a consequence, the company was only able to use the ship for the harbor scenes about an hour a day.

After four weeks, the cast and crew moved to Fishguard, Wales, to shoot the episodes at sea. That's where the real problems began. For starters, the generators installed on the *Rylands* made so much noise they interfered with the sound track. The company had to hire a second ship to generate power, with cables running from its deck to the lights, cameras, and other equipment used by the crew.

The weather was terrible in Fishguard, with an unprecedented seventy consecutive days of rain. The cast and crew often holed up in their small hotel, playing cards, drinking, and rehearsing. When they were able to take to the sea, high winds and choppy waves often prevented them from filming. Moreover, many company members became seasick. And twice gale forces demasted the venerable *Rylands,* mandating yet more delays for repairs.

An even worse mishap occurred when foul weather caused the two-inch-thick cable attached to the rubber whale to snap, the result of the mechanical creature's tremendous weight. At the same moment, actors and cameramen in longboats needed help returning to the ship. Huston was faced with the choice of saving his colleagues or his title character, and the whale lost. A replacement was ordered, for another $30,000.

Although Greg genuinely liked Huston, the difficult working conditions put a strain on their relationship. The director's friend Peter Viertel found the actor "tense and disenchanted with his director, who, it seemed to Peck, was accepting the endless rain too philosophically."

Adding to Greg's frustration were his difficulties with the role that John had talked him into doing. The director wasn't much help. "Huston was not that great an actor's director," Greg later said. "When people were perfectly cast, like Bogart and Lorre and Greenstreet, he was great with them. But he was not very good at helping actors to find a performance." Typically, John's suggestions would be along the lines of "Make it bigger, kid," or "More brimstone," which were of little use to the Method actor. Once, when Peck had an important scene with a long speech, Huston told him, "Kid, if you ever deliver the goods this has got to be the time." Greg later asked rhetorically, "Is that direction?"

What Huston lacked in communication skills he more than made up for in bravado. A tough, hard-drinking man, he had a reputation for endangering the safety of his cast members. Peck was no exception. Instead of using a stunt double for the climactic sequence in which Ahab clings to the massive Moby Dick, Huston wanted his star to do it. That way, he could get close-ups of Ahab's face. Peck was game. But neither man had anticipated the rubber whale breaking loose from its cable with Peck strapped on board and getting lost in a dense fog. As he slithered around on the mechanical contraption, Peck had only one thought; "Oh, my God, I'm going to die, tied to the back of a rubber whale out in the middle of the Irish Sea!" Finally, after about ten minutes, the camera crew found him, and he was able to extricate himself. The rubber whale then drifted away, never to be seen again. Another replacement was ordered.

After about eleven weeks and only about ten good weather days, Huston gave up, and the company returned to London. There, they filmed interiors at the Elstree Studios. They also shot some shipboard sequences, as two sections of the *Pequod* were reconstructed on a soundstage and set on hydraulic rockers. According to Oswald Morris, filming in London was a major strain for Peck and Huston, as their visas entitled them to work in England for only brief periods. So they had to fly to Paris each Friday evening and return each Monday morning.

In December, the company was ready to go to sea again. With the arrival of winter, a warm-water location was clearly needed, and Huston chose the Canary Islands. Despite the near loss of a third mechanical whale, the requisite footage was obtained. At last the ordeal was over!

It took some fifteen months for Huston and editor Russell Lloyd to reduce the 400,000 feet of exposed film to an 11,000-foot, 116-minute movie. Appropriately, the world premiere was held in New Bedford on June 27, 1956. When Peck and the director arrived at the airport on the twenty-fifth, 10,000 people were there to great them, with 25,000 more lining the road into town. The following day, there was a host of film-related activities, capped on the twenty-seventh by a parade, with an estimated 100,000 people on hand. That evening, *Moby Dick* was screened at three local theaters. "I've been to premieres in Hollywood and New York," Greg told the crowd at one of them, "but nothing has ever matched this."

The New York opening—at the Sutton and the Criterion theaters—

came on the Fourth of July. Often with a project as problem-plagued as *Moby Dick,* the best the producers can hope for is a finished product of any kind. By contrast, Huston's sea saga turned out exceedingly well. Bosley Crowther of the *New York Times* called it "one of the great motion pictures of our times," adding, "Space does not possibly permit us to cite all the things about this film that are brilliantly done or developed, from the strange, subdued color scheme employed to the uncommon faithfulness to details of whaling that are observed." The *New York Herald-Tribune*'s William K. Zinsser went even further, arguing that *Moby Dick* "may just be the finest film that this country has achieved."

Moby Dick managed to capture ninth place among the top ten money-earners for 1956, with a gross of $5.2 million. Had the film come in on budget—$3 million—its earnings would have been acceptable. But at approximately $4.5 million, before negative and advertising costs, it failed to break even.

The box-office showing disappointed Peck, who had a 10 percent share of the profits. He also faulted the film on artistic grounds, arguing that Bradbury and Huston tried to "say something cosmic," but ended up with something merely "sophomoric and static."

As for his performance, most of the critics agreed with Wanda Hale of the New York *Daily News*, who found him "stiff and stagey." In fairness, he had a number of strikes against him. To begin with, his costume and makeup immediately evoked the image of Abraham Lincoln, a fact noted in virtually every review. Why no one on the production team attempted to redress this distraction is a mystery. Secondly, the screenplay made Ahab essentially a one-note character. Perhaps an actor with greater technical underpinnings—Olivier or Welles, for example—might have made more interesting choices within a very narrow range, but perhaps not. As Father Mapple, even Welles failed to sustain an interminable sermon based on the story of Jonah. Finally, Peck himself couldn't identify with the character. Years later, he said, "I was unable to overcome the feeling that Ahab was an old lunatic."

Perhaps the best that might be said of his performance is that it was a noble effort. He deserves credit for trying to tackle a role so far from his age and persona and for attempting to reach the character's fevered emotional pitch, which played to his weakest point as an actor. Huston always defended Peck's work, but Ray Bradbury was probably right when he stated, "Greg Peck is never going to be a paranoid killer or a maniac devourer of whales."

For a time after the conclusion of principal photography, Huston and Peck remained close friends. "Greg is one of the nicest, straightest guys I ever knew," the director wrote in his autobiography, "and there's a size to him. I conceived a great affection for him during the making of this picture—I had a chance to observe him closely and he was not found wanting in any department."

They shared common interests, including primitive art and racehorses. In fact, Peck invested in several of Huston's thoroughbreds, the start of a long-standing hobby. They also wanted to work together again. Melville's *Typee* and *The Bridge in the Jungle* were two of the projects they explored. Then, suddenly, Peck turned cold. Huston couldn't figure out what happened. "Had it been almost anyone else," he wrote, "I would have said, 'The hell with it,' but not with Greg. I valued our friendship too much. I searched my memory for some clue to his behavior." But he was unable to determine what he had done. After being rebuffed by Peck in several subsequent encounters, he finally gave up.

What Huston never learned was that, several years after the making of *Moby Dick,* Greg discovered that the director had really wanted Orson Welles for Ahab and that he talked Peck into doing the role because it was the only way Warner Bros. would finance the picture. Greg couldn't stand the feeling of betrayal. In a very revealing moment, he told Dennis Brown, who worked with him decades later on his one-man show, *A Conversation with Gregory Peck,* that such "deceit" reminded him of his youth when he felt "abandoned or . . . at least without stability." As a consequence, he told Brown, if someone appeared to be using him for his or her own gain, his tendency was "simply to separate myself from them."

In a town like Hollywood where people mislead and use one another all the time, Peck's attitude offers an important insight into his psyche. No matter how famous and popular he became, he would always carry lonely Eldred within him.

CHAPTER 13

Back Home

On December 29, 1954, while Greg was battling a rubber whale in the Canary Islands, Greta was testifying on behalf of her divorce petition in a Los Angeles Superior Court. Questioned for thirty minutes by her attorney, James C. Sheppard, she cited instances of spousal neglect and cruelty, including the housewarming party in France when Greg had stormed out. By 1952, she told the judge, A. A. Scott, her husband was frequently staying away from home all night, although she refrained from any mention of infidelity, having no wish to jeopardize Greg's reputation or popularity. Peck subsequently denied the charges of cruelty. Through his attorney, Lawrence W. Beilenson, he issued a one-page statement asserting that Greta's allegations were offered simply to facilitate a speedy trial.

The split was amicable. A financial settlement had already been worked out that called for Greg to pay $750 a month in child support. Greta was to retain their Pacific Palisades home plus half of all other community assets, including insurance policies and an automobile. "As alimony," reported the *Los Angeles Times,* "Mrs. Peck will receive in excess of $65,000 a year, by conservative estimate. The contract specifies Peck will pay her from his earnings as follows: 20% of the first $100,000; 12% of the second $100,000; 10% of the third $100,000; 7.5% of the fourth $100,000 and 5% thereafter—until the year 1965. After 1965, she gets a flat 10% of his earnings until she remarries."

Greta was also awarded custody of the children, who were ten, eight, and five at the time. Acknowledging that Greg was a "wonderful father," she approved loose visitation rights. Peck said at this point, "I want to do a good job with the boys. I hope to teach them the right values, to work and develop their minds. I don't want them loaded with spending money. They'd miss all the good things that form character in kids."

Judge Scott granted the divorce petition, but, under California law, it would take a year to become final. Over the ensuing decades, the former husband and wife enjoyed an amicable relationship, centered on their mutual love and concern for their sons. Greta never remarried.

Shortly after the New Year, Greg and Veronique were back in Paris.* But, as 1954 gave way to 1955, it was time to return home. Not only were Peck's kids in the States, the tax loophole that had fostered his foreign sojourn was eliminated. Worse, income earned abroad during that presumed window was now deemed taxable on a retroactive basis. Greg told a journalist at the time, "One day, I was a millionaire. Then the phone rang and I was told the tax law had been changed. I don't think anyone ever said 'goodbye' to $900,000 as suddenly as that before."

Aside from the dramatic loss of income, Greg had done his career little good since leaving Los Angeles in 1952. Of the five features he had made abroad, three—*The Man with a Million, Night People,* and *The Purple Plain*—were overlooked entirely, and, in the remaining two—*Roman Holiday* and *Moby Dick*—he was overshadowed by other elements.

But, on a personal level, there had been significant growth and change. Casey Robinson might have gone too far in suggesting, with reference to *The Snows of Kilimanjaro,* that the pre-Europe Peck lacked a worldview. Greg was well read and devoted considerable thought to history and current events. But, aside from his sojourn in England and the South of France during the making of *Captain Horatio Hornblower,* he had previously spent almost no time outside of the continental United States. Nor had he enjoyed much exposure to people beyond the entertainment industry. While abroad, he not only lived for months at a stretch in Rome, London, and Paris, he sojourned in Berlin, Munich, Switzerland, Ireland, Wales, Ceylon, and the Canary Islands. As he put it in August 1954, "In two years, I have covered a lot of ground, met a lot of people. . . . I'm glad . . . to have had the opportunity to see all those foreign places I'd always read about."

This broadening experience added a veneer of sophistication to Peck's already reserved, gentlemanly demeanor. Visiting some of the world's major museums had fostered an interest in art. He developed a consuming passion for thoroughbred racing; in the years to come, he would own interests in several potential champions. He began having his suits tailored in London. And, of course, he formed a close personal relationship with a younger, sophisticated French woman who was well acquainted with major political and cultural figures in her own country and on the world stage. If Greta was a fit companion for a lonely, impoverished, novice actor, Veronique Passani was an appropriate consort for a digni-

**Moby Dick* didn't wrap until March, but Peck was released early.

fied, mature man of breeding and culture. Greg had grown into such an individual. Indeed, the grandson of Black Irish immigrants had, in effect, become lord of the manor.

Nevertheless, at the outset of 1955, he was still a married man and would remain so until the end of that calendar year. Thus, when he left for America on January 24, he traveled alone. He said upon his arrival in the States, "I am very fond of Veronique. We have the same tastes in art, sports, and everything. . . . We enjoy each other's company, but we did not discuss marriage plans."

He hoped she would soon visit him—which she did on March 9. Greg arrived in New York the day before to meet her flight when it landed at Idlewild (now Kennedy) Airport, but, in the name of discretion, he remained in the terminal at a luncheonette while a friend went to the gate to greet her. After clearing customs, she left with the emissary in a chauffeur-driven Cadillac. At the outskirts of the airport, Greg joined them in the car.

The couple spent about a week in Manhattan, enjoying the city. Greg also spent some time publicizing *The Purple Plain*, which would open in New York the following month. Then, on March 18, he returned—alone—to a rented home in Mandeville Canyon; Veronique arrived the following day, checking in at the Bel-Air Hotel.

"I have no plans to marry Miss Passani," Greg told Louella Parsons in L.A. "I want to spend a lot of time with my three boys for the next year. My house is very close to where they live with their mother; so close in fact that they bicycle over to see me every day." Parsons wasn't fooled regarding Peck's feelings for Veronique. "Although Greg insists they are not engaged," she told her readers on March 19, "it's my personal opinion that when he is free they will marry."

In a crafty public-relations exercise, Peck invited the powerful columnist to his home the following week, where he introduced her to his girlfriend. "She is entirely unlike what I had expected," Parsons reported on March 25. "She is a very pleasant girl, without any affectation, and she is not a great beauty. Her eyes, almost violet in color, are her best feature. For a girl who has lived in Paris most of her life I expected a fashion plate. But she wore a very simple dark dress and a mushroom shaped pink hat." (Perhaps Veronique was not at her best that day, but most people would consider her extremely well dressed and, if not a great beauty, inordinately attractive.)

Parsons' prediction about the couple's marital plans proved correct. On December 30, 1955, Superior Court Judge Elmer D. Doyle signed the decree finalizing the divorce between Greg and Greta. At 7 P.M. the following day, Greg and Veronique were married by a justice of the peace, Judge Arden Jensen of the Santa Barbara Circuit Court. The ceremony took place in Lompoc, California, at the ranch of one of Greg's friends, artist Channing Peak. Also present were the Peaks' four children, Greg's mother and her husband, and Mr. and Mrs. Pida Pedotti, associates of Peck's in the cattle business. After ringing in the New Year, the couple went on a three-day honeymoon. There wasn't time for more, as Greg was in the middle of filming his first feature since coming back to the United States. Appropriately, *The Man in the Gray Flannel Suit* represented a return to the large canvas and class-A production values of his pre-European offerings. It was also the first project under a new contract with Fox, which called for him to star in five pictures over three years with a large salary jump—to $250,000 per picture.

The United States at midcentury was enjoying unprecedented prosperity. The nuclear threat posed by the Soviet Union required constant vigilance, but, for the most part, Americans appeared content with their lives and optimistic about the future. Here and there, however, voices were raised to suggest that the suburban ranch houses dotting the country represented something less than utopia.

One of the dissenters was Sloan Wilson, a thirty-five-year-old Harvard-educated World War II veteran then teaching English at the University of Buffalo. Wilson drew on his experience with Time-Life to write a novel in which a decent, intelligent man, Tom Rath, becomes part of an endless line of breadwinners marching off each day in their civilian uniform—the gray flannel suit—to jobs they neither like nor hate, talking alike and acting alike, in order to earn paychecks that barely cover their material needs. Like many other men of his generation, Rath is haunted by his experiences in World War II, during which he killed seventeen men and drifted into an affair with a young Italian woman. She later gave birth to his child, a son he's never seen. His wife, Betsy, senses her husband's emotional detachment but doesn't understand its cause or know how to breach it. Rath's personal, marital, and professional problems come into focus when he takes a job as the assistant to Ralph Hopkins, the dynamic head of a broadcasting company. Wilson based Hopkins on his boss at Time-Life, Roy Larsen.

Published "just as a major intellectual debate was forming on the issue of conformity in American life," to quote David Halberstam, author of *The Fifties*, a major study of the United States at midcentury, *The Man in the Gray Flannel Suit* touched a nerve in the American psyche. As a consequence, the book became a mega-best-seller and one of the most influential novels of the decade.

Darryl F. Zanuck purchased Wilson's tale, published in 1955 by Simon

& Schuster, for $175,000 plus escalators tied to its book club and hardcover sales. Zanuck, who produced the picture himself—his last project before leaving Fox—assigned the screenplay to Nunnally Johnson. Johnson adhered faithfully to Wilson's major characters, themes, and incidents, while reshuffling the order of some episodes and eliminating others. As with *Night People* and two subsequent films, Nunnally was allowed to direct his screenplay.

Peck arrived in New York at the end of September 1955, several weeks before the start of filming, in order to soak up Rath's milieu. He not only visited several advertising agencies and the executive offices at NBC, he also took an afternoon commuter train to Larchmont, one of the nearby bedroom communities. *Life* magazine assigned a photographer to cover his "research" trip, and the photo spread ran in its November 7 issue.

Principal photography began on October 11 in Westport, Connecticut, site of the Rath home. At that point, the role of Betsy Rath hadn't been cast, so an extra by the name of Christine Linn was hired as a stand-in. Wearing a kerchief on her head so that she could pass for either a blonde or a brunette, she was photographed only in long shots—which do appear in the film. When the company returned to Los Angeles in November, Jennifer Jones, who had a three-picture contract with Fox, was given the role.

The Fox publicity department eagerly trumpeted the reunion of the stars of *Duel in the Sun,* but *The Man in the Gray Flannel Suit* was hardly another "Lust in the Dust," and Betsy Rath, a practical homemaker and mother of three, was a far cry from the earthy, amoral Pearl. Jones didn't particularly care for the character, whom she considered shrewish. Nevertheless, she threw herself into Betsy's emotional scenes, too much so in Johnson's opinion. The director recalled one problematic sequence, that in which Tom tells Betsy about his affair during World War II. At that point, Jones, acting distraught, was supposed to run out of the Rath house onto the front lawn with Peck as Tom in pursuit. "She came out like an impala," Johnson told his daughter, Nora, dashing right past the mark where Peck was supposed to catch her. After calling "Cut," Johnson said to her, "You must have forgotten, honey, we've got to get you in the camera," to which Jones replied, "Well, I thought I was supposed to be real." In the next take, she hit her marks but scratched Peck's face when he grabbed her. "There were big claw marks there," Greg said. None too happy, he told Johnson, "I don't call that acting. I call it personal. Can't you get her to do the scene right?" According to the director, they were never able to bring her fully under control.

Johnson's relationship with Peck was less turbulent. As with *Night*

People, the director and star worked harmoniously together but neither would ever be the other's favorite collaborator. Peck preferred directors who were more in tune with an actor's needs, and Johnson sometimes grew impatient with Greg's questions about motivation and behavior. As he wrote his daughter at the time, "Peck does a good deal of deep thinking, which slows up progress while we discuss the psychology of a scene." Moreover, Greg often wanted to compare the screenplay with the novel. According to Johnson, he always had Wilson's book close at hand, with "all kinds of notes and little pieces of paper sticking out" of it.

The Man in the Gray Flannel Suit wrapped on February 3, 1956, five days behind schedule. So swift was the New York opening—which came on April 12—that the picture beat *Moby Dick* to the screen by almost three months.

At 153 minutes, the CinemaScope production was long and overly crammed with incidents, but most of the critics treated it kindly. Bosley Crowther of the *New York Times* called it "a mature, fascinating and often quite tender and touching film," and *Cue* predicted that it "may turn out to be the best dramatic film to come out of Hollywood this year." But William K. Zinsser of the *New York Herald-Tribune* probably came closer to the truth, asserting that "there are enough people here for two or three movies, and each scene is an emotional crisis. The movie is a series of tiny soap operas laid end to end."

Peck was very good as the sober, thoughtful Tom, although he was arguably a little short on humor and affability, perhaps a bit too much the straight arrow. His performance is particularly interesting when set against his role as that other New York working stiff, *Gentleman's Agreement*'s Phil Green. Whereas the latter is consumed with zeal for his story no matter the personal cost, Tom is much more conservative, a man who wants to follow the dictates of his conscience but fears jeopardizing his paycheck. He also wants his work to have personal meaning but not at the expense of his home life. He's a more complex and commonplace character than Phil but somewhat less admirable.

The Man in the Gray Flannel Suit grossed $4.35 million and ranked fourteenth among the hits of 1956, five places behind *Moby Dick.* But Peck was disappointed with the result. He had hoped that the picture would be something of a sequel to William Wyler's award-winning *The Best Years of Our Lives,* offering a meaningful look at the problems of the World War II veterans a few years further on. Instead, he thought, like William K. Zinsser, that the domestic story was too much of a soap opera. In his opinion, the best moments were the flashbacks to Rath's World War II experiences.

* * *

It may well be that Gregory Peck has portrayed more writers on screen than has any other star in Hollywood. By the mid-fifties, he had already done so four times, not counting *The Man in the Gray Flannel Suit,* where Rath's written communications skills were of paramount importance. But *Designing Woman* offered the first—and only—time in which he played a writer for laughs.

Specifically, he was sports reporter Mike Hagen, who meets, falls in love with, and marries the title character, a dress designer named Marilla, while they are both in Los Angeles on business. Complications set in when they return to their jobs in New York and try to reconcile their divergent lifestyles and circles of friends.

The war-between-the-sexes comedy was the brainstorm of a two-time Academy Award–winning MGM dress designer named Helen Rose. Written by George Welles, whose credits included several Metro musicals and comedies, it was conceived as a vehicle for James Stewart and Grace Kelly, who had previously costarred in Alfred Hitchcock's thriller *Rear Window.* When Kelly married Prince Rainier of Monaco and retired from acting, Stewart bowed out of the picture as well. Thereafter, Dore Schary, who succeeded L. B. Mayer as the head of the studio in 1951 and who produced *Designing Woman* himself, brought Peck back to Metro for the first time since *The Great Sinner* seven years earlier. Schary replaced the blond Kelly with a sultry brunette, Lauren Bacall.*

Vincente Minnelli was assigned to direct. Best known for his musicals, which included *Meet Me in St. Louis, An American in Paris,* and *The Band Wagon,* Minnelli had also helmed several comedies, including *Father of the Bride* and its sequel as well as *The Long, Long Trailer* starring TV's hottest duo, Lucille Ball and Desi Arnaz. A former set and costume director, Minnelli invariably brought a lavish visual style and impeccable good taste to his projects. Peck also learned to admire Minnelli for "a wonderful sense of pacing, of keeping things moving, of not letting things get boring, keeping it dancing along."

Minnelli came to appreciate Peck's zest as well. As he recalled in his autobiography, *I Remember It Well,* he found that "Greg . . . was raring to go, like a banker at an American Legion convention. Pratfalls, double takes . . . he was ready to do it all. I never thought he would have to be held back."

**Designing Woman* was the last film Schary produced for MGM; he was fired shortly thereafter. Thus, for the second picture in a row, Peck participated in a mogul's farewell project.

Bacall was also eager to participate in the fun. Having put her career on hold to care for her husband, Humphrey Bogart, who was battling cancer of the esophagus, she took the job solely because Bogie convinced her that the work would do her good. The support and understanding of her gentle director and down-to-earth costar helped as well. Indeed, she later called *Designing Woman* a "godsend."

Peck became friendly with Bogart, who occasionally visited the set with his and Bacall's two children. As the actor's illness worsened, Greg took to visiting him at his home. In fact, he saw Bogie just a few days before his death. To cheer him up on that occasion, Peck launched into a joke. It was a long one and, even though he pruned the story as he went along, it could only be condensed so far. Finally, Bogart interrupted to say, "If you don't get to the end of this soon, I won't be around for the punch line." Bogart died on January 14, 1957.

Peck and Bacall also became close friends. "Betty Bacall is one of my favorite people," Greg said years later, adding, "No one else has her looks, her style, her way of moving and wearing clothes, her sharp mind."

But his favorite scene in the picture was not with Lauren; it was with Dolores Gray, who was playing Mike's hot-tempered girlfriend, entertainer Lori Shannon. After his spur-of-the-moment marriage to Marilla, the reporter takes the unsuspecting Lori to a high-toned Manhattan restaurant where he breaks the bad news. She responds by calmly dumping an entire plate of ravioli in his lap. Following the film's release, the great comedian George Burns told Peck that his deadpan reaction to being covered in hot pasta had him in stitches. "Well, to me it was worth as much as the Academy Award," Peck said gleefully, "to have George Burns tell me that I could make him laugh." It was a delightful moment, but it set up an even funnier bit later on: the next time Mike encountered Lori, Peck immediately covered his crotch with his hands.

There weren't too many other chuckles to be had, however, when *Designing Woman* opened on May 16, 1957. William K. Zinsser of the *New York Herald-Tribune* went so far as to call the film "a two-hour endurance test." Despite the usual MGM/Minnelli gloss, everyone seemed to be working just a bit too hard.

Although George Welles would inexplicably win an Oscar for his screenplay, his plot and characters were highly reminiscent of the 1942 Spencer Tracy–Katharine Hepburn comedy *Woman of the Year*—a fact that virtually every critic noted in reviewing *Designing Woman.*

The Peck-Bacall comedy failed to score with audiences, in part because it was competing with the latest Tracy-Hepburn pairing, *Desk Set,* which opened in New York one day after *Designing Woman.* Ending up in fortieth place among the top grossers of 1957, it is probably best remembered today for Bacall's character's favorite form of foreplay, nibbling on Peck's earlobe.

After *Designing Woman* wrapped on November 23, 1957, Peck enjoyed seven months off before the start of his next project, which gave him time to concentrate on personal matters.

For starters, he had a new home. Earlier in the year, he and Veronique had purchased a house on Summit Ridge Drive in Brentwood for $95,000. Formerly owned by bandleader Artie Shaw and Lana Turner, as well as boxer Kurt Frings and his wife Ketti, it featured three bedrooms, one of which was reserved for Greg's children, who usually came to stay on weekends. At first, there was some tension between the boys and their father's new wife. But Veronique was patient. Her stepbrother, Cornelius, was roughly in their age group, so she felt comfortable around preteens. She also made clear at the outset that she didn't see herself as the boys' new mom but a friend. Eventually, Jonnie, Steve, and Carey began to come around. "[I]t took a while," Peck conceded. "But she was successful. So much so that I think each one of the boys came to her at various times when they had a problem, to confide first in Veronique even before they confided in me."

The second bedroom in the new home was the master suite. And the third was converted to a nursery, for on October 24, 1956, Veronique had given birth to their first child. Weighing seven pounds, fourteen ounces, the baby, Greg's fourth son, was named Anthony.

Although Veronique had been a career woman, she settled happily into domesticity. As Jean Libman Block observed a few years later in *Good Housekeeping,* the former reporter had "the continental woman's conviction that the home is all. To cook an exquisite meal, create an atmosphere of serenity for her husband, open her children's eyes to beauty—to her these comprise the ultimate feminine purposes." The need for a harmonious environment became particularly important when Greg was working. As Block noted, "When he is before the cameras . . . the household becomes considerably more tense. His easygoing, relaxed manner disappears and an obsessive perfectionism seizes him. Veronique and the children hear him walking up and down by the hour, memorizing his script, pacing out the action."

Domestic peace after his stormy first marriage produced a change in the actor. "In the years I've known Gregory," Louella Parsons wrote in 1958, "I've never known him to seem as contented as he is now. He is that rare thing, a happy man who knows and appreciates the good things in life which he possesses." Years later, he would say that meeting

Veronique "was the best thing that ever happened to me. I learned from her who I was, and I also learned from her how it is possible to be happy."

But he remained a complicated fellow. "Gregory can be as quiet as a meditating monk," Veronique told readers of the *Hollywood Citizen-News* a few years later. "But he can also talk a blue streak. He is very sophisticated; he also is a person of basically simple tastes. He is methodical—and also unregimented. He can confound the man who has classified him as a confirmed introvert by breaking out in a surge of joke-telling, elbow-nudging extroversion. He is conservative about financial matters. But he can spend money with reckless abandon. In other words, he more complex and contradictory than Hollywood shows him."

Even more than in the past, he eschewed the Hollywood social scene, preferring to simply talk with his wife, or perhaps listen to records with her, in the comfort of his own living room. To the extent that they entertained, they liked to restrict themselves to eight or ten guests. On those occasions, Peck said, Veronique took care of everything. "I don't have to do anything but enjoy myself."

His circle of friends changed, however. As one of his pals from earlier days noted, "When they got married, a lot of the guys he used to see a lot no longer were—I wouldn't say not welcome—but were sort of cut off. I guess that's the way she is. She didn't want him hanging around with his old buddies or something. I had the impression that she wanted a more select group of friends for Greg." Whether it was due to Veronique's influence or not, Peck returned from Europe with broader interests and a more cosmopolitan air than he had known previously, and he sought companions with whom he could share his current pursuits and outlook.

One of those was William Wyler. Greg and Willy had become extremely close during the making of *Roman Holiday*. "We spent holidays together at Sun Valley with our families," Peck recalled. "We were always dining out together. It would be the Wylers at the Pecks and the Pecks at the Wylers. Veronique and Talli [Willy's wife] really liked each other. We were a foursome."

The director and actor also wanted to work together again. But instead of being hired guns as they were with *Roman Holiday*, they decided to produce their own project. Actually, Peck had been thinking about getting into production for several years. Around 1956, he told gossip columnist Sheilah Graham, "Everybody is doing it—setting up their own companies. You can incorporate yourself for $25, rent an office, and put your name on the door and you're in business." That year, he formed just such a company, Melville Productions. His partner was screenwriter Sy Bartlett, the coauthor of *Twelve O'Clock High*. Shortly thereafter, Peck and Bartlett announced a two-picture production-distribution deal with United Artists. They intended their first project to be *Affair of Honor,* based on upcoming Broadway play about the American Revolution. But the play failed, and the project was abandoned.

Then Greg and Wyler decided to coproduce *Thieves Market,* an adaptation of Edward Anderson's 1937 novel, *Thieves Like Us,* which had been filmed as *They Live by Night* in 1949. They commissioned a script but weren't happy with the result, and that project was also dropped.

Finally, Peck discovered a Western story by Donald Hamilton called "Ambush at Blanco Canyon," which had been serialized in the *Saturday Evening Post* and later expanded into a novel called *The Big Country.* Peck liked the story, which dealt with an Eastern seaman who gets caught up in a range war in 1880s Texas after becoming engaged to the daughter of one of the feuding ranchers. Greg saw the piece as "sort of a 'Grand Hotel' Western" with "a whole gallery of characters." Wyler liked the property as well.

Instead of using Melville, Peck formed a separate company for *The Big Country,* which he called Anthony Productions, after his infant son. Wyler set up an entity of his own, World Wide Productions. Through these two companies, the director and star coproduced the picture in conjunction with United Artists. It was clear from the outset that Willy would have final say in all artistic matters. Peck would have casting and script approval, and, given his experience in the cattle business, would hire the wranglers, rent the livestock, and select the horses.

Wyler would also direct and Peck would play the peace-loving seaman, Jim McKay, arguably his most heroic role since *Captain Horatio Hornblower.* Following the "Grand Hotel" format, he and Willy went after—and got—major names for every other principal role: Charles Bickford and Burl Ives as the feuding ranchers, Major Henry Terrill and Rufus Hannassey; Charlton Heston as Terrill's foreman; Chuck Conners as Ives' oldest son; Jean Simmons as Julia Maragon, the schoolteacher who owns the water rights that Terrill and Hannassey need; and, one of the hottest new female stars at the time, Carroll Baker, as Jim's fiancée, Patricia Terrill. Before finalizing her decision, Baker met with the producers. "At the meeting," she recalled in her autobiography, *Baby Doll,* "impressed as I was with Wyler and his films, it was Peck who got most of my attention. I couldn't keep my eyes off him. He was so tall, handsome and immaculately dressed, so charming and funny and such a perfect gentleman—he would have turned any girl's head." By the time Greg and Willy got through casting, they had to add an extra $500,000 to the initial budget of $2.5 million.

Principal photography began on July 30, 1957, and lasted five months.

Although the interiors were shot at the Goldwyn Studios in Los Angeles, the company spent the majority of the shoot at two locations in California. One was Red Rock Canyon in the Mojave Desert, where the gun battle between the two old ranchers, Terrill and Hannassey, was filmed. The other was about thirty miles east of Stockton in the central part of the state. On this distinctive, flat brushland, Wyler shot the range sequences, using a real working ranch, the 3,000-acre Drais spread. There the company constructed a sprawling Victorian house to serve as the Terrill home and a small Western village, which Wyler used for the town sequences. As filming around Stockton took place in summer, Greg brought Veronique, baby Anthony, and his three older sons with him to the location. Jonnie, Steve, and Carey even earned a bit of money playing extras; they can be seen in the opening sequence, passing disdainful remarks as their dude father arrives in town.

Making *The Big Country* turned out to be almost as problematic as *Duel in the Sun.* The screenplay was a major headache. Before filming began, several writers—Jessamyn West, Leon Uris, Wyler's brother Robert, and Robert Wilder—had contributed to the effort. But the result was overlong and unsatisfactory. As the cameras turned, the author of the original story, Donald Hamilton, worked with Peck on rewrites at night, after Greg completed his acting chores. But Hamilton was no screenwriter. Eventually, Sy Bartlett and James Webb, an old hand with Westerns, were hired. They and Wilder would share screen credit, and West and Robert Wyler were cited for adapting the novel.

In addition to script problems, the remote locations offered the cast and crew few outlets for after-hours fun. And, of course, Wyler filmed in his usual methodical fashion, calling for numerous takes. His way of working didn't sit well with some members of the cast, notably Charles Bickford, who had a major blowup with the director and stalked off the set. He returned only after Wyler threatened to report him to the Screen Actors Guild. There was also tension between Willy and Jean Simmons, and Carroll Baker, who was pregnant at the time, was occasionally ill humored. As if all this weren't bad enough, principal photography ran about a month over schedule and drove the budget from \$3 million to \$4.1 million.

While on location, the production problems took their toll on Peck and Wyler. At one point, they were shooting a scene in which Pat and Jim ride to the Terrill ranch in a buckboard. En route, McKay is hassled by the sons of Rufus Hannassey, led by Chuck Conners as Buck. When Peck saw the rushes of this encounter, he was unhappy with a close-up, in which he thought he looked like a "cretin." He asked Wyler if they could do a retake. "I'll think about it," the director replied. Peck reiterated the request several times as filming progressed, and on each occasion, Wyler remained noncommittal. Finally, as the company was about to wrap at the location, Greg again reminded the director of the close-up. At that point, Willy said, "Well, to hell with it. I'm not going to do it. I can cut around it, and anyway, I'm *directing* this picture."

Peck was furious. He felt that as the star of the picture, he was entitled to the courtesy of a retake. But he wasn't just the star; he was Wyler's coproducer and friend. Given their relationship, Willy's attitude was inexplicable. Unable to contain his hurt and disappointment, Greg went to his Winnebago, changed into his civilian clothes, and, without telling anyone, drove back to Los Angeles, about 400 miles away. A few days earlier, Veronique had returned with the kids. When Greg came through the door late that night, she was stunned. "What are you doing here?" she asked. He confessed to walking off the picture. "But it's your own picture," she replied. "How can you walk off your own picture?" "I don't know," Greg said, "but it just seemed like the right thing to do."*

Shortly thereafter, Wyler and the rest of the company returned to Hollywood for several more weeks of filming. He and Peck went about their business without speaking to one another. "He'd be six feet away from me," Greg told Wyler's biographer, Jan Herman, "not looking at me. He'd direct everyone else in the scenes, not me. But I coped. By that time I was so into the character, I didn't need to be directed. I was all revved up, full of adrenaline. I think I did my best acting in those scenes."

The feud continued in postproduction, during which Wyler tried to take sole credit as producer, arguing that Peck hadn't earned co-billing. In a letter dated March 27, 1958, he offered the actor three alternatives: 1) no credit at all; 2) credit as Associate or Assistant Producer; or 3) the removal of Wyler's name entirely from the film.

Peck replied on April 8, firmly rejecting the first two options. In a long iteration of his involvement with the project, he wrote, "I performed, for eleven months, from the finding of the original story material through to the completion of the shooting, all the functions of a co-producer." He cited numerous examples of his contributions to the screenplay: supervising one of the screenwriters, Leon Uris, after Wyler refused to do so for personal reasons; working intensely for several weeks with one of Uris' successors, Robert Wilder, "often staying up all night and dictating memos on the phone at 6:00 and 7:00 in the morning to my secretary, who would then type up my work and submit it to Wilder when he came to the office"; assisting Donald Hamilton in Stockton; and, finally, recommending Webb and Bartlett, who gave the screenplay its final shape. He

*The close-up that Peck found so distasteful was not used in the final cut.

also cited numerous specific instances of scenes that he had suggested, labored over, and/or fought for, adding, "I did everything I could in my work with the writers, to build stronger characterizations for every player in the picture," including Heston, Baker, and Ives. He cited as well his contributions beyond the script, from forming a coproduction deal with United Artists before Wyler and he joined forces to his suggestions regarding casting, publicity, wardrobe and makeup, the choice of locations, the budget, and the hiring of technical personnel.

Encouraging Wyler to share the producer's credit as originally planned, he concluded by acknowledging that the "the overlapping of director-producer and actor-producer function was, in our case, a serious mistake. If it had not occurred we would probably still be the best of friends. I am not going to opinionate in this letter on the reasons for our mutual personal resentment. Since it exists, I suggest we finish up our relationship in a business-like way and resolve this producer credit matter without rancor." Peck got his coproducer's credit.

In mid-April, Wyler washed his hands of the Western, announcing that he was leaving for Rome to start work on his next film, *Ben-Hur*, and would therefore be unable to devote "further time to matters pertaining to *The Big Country.*" He asked that he not be disturbed in Rome for any reason, adding that he had authorized his longtime editor, Robert Swink, to do whatever was necessary to ready the picture for release.

The biggest problem Wyler left to his associate was how to end the film. During principal photography, the writers had been unable to come up with a satisfactory resolution. As Carroll Baker's contractual stop-date neared, Wyler and Peck even halted filming for two days in order to work on the final sequence. At the end of that interval, they had yet to solve the problem and had to dismiss Baker without shooting any additional footage. Consequently, in the finished picture, her character just disappears. After Wyler left for Rome, Peck tried to rehire the actress for a day, so that her character could be inserted into the final showdown between the two old ranchers, but was unable to do so. Instead, the film winds down with the Hannasseys' kidnapping the schoolteacher, Julia. She is rescued by Jim, culminating in a gun battle between the seaman and Buck. Almost immediately thereafter comes another gun battle, between the Major and Rufus, after which Julia and Jim survey the land on horseback, suggesting that peace at last has come to "the big country." Swink shot this footage of Greg and Jean Simmons.

Wyler later wrote the editor from Rome to express his approval. Peck, however, found the ending anticlimactic. The problem, in his view, was that there were too many characters with unresolved conflicts near the picture's end, causing the story to bounce back and forth between Jim and the schoolteacher and the two ranchers. He wanted to eliminate the showdown between the old men. Thus, the saving of Julia would have led directly to the finale.

The idea had some merit. Not only would it have eliminated the story's seesaw problem, which *is* somewhat ragged, it would have prevented the back-to-back gun battles between Peck and Conners, and Ives and Bickford, the proximity of which diminishes both. Finally, the deletion would have somewhat reduced the film's substantial running time of 166 minutes. Peck, however, was unable to elicit support for his idea.

On October 1, 1958, *The Big Country* debuted at the Astor Theatre in New York. Despite the myriad production difficulties and the absence of the director at a crucial postproduction phase, the Western had much going for it. In addition to the engaging stars in the cast, it was beautiful to look at, having been shot in a wide-screen format known as Technirama. It was also highly entertaining, with such memorable set pieces as Peck's determined battle of wills with a wild horse, his fistfight with Heston, much of which Wyler showed in a daring long shot, and his gunfight with Conners. A standout among the stellar supporting cast was Burl Ives, who would win an Oscar for his ornery, self-righteous Rufus Hannassey. Overall, the reviews were respectable and the audience response was enthusiastic, taking the Western to eleventh place among the hits of 1958. But, given its outsize budget, the initial earnings of $5 million barely put *The Big Country* in the black.

The Western was behind them, but the feud between Wyler and Peck continued. Their wives tried to bring them together, to no avail. When the two men saw one another at social events, they maintained an awkward silence. "I missed Willy," Peck confessed. "I don't know whether he missed me. Maybe he did." Nearly two and a half years later, Greg was standing in the wings at the Academy Awards, waiting to go on as a presenter, when Wyler came off stage, having just won an Oscar as Best Director for *Ben-Hur.* Peck extended his hand and said, "Congratulations, Willy, you deserve it." Wyler took Greg's hand and said "Thanks." Then he grinned and added, "But I still won't retake that buckboard scene." That ended the feud.

Peck embarked on a second Western while *The Big Country* was in postproduction. Less epic in scope, about $2 million cheaper, and roughly an hour and fifteen minutes shorter in running time, *The Bravados* brought Greg back to Fox.

By coincidence, his characters in the back-to-back Westerns were both named Jim. But whereas *The Big Country*'s McKay was a peace-loving man, *The Bravados*' Jim Douglas was a taciturn small-time rancher out to track down and kill the four men who had raped and murdered his wife.

Based on a paperback novel by Frank O'Rourke published by Dell in February 1957, this revenge drama went through several screenwriters, including John O'Hara and Richard Breen. Only a third writer, Philip Yordan, received screen credit. The result was faithful to O'Rourke's story up to the point near the end when Douglas confronts the last of the four outlaws, an Indian named Lujan. Originally, the rancher allowed the man to live because he'd lost the thirst for revenge. When asked to direct the picture, Henry King refused, arguing that Douglas' motivation in this scene didn't ring true. "Why did he chase him that far and then not kill him?" the director asked. Eventually, King came up with a far richer solution: in confronting Lujan, Douglas learns that neither the Indian nor the three men he's already killed were the ones who butchered his wife. Thus, he himself is a murderer. Stricken with remorse, Douglas goes to church to seek redemption. After working with Yordan on this resolution, King agreed to make the picture.

The director and the film's producer, Herbert B. Swope Jr., assembled a solid group of character actors for Peck to track down—Stephen Boyd, Albert Salmi, Lee Van Cleef, and Henry Silva. But for the young woman who falls in love with Jim, Josepha Velarde, they made an unusual choice—the chic British actress Joan Collins. Seventeen years Peck's junior, Collins had made her American debut in 1954 in *Land of the Pharaohs,* following appearances in seven British films in two years. The actress campaigned for the part of Josepha. As she later recalled in her autobiography, *Second Act,* "I was totally wrong for the role of a tough frontier woman whose life was only complete when she was roping a horse or striding the dusty plains, but, even though horses and I are like oil and water, I still wanted to do it."

Principal photography began on February 3, 1958. The studio had wanted to shoot in Arizona, but King insisted they film in southern Mexico, an area that he had flown over and fallen in love with many years earlier. He felt the additional cost was worth the trade-off in fresh visuals. As it turned out the company saved about $250,000 because the weather was perfect during the forty-eight days of location filming, while Arizona experienced rain much of the time.

The picture wrapped on April 1, five days behind schedule. On May 1, Veronique gave birth to a six-pound, eight-ounce baby girl, whom she and Greg named Cecilia. "I'm such a lucky fellow," the actor told the press. "It's my first daughter in five tries." Less than two months after that, on June 25, *The Bravados* debuted at the Paramount Theatre in New York.

Although Peck didn't particularly care for his character, which he found "unbelievably grim and straight-faced," he was fine, delivering another of his patented martinet-hero performances. But he was pleased by his work in the film's final scenes, in which Douglas learns he's been hunting the wrong men and seeks forgiveness from God. "I think my realization of the enormity of what I had done," Greg said years later, "three or four minutes on the screen, was as good as any work as I've ever achieved. The picture wasn't very successful, and it's certainly not seen today. But an actor does have little ornaments hanging on the tree here and there, work that he's proud of that maybe no one really noticed."

As Peck observed, *The Bravados* was not a success. It drew a mixed response from the critics. Some liked the emphasis on action, the lush color photography, and the attempt to grapple with the kind of moral complexities that most horse operas avoid. But others found the pace too slow, the romance between Jim and Josepha tacked on for the sake of a love story, and the characters portrayed by Boyd, Salmi, Van Cleef, and Silva poorly developed. The Western took in only $2.2 million, which didn't cover the costs of production, distribution, and promotion.

CHAPTER 14

Two for United Artists, Two for Fox

Melville Productions finally got off the ground on May 26, 1958, nearly three months after *The Bravados* wrapped. Peck and Sy Bartlett chose to launch their independent production company with a gritty war story focusing on the U.S. Army's confused and costly attempt to capture a Communist-held outcropping known as Pork Chop Hill during the waning days of the Korean War.

The screenplay by James Webb, coauthor of *The Big Country,* was based on the book *Pork Chop Hill: The American Fighting Man in Korea, Spring 1953* by Brigadier General S. L. A. Marshall, described by *Saturday Review*'s Hollis Alpert as the "best writer of our time on men of war." Webb, who brought the project to Peck's attention, focused on one chapter of the book, "All the King's Men," which followed the exploits of K Company. Under the command of Lieutenant Joseph P. Clemons Jr., the company was one of several units to take Pork Chop during the seesaw battle.

Peck and Bartlett determined from the outset that they wanted to produce an unvarnished portrait of soldiers in combat, avoiding the typical war movie clichés. Said Bartlett, "We wanted people who saw the picture to say, 'this is the way it was,' and 'these must be real GIs we're looking at.'"

To that end, the producers cast—aside from Peck, who would play Clemons—a group of unknown actors.* "Sy started screening some 640 applicants," said Greg at the time. "When he got less than 100 I sat in on the interviews. Sy insisted on allowing each candidate at least fifteen

*As Peck was a principal in Melville Productions, it is appropriate to refer to him as one of the film's producers. Unlike with *The Big Country,* however, he took no producer's credit on this or a subsequent Melville film. Only Sy Bartlett was so acknowledged.

minutes to detail his background and ambitions. We wanted to give a chance to as many unfamiliar faces as possible." A remarkable number of those cast went on to notable film and TV careers, including Robert Blake, Norman Fell, Harry Guardino, Martin Landau, Gavin McCloud, George Peppard, Rip Torn, Henry Dean Stanton, and Woody Strode.

Casting relative unknowns had a salutary effect on the budget. Having learned his lesson from the excesses of *The Big Country,* Peck was determined that *Pork Chop Hill* be produced on a sound economic basis. The extent of his concern can be seen in a memo to Bartlett, Webb, production manager Tom Andre, and the film's director, Lewis Milestone, on May 20, six days before the start of principal photography. Discovering that the budget had reached $1.8 million, Peck wrote, "This is an absolutely impossible figure. If this picture cannot be made for $1,300,000 it should not be made at all. . . . [O]ur basic story has limited audience appeal and we cannot gamble on such an intangible as the hope that we will come off with a classic war picture." He insisted that $500,000 be cut. The Melville team members sharpened their pencils and met this objective. It proved to be something of a Pyrrhic victory, however, as the final cost of the picture climbed to $1.75 million. Still, that was remarkably low for a feature in 1958.

The producers' cost-cutting measures included filming in black-and-white and close to home. The few interiors were shot at the Goldwyn Studios, but most of the work took place at the Albertson Ranch in Thousand Oaks, California, about twenty-five miles from the heart of Los Angeles. Roughly $100,000 was spent to turn a 300-foot outcropping at the ranch into a battlefield, complete with wood-and-stone bunkers and a network of trenches that zigzagged from the base of the hill to its crown. Track was laid along the side of the mound. This enabled cinematographer Sam Leavitt, utilizing a camera mounted on a wheel-based platform, to move alongside the actors as they pursued their characters' objective.

As with the makers of any military-related story, Peck and Bartlett were dependent upon support from the Pentagon, which, in this case, came readily. The army even made Joseph Clemons Jr. himself a technical advisor. The commander of K Company was then a captain on duty at Fort Campbell, Kentucky. "Clemons taught me how to crawl on my belly under fire," said Peck at the time, "how to cut barbed wire, how to get rid of a hand grenade—and if we weren't in shape *before* the picture we were *after.*" He realized how unusual it was for an actor to take on a real-life character with the actual person on hand to offer pointers. As Peck put it, "It's quite a thrill to play a part such as this, and at the end of the scene, turn to the man you are portraying, a few feet behind you, and ask how it looked."

Although K Company's assault on, and defense of, Pork Chop Hill took place over three days and two nights, Milestone was accorded forty days' shooting time to replicate the battle, and he ended up going fifteen days over schedule. "It was physically tough for everybody," recalled assistant director Ray Gosnell Jr. "It was all night shooting. We were climbing this hill in Thousand Oaks and every shot was a monster to do because you had smoke in it, you had night shooting, you had to light everything, and everything was a moving shot going up this hill."

Peck relished the experience, particularly working with the relative newcomers who were his costars. According to Bartlett, "Greg was generous in giving of himself on the set to help those young actors. He was excited over their fresh approach to assignments—lines memorized, well trained, and continually offering good suggestions."

Oscar-winner Lewis Milestone, age sixty-three, hadn't directed a feature for five years, but he was an appropriate choice to take the helm of *Pork Chop Hill,* having been responsible for two classic war dramas, *All Quiet on the Western Front* and *A Walk in the Sun.* As the former was about World War I and the latter about World War II, the director considered his new assignment the third leg in a trilogy on America's major twentieth-century conflicts (this was, of course, prior to Vietnam).

There were no overt problems between Milestone and Peck on the set, but they disagreed over Greg's performance. At the time of the battle, Clemons had been a recent West Point graduate with virtually no combat experience. In Marshall's book, he came across as, to quote Joseph Millichap, author of a study of Milestone's work, "a rather confused individual . . . a greenhorn officer who makes some rather fundamental military errors." The director wanted to adhere to this interpretation. But Peck, at forty-two, portrayed the lieutenant in typically heroic fashion, neither indecisive nor prone to mistakes.

Peck and Milestone also differed over the film's tone and pacing, which became more obvious after the director delivered his edited version of the picture. "Milly had a right to his cut," Peck said years later. But he, Bartlett, and James Webb found it, in Peck's words, "a bit self-conscious and artsy." They took over the final editing, and, as Peck put it, "sharpened it up and speeded it up," which displeased Milestone. "*Pork Chop Hill* became a picture I am not proud of," the director stated, "because it looked as if it were 'cut with a dull axe.' All that remained was Gregory Peck and a gun."

Milestone may have been unhappy with it, but the final cut of *Pork*

Chop Hill is certainly true to the producers' expressed intentions at the outset of the project: it offers an unvarnished, unsentimental portrait of the turmoil and folly of war, and, at the same time, depicts the courage of ordinary individuals in one particular combat setting. When the picture opened in New York on May 29, 1959—just in time for the Memorial Day weekend—critics applauded the result. *Variety* asserted "Hollywood has come a long way to be able to make war films such as *Pork Chop Hill.* The pretense and the heroics have been stripped from this picture. What is left is a grim, utterly realistic story that drives home both the irony of war and the courage men can summon to die in a cause which they don't understand and for an objective which they know to be totally irrelevant."

Although *Pork Chop Hill* was overlooked by the Academy, *Time* magazine named it one of the year's five best pictures. It also became one of Peck's personal favorites. "I like it because of the extreme tragic irony," the actor said. But his preproduction estimate of the film's box-office potential proved prescient. Focusing on an unpopular war with little to attract women moviegoers, *Pork Chop Hill*—despite the glowing reviews—placed a mere forty-fifth among the hits of 1959, with box-office revenues of only $1.7 million—exactly the cost of production.

Before the release of their war film, Peck and Bartlett decided to break with United Artists. When Melville went into production next, it was in partnership with Universal. But this venture wouldn't commence until 1961, nearly three years after the start of the company's first project. That was fine with Peck. "I have no wish," he said around 1957, "to turn my company into the dimensions of a major studio where operation is concerned. Nor do I wish to be as ambitious as my contemporary and friend, Burt Lancaster, with his vast program of films for Hecht-Hill-Lancaster. I intend to keep on producing when I find the story that appeals to me and I'm certain that I can transmit that appeal to the public." In the meantime, he was content to work as a freelance actor, increasingly taking a percentage of his projects' profits as part of the deal. Such was the case with his next film, *On the Beach,* which went into production about six weeks after *Pork Chop Hill* wrapped.

Where Peck's combat movie demonstrated the devastating impact of ground warfare on a single infantry company, *On the Beach* considered the result of nuclear holocaust on the whole of humanity. In his best-selling novel, published by William Morrow in 1957, Nevil Shute depicted a postwar world in which most of the population has been killed in an exchange of missiles. For the moment, only remote Australia remains untouched. But scientists expect that wind-borne radioactive fallout will arrive there shortly with devastating results. How the doomed populace confronts its final days is portrayed through the interlinked stories of several characters—Dwight Towers, the commander of an American nuclear submarine berthed in Melbourne; Moira Davidson, an attractive but lonely Australian woman who falls for Dwight; Julian Osborn, a British scientist who fantasizes about being a racecar driver; Ensign Peter Holmes, liaison officer between the Australian Navy and the U.S. sub; and Peter's wife, Mary, a young mother who refuses to accept the future they all face.

The film's producer-director was Stanley Kramer, known for projects that dramatized important social issues, such as *The Defiant Ones* and *Inherit the Wind.* At a time when the United States and Soviet Union had arsenals of missiles aimed at one another and the threat of mass destruction was ever-present, the antinuclear message of *On the Beach* ideally suited Kramer's liberal agenda.

United Artists, which had a coproduction agreement with Kramer, didn't think much of the subject's commercial prospects, but Kramer was optimistic. Still, he hedged his bets by peppering the cast with big names: Peck as the sub commander; Ava Gardner as Moira; Anthony Perkins, then a hot young actor thanks to films like *Friendly Persuasion, Fear Strikes Out,* and *The Matchmaker,* as the ensign; and Fred Astaire—in his first dramatic role—as the racecar-driving scientist.

Kramer decided to film virtually the entire picture in Australia, with Melbourne as his principal location (the harbor scenes were shot in Sydney). The Aussies, having never witnessed the making of a Hollywood film before, turned out in droves to watch the company work. But, for the final scene, depicting the city's deserted streets due to radioactive fallout, Kramer needed the locals to leave them alone. Using the newspapers and radio, the director asked everyone to stay off the streets for a designated hour on a designated day—and they did. "Bearing in mind that this was a very real, very large, and very busy city," he recalled, "it was a huge favor to ask, a huge operation, but it went off without a hitch."

The producer-director's base of operations was the Royal Showgrounds, a seventy-two-acre facility normally used for an annual agricultural fair and the occasional sporting event. A soundstage was erected in the mammoth Agricultural Hall, and there the company filmed the picture's interiors, including that of the submarine, which was designed from photos of the real thing and constructed at a cost of $100,000. For exteriors of the sub, Kramer, unable to obtain cooperation from the Pentagon due to the picture's antinuclear message, borrowed the HMS *Andrew* from his Australian hosts.

Rather than stay at a hotel during principal photography, Greg and Veronique rented a large Victorian house owned by a former tennis star, Sir Norman Brooks. The Pecks also brought their French cook and Greg's secretary, Bella Rackoff. The star and his wife were invited to dozens of local parties and events, but they declined to attend most of these affairs. On his few days off, Greg took Veronique to Melbourne's numerous antique shops. They also attended the races whenever possible.

Melbourne lacked the cosmopolitan air of its Northern Hemisphere counterparts. Pubs shut down promptly at 6 P.M. Moreover, the months of filming—January, February, and March—coincided with Australia's summer, and Melbourne experienced a seventeen-day hot spell, during which temperatures exceeded 100 degrees. Uncomfortable and bored, the company's principals tended to gather at the Peck residence, enjoying good French food, free-flowing liquor, lively conversation, and spirited card games. "Fred Astaire spends many evenings here," Bella Rackoff noted in a letter to Sy Bartlett, "and they have hot gin rummy games." Greg and Fred, who hadn't known one another beforehand, formed an enduring friendship Down Under.

Ava Gardner also spent much of her free time with the Pecks. Since *The Snows of Kilimanjaro,* she had divorced Frank Sinatra and moved to Madrid, where she had become part of the international jet set. She found staid, hot Melbourne particularly stultifying. Miserable though she was, she was well suited to her role, and Peck enjoyed working with her again. Looking back, he considered Moira Davidson "one of her finest performances."

The reunion was marred only by his disagreement with Stanley Kramer over the nature of the sub commander's relationship with the Aussie woman. Kramer insisted that the Dwight-Moira affair be consummated whereas, in the book, Towers abstains out of respect for his deceased wife. Peck argued that the change was "out of character," and that "self-denial on a matter of principle was romantic." But the director wanted to give the audience some relief from the story's downbeat theme, and the romance between Towers and Moira provided such an opportunity. Reluctantly, Peck acquiesced.

Otherwise, the star and director got along extremely well. Peck shared Kramer's hope that the film might alert the public to the dangers of the arms race. "I think we all became somewhat imbued with Stanley's mission," the actor said, "we all wanted to help him do it." For his part, Kramer admired Greg's discipline and dedication. "The precision and thoroughness of Peck is well known," the filmmaker asserted. "If he played the commanding officer of a nuclear submarine, he demanded complete background knowledge of what was then top-secret information. How fast could the vessel travel? How much fuel was necessary? How long could it stay beneath the surface? I passed on to him the details that had been furnished me by the navy. They were approximate figures. That made Peck uncomfortable. He needed to know the exact implication of each order he issued. Fortunately, a confidential talk with the navy technical advisor settled the situation. I must say, I admired his tenacity and insistence on total accuracy in the preparation for his role."

Principal photography wrapped on April 2. Eight months later, on December 17, 1959, *On the Beach* premiered. Given the picture's theme, Kramer decided to open it simultaneously in seventeen major world cities, including New York, Berlin, Caracas, Johannesburg, Lima, London, Melbourne, Paris, Rome, Tokyo, Toronto, and Zurich.

Although Moscow wasn't on the list for obvious reasons, Kramer pulled off a diplomatic coup by arranging a screening in the Soviet capital on the same December evening; he dispatched the Pecks as his representatives for the occasion. "We flew to Moscow in a blizzard on December 17," said Greg, "and the policemen at the airport were on horseback dressed as though they were going to the North Pole, fur hats and fur collars. I don't know what the temperature was, but it was certainly maybe twenty or thirty below zero. It was a strange experience, the sky was very dark, the blizzard was blowing and it was freezing cold." Knowing that their time in Moscow would be brief, the Pecks asked if they could possibly catch a performance of the Bolshoi Ballet that evening. They were driven directly from the airport to the theater and, within moments, were seated in one of the boxes reserved for government officials, watching *Romeo and Juliet.* Afterward, they were taken to their hotel, a large suite at the National, on Red Square. Too excited to sleep, they asked their Intourist guide if they could take a walk outside. Permission granted, they strolled for about two hours. Peck described the whole evening as a "[m]arvelous, glamorous experience."

The Moscow screening was held under tightly controlled circumstances in the auditorium of a workers' club before an invited audience of 1,200 Soviet officials, the international press corps, and foreign diplomats including U.S. Ambassador Llewellyn Thompson. Unlike the other premieres, it wasn't the kickoff for a regular commercial engagement; ordinary Soviet citizens would never see the picture. Still, the event was a success. "They loved us in Moscow," Greg told *Variety.* "It was the best reaction I've seen in the showings I've attended. They laughed in all the right places, and applauded after many dramatic sequences."

The American critical response was almost as enthusiastic. Although *Time* magazine called the picture "a sentimental sort of radiation romance," most critics sided with *Saturday Review*'s Arthur Knight, who asserted that *On the Beach* "aims at something big and emerges as something tremendous." Peck, donning a military uniform for the second picture in a row, brought his usual dignified brand of heroism to Captain Towers. But Ava Gardner and Fred Astaire in flashier roles were the standouts among the cast.

Somewhat surprisingly, *On the Beach* earned only one Academy Award nomination, for its editor, Frederic Knudtson, who lost. But it scored well with the public, taking in $6.2 million in its initial release to become the eighth-highest-grossing film of 1960. It was the first of Peck's films to rank in the top ten since *Moby Dick* four years earlier.

Although the majority of people who have worked with Gregory Peck over the years describe him as a consummate professional, a gentleman, and a friendly, if somewhat remote, human being, he is a passionate advocate for his ideas about a project. Ask Gottfried Reinhardt, who tangled with him over the editing of *The Great Sinner.* Or Nunnally Johnson, who called him "stubborn." Or William Wyler, who said after the making of *The Big Country,* "I wouldn't direct him again for a million dollars and you can quote me."

Aside from the Wyler-Peck Western, the two projects that put Greg at the greatest odds with his colleagues were biopics, one based on the life of F. Scott Fitzgerald, the other the story of General Douglas MacArthur. About twenty years separated them. The story of the writer came first.

Actually, *Beloved Infidel* was as much about gossip columnist Sheilah Graham as it was about the author of *The Great Gatsby, This Side of Paradise,* and *Tender Is the Night.* Graham was romantically involved with Fitzgerald during the last four years of his life. In fact, he died in her home shortly before Christmas 1940.

To portray Graham, independent producer Jerry Wald chose British actress Deborah Kerr, the popular star of *From Here to Eternity, The King and I, Tea and Sympathy,* and *An Affair to Remember.* Kerr had one film left in her contract with 20th Century–Fox, and Wald had a coproduction agreement with the studio. Peck, who still owed Fox three pictures, was impressed, somewhat reluctantly, into playing the writer. He bore no resemblance to Fitzgerald, but relatively few people in 1959 even knew who the author was let alone what he looked like. To direct, Wald went with Greg's favorite, Henry King.

Filming began about two and a half months after *On the Beach* wrapped. But the project's origins dated back to 1956, when Jerry Wald was considering a film of Fitzgerald's unfinished novel about Hollywood, *The Last Tycoon.* Writer John O'Hara suggested that the producer contact Graham on the theory that she might know how Scott would have completed the story had he lived. Until O'Hara mentioned Sheilah's relationship with Fitzgerald, Wald was unaware of any connection between the two of them. Then he met with the gossip columnist and, as he listened to her reminisce about Scott, he became fascinated. He urged her to write a book about the author, promising to produce the film version. At first, she demurred, but Wald persisted, and eventually she consented to do it.

Published by Henry Holt in November 1958, the memoir, cowritten by Gerold Frank, detailed the columnist's life prior to meeting Fitzgerald as well as their stormy years together. Many of those who knew the poised, self-confident Hollywood insider were surprised to learn that she had been born in a London orphanage, worked as a maidservant at sixteen, then became a saleswoman, and later a chorus girl. An article she wrote about stage-door Johnnies led to her career in journalism. In time, she landed a job in New York, eventually becoming a syndicated columnist carried in 150 American papers. It was on Bastille Day—July 14, 1937—that she met Fitzgerald; he was a guest at her engagement party to a British lord (the wedding was never held). At that point in his life, Scott, an alcoholic burdened by debts due to the institutionalization of his wife, Zelda, was trying, not very successfully, to earn a living as a Hollywood screenwriter. He not only became Sheilah's lover, but also her teacher, introducing her to literature, music, and other cultural achievements that her orphanage education had overlooked.

Alfred Hayes incorporated much of Graham's background into his screenplay, completed in April 1959. In essence, he created a Cinderella story, chronicling the columnist's rise from rags to riches thanks, in part, to the love and support of a once-famous novelist. Peck wasn't at all happy with this concept, which relegated Fitzgerald to a secondary character.

Shortly thereafter, Robert Alan Arthur replaced Hayes, but he, too, failed to solve the script's problems. So Wald brought in Sy Bartlett for another rewrite. Greg's Melville partner dropped the scenes depicting Graham's developmental years, opening with her arrival in New York; in the final cut, Fitzgerald would make his first appearance about fifteen minutes into the story. Otherwise, Sy's version also failed to satisfy; the scenes were plodding, and the characters remained paper-thin. Finally, Wald asked for input from Henry King, who often doctored the screenplays of his films. But even King was unable to breathe life into *Beloved Infidel.*

Peck favored postponing principal photography until the screenplay was satisfactory, but the window of opportunity on Kerr's contract was drawing to a close. She was supposed to be released on September 4 because she was due to begin shooting her next feature, Warner Bros.' *The Sundowners,* shortly thereafter. Since the studio didn't want to lose her as Graham, a start date was set for July 22. Bartlett continued rewriting while the picture was in production.

Making the film was not a happy experience. Tensions always run higher when scenes are being reworked from day to day. Moreover, Kerr was going through a divorce; she received her interlocutory decree the day before she started work on the picture. Given her personal situation, she would have preferred to pass on *Beloved Infidel,* but she was advised by her agent to cooperate rather than face suspension.

Trying to complete the actress' scenes in time for her stop-date exacerbated the difficulties. When Wald agreed to the commitment, the screenplay was about 130 pages long, which allowed for a decent, if not comfortable, shooting schedule. As Bartlett continued to rewrite, however, the script grew to nearly 180 pages. Clearly, Wald would be unable to release Kerr on time. Thereafter, the actress graciously told the producer that she wouldn't hold him to the original target, arranging to postpone her *Sundowners* commitment with the picture's director, Fred Zinnemann.

Deborah was also caught between the forces who wanted *Beloved Infidel* to focus on Fitzgerald—namely Greg—and those who felt it should be about Graham. She understood her costar's motivations but was disappointed that the result left with her with little opportunity to convey the full spectrum of Sheilah's background and personality. Nevertheless, she was a model of cooperation on the set. Wald told Fox executive Lew Schreiber shortly after the picture wrapped, "She has had to put up with a great deal of 'guff,' more than many an actress in her position would do." The producer was referring, at least in part, to the behavior of her costar.

Indeed, Peck was not himself during filming. "I had never seen him going through such an internal combustion about anything," Veronique said shortly thereafter. Aside from the script problems, he felt that the rush caused by Kerr's scheduling conflict was forcing him to give less than his best. On August 7, he protested in writing to King, Wald, and Buddy Adler, informing them, "I must have more careful rehearsal and more takes until I am able to put across the character and story values I see in each scene. With more rehearsing I become less mechanical, more spontaneous. . . . If I can't be allowed to do my best, then I want you to replace me. I will not go on this way, doing half-baked scenes."

He was also displeased by what he considered the film's shoddy production values. On September 17, eight days before the end of principal photography, he wrote Wald again, requesting that four scenes be refilmed before Kerr was released. These included a sequence set in Tijuana, Mexico, which was done on a studio soundstage. Not only was the set tacky in his opinion, it was so small that it severely restricted his and Deborah's movements and, by extension, their spontaneity. He urged that they go to a Hispanic area of Los Angeles, hire some extras to create a crowd, and use a crane for an overview shot. As he put it, "We have had every 'production number' planned for the picture taken away from us. . . . My fear is that . . . the audience doesn't get a chance to breathe, get away from us, and look at something else now and then." The scene wasn't reshot.

Although Peck's inputs and suggestions made life difficult for Wald, King, and Buddy Adler, it must be said that his motives were pure—to make his performance and the film as good as possible. As Henry King later put it, "He knocked himself out from one end of the picture to the other to try to be Fitzgerald." He worked particularly hard on the several scenes in which the writer becomes drunk and abusive. He even prepared for one of the drunk scenes by getting inebriated. It didn't work too well. "He scared Deborah Kerr half to death," recalled Henry King. "You would think he was a drunken demon." Another sequence, which called for an inebriated Scott to assault Sheilah, required two days to film; it left Greg hoarse and Kerr black-and-blue. "I'd rather fight ten men than lay a hand on a lady," Peck said shortly thereafter, but Deborah had encouraged him to play the scene full out.

The picture wrapped on September 25, but the star continued his fight for the best possible product into the postproduction period, peppering Wald with memos in response to the rough cuts that he viewed.

In the end, all of the wrangling and hard work amounted to relatively little. Opening on November 17, 1959—one month before *On the Beach*—*Beloved Infidel* earned a mere $1 million at the box office, making it one of the least successful features of Peck's career. In his critique, *Saturday Review*'s Arthur Knight offered a cogent diagnosis of the picture's problems: "Gregory Peck . . . and especially Deborah Kerr . . . move through the piece with superhuman loftiness, groomed and coifed and costumed to storybook perfection. Despite the names, despite the fact that Sy Bartlett's script hews fairly close to the line of Miss Graham's disarmingly frank autobiography, these people have been drained of life. They speak the language of romantic novels; they live in a Technicolored dream world. The fault, I should say, is only partially in the performances. . . . [I]t is because that is the way the roles were conceived in the writing and direction."

Even Henry King wouldn't have disagreed. "After I got it finished," he said years later, "it sort of left me a little flat." Although he and Peck continued to like and respect one another, the biopic would mark the last of their collaborations.

Meanwhile, Greg was so disheartened by the experience of making *Beloved Infidel* that on the last day of filming, he hurried home and without a word dropped two airplane tickets on Veronique's dinner plate. They were for Hawaii, and the plane was leaving that very night! "With barely time to throw a few things together," Mrs. Peck recalled, "we were off to the airport and away on three of the most exhilarating weeks of our lives."

When Peck left Fox for Hawaii, he kept his belongings in his studio dressing room. He expected to return shortly thereafter to begin preproduction work—costume fittings, makeup tests, and so forth—on his next picture, *The Billionaire,* a comedy about a wealthy man who pretends to be an entertainer in order to woo a showgirl. As Fox had only one contractual claim on Peck's services per year, and it had used that for *Beloved Infidel,* he was doing *The Billionaire* under a separate—and more favorable—agreement that called for him to receive a $250,000 guarantee against a percentage of the gross.

Peck liked the project's earnings potential as well as the chance to do another comedy. He also wanted to work with Milton Berle, Bing Crosby, and Gene Kelly, who, as themselves, would instruct the billionaire in the arts of comedy, song, and dance, respectively. Nevertheless, Greg withdrew from the project shortly before the start of principal photography. The official reason was that a postponement in its start date made it impossible for him to complete his scenes in time to be in Greece for the beginning of his next project, *The Guns of Navarone.* That wasn't the real reason, however.

What happened was that Fox assigned the role of the billionaire's love interest to Marilyn Monroe, the blond bombshell who had replaced Susan Hayward as the hottest actress on the lot. Unhappy with the size of her part, Monroe insisted upon a rewrite. Peck, who had script approval, agreed to some changes, but he got much more than he bargained for. "My part began to diminish," he recalled. "Marilyn's part kept getting bigger and bigger and the whole thing stopped being funny." When he went to the film's director, George Cukor, to find out what had happened, he learned that Monroe's husband, Arthur Miller, had done the rewrite. "I've always wanted to work with Arthur Miller," Peck told the director, "but he's hardly the man for this piece of fluff."

Not only had Miller reduced the size of Greg's part, he'd transformed the billionaire from a rogue who could buy anything to a stuffed shirt. Greg decided that the best thing to do was part with Monroe and company. French actor Yves Montand took Greg's place, and the film was released as *Let's Make Love* in 1960. Peck's assessment proved correct; it wasn't very funny.

On this disappointing note, the actor's creative output during the 1950s came to an end.

Looking back over the seventeen films he made during the decade, one finds a narrower array of roles than those he assayed in the forties. Mostly professionals and rugged individualists from America's past, they included five military figures, four writers, three sailors, and several Western archetypes. Except for the tragic F. Scott Fitzgerald and *Moby Dick*'s Captain Ahab, the characters shared a decidedly heroic bent. In some cases, such as King David, *The Bravados*' Jim Douglas, and *Roman Holiday*'s Joe Bradley, the men had significant flaws. In other instances, notably Horatio Hornblower, *Night People's* Colonel Steve Van Dyke, and *The Big Country*'s Jim McKay, they were downright admirable. But flawed or not, they played to Peck's strengths, allowing him to convey dignified, intelligent, intensely inner-directed people who basically keep their emotions in check. Thanks to such vehicles, his screen persona came into sharp relief in this decade. It was hardly a coincidence that Peck chose most of his own projects in the fifties; that hadn't been the case when he was under contract to others.

Viewed another way, Peck's fifties oeuvre included mostly middle-of-the-road commercial fare, among them three Westerns, two comedies, and a number of period costume dramas. Overall there were fewer blockbusters commercially or critically. Out of the releases between 1951 and 1960, only four were top ten box-office hits and only one, *Roman Holiday,* earned an Oscar nomination for Best Picture. By contrast, four of the thirteen Gregory Peck pictures released between 1944 and 1950 landed in the top ten, and four were Academy Award nominees. Peck personally earned four nominations for Best Actor during this partial decade. He was overlooked entirely during the fifties.

These statistics shouldn't be taken to mean that his popularity was in decline. On the contrary, he was at least as well regarded by the public in 1959 as he was in 1949. As one Los Angeles theater manager observed in 1956, "Peck's name on our marquee is the best box-office insurance we can have." Moreover, Peck wasn't necessarily looking to be the biggest draw in town. "I'd rather do a small picture," he told Hedda Hopper in 1954, "with a well written interesting up to date part and get satisfaction out of it, even if it doesn't gross enough to make me number 1 box office boy of the month. That only means that your picture grossed more than any others—it has nothing to do with you really."

As the new decade dawned, he was approaching forty-four years old. One had to wonder how long he could count on the kind of romantic leads that were at the core of his popular appeal. To be sure, the gap between his age and the ages of some of his leading ladies was starting to widen—Audrey Hepburn, Carroll Baker, and Joan Collins were thirteen, fifteen, and seventeen years younger than he, respectively.

But there was no immediate worry. At the outset of the 1960s, he still looked fabulous. Moreover, he was about to embark on several films that would have more in common, in terms of quality and popularity, with his forties fare than with those of more recent vintage. These would keep him at the top of his profession, perhaps even take him to an even higher plateau. The first of these started filming in March 1960.

Part Four

Citizen Peck

CHAPTER 15

Going Commercial

In 1957, Columbia Pictures scored a smash hit with a high-adventure drama entitled *The Bridge on the River Kwai.* Directed by David Lean, this World War II thriller won seven Oscars, including the awards for Best Picture, Director, and Actor (Alec Guinness).

Eager to duplicate its success, Columbia seized on a 1957 novel, *The Guns of Navarone* by Alistair MacLean, which producer-screenwriter Carl Foreman brought to the studio. A victim of the blacklist, Foreman had scripted such celebrated dramas as *Champion, The Men,* and *High Noon* and he coauthored the *Kwai* screenplay without credit. So confident was production chief Sam Briskin of the project's commercial potential, he gave Foreman a budget that exceeded even *Kwai*'s—$5 million—the most money ever for a Columbia film to that point.

Like its epic predecessor, *The Guns of Navarone* involved the exploits of a small commando squad during World War II. In this case, the unit's mission was to blow up two gigantic, state-of-the-art Nazi weapons blocking traffic through the Aegean Sea, so that a fleet of destroyers could rescue two thousand British soldiers trapped on a nearby island. Thanks to a traitor in their midst, the commandos are dogged by German troops every step of the way.

In keeping with the Anglo-American casting of *The Bridge on the River Kwai,* Foreman wanted to people his commando unit with an international array of stars. In addition to Peck, the team members would be played by David Niven; Greg's *World in His Arms* costar, Anthony Quinn; Stanley Baker; Anthony Quayle; and, for the younger viewers, teenage heartthrob James Darren.

Although Foreman adhered to the basic tenets of MacLean's suspenseful plot, he tinkered in significant ways with the novelist's characters. For starters, he turned the book's two male Greek partisans into females, linking them romantically to the commandos portrayed by Peck and Quinn (Gia Scala and Irene Papas were cast as the partisans). He also turned Niven's explosives expert, Corporal Miller, from a gung-ho Californian into a much more diffident Englishman. MacLean's Andy Stevens, the young son of a British lord who is badly injured early on, was scrapped in favor of a more mature major named Roy Franklin (portrayed by Quayle). Moreover, Franklin became the team's leader, a role performed in the novel by Peck's character, Captain Keith Mallory. Foreman's thinking, which he explained in a letter to Peck on February 23, 1960, was that Mallory would be more interesting if he started out in a nonleadership capacity and was then forced by circumstances to take command. In deference to Peck's casting, the New Zealand mountain climber became an American. Foreman also introduced another layer of tension in his handling of Quinn's character, Andrea. In the novel, the Greek commando and Mallory are best friends. Foreman made them former friends, now enemies bound together solely by the mission. Peck, who consulted regularly with Foreman during the project's preproduction phase, objected to this alteration. He considered the enmity between the commandos "tacked on." Finally, the screenwriter created a strong bond between Quayle's and Niven's characters, Franklin and Miller, which produced further tensions between the latter and Peck's Mallory. Greg jokingly described the complications thus: "David Niven really loves Tony Quayle and Gregory Peck loves Anthony Quinn. Tony Quayle breaks a leg and is sent off to hospital. Tony Quinn falls in love with Irene Papas, and David Niven and Peck catch each other on the rebound and live happily ever after."

To direct his international band, Foreman chose Alexander Mackendrick, a British filmmaker better known for his intelligent comedies and hard-edged dramas than for action-driven fare.* One of his few American films was the 1957 cult favorite *Sweet Smell of Success,* a cynical look at the underbelly of Manhattan's celebrity journalism.

Foreman chose to shoot the thriller on Rhodes, an island in the eastern Aegean about 225 flying miles from Athens. An enthusiastic Greek government provided the production company with tanks, planes, helicopters, ships, technical advisors in the form of generals who had fought in World War II, and more than one hundred soldiers to portray Nazi Alpenkorps troopers.

In anticipation of the start of principal photography, Peck arrived in Athens on March 7, 1960. He was scheduled there for two weeks of preproduction press interviews.

Meanwhile on Rhodes, Mackendrick commenced filming second-unit

*Mackendrick was actually born in Boston to Scottish parents who were visiting the United States at the time.

footage, but after only a couple days' work, the director left the production. Although a serious back ailment was given as the official explanation, he was fired. Foreman told Peck at the time that Mackendrick was suffering from personal emotional problems.

Initially, Foreman considered taking over the picture himself. Peck, who had director approval, wasn't comfortable with that idea. He respected Foreman, but the producer-screenwriter had never directed a film before, and *Navarone* was a big, complicated job. Quinn and Niven, with whom Greg consulted, shared his concern. Peck tactfully communicated his feelings to Foreman, who deferred to the star's wishes.

The producer quickly settled upon three alternative candidates, British directors all: Michael Anderson, Guy Hamilton, and J. Lee Thompson. He arranged for samples of their work to be sent to Athens, so that Peck could draw his own conclusions about their talent. Based on what he saw, Greg opted for Thompson, who was a few years older and somewhat more experienced than the other two. Lee was the producer's first choice as well.

Thompson arrived at the end of the following week, just a few days before he had to take the helm of the picture. When the time came for the cameras to turn on March 21, the forty-six-year-old former actor was obviously, in Peck's words, "frightened to death." Not only was Thompson "a highly strung individual," to quote Greg, he had a fondness for drink. Still he dug in, determined to master the production. That didn't mean that he became conversant with the script, however. According to Anthony Quinn, he seemed to approach each shot on "a whim." Still, his spontaneity helped keep everyone else fresh.

The company spent five months on Rhodes, where some locations were so remote they needed donkeys to transport the equipment and personnel. The base of operations was the Hotel Miramare, a series of detached bungalows with a restaurant, a bar, and a swimming pool. The amenities came in handy, for, as one British journalist told his readers, "Nothing much happens here at night. The food is awful, everything shuts up early, and unlike most Greeks, the islanders tether their daughters and let the goats wander free. So the chief *divertissement* among the stars is playing chess."

Quinn was credited with introducing the game by means of several portable sets that he brought from home. Not only did chess help the stars kill time, it served to lesson the tension among them. Not that there were major personality conflicts, but, before the start of the game playing, Peck, Quinn, and Niven were, in Lee Thompson's words, "all eyeing each other warily and wondering which of them was going to come out ahead." Thereafter, Peck and Niven became good friends.

Hard as the filming was in Rhodes, one of the most difficult scenes was shot at the Shepperton Studios in London, where work commenced in August. This lengthy sequence featured a raging storm that causes the destruction of the commandos' fishing boat. "Here, on an indoor marine set," reported Jan Whitcomb in *Cosmopolitan* magazine, "the actors were buffeted by wind machines, slugged with tons of water from overhead chutes, and battered by the heaving decks of a studio-built boat. Before they were through, Peck sustained a three-inch gash on his forehead; Quinn and Niven twisted their spines; Baker wrenched his neck; and Darren was completely knocked out by a wave, and almost drowned. One of the still photographers suffered three crushed toes; another broke his arm."

As if this weren't punishment enough, the tank wasn't heated, and the water was freezing. "We were in it for many hours," Peck recalled, "and David Niven took deathly sick, he was out for a week at one time with the flu." To keep warm, the actors imbibed brandy. By afternoon, some found themselves barely able to function. "But Greg," Niven asserted, "would match anybody drink for drink, and never so much as stagger or muff a line. Really quite disgusting to see a man able to handle liquor like that."

While in London, Peck rented a home on Burleigh Road in Ascot, about forty-five minutes outside of London. Thus, he and Veronique could catch the races whenever his schedule permitted. Niven recalled that for Ascot's opening day, Greg was fully prepared with the customary outfit, a pearl-gray tailcoat, striped pearl-gray trousers, and a top hat—all of which he had custom-made—plus gloves and a walking stick.

Initially, the picture had been scheduled to wrap by July. Anticipating a vacation thereafter, Greg rented a villa in Cap Ferrat in the South of France. However, the shoot continued throughout the summer, so he was able to visit only on weekends. He had also arranged for his three oldest sons to attend the Olympics in Rome, but an assistant and his mother had to accompany them in his stead. He didn't fault Thompson for the delays. As he put it, they "were not due to anything but the fact that it was a big, big picture with a lot of stuff to be covered."

Finally, after seven months, the picture wrapped. The world premiere came in London on April 27, 1961, followed by the New York opening on June 12. While the thriller lacked *Kwai*'s sharply etched characterizations and thematic overtones, no one denied that it was exciting. Archer Winsten of the *New York Post* wrote "The picture grips you in its vise of daring action and danger with an astonishing power." Winsten's colleague, Paul V. Beckley of the *New York Herald-Tribune*, agreed, calling the film "a textbook example of how to manipulate the elements of suspense."

The Guns of Navarone didn't match the earnings of *The Bridge on the River Kwai,* but it was a great success, grossing $12.5 million to become the biggest hit of 1961. As Peck had a share of the profits, it was his most financially rewarding project to that point. He used some of his earnings to purchase a vacation house in Cap Ferrat, a bit of poetic justice, considering the disruption to his vacation plans during filming.

In addition to its box-office take, *The Guns of Navarone* earned six Oscar nominations, including those for picture, director, and screenplay, but it won only for special effects. The competition was particularly strong in 1961, with the musical *West Side Story* dominating the field.

In April 1967, six years after the picture's world premiere, Carl Foreman announced a sequel, *Force 10 from Navarone,* which would reunite Peck, Niven, Quinn, and J. Lee Thompson with a screen treatment provided by Alistair MacLean. It was supposed to start shooting in the spring of 1969, but the project failed to materialize. When it finally went into production in 1977, Robert Shaw had replaced Peck and Edward Fox took over from Niven. Guy Hamilton, one of the choices to succeed Mackendrick, was the director. The sequel was not a success.

Peck had been unable to attend either the world or the American premiere of *The Guns of Navarone.* At the time, he was hard at work on his next film, the second feature from his own Melville Productions.

This time he and Sy Bartlett opted for more commercial fare than *Pork Chop Hill.* They chose a 1958 paperback thriller called *The Executioners* by John D. MacDonald, best known today as the creator of Florida private eye Travis McGee. Again they engaged James R. Webb to turn a book into a viable screenplay. He fashioned a creepy suspenser in which a clever ex-con, Max Cady, terrorizes an attorney named Sam Bowden and his family as payback for Bowden's eyewitness testimony at the psychopath's trial for sexual assault.

Peck was ideally suited to play the upstanding family man and lawyer, another white-collar professional to go with his myriad writers and military figures. But the cunning ex-con was the flashier role. It was originally offered to Ernest Borgnine. After the Oscar-winning actor declined, it went to Robert Mitchum. The sleepy-eyed star, a year younger than Peck, usually portrayed leading men, but once before, in 1955's *Night of the Hunter,* he had tackled a psychopathic killer, with chilling results.

On the order of "been there, done that," Mitchum initially passed on Cady. He changed his mind based on Peck's willingness to make him a coproducer of the picture (without his having to actually do anything except act). Thus, *Cape Fear,* as the film was ultimately called, became a

Melville-Talbot coproduction. It was released in association with Universal-International, with which Peck and Bartlett had signed a two-picture deal following their departure from United Artists.

Filming began in Savannah, Georgia, on May 2, 1961. The company utilized a variety of sites, including Grove Point Plantation, which served as the exterior of Sam's home.

It is hard to imagine two more contrasting personalities than *Cape Fear*'s costars. Peck took his craft as seriously as anyone in Hollywood, investing countless hours in preparation. Mitchum was as cavalier about acting as one could be. He liked to work fast and go home, earning as much money along the way as possible. He didn't even need to spend time memorizing his lines. Blessed with a photographic memory, he could scan his dialogue just before a scene was shot and be word perfect.

The difference between the stars was manifest in their behavior in Savannah. Each evening, Greg returned to his rented home, spending most of his free time quietly with Veronique. Mitchum stayed in a hotel and was out every night. "We had one assistant director who was sort of assigned to him, to go out drinking with him," recalled assistant director Ray Gosnell Jr., "to keep track of him just so we knew where he was."

The last time Mitchum had been in Savannah, before he became a movie star, he'd been arrested for vagrancy and sentenced to hard labor on a chain gang. He wasn't happy to be back. Peck, by contrast, enjoyed the town's sultry Southern ambiance and its amiable citizenry.

Although the location was pleasant for all but Mitchum, the company cut short its stay for financial reasons; scenes scheduled for filming in Savannah had to be done in Hollywood, to which the cast and crew repaired on May 20. The shoot continued, primarily at Universal, through July 5, well beyond the original wrap date, June 8.

At the studio, the differences between the two stars continued to manifest themselves. According to Ray Gosnell Jr., Greg quite reasonably asked that there be no offstage distractions in his sight lines when he was working. On one occasion, Mitchum stood just to the side of the camera and stripped naked while his costar played his scene. "As far as I know," Gosnell added, "Peck never commented upon it. We did another take, of course."

Mitchum's prank was atypical. When not working together, the stars mostly avoided one another. "I don't remember seeing them have a lot of contact," recalled Polly Bergen, who played Peck's wife in the film.

With Bergen herself, Greg was far more accessible. The twenty-nine-year-old singer-actress hadn't made a film in eight years, having spent the interim performing on the New York stage and in TV, and she was very nervous about her return to the big screen. "Greg spent an enormous amount of time with me," she said. "He was wonderful, and he was very, very supportive. . . . I wouldn't have let anyone know how insecure and frightened I was. But he, I think, knew that instinctively, and was there to set me at ease and to help me and to be nurturing."

Greg also spent considerable time with the film's director, J. Lee Thompson, the Englishman who had just saved *The Guns of Navarone.* Said Ray Gosnell Jr., "I always had the feeling that he was Peck's man, that he was shooting what Peck wanted to have shot." Polly Bergen added, "They appeared to be very close."

The tight collaboration continued during postproduction, when Peck, like most producers, supervised the film's editing. To his credit, he didn't want the picture weighted in his character's favor—which he certainly could have done. On the contrary, he combed through Mitchum's footage, "making sure" that, in his words, Bob's "best moments were on the screen."

Peck did his job well, for when *Cape Fear* opened in New York on April 18, 1962 (six days after the world premiere in several Florida cities), Mitchum drew praise from most quarters. Greg held his own, however. *Saturday Review*'s Arthur Knight lauded Mitchum but found Greg "equally commendable in a role that is, I suspect, far more difficult—that of the man who is acted upon."

In contrast to the performances, the picture drew a surprising amount of vituperation. Paul V. Beckley of the *New York Herald-Tribune* called it a "masochistic exercise," while Brendan Gill told readers of the *New Yorker,* "In case you were thinking of dropping in on *Cape Fear,* don't. It purports to be a thriller, but is really an exercise in sadism, and everyone concerned with this repellent attempt to make a great deal of money out of a clumsy plunge into sexual pathology should be thoroughly ashamed of himself. What on earth is Gregory Peck doing in such a movie?"

These comments suggest something akin to a B-movie exploitation film, but this wasn't the case. *Cape Fear* was well made, arguably on a par with *The Desperate Hours,* William Wyler's 1955 depiction of three escaped convicts terrorizing a middle-class family. Moreover, the thematic question it raised—what does a law-abiding citizen do when society's instruments can't protect him from a diabolical terrorist?—neatly anticipated the angst of many modern suburbanites. Arguably, what made *Cape Fear* unpalatable was Cady's repulsive nature. Watching him maintain the upper hand through most of the picture made critics and moviegoers alike distinctly uncomfortable.

Cape Fear performed terribly at the box office. Grossing somewhere between $1.6 and $1.9 million against a cost of $2.6 million, the picture brought an end to Melville Productions. Even though Peck and Bartlett had one more film commitment from Universal, the partners channeled their energies into separate ventures thereafter.

Times change. What seemed repugnant in 1962 was welcomed by audiences thirty years later. A 1991 remake of *Cape Fear* directed by Martin Scorsese, with Robert De Niro as Cady and Nick Nolte as Sam, was a smash hit, taking in more than $77 million in just 150 days. As the owner of the original property and a featured player in the remake, Peck reaped the benefits of this success.

Greg enjoyed a three-month vacation after *Cape Fear* wrapped, which he mostly spent with his family in the South of France.

"We completely relax down here," the actor said a few years later. "We golf, swim, lie in the sun, have a few friends in—it's all very casual and idyllic. I spend a lot of time gardening, because that's one of my favorite hobbies. Veronique cooks while I garden. We are a great combination. She makes great fish casseroles, marvelous salads and my favorite of favorites, Boston cream pie."

He also liked to stroll around the nearby village, where the locals quietly accepted his presence. That didn't mean, however, that life at Villa Doma Alles Des Brises, as the Peck home was called, was ordinary. Among Greg and Veronique's friends were the Prince and Princess of Monaco. The Peck youngsters, Anthony and Cecilia, even went to the palace to play with Albert and Caroline, the children of Grace and Rainier. One day, Greg recalled, Anthony punched Albert in the nose. Like any parent, he was concerned about his kid's fisticuffs, but the stakes were naturally a bit higher when one of the combatants—and the loser, at that—was of royal blood. Grace, however, alleviated Greg's concern, saying, "Don't be silly! It was the best thing that ever happened to him! It was the first bloody nose he's ever had, and the first time anyone has ever punched him!" Eventually, the boys became friends, even attending Amherst at the same time.

Peck's idyll in Cap Ferrat provided a wonderful restorative, but, for him, the greatest pleasure was work. In September, he returned to the U.S. for his next film, a Western. Indeed, the biggest Western of them all.

If Peck had embarked on *The Guns of Navarone* and *Cape Fear* in the hope of personal financial gain, he agreed to participate in *How the West Was Won* because a portion of its profits were earmarked for St. John's Hospital. Many members of the motion picture industry, including Greg and Veronique, patronized the Santa Monica facility.

St. John's unlikely involvement in the making of a feature film came at the behest of Bing Crosby. The singer-actor had acquired the rights to a series of pictorial essays on the settlement of the western United States that ran in *Life* magazine in 1959. Crosby had been planning on turning the series into a television special to benefit St. John's but agreed to sell his option to MGM, providing the studio honored his commitment to the hospital. Sol Siegel, who had replaced Dore Schary as Metro's studio chief, readily agreed.

Siegel had been looking for just such a property, something spectacular with which to launch a four-picture deal with the Cinerama company. Introduced at the 1939 New York World's Fair as Vitarama and perfected in the early fifties, Cinerama was a wide-screen process that dwarfed even CinemaScope and its competitors. It utilized three cameras, one facing center, one pointing slightly to the left, the other pointing slightly to the right. Likewise, three projectors were required to show the result, a giant image interrupted by thin vertical spaces, reflecting the gaps between what each camera could capture. To give the image a greater sense of depth, the screen was curved at an angle of 165 degrees.

The first five Cinerama features had been travelogues. They were enormously popular, but, by the beginning of the sixties, the novelty was wearing off. MGM's idea was to use the format to tell a story. Hence, Siegel's enthusiasm for the *Life* series.*

He turned the project over to producer Bernard Smith, who in turn engaged one of Peck's favorite writers, James R. Webb, to fashion a screenplay. What Webb devised was an episodic overview of the taming of the West between 1838 and 1889 as witnessed by three generations of a single family, the Prescotts. Breaking up the story into six segments, each introduced by voice-over narration, Webb focused on the eras of the riverboat, the covered wagon, the Civil War, the railroad, the cattle drive, and the gunfighter (eventually, the cattle drive segment was eliminated). As Smith planned to shoot the $15 million epic at a host of locations with a veritable cast of thousands, he chose three directors. John Ford was assigned the segment covering the Civil War, George Marshall the episode depicting the coming of the railroad, and Henry Hathaway the other three (a fourth director, Richard Thorpe, shot some transitional footage without credit).

Once the concept was set, a committee of St. John's boosters, including Louella Parsons, Mrs. James Stewart, Mrs. Clark Gable, and actress Irene Dunne, endeavored to entice the biggest stars in Hollywood to

*Although Sol Siegel had intended *How the West Was Won* to be the first MGM-Cinerama offering, the second of the company's joint projects, *The Wonderful World of the Brothers Grimm*, debuted first. Owing to difficulties between the two companies, the final two films were never made.

appear in the Western—at a weekly salary of $5,000 apiece (less than a third of Peck's usual asking price by this point). They were extremely successful advocates. In addition to Greg, who was corralled by Irene Dunne, the participants included Carroll Baker, Lee J. Cobb, Henry Fonda, Carolyn Jones, Karl Malden, George Peppard, Debbie Reynolds, James Stewart, Eli Wallach, Richard Widmark, and John Wayne, with Spencer Tracy providing the narration. When Peck heard the lineup, he told Dunne that she should ask MGM to increase St. John's profit participation from 5 percent to 10 percent. She took his advice, and the studio complied.

Filming began in May 1961 with the first episode, "The River," which was shot in and around Paducah, Kentucky. It was followed in September by the segment involving Peck, for which the company—helmed by Hathaway—set up shop in Montrose, Colorado. Known as "The Plains," it featured Greg as a tinhorn gambler, Cleve Van Valen, who pursues one of the Prescott girls, saloon singer Lillith (Debbie Reynolds), on a wagon train bound for California in the hope of getting control of a gold mine she's inherited. His rival for her affections is the wagon master, played by Peck's *Macomber Affair* costar, Robert Preston.

A former child actor, Hathaway's directing career dated from 1932 and encompassed a variety of genres, but horse operas were his specialty. Peck found the director "a charming fellow at dinner," but hell-on-wheels at work. Said the actor, "He just yelled and screamed and foamed at the mouth and chewed cigars all day long. The terrible tempered Mr. Hathaway." But, like William Wellman, Raoul Walsh, and Henry King, Hathaway knew how to tell a story. Peck admired the director's "use of the camera, his sense of where people ought to move, where they should stand, his visual sense, his kinetic sense . . . everything just dovetailed."

Hathaway was about all that Greg respected about *How the West Was Won.* He later described the picture as "cornball," adding, "I didn't even like my role particularly." He also hated Cinerama. As he put it, "I found it impossible to act realistically in front of that giant machine with three lenses." Particularly disconcerting was that, for technical reasons, an actor couldn't look directly at someone in a scene with him. In order for the result to look normal, he had to gaze off to the side a bit. Consequently, Greg "couldn't see anything in the eyes [of his fellow actors], or take anything from the facial expression." He likened the result to "talking to a fireplug." A number of his costars, including Carroll Baker, Karl Malden, and Thelma Ritter, felt the same way.

Peck had hoped to complete his assignment in five weeks, but it took a bit more; he was released on November 10. But principal photography continued on the rest of the picture until the beginning of January 1962, encompassing, in total, location filming in nine states. *How the West Was Won* finally opened at New York's Loew's Cinerama (formerly the Capitol) on March 28, 1963, following the world premiere in London the previous November and the Los Angeles premiere in February.

The critics were equally divided between those who found it a compendium of Western clichés and those who enjoyed the all-star cast, the stunning photography, and the story's epic sweep. Most agreed that whatever level of success the film achieved, it was due not to the acting—which was merely serviceable—but to the spectacular scenery and to such action sequences as a flatboat caught in the rapids of a raging river, a buffalo stampede, and a train robbery.

Despite the mixed critical response, the public loved *How the West Was Won.* With domestic box-office earnings of $17 million, the Western became the biggest hit of 1963, besting such other epics as *The Longest Day* and *Lawrence of Arabia,* as well as lavish remakes of *Cleopatra* and *Mutiny on the Bounty.* It also earned eight Oscar nominations, including those for best picture, original screenplay, color cinematography, sound, and editing—and it won three (screenplay, sound, and editing).

Although Peck didn't care for the picture and, in fact, regretted having done it, it gave him another box-office smash—and Best Picture Oscar nominee—to go with *The Guns of Navarone.*

But neither of these narrative-driven epics challenged him as an actor. Nor, for that matter, did the picture in between, *Cape Fear.* His next assignment, however, would not only offer him a wonderful role, but also the film would prove hugely popular. Indeed, it would become the defining performance and the best-remembered picture of his career.

CHAPTER 16

Atticus

In 1961, Peck received a copy of *To Kill a Mockingbird*, a recently published novel by an Alabama woman named Harper Lee. It came to him by way of producer Alan J. Pakula and director Robert Mulligan, associates in an independent production company that was, like Peck's Melville Productions, partnered with Universal. Pakula and Mulligan wanted to know if Greg would be interested in playing the principal adult character in Lee's novel, a widower and attorney by the name of Atticus Finch. The story was narrated by Finch's adult daughter, Scout, who looked back on her Depression-era childhood in the fictional town of Maycomb, Alabama. The narrative encompassed her adventures with her older brother, Jem, and a visiting friend, Dill Harris; Scout and Jem's loving relationship with their widowed father; and their father's controversial defense of a black man, Tom Robinson, for the rape of a white woman.

After reading *To Kill a Mockingbird* straight through in one night, Peck knew that the role of Atticus was very special indeed. As he later put it, "God was smiling on me."

Beyond the opportunity to address American race relations, he identified with the attorney, saying "I felt I could climb into Atticus's shoes without any play-acting, that I could *be* him." Moreover, the story's milieu reminded him of his youth in La Jolla. It wasn't in the South, but it had afforded him the same kind of small-town childhood where kids make their own fun and everyone knows everyone else. He could even relate to growing up in a single-parent household with his grandmother. As soon as he finished reading the book, he phoned Pakula and Mulligan to say, "If you want me, I'd love to do it."

With their star in place, the producer and director set about acquiring the novel. At that point, it had been a *New York Times* best-seller for about six weeks (spurred by its subsequent receipt of the Pulitzer Prize, *To Kill a Mockingbird* would remain on the list for more than a year and a half, garnering sales in excess of 3 million hardcover copies). Major studios were in the bidding as well. But Mulligan and Pakula prevailed. Peck formed a new production company called Brentwood to make the venture a three-way partnership.* Initially, the hope had been to have Harper Lee write the screenplay, but she demurred. A very suitable replacement was found in another Southern writer, playwright-novelist Horton Foote.

Within the obvious scope of translating a work from one medium to another, Foote remained faithful to the novel. Like the book, the action of the film would primarily unfold from the kids' point of view. It would also seek to preserve the gentle quality of Lee's memory piece.

Given Peck's popularity and that of the novel, the producer and director cast the rest of the picture with unknowns, primarily from the New York stage. These included Frank Overton as the local sheriff, Brock Peters as Tom, and Robert Duvall as the Finchs' gentle but reclusive neighbor, Boo Radley. An extensive search was conducted to fill the demanding roles of Scout, Jem, and Dill. Eventually, they went to nine-year-old Mary Badham, thirteen-year-old Phillip Alford, and nine-year-old John Megna. Megna had been on Broadway, in *All the Way Home*, but Badham and Alford, both of Birmingham, Alabama, were novices. They had only acted in school and community theater productions.

As Lee had based her novel on her own youth, Peck visited her hometown of Monroeville, Alabama, before filming began. There, he met the prototype for Atticus, Amasa Lee. "He was a fine old gentleman of eighty-two," Peck said, "and truly sophisticated although he had never traveled farther than a few miles from that small Southern town. I studied him intently."

Pakula and Mulligan also visited Monroeville, hoping to film the picture in its real-life setting. But the town had changed too radically since the 1930s. After considering other locations, with similar results, they decided to shoot entirely at Universal. Based on sketches and photos of Monroeville, art directors Alexander Golitzen and Henry Bumstead spent $225,000 to erect thirty buildings over fifteen acres on the studio's backlot. Some of the structures were wooden turn-of-the-century Los Angeles homes targeted for demolition due to freeway construction. One became the Finch house.

*Unlike Melville Productions, which was created to locate, develop, and produce motion pictures, Brentwood Productions was initiated as a vehicle through which Peck could channel his profit participation in *Mockingbird*. He had input in the film's casting, the development of the screenplay, and other creative decisions, but he would have been involved in those realms anyway, partner or not. After *Mockingbird*, he would use Brentwood to be more proactive in project initiation and development.

As set construction progressed, Mulligan worked closely with his young charges, Mary Badham, Phillip Alford, and John Megna. "It was about four or five weeks of rehearsal," recalled Megna, "and mostly what we did was play together. My recollection is that they observed what we did very closely and then crafted the scenes around the chemistry." Eventually, Mulligan brought a camera into the rehearsals, stationing it far away from the kids and then moving it closer and closer until it was right on top of them. By then, they took it for granted.

Principal photography began on February 12, 1962, three months after Peck finished *How the West Was Won.* Harper Lee was on hand to watch as the cameras rolled. The first setup was simple. Peck as Atticus is walking home from a day's work and is greeted en route by his exuberant kids. "While we were walking along," Greg recalled, "and playing the scene I caught a glimpse of Harper across the street standing there watching and, even though it was the middle of the scene, it registered on me there were tears on her cheeks." When the take ended, Peck walked over to the novelist, thinking to himself, "Oh, we just killed her, we just got to her something terrific." Instead of praising his performance, however, she said, "Oh, Gregory, you've got a little pot belly just like my daddy!"

Mulligan's preproduction work with his young actors paid off. "Acting with Mary and Phil is like living the part," said Peck. "They believe in their portrayals and they don't pretend. They play themselves no matter what the dramatic situation. It is the most refreshing experience I have had in a long time." The pleasure was mutual. Years later, as an adult, Mary Badham called Peck "every little girl's dream of a father, kind, considerate, patient, a total delight to work with." To which Mulligan added, "Gregory Peck brought the kids into him. Within several days, I would see Mary Badham go over and crawl up and sit in his lap. There was no plan for this to happen. Greg just behaved like the decent man that he is, and both the children sensed that."

There were occasional problems, however. Alford liked to tease Badham, and Megna followed his lead. Today, Phillip attributes his behavior to the difference in their ages; he was a teenager, Mary was only nine. Moreover, Badham had the habit of silently mouthing the lines of her costars, including Peck's. "Mary . . . never could get used to what, I suppose, is my slow and deliberate way of speaking," the actor said. "In our scenes together her mind often raced ahead and her lips would silently form my words ahead of me."

Although more restrained in their reaction, others also noticed the star's considered delivery. Assistant director Terry Morse remembered the scene in which a judge asked Atticus to represent Tom Robinson. "I think it took Peck fifteen to twenty seconds to answer," said Morse. "He just sat there and pondered and pondered. . . . Everybody on the crew was wondering, 'Was he ever going to answer?'"

Peck's deliberate pacing wasn't restricted to *Mockingbird.* While never exactly speedy, he'd been injecting a slower, more thoughtful—and arguably more stylized—process of reaction and delivery into his performances for some time; it can be seen in such diverse roles as Jim McKay in *The Big Country,* Keith Mallory in *The Guns of Navarone,* and Sam Bowden in *Cape Fear.*

The Robinson trial, which serves as the centerpiece of *To Kill a Mockingbird,* took about two weeks to shoot. For Greg, questioning Atticus' client on the stand proved particularly difficult. As the scene played out, Brock Peters as Tom started to cry, as did the African-American extras. It caused Peck to choke up as well. "That was one of my toughest moments as an actor," he recalled, "fighting back the tears."

The sequence climaxes with Atticus' closing argument. Actors relish the opportunity to perform a passionate speech, and Peck was no exception. "It's like getting back on the stage," he said years later. "I'd rehearsed a lot at home. Would you believe two or three hundred times? Sure. I was ready and everybody was ready and we just started rolling. I don't know how many times we did it from different angles and points of view, but I enjoyed it."

By the time the courtroom scene was in the can, many members of the *Mockingbird* company believed they had witnessed an Oscar-winning performance.

The last scene to be shot was that in which Atticus spends the night before the trial outside the jail guarding Tom from a would-be lynch mob. As Peck later admitted, he didn't really know what his character should be feeling in that sequence, so he simply fell back on technique. "I know, if nobody else does," he said, "that I played that scene without understanding it and I can see the flaws in the acting. Once you understand a part, then everything falls together without any effort—voice, expression, gestures. When you don't understand it, you bluff through."

Mary Badham, whose long speech in the scene defuses the anger of the mob, didn't help matters. Not wanting filming to end, she kept muffing her lines, thereby delaying the inevitable until, finally, her mother told her, "Look, enough is enough. Let's get this done and get it over with. You're a professional now."

Principal photography ended on May 3, eight days behind schedule. Peck was pleased with the way the shoot had gone. "It felt good while we made it," he recalled. "It seemed to just fall into place without stress or strain." His confidence ebbed, however, when he viewed a rough cut. In a lengthy memo to his agent George Chasin and Universal executive Mel Tucker dated June 18, 1962, he cited forty-four points of concern, the essence of which suggested that, in the effort to preserve the kids' point of view throughout the film, there was too much footage of Scout, Jem, and Dill, and not enough of Atticus. At one point he wrote, "Atticus has no chance to emerge as courageous or strong. Cutting generally seems completely antiheroic where Atticus is concerned, to the point where he is made to be wishy-washy. Don't understand this approach."

Thereafter, Robert Mulligan and the film's editor, Aaron Stell, undertook another cut, which left Peck feeling better, but he wasn't completely satisfied. On July 6, he wrote Tucker, "I believe we have a good character in Atticus, with some humor and warmth in the early stages, and some good emotion and conflict in the trial and later on. . . . In my opinion, the picture will begin to look better as Atticus' story line emerges, and the children's scenes are cut down to proportion."

Once more, Peck's criticisms were given due consideration by Alan Pakula and Robert Mulligan and did nothing to tarnish his relationship with them. In fact, Peck considered Mulligan one of the best directors with whom he'd worked and he wanted to do another picture with the duo.

In order to qualify for Academy Award consideration, *To Kill a Mockingbird* opened at a few theaters in Los Angeles on Christmas Day 1962. The official premiere came at New York's Radio City Music Hall on February 14, 1963—Valentine's Day—about six weeks before the Manhattan opening of *How the West Was Won.* A few critics, including the *New York Times'* Bosley Crowther and a *Newsweek* critic, argued that the picture was at its most appealing when focusing on the children and that the trial sequence dragged the story down, but on the whole, the reviews were quite enthusiastic. *Variety* called it "a major film achievement, a significant, captivating and memorable picture that ranks with the best of recent years."

There was also universal acclaim for Peck's performance. Leo Mishkin of the New York *Morning Telegraph* spoke for most of his colleagues in writing, "As Atticus, Mr. Peck . . . creates a remarkable figure of innate strength and nobility, one far removed from some of his more recent swashbuckling screen appearances."

It wasn't that the Southern lawyer took Greg into fresh territory. Aside from the lack of any romantic involvement and Peck's use of round, black spectacles, which both softened and deglamorized his features, Atticus was, in fact, a synthesis of much that he'd explored before—the wise, understanding father of *The Yearling;* the staunch opponent of prejudice in *Gentleman's Agreement;* the ordinary citizen wanting to make a positive contribution in *The Man in the Gray Flannel Suit;* the skilled litigator in *The Paradine Case* and *Cape Fear;* and the soft-spoken man of peace in *The Big Country.* But all of these elements combined in *Mockingbird* to create something more genuine, more human, more sympathetic than anything that he'd done before, the best distillation of the persona Gregory Peck had been developing for nearly twenty years. As Harper Lee put it, "In that film, the man and the part met."

Over the years, *To Kill a Mockingbird* has remained the star's favorite of his films. He has also stayed close to many of those involved in its making, including Harper Lee, Mary Badham, Philip Alford, and Brock Peters. Moreover, it is the picture with which he is most closely associated. The enduring popularity of the novel is, of course, a contributing factor. Students read the book for school and then watch the film. As Peck put it, "The movie is my little pipeline to an entirely other generation."

To Kill a Mockingbird performed extremely well in its initial release, coming in eighth place for the year with earnings of $7.5 million. This was no small feat for an intimate black-and-white drama, considering the number of large-scale, high-budget wide-screen epics competing for audience attention in 1963, not the least of which was Peck's own *How the West Was Won.* The picture also earned eight Academy Award nominations, including those for best picture, director, supporting actress (Mary Badham), screenplay (adaptation), black-and-white cinematography, musical score, and black-and-white art decoration–set decoration. Peck was nominated as well, for the first time in thirteen years. Having been so recognized on four previous occasions without a single win, he didn't rate his chances very highly this time.

After *To Kill a Mockingbird* wrapped at the beginning of May, Peck took the rest of 1962 off. The year brought several significant developments. First, in July, he found himself without professional representation. Having purchased Universal Studios, MCA could no longer operate as a talent agency, which would have been a conflict of interest. At the end of the year, Greg signed with the William Morris Agency. He and MCA hardly parted company, however; three out of his next four films would be Universal productions.

Another professional divorce came at the end of the year. Peck hadn't made a film at Fox since *Beloved Infidel* wrapped more than three years earlier. Since then, the studio had fallen on hard times due to one mammoth production, *Cleopatra.* The epic starring Elizabeth Taylor became so expensive it nearly bankrupted the studio. In an effort to save the company, Darryl F. Zanuck took over as president earlier in the year. He shut down production entirely while he reorganized the studio and evaluated the properties in the pipeline, a process that took nine months. By then, Peck wanted out, even though he was contracted to Fox for two more pictures.

What allowed him to abrogate the agreement was a stipulation in the federal labor code—Section 2855—which declared that personal service contracts couldn't extend beyond a seven-year limit. He had signed the contract with Fox in 1953, but it didn't take effect until the beginning of 1955. Thus, the seven years were up in 1962. Zanuck acknowledged that Greg had a legal right to end his relationship with the studio but urged him not to do so, reminding him of the role that their first venture, *The Keys of the Kingdom,* had played in his career.

Zanuck had a good reason to want to hold on to Peck, for, on November 10, 1962, the Theatre Owners of America had named him the most popular actor of the year, indicating that his films had been more profitable financially than those of any other star.

Peck, however, was not swayed by Zanuck's appeal. By 1962, the seven-year studio contract was essentially a thing of the past. Actors in demand, like Greg, could make more money per project with more control over their creative choices by coproducing pictures through their own independent companies or by freelancing on a combined salary-profit participation basis. Peck was doing both.

Although Greg's career was in high gear in 1962, the passing of his father on August 25 marred his elation.

While Doc had initially opposed his son's chosen field of endeavor, he was proud of what Greg had accomplished, and the two remained close over the years. Even as a white-haired, elderly man, Peck Sr. retained a lively sense of humor. Popping into stores and gas stations, he'd present his credit card to pay for his purchase, relishing the moment when the salesperson would look down and catch the name on the card. "You're Gregory Peck?" the astonished clerk would usually ask, eyeing the senior citizen with suspicion. "Ah, yes," Doc would reply, his voice still carrying a hint of an Irish brogue, "but I've not been at all well lately." Greg asserted with a chuckle, "He must have done that a hundred times. Never got tired of it."

Doc was seventy-six when he was felled by a heart attack at his home in San Diego. He had been suffering from cardiac trouble for a number of years.

Greg resumed work on February 18, 1963, four days after the New York premiere of *To Kill a Mockingbird.* He was once again in military uniform. But *Captain Newman, M.D.,* set in a 1944 southwestern Air Corps mental ward, was different from his previous service-related fare.

Greg played the head of the ward, Josiah Newman, an amiable psychotherapist willing to bend the hospital's rules when it comes to his duties as an administrator but totally dedicated to his troubled patients. Like the 1961 Leo Rosten novel on which it was based, the screenplay featured dollops of zany humor. These were borne primarily by a Sergeant Bilko–like orderly named Jackson Laibowitz and his hapless foil, orderly Pepi Gavoni.

But the film also had a serious side, in its depiction of Newman's treatment of three seriously ill patients coping with the horrors of combat. Sandwiched between the laughs and the pathos was a gentle romance between Newman and Lieutenant Francie Corum, a caring nurse whom he steals from another ward.

Having discovered the book initially, Peck took *Captain Newman* to Universal, which produced the film in association with his Brentwood Productions. Unlike most of its competitors, the studio continued to maintain a large roster of contract players, two of whom were assigned to principal roles in *Captain Newman*—Angie Dickinson, fifteen years Peck's junior, as Francie, and Tony Curtis as Laibowitz. Curtis, who customarily played dashing leading men, had demonstrated a deft comic touch in *Some Like It Hot* and *Operation Petticoat.* Rounding out the cast as Newman's three principal patients were Eddie Albert, singer Bobby Darin, and Robert Duvall in his follow-up to *To Kill a Mockingbird.* To direct, Universal turned to David Miller. Miller worked in a variety of genres, as evidenced by his three prior productions for the studio: *Midnight Lace,* a thriller starring Doris Day; *Back Street,* a sudsy drama based on a Fannie Hurst novel; and *Lonely Are the Brave,* a Western featuring Kirk Douglas.

As usual, Peck prepared carefully. He read numerous articles and journals pertaining to mental health, conferred with several psychiatrists, and visited the wards of a nearby mental institution. He also utilized the film's technical advisors, including a Beverly Hills shrink named Barnie Greensom, whose wartime experiences had inspired Rosten's novel. Poring over his script with customary thoroughness, he made frequent comments, cautioning himself not to be "sharp" and not to "rush." He also reminded himself to "relax," and to show concern for Newman's patients but not play a saint. "Find the spots for a bit of anger and variety," he noted.

On April 1, after filming at Universal for about six weeks, the company moved to Arizona. There, the U.S. Army Hospital at Fort Huachuca stood in for the fictional Camp Colfax. The fort, established in 1877 to protect white settlers against Apache Indians, extended over 74,000 acres of barren desert.

That spring, Peck had a horse, Owen's Sedge, in the Grand National in England. The race was held just as the *Newman* company's stay in Arizona was drawing to a close. Two days thereafter came the Oscar ceremonies. Juggling his work, the sporting event, and the awards gala required precision timing, but Peck was determined to do all three.

First came the race. Arriving in London at around one o'clock in the morning, Greg and Veronique had sufficient time to attend the ball customarily held the night before. After about two hours' sleep, they were up for the traditional walk around the racecourse. The day was rainy and misty, and Owen's Sedge finished a disappointing seventh in a field of forty-three, but the Pecks enjoyed themselves nonetheless. As the sun set, they flew to Tucson and from there, took a helicopter to Fort Huachuca—thus enabling Greg to check in for the final day of location work.

The next day, Monday, April 8, the *Newman* cast and crew were back in Los Angeles, just in time for the Oscar telecast that evening from the Santa Monica Civic Auditorium.

Earlier in the day, Greg had received a gift from Harper Lee, her father's gold watch and chain, Amasa Lee having died while *Mockingbird* was in production. Greg carried the watch with him to the ceremony, along with a rabbit's foot given him by his daughter, Cecilia. Even with these good-luck talismans, he didn't expect to win the statuette. His competition was formidable—Burt Lancaster as a real-life convict avian expert in *Bird Man of Alcatraz;* Jack Lemmon as an alcoholic in *The Days of Wine and Roses;* Marcello Mastroianni as a scheming unfaithful husband in *Divorce—Italian Style;* and Irish newcomer Peter O'Toole as the World War I hero, *Lawrence of Arabia.* Peck was betting on either Lemmon or O'Toole. As the evening progressed and *Lawrence of Arabia* garnered a number of wins, including those for editing, color cinematography, and direction, it looked as though O'Toole might indeed be swept along in the groundswell.

Then came the big moment when Sophia Loren, the previous year's Best Actress, announced the names of the Best Actor nominees in alphabetical order. A hush fell over the house as she looked at the audience and announced the name of the winner—Gregory Peck!

"I wasn't nervous until I heard my name," Greg told the Associated Press' Bob Thomas the next day. "Then I fell to pieces. I don't know how I got on the stage." He hadn't prepared any remarks, but on his way up the aisle, he told himself not to "say anything mushy or foolish." Clutching Amasa's watch, he thanked, among others, the press for their reviews of the picture, and got off quickly. On their way toward the wings, Sophia Loren asked him, "Now when are we going to do a movie together?"

Earning the ultimate recognition from one's peers is bound to affect any actor, and Peck was no exception. As he put it a few years later, "Having won it makes you feel at home with yourself." He knew that it wouldn't change his career in fundamental ways; his asking price was already on a par with that of the industry's other major stars, and he would continue to receive the same spectrum of material, good and bad, that he'd received before. But the award was kind of a demarcation, representing membership in an exclusive club, or, in his words, "a landmark—you know it's going to be in your obituary."

The day after the ceremony, he was back on the set of *Captain Newman,* even though he'd partied until 4 A.M. A month later, on May 7, the picture wrapped. He had enjoyed the shoot, "particularly, he said later, "for its comic aspects, the scenes with Tony Curtis, and some of the wild comedy with the patients." He also liked working with Angie Dickinson.

The critics were somewhat less enthusiastic upon the picture's debut on February 20, 1964. Several argued that the mix of comedy and drama prevented the film from operating successfully in either genre. Some also found the depiction of psychiatry rather superficial. *Cue,* on the other hand, called the film "a continually interesting, frequently absorbing, and often very funny comedy" in which the "mixture of fun, frenzy and solid drama is neatly balanced."

Peck's performance drew adjectives like "restrained and intelligent," but he was better than that. He brought an unusually relaxed quality to the psychologist, often getting the best of Tony Curtis in their running banter while, at the same time, conveying confidence and maturity with Newman's patients. Not only did he handle the humor nicely, he was effective in the heavier moments, as in his controlled but heartbroken reaction to the combat death of a former patient.

Caught in the large shadow cast by *To Kill a Mockingbird, Captain Newman, M.D.* is often overlooked in Peck's oeuvre—although it managed to place a respectable twenty-first among the year's box-office champs. Still, it is a pleasant comedy-drama with one of the actor's most well-rounded performances, certainly his best attempt at humor.

In the sixties, Peck was asked if he ever got tired of playing the good guy. "Not exactly," he replied. "I know that I'm usually the solid dependable one who carries the plot along while the other actors dash in and out with their big scenes. But there seems to be money and billing in what I do and I'm not yearning to play a crook or stab somebody in the back or punch an old lady in the nose. Also, I don't think I could stay interested for a couple of months in a character of mean motivation. I would avoid such a fellow in my private life, and I don't like to find myself playing one."

But a character of "mean motivation" is precisely what Peck agreed to play in his next film, *Behold a Pale Horse.* The role was that of a cold, autocratic Spanish Civil Guard officer, Captain Vinolas. This glorified policeman is determined to capture Manuel Artiguez, a onetime hero of the anti-Fascist forces during the Spanish Civil War, now retired to a mountain village across the border in France. Set in 1959, J. P. Miller's screenplay was loosely based on the novel *Killing a Mouse on Sunday* by Emeric Pressburger, which, in turn, was based on the exploits of a real-life Civil War revolutionary named Zapater.*

Peck had several reasons for accepting this unusual assignment. First, his costars would be Anthony Quinn as the revolutionary, and the hot Egyptian costar of *Lawrence of Arabia,* Omar Sharif, as an idealistic priest. Second, he wanted to work with the film's director, Fred Zinnemann, one of the leading filmmakers of the postwar period and winner of two Academy Awards—for *High Noon* and *From Here to Eternity.* Finally, Greg would receive a salary of $400,000 and split 60 percent of the profits with Zinnemann. The film would be coproduced by their companies, Brentwood Productions and Highland Productions, in association with Columbia Pictures.

Then, before filming began, something odd happened: the casting changed. Peck may have reconsidered the implications of playing a villain or, as J. P. Miller would have it, Zinnemann had an "epiphany." In any event, the director decided to switch the hunter and the hunted so that Peck became the revolutionary and Quinn the policeman. Miller hated the idea. He saw Vinolas as "very self-contained, very icy and controlled" and Artiguez as "a passionate, emotional, violent man who would scare the living hell out of you." In his opinion, Peck lacked the emotionality for Artiguez. In point of fact, Greg wasn't really right for the cop either. Who in 1964 wanted to see Gregory Peck as a Spanish Inspector Javert?

In any event, Peck was satisfied with the reversal. "I've got a real juicy character here," he told *Seventeen* magazine. "They're graying down my hair, adding lines to my face, putting circles under my eyes. I don't have to worry about staying slim, so I can eat all the French food I want to."

*Pressberger, himself a highly regarded screenwriter, producer, and director of British films (notably those created in partnership with Michael Powell), initially adapted his own novel. When J. P. Miller, best known as the author of *The Days of Wine and Roses,* was hired for a rewrite, Pressberger withdrew from the project, and only Miller is credited for the *Behold a Pale Horse* screenplay.

His character was also a smoker. Anticipating today's social service announcements on TV, he made a point of telling the press. "Except for film roles, I never smoke. . . . I quit smoking years ago. One of my boys had the habit of chewing his fingernails. We made a pact that if I would quit smoking he would quit biting his nails."

Zinnemann had hoped to shoot the picture in Spain, but the Franco government vehemently opposed the project. Not only did it refuse to grant the necessary work permits, it also placed a ban on all of Columbia's pictures and froze the studio's Spanish assets. Left with little choice, Zinnemann set up shop across the border in Basque France.

With principal photography scheduled to begin in the town of Pau (pronounced "Po") on June 13, 1963—about five weeks after *Captain Newman, M.D.* wrapped—Peck stopped at the Cannes Film Festival in May for a screening of *To Kill a Mockingbird.* The following day, he held a press conference at which several French reporters questioned him about American race relations. One asked rather baldly, "Do you like Negroes as you did in the film?" The actor thought for a moment and then said, "For one reason or another I have never felt intolerance. I judge Negroes on personality, intelligence and quality as I would anyone else. I'm thankful that I was born in an area where this type of prejudice doesn't exist." After the press conference, screenwriter Allen Rivkin, head of the American delegation to the festival, said, "I was proud of Peck. This was the first time an American performer has been questioned by the European press on the U.S. race question that has been pointed up recently by Birmingham."*

Budgeted at a modest $3.9 million, *Behold a Pale Horse* was shot in black-and-white on a relatively brisk seventy-six-day schedule, which Zinnemann exceeded by about thirty days. With Pau and Biarritz as their bases, the *Pale Horse* cast and crew worked in a variety of locales, including several picturesque towns at the foot of the Pyrenees, in the mountain area around Col d'Aubisque, and in Lourdes, where they became the first motion picture company to photograph the religious center. In mid-July, the cast and crew moved to Studio St. Maurice outside of Paris for the film's interiors. Because Anthony Quinn had to start work on another picture in early September, the schedule was adjusted to complete his scenes first.

"It was a marvelous experience," Peck said of the making of *Behold a Pale Horse.* He found his role a challenge, and he loved working with

*In 1963, demonstrations by African-Americans in Birmingham, Alabama, resulted in rioting and severe police reprisals as well as the arrest of civil rights activist Martin Luther King Jr., requiring then-President John F. Kennedy to send in 3,000 troops to restore order.

Zinnemann. He considered the director a master technician whose penchant for "planning and precision" exceeded even that of Hitchcock.

When Columbia previewed the picture in February 1964, it became apparent that American moviegoers lacked a clear understanding of the dynamics of the Spanish Civil War. To help them place the story in its historical context, Zinnemann asked J. P. Miller to write a short prologue explaining the issues at the root of the conflict. Images from a French documentary, *To Die in Madrid,* were blended with Miller's words, and a brief new scene was shot, showing the refusal of Peck's Artiguez to lay down his arms in defeat.

With this adjustment, *Behold a Pale Horse* debuted at the Sutton and Victoria theaters in New York on August 13, 1964. Columbia opened the picture with considerable fanfare and a generous publicity budget, but the film took in a mere $900,000 between its opening day and the end of December.

If moviegoers lacked interest in the drama with the strange title—drawn from chapter 6, verse 8 of the Book of Revelation—the critics were disappointed by it. Although *Newsweek* called it a "handsome, impressive picture," some argued that the adversaries played by Peck and Quinn should have met in a face-to-face showdown. Others felt the filmmakers failed to take a sufficiently strong stand on the politics and personalities behind the drama, an opinion Peck shared. Finally, some believed—like J. P. Miller—that the casting was off. Richard Schickel noted in *Life* magazine, "What is needed is the internal stimulus of a powerful performance from Artiguez. The role cries out for the crude energy of an animal caged by circumstances he cannot understand. What we have instead is gentle, attractive, intelligent Gregory Peck, an actor who sometimes smolders but is quite incapable of bursting into angry flame."

Naturally, Peck was disappointed by the failure of *Behold a Pale Horse*—if for no other reason than his profit participation in the outcome. But he looked at the experience in a positive light, telling reporter Leonard Harris, "I think I managed to change my 'American boy' image—you know, I'm usually the commander of an American sub—without tricks or gimmicks like an accent or external mannerisms. I can do those tricks as well as the next man, but I wanted to do the character from the inside."

CHAPTER 17

Playing a Public Role

Behold a Pale Horse wrapped on October 11, 1963. Having starred in four pictures in little more than two years, Peck took a break. "I felt I needed a good rest," he explained. "I also felt I wanted to spend more time at home enjoying my family. So that's what I did."

But he was hardly idle during this interval. For one thing, he narrated two documentaries for the United States Information Agency (USIA). Then under the purview of journalist Edward R. Murrow, the federal agency produced pro-American films, radio programs, and other material for dissemination abroad. The larger and more significant of the documentaries was an eighty-five-minute portrait of President John F. Kennedy, who was assassinated about six weeks after *Behold a Pale Horse* wrapped. Ironically, Greg and other members of the motion picture community had been scheduled to lunch with the president in Washington, D.C., on December 10.

According to George Stevens Jr., then chief of the USIA's motion picture section, Murrow proposed a short ten-minute portrait of the new president, Lyndon B. Johnson, in order to win Johnson's support for the film on JFK—which at $100,000 would be the most expensive in the agency's history and its first feature-length project. Peck also narrated this short film, entitled *The President.* The result so pleased LBJ it marked the start of a friendship between Greg and the chief executive. One immediate consequence of their relationship was the actor's invitation to the White House on September 3, 1964, to watch Johnson sign the National Arts and Cultural Development Act, a major piece of legislation that established for the first time in U.S. history direct federal financial support for extant nonprofit arts and cultural institutions.

Two months later, on November 16, the Kennedy film, called *John F. Kennedy: Years of Lightning, Day of Drums,* was unveiled in an auditorium in the Department of State before an invited audience of diplomats and government officials. Screenings were held that same evening in Rome, Beirut, and Mexico City.

By statute, USIA films could not be shown domestically. But so many American citizens petitioned for the right to see *Years of Lightning, Day of Drums* that Congress waived the regulation, and the feature was commercially released in the spring of 1966—with all the profits benefiting Washington, D.C.'s newly established Kennedy Center for the Performing Arts. The documentary, directed by George Stevens Jr., was extremely well received. Bosley Crowther of the *New York Times* called it a "magnificent motion-picture tribute."

Peck was not paid for his services for the USIA. In the case of the documentary on JFK, he received by way of thanks a 16-mm print of the picture and a three-volume set of Kennedy's public papers issued by the government.

By the time *Years of Lightning* premiered, Peck was immersed in another project. As the 1964 California fund-raising chairman for the American Cancer Society (ACS), he used his celebrity for the first time to actively promote a charitable endeavor. He had taken the job at the urging of two friends, actors William Lundigan and William Gargan, the latter a victim of cancer of the larynx. Greg was no stranger to the disease, having witnessed his grandmother's agony when he was in college and the final, horrific days of Humphrey Bogart in 1957. Moreover, his stepmother, Harriet, was suffering from cancer at the time he took the job (she passed away, at age sixty-seven, on June 26, 1964).

Beyond combating something that had impacted him directly, he wanted to make a positive contribution to the community. As he neared fifty, he had begun to reflect on what he had accomplished and what he still wanted to do and, while he loved acting, he didn't want just to drift from picture to picture.

During his California ACS chairmanship, Greg toured the state, making thirty-five speeches in eighteen communities. Throngs of fans attended his rallies and the organization's volunteers told him how much his participation meant to them. "This is the most rewarding work I've ever done," he told friends. "I don't care how much time it takes—I have to do it."

In addition to his work for the ACS in 1964, he was elected to the Board of Governors of the Academy of Motion Picture Arts and Sciences. This nonprofit organization was founded in 1927 to promote the quality of films, provide a meeting ground for the various disciplines engaged in the motion picture industry, encourage technical innovations, and other related objectives. Of course, the Academy is best known for its annual awards for excellence, commonly known as the Oscars. Directing the ceremonies and the organization's other activities is its Board of Governors, which consists of two members from each of the thirteen areas of film craftsmanship—Actors, Art Directors, Cinematographers, Directors, Executives, Film Editors, Composers, Producers, Public Relations, Short Film and Feature Animation, Sound, Visual Effects, and Writers. Elected by the Actors branch, Peck became the Board's first vice president in 1966.

Despite his busy schedule, Greg fulfilled his primary goal for his hiatus, spending time with his family. That August, he told one reporter that he had enjoyed "wonderful weeks of leisure . . . with Veronique and the children at our home and the ranches." In October, a year after he finished *Behold a Pale Horse,* he went back to work.

Most actors spend their entire careers without ever portraying an amnesiac. Peck explored the terrors of this condition twice.

Like *Spellbound, Mirage* was a thriller. But where the Hitchcock-Selznick film was inner-directed, using traumatic memory loss to portray the psychoanalytic method at work, *Mirage* was outer-directed, underscoring a principal concern of the early sixties—the ever-present threat of nuclear holocaust.

The social message came wrapped in a tantalizing puzzle. The picture opens during a blackout in a Manhattan skyscraper. Peck is David Stillwell, a cost accountant whose office is in the building. Descending twenty-seven floors to the ground, he encounters a beautiful woman named Sheila who seems to know him, but he doesn't recognize her. Outside, he learns that the head of a world-famous foundation for peace has just plummeted to his death from an office window in the building. Later, at his apartment, he encounters a pudgy man who holds a gun on him and tells him he is expected to board a plane to Barbados to meet someone known as the Major. Stillwell eludes the man, but gradually begins to realize that he has no memory of the last two years. As the rest of the film plays out, he tries to piece together the elements of his lost identity. Eventually he comes to realize that he isn't a cost accountant but a physiochemist working on a way to neutralize nuclear radiation and that the man who plummeted from the skyscraper was a close friend. Along the way, he's pursued by several very dangerous men and gets some badly needed assistance from a novice private eye and the mysterious Sheila.

Peter Stone, the author of *Charade* and the Oscar-winning *Father Goose,* crafted the screenplay in a style somewhat reminiscent of a *Twilight Zone* episode. It was based on the novel *Fallen Angel* by Walter Ericson, a pseudonym for Howard Fast.

Produced by Universal (this time without the involvement of Peck's Brentwood Productions), *Mirage* was shot in black-and-white in forty-four days, quite a short schedule for the 1960s, including fifteen days on location in New York.

Cast as Sheila was Diane Baker, who had just signed a nonexclusive, multiple-picture contract with Universal. Nearly twenty-two years younger than Peck, the pert brunette had made her screen debut in *The Diary of Anne Frank* and gone on to noteworthy roles in *The Best of Everything, The Prize,* and Alfred Hitchcock's *Marnie.* She genuinely liked working with her leading man, whom she called Mr. Peck off-camera. Not only did he amuse her with the occasional joke, he was always eager to rehearse, as was she. And, unlike some major stars, he didn't need to dominate every scene. As she put it, "He was a sharing actor. He liked the joint effort of making the scene work."

Edward Dmytryk, one of the Hollywood Ten, was at the helm of the production. Before the blacklist, he'd established himself as a skilled stylist with such dark films as *Murder, My Sweet; Cornered;* and *Crossfire.* After cooperating with HUAC—a move that infuriated many Hollywood liberals—he was allowed to resume his career. His ensuing output included commercially successful, albeit more mundane, fare, including *Raintree County, A Walk on the Wild Side,* and *The Carpetbaggers.* According to Diane Baker, "He was a really bright man and very talented, but he was very calm and quiet during the making of this. It was almost as if he was subdued." Peter Stone went a step further, asserting, "I don't think he was concentrating on the picture. It doesn't have any directorial style."

The lack of panache was Peck's biggest criticism of *Mirage* as well. The actor later explained, "It needed a much more modern kind of photographic approach and less literalness. . . . It was all a trick—a shell game. So I think it should have been treated more as a cinematic ballet of suspense."

Few of the major critics harped on the picture's lack of style when the thriller opened in New York on May 26, 1965. Some of the notices, including those from *Time, Life*'s Richard Schickel, the *New York Times*' A. H. Weiler, and the *New York Post*'s Archer Winsten, were quite strong, while those in *Newsweek, Cue,* and *Variety* were less fulsome. For the film's detractors, a particular sore point was the root cause of Stillwell's amnesia, revealed at the climax.

Greg acquitted himself nicely in a role that made little demand on his well-honed persona. As Kathleen Carroll of the New York *Daily News* put it, "Peck is everybody's affable, straightforward guy and the character he plays, at his understated best, immediately arouses sympathy."

Baker was also well received. However, the strongest notices went to Walter Matthau as the private eye. Although he was not yet a star, the forty-five-year-old character actor was slowly moving from supporting heavies to comic leads; *Mirage* offered another step in that direction.

Despite Peck's popularity, some solid notices, the location photography, and a strong supporting cast that also included George Kennedy and Jack Weston, *Mirage* failed to score at the box office, taking in only $1.5 million in its initial release.

Peck fared much better with his next thriller, which went into production four months after *Mirage* wrapped.

Arabesque was inspired by *Charade,* one of the biggest hits of 1963. Both Universal films were frothy concoctions blending romance, suspense, and sophisticated humor with a major male and female star, a glittering foreign location, and a sumptuous wardrobe for the female lead. In the case of *Charade,* the duo at the top was Cary Grant and Audrey Hepburn; the wardrobe was by Givenchy; and Paris the principal locale. In *Arabesque,* the couturier was Christian Dior; the setting England; and the stars Peck and Sophia Loren, thereby answering the question posed by the actress after presenting Greg his Oscar.* As with *Charade,* *Arabesque*'s director was Stanley Donen, the score was by Henry Mancini, and the screenplay involved Peter Stone.

Arabesque's plot, based on Gordon Cotler's 1961 novel, *The Cipher,* involved the efforts of several individuals, including a well-respected Arab politician (Carl Duering) and a ruthless oil magnate (Alan Badel), to possess an ancient cipher with import for the present-day Middle East. Caught between them is an American scholar, David Pollack, hired to translate the hieroglyph, and an Arabian beauty, Yasmin Azir, the oil magnate's mistress who has an agenda of her own.

The book was rather dull but had a clearly delineated plot and characters. Screenwriters Julian Mitchell and Stanley Price whipped the story into a frothy mélange, but, along the way, they so muddied the plot and the personalities of the principal characters that, with about three weeks left before the start of principal photography, Donen sought help from Peter Stone. "If you will trick up the dialogue as much as you can," the director told the *Charade* screenwriter, "I will trick up the camera as much as I can. I'll photograph everything reflected off of the lamp of a Rolls Royce, you know that sort of thing, and maybe we can make a pic-

*According to Sophia Loren biographer Warren G. Harris, Cary Grant was originally slated to reteam with Donen for *Arabesque.* But after drawing some criticism for playing opposite the much younger Hepburn in *Charade,* he decided it was time to retire from romantic leads and recommended his friend, Gregory Peck, in his stead.

ture that's so heavy on style nobody will care what it's about." Working from the extant script, without reference to Cotler's novel, Stone did the best he could. He was billed after Mitchell and Price under the pseudonym Pierre Marton.

Greg arrived in London on April 11, 1965. Nine days later, new script in hand, he started work at the Pinewood Studios in London. He and Donen had to begin with the scenes that didn't involve Loren, as her previous film, *Lady L,* had gone over schedule. Contractually entitled to a four-week vacation before returning to work, she joined the *Arabesque* company around May 6.

Peck hadn't played opposite such a major international star since the ill-fated *Beloved Infidel,* released six years earlier. His agent, Phil Kellogg of William Morris, felt the pairing would be good for the actor's image as a romantic leading man. But Greg was just happy to be working with Loren, who was at home with both comedy and drama. In fact, according to Kate Cameron of the New York *Daily News,* it was he who suggested the Italian actress for the enigmatic Yasmin.

One of the first scenes they filmed together was among the comic highlights of the picture, the sequence in which Peck's David Pollack hides in Yasmin's shower stall. When her lover arrives, she is forced to join him, blithely chatting with the oil magnate as the water courses down her naked body, much to the professor's discomfort. The two stars barely knew one another at that point, so Greg tried to make light of Loren's state of undress, saying, "Don't be embarrassed. It's all in the game. Strictly professional." To which Sophia replied, giggling, "What makes you think I would be embarrassed?" Greg gulped and answered softly, "Absolutely nothing. Nothing at all."

The stars had a good time together, spending the lulls between setups in a running cutthroat game of gin rummy—which she won handily. Peck later called her "a terrific woman, in many ways my favorite leading lady. In just her femininity and sense of fun and health and sensuality and beauty. She's just a terrific girl to be around for a few months."

For her part, Sophia found Greg amiable and easy to work with, but she realized that he lacked the impeccable comic touch of Cary Grant, with whom she'd costarred in the comedy *Houseboat.* Peck himself knew that he wasn't in the same league as his urbane friend. As he occasionally reminded Donen during filming, "Stanley, there's only one Cary Grant."

If Peck found Dmytryk's style wanting during the making of *Mirage,* he had no complaint with Donen. Having started as a dancer and then a choreographer, *Arabesque*'s director was best known for his lavish color musicals. These included two classics codirected by Gene Kelly, *On the Town* and *Singin' in the Rain,* plus *Royal Wedding, Seven Brides for Seven*

Brothers, and *Funny Face.* "Stanley had a terrific instinct," Peck said, "like a choreographer, which, of course, he had been. But even in an ordinary dramatic sequence he'd use the body to punctuate what was happening—standing, relaxing, everything, it was all choreographed. If you look at the picture, we were always moving, because Stanley just wanted to keep the ball in the air the entire time."

About 75 percent of *Arabesque* was shot on location—at, among other sites, Oxford University, the London Zoo, and one of Peck's favorite hangouts, Ascot. Principal photography continued through September 24, although Greg was released ten days earlier. The picture opened in New York on May 5, 1966, about a year after the debut of *Mirage.*

Both Peter Stone and Stanley Donen did what they had set out to do. The former injected the script with considerable urbane banter while the latter used unusual camera angles and photographed his subjects through windows, fence posts, fishbowls, and off every conceivable object capable of reflection, from sunglasses to TV sets to the lenses of a microscope. He also utilized extreme close-ups of faces, hands, and other body parts. At one point, he created a visual pun, cutting from a tight shot of Loren's mouth to the closing teeth of a bulldozer. In addition, the sets, notably the rooms in Yasmin's townhouse, were spectacular, and Loren's $100,000 Dior wardrobe was stunning. The actress never looked more ravishing.

But neither the physical production nor the wizardry of Stone and Donen could disguise the silliness of the story, which, in addition to its other flaws, invited unfavorable comparisons with Alfred Hitchcock's *North by Northwest* (and, to a lesser extent, *The Man Who Knew Too Much*). The critical reaction accordingly diverged between those who felt that the lack of a coherent plot was the picture's chief flaw and those who found it the principal virtue. Taking the latter position was Richard Schickel, who told readers of *Life* magazine, "This is only commercial film-making at its mindless, marvelous best, a movie to lighten a dreary afternoon or briefly lift life's burdens from your twitching shoulders." By contrast, the *New Yorker* postulated that the thriller "gets lost in the maze of a plot so convoluted that it would outwit the brightest laboratory rat who ever lived. . . . Mr. Donen and his innumerable helpers hadn't the slightest idea of how to end a movie that, all things considered, should never have been begun."

Still, the allure of the chic proved hard to resist, and *Arabesque* ended up with respectable earnings of $5 million. Some critics may have found Peck wanting in the light-comic-touch department, but Greg had one compensation: he had a share of the profits, and *Arabesque,* as he put it, "brought me a lot of money."

* * *

Greg devoted five months to the making of *Arabesque.* He spent the rest of 1965 on the sort of public service endeavors that had engaged him the previous year.

After attending the inauguration of President Johnson in January, he returned to Washington, D.C., on April 9—shortly before starting work on *Arabesque*—to attend the preliminary meetings of the National Council on the Arts. The council was an advisory body appointed by LBJ to oversee the disbursal of the endowment allocated by the National Arts and Cultural Development Act of 1964.

Greg was one of twenty-four council members. His colleagues included many of the leading figures in American arts and letters, among them actress Elizabeth Ashley, composer-conductor Leonard Bernstein, TV journalist David Brinkley, choreographer Agnes de Mille, novelist Ralph Ellison, composer Richard Rodgers, sculptor David Smith, set designer Oliver Smith, violinist Isaac Stern, and film director George Stevens. Their chairman was Broadway producer Roger L. Stevens, then-director of the newly established Kennedy Center. Looking back on both the council and its enabling legislation, George Stevens Jr., the present director of the Kennedy Center (no relation to Roger), said, "It was a landmark. The National Council on the Arts . . . was an amazing confluence of talent, ideas, and opportunity. It was bringing people from different worlds, and those worlds had never been brought together before in this country. It was tremendously invigorating, a golden moment."

The moment may have been golden, but the endowment was not, initially encompassing a mere $4.1 million. It was, in the words of council member Isaac Stern, "a pittance compared to the need." By contrast, the concurrent annual bequests of the Ford Foundation amounted to around $25 million.

After a swearing-in ceremony at the White House, the council got down to the business of deciding how to target its allocation, with a series of meetings over a two-day period. The members quickly realized that they faced two alternatives: one, to offer support to a wide variety of small, struggling institutions; or, two, to bolster the large, well-established bulwarks of American arts and culture. Peck and the majority of the other council members favored buttressing the major established concerns. "In the long run," explained Isaac Stern, "their influence was much greater."

As one of the few actors involved, Greg wanted to ensure that an appropriate portion of the endowment benefited the country's numerous nonprofit theaters. These institutions, loosely amalgamated under the banner of the League of Resident Theaters (LORT), covered a broad range. Some had resident companies; others hired casts, directors, and other personnel on a show-by-show basis. Some staged revivals of classics, some introduced new works, others focused on recent Broadway fare, and some offered a combination of all three.

Shortly after his appointment, Greg undertook an extensive tour of these institutions, visiting twenty-six cities in total. At the conclusion of his fact-finding mission, he wrote a report to the council recommending funding for sixteen theaters, including the Long Wharf in New Haven, the Arena Stage in Washington, D.C., and the Boston Theater Company. "Greg's authority was never doubted," recalled Isaac Stern, "so whatever he had to say was accepted immediately." Like everyone else on the council, Greg realized that the grants were tiny compared to the need. As he said, "It was small potatoes, $10,000 to $15,000 for a theater, but it helped them elevate their standards. And that was our idea. In some cases, like the Cleveland Playhouse, it made it possible to put two more experienced actors under contract for a season."

As the council worked to establish objectives and funding criteria, the most difficult discipline to target was film. The medium had not even been mentioned in the original draft of the National Arts and Cultural Development Act; it was added later, principally at the behest of George Stevens Jr. This oversight was symptomatic of the way motion pictures were regarded in the sixties, not as an art form but simply as popular entertainment. As Stevens pointed out, in the United States, "the movies were about movie stars, whereas in Europe there was a real film culture and a tremendous appreciation of American films."

Peck was strongly in favor of elevating film to parity with theater, dance, and the other recognized performing arts. So was LBJ. At the signing of the National Arts and Cultural Development Act, the president announced plans to form an American Film Institute. But no one, including Johnson, knew exactly what such an organization should be or do. Roger Stevens appointed Greg, George Stevens, and Elizabeth Ashley to study the problem and make recommendations to the council.

Greg pursued the job with his usual thoroughness. According to George Stevens Jr., he was "very thoughtful, very sober, very curious, gathering information, wanting to understand the landscape." Among other things, he discovered that more than half the films produced in the United States up to that point were either missing or decaying or in danger of disappearing. He wanted to redress that situation, becoming a strong advocate for film preservation.

What Peck, Ashley, and Stevens ultimately recommended to the National Council on the Arts was that the American Film Institute (AFI) should: 1) take an active role in the preservation of motion pictures; 2) foster studies of the medium as an art form; 3) encourage excellence in the making of films; and 4) train aspiring practitioners in the related crafts. Once these recommendations were accepted, the council then engaged a private organization, the Stanford Research Institute (SRI), to undertake a one-year study of such institutions in other countries and suggest ways that the expressed goals for the AFI could be achieved.

Peck supplemented the SRI's research with some fact-finding of his own. Among other things, he considered the question of where the new institution should be located, meeting with officials at UCLA, who wanted to house the AFI on their campus, and with Schuyler Chapin and Amos Vogel, who lobbied in favor of their institution, New York's Lincoln Center. Eventually, Peck concluded that the AFI should be on the West Coast, and the council agreed. Until a proper home could be found, however, it would be housed in Washington.*

In October 1965, just before his trip to New York, Peck undertook yet another assignment. He became the general chairman of a massive fund-raising effort on behalf of the Motion Picture Relief Fund, a nonprofit organization that provided medical assistance and convalescent care for indigent members of the motion picture industry.† At the time, the Fund maintained the Motion Picture & Television Country House and Hospital outside of Los Angeles in Woodland Hills plus a rest home, a welfare center, and several beds at Cedars of Lebanon Hospital. The goal of the fund-raising drive was very ambitious, to raise $40 million over fifteen years. This income would be used to expand and upgrade the Woodland Hills facility and as an endowment to meet rising operating costs.

Once again, Peck threw himself into the challenge. In addition to lending his name to an appeal letter mailed to members of the Hollywood community, he attended a series of parlor meetings—small gatherings at the homes of prominent industry figures—where he spoke informally about the Fund and its needs. Toward the end of the year, he also chaired a series of luncheons with key studio executives in order to get them and their studios to support the drive. At these sessions, he encouraged the studios to establish systems whereby employees could direct portions of their paychecks to the Fund. Greg also supplied considerable financial backing of his own, in 1966 donating 2 percent of all of

*A training conservatory opened at Greystone Mansion in Beverly Hills in 1968, but it wasn't until 1981, when the AFI acquired the campus of Immaculate Heart College in Hollywood, that the institution was permanently ensconced in the heart of the motion picture community.

†In January, 1967, the organization became the Motion Picture and Television Relief Fund.

his earnings to the campaign. This included residuals, profit participations, and the earnings of his Melville and Brentwood films.

Busy as he was with his civic responsibilities, Greg ended 1965 on a personal note: December 31—New Year's Eve—marked his and Veronique's tenth wedding anniversary. At one point he said of his life, "I've had my ups and downs. There have been times when I wanted to quit. Times when I hit the bottle. Girls. Marital problems. I've touched most of the bases." But those days were long behind him. In his second marriage, he'd found the kind of stability that he'd never known before and that he'd yearned for all of his life. And, in place of the frequent battles royale with Greta, he now enjoyed serenity. This was important to him. As his son Stephen once said, "Dad doesn't like conflict. He is where he is because he's got ego, ambition, and drive. But the man I see is still basically a small-town boy. He's shy and very sensitive to people's feelings. He doesn't want them to be hurt the way he was hurt."

Greg and Veronique were as much in love in 1965 as they'd been on the day of their nuptials. "The Pecks are the happiest married couple I know, in or out of show business," asserted columnist Wanda Hale the previous year. "After nine years of marriage, Veronique still flirts with her husband as if they had only met yesterday and fell in love at first sight, which they did. She looks at him adoringly, with those big, soft, amber eyes and he looks at her lovingly."

Where Greg's first marriage represented what he called "an attraction of opposites," his relationship with Veronique reflected the coming together of people with similar tastes and interests. They were each intelligent, family-oriented, and loved to laugh. Of the two, she was more outgoing and less introspective and kept Greg, the loner, from taking matters too seriously. "When I'm overtaken with myself," he explained, "and think that something's very heavy to deal with, she will pull off an imitation of me in a dark mood and suddenly I'll find myself laughing."

By this point, the Pecks were living on Cliffwood Drive in Brentwood, having moved from Summit Ridge Drive in the late fifties. Formerly owned by director Charles Vidor, the house was a lovely two-story, red-brick French Provincial structure surrounded by brick walls and gardens. It was a soothing place, which the Pecks decorated in light colors, primarily beige, light green, and yellow, with paintings from their extensive art collection dotting the walls and views of the gardens from every first-floor room. Greg and Veronique enjoyed entertaining here. The star recalled one evening when the guest list included Groucho Marx and his wife, Mike Nichols, Rosalind Russell and her husband Freddie Brisson,

Simone Signoret and her then-husband, Yves Montand. "After dinner we ran *A Night at the Opera,*" the host recalled, referring to one of the Marx Brothers' classic features. "Mike Nichols said he *had* to see it once a year. Groucho saw the beginning of it and disappeared. I went looking for him and found him sitting in the garden alone. He said, and this was a surprise, 'I feel shy with all those pros watching . . .' I think it was the only time Groucho admitted to anything like shyness."

Not content to simply stay at home and tend house, Veronique became an integral part of Greg's professional endeavors. "I get a lot of my best ideas from my wife," the actor told reporter Samantha Dean a few years later. Indeed, by the mid-sixties, she'd become a familiar presence on the set of his films and in the screening rooms where his rushes were viewed. "In the background, you saw her," said Frederick Fairfax, assistant director of Peck's 1969 feature *The Chairman,* "looking immaculate, with the dark glasses on. . . . And I wouldn't think anything got by her." Protecting her husband was Veronique's first priority. If she didn't think he was being shown to his best advantage or she felt his amenities on location were lacking, she made her feelings known. A friend, film composer Elmer Bernstein, called her "formidable," adding, "I don't think she suffers fools gladly."

Veronique not only helped foster Greg's career, she supported his public service activities as well, accompanying him, for example, on his multi-city tour of the nation's LORT theaters in 1965. "I just participate in everything Greg does," Veronique explained at that time. "I like it this way; I am not a career woman." However, *Los Angeles Times* reporter Maggie Savoy pointed out that "beneath this 'I'm-just-a-housewife' exterior is massive and professional devotion. She can run a press conference, give interviews, arrange schedules and packing and details in three cities in one day."

Elmer Bernstein once described Peck as "a great humanist. He believes in people. He always believes that things can be better, and he's willing to help in various causes to try to make things better—and in a quiet way, by the way." As 1965 gave way to 1966, Greg continued to expand the realm of his nonacting involvements.

In January, he became the National Crusade Chairman of the American Cancer Society. He began his term by producing a short informational film for the organization called *Investment in Life.* Shot at the Strang Cancer Detection Clinic in New York, it debuted in March.

He also built upon his efforts for the ACS in California two years earlier, traveling throughout the United States, visiting patients in cancer wards, and observing surgical procedures. As if preparing for a film role, he delved into the available research with gusto and met with experts in the field. Thus, when he addressed a gathering, he could speak knowledgeably and convincingly, explaining specifically the kinds of research and other activities supported by contributions. He also spoke out against smoking. This posture was nowhere near as socially acceptable then as it is now, but he didn't mince words. "We say cut it out," he told audiences, "forget it. We say that Marlboro Country is just on the outskirts of town. It's the cemetery." Typically, he concluded his remarks by remembering film stars lost to cancer, including Humphrey Bogart, Gary Cooper, Charles Laughton, and Ann Sheridan.

Such was Peck's dedication to the ACS that he even devoted his fiftieth birthday—April 5, 1966—to the cause. He began the day with a breakfast for about 1,200 people in Atlanta, spoke at a lunch engagement for 600 in New Orleans, and attended a dinner in Houston for 1,000. When he left office at the end of the year, the American Cancer Society was $50 million richer.

He also found time in 1966 to narrate a third film for the United States Information Agency. A twenty-eight-minute documentary called *A President's Country,* it focused on the land, people, creatures, and climate of the Texas Hill country where LBJ was raised. The president's boyhood was recounted as well. In October, prints were sent to ninety-eight nations around the world for screenings at U.S. embassies. At the end of the year, President Johnson had an opportunity to thank Peck for his involvement with this project; Greg and Veronique were present at the White House on December 13 for a formal dinner honoring the members of the National Council on the Arts.

In addition to bolstering theaters through his Arts Council membership, Peck became directly involved in the formation of a Los Angeles performing arts center in the fall of 1966.

For many in southern California, the 1965 riot in the African-American community of Watts served as a dramatic wake-up call. Dr. J. Alfred Cannon and C. Bernard Jackson, two black men affiliated with UCLA, believed that a potential solution to minority disenfranchisement was the creation of an inner-city facility for theater, dance, and music. They wanted to feature predominantly African-American, Latino, and Asian performers in programs directed at minority audiences.

With this goal in mind, they incorporated the Inner City Cultural Center (ICCC) on April 15, 1966, taking up residence in a former movie house, the Boulevard Theater, in the heart of South Central Los Angeles. In addition to a schedule of public performances, the ICCC planned to create courses for youngsters in acting, music, dance, writing, the graphic arts, and film appreciation. Furthermore, a series of performances would be offered free of charge for L.A.'s junior high school and high school students. This program, known as Project Discovery, was part of a national initiative called the Educational Laboratory Theater Project and was modeled on extant programs in New Orleans and in Providence, Rhode Island.

Like many white liberals, Peck was sympathetic to the aims of the ICCC. Accordingly, he donated approximately $50,000 to the organization, and Veronique helped raise a like amount by staging the first U.S. showing of the collection of Paris designer André Courreges. In addition, as a director of the organization's board, Greg helped obtain funding from the National Council on the Arts. He also spoke before the Los Angeles school board to win crucial support for Project Discovery, which he oversaw as chairman of the ICCC's Theater Committee, and he met with Joseph Papp and Bernard Gersten of New York's acclaimed Public Theatre. Papp, impressed with the sincerity of Peck's efforts, wrote on his return to Manhattan, "There is no question in our minds that your organization holds great promise for that culturally blighted city [Los Angeles], and we want to do all we can to help."

Peck initially derived enormous satisfaction from this organization, particularly the program of performances for school kids. He also enjoyed helping to select and cast the plays, a return of sorts to his days with the La Jolla Playhouse. "In my years in the theater and in films," he shared with readers of an ICCC appeal letter, "no single role has excited me more than the part I am now playing in helping to establish the Inner City Cultural Center as a permanent part of the Los Angeles cultural community."

In 1967, the ICCC launched its inaugural season, which included *Slow Dance on a Killing Ground,* Jean-Paul Sartre's *The Flies, Tartuffe, The Glass Menagerie, The Sea Gull,* and *A Midsummer Night's Dream.* In addition to the center's regular weekly performance schedule, Project Discovery offered free matinees during the 1967–68 school year to every tenth-grade student in the city, some 35,000 of them.

Slow Dance on a Killing Ground was a major success, so much so that its run was extended by a full month. Nevertheless, at the end of the season, the ICCC was in trouble. Andre Gregory, the talented artistic director of Project Discovery, had departed. And members of the Los Angeles minority community were unhappy with the company's policies. Particularly vocal was Philip Carey Jones, who chaired the West Coast Ethnic Minorities Committee of the union, Actors' Equity. He felt that the ICCC had failed to hire an appreciable number of minority actors and technicians and had selected a repertory that, except for *Slow Dance*, had no significance for its target audience. Worse, the ICCC was in jeopardy financially. At one point, in January 1968, it appeared that the company would be unable to meet its payroll. Shortly thereafter, producing director David Lunney was dismissed. Peck, who wasn't consulted before the firing, resented the manner in which this action was taken. On April 13, he resigned as chairman of the Theater Committee.*

Lunney's firing was merely the final episode in a series of events that dramatized the gulf between Peck and the organization's founders, in particular executive director C. Bernard Jackson. According to Ernest Dillihay, presently the Director of Performing Arts for the City of Los Angeles Cultural Affairs Department and the author of a history of the ICCC, Peck and Jackson differed over the most fundamental tenets of the center's direction. "Jackson," explained Dillihay, "thought local minority artists deserved a chance at the performing opportunities the organization provided. Peck, wanting the productions to be as professional as possible, was in favor of importing professionals from other places, notably New York, at relatively high salaries." In other words, where Greg was result-oriented, Jackson was willing to sacrifice short-term quality in order to train local individuals who might provide excellence later on. The executive director also wanted to ensure that badly needed income stayed in the community. Most of the ICCC staff agreed with him.

Beyond substantive issues, the conflict between Peck and Jackson was reflective of what was transpiring all over the country in the late 1960s, as many African-Americans became increasingly resentful of assistance from Caucasian liberals. After marching shoulder to shoulder with blacks in the civil rights struggles of the fifties and early sixties, few whites knew how to react when they suddenly found themselves cast as patronizing do-gooders. Peck, like many of his peers, retreated in anger and confusion. Although he temporarily remained on the ICCC's board of directors, he withdrew from active involvement in the institution after the spring of 1968. A year later, on March 31, 1969, he quietly resigned.†

* * *

*The ICCC's financial problems didn't end with Lunney's departure. The following year, the General Accounting Office, the watchdog agency that oversees the spending of U.S. Congressional funds, accused the organization of financial improprieties.

†The ICCC continued to function, at several different locations, into the 1990s. Its last production was in 1996, around the time of Jackson's death. Although it is not technically defunct, it was nonoperational as of the spring of 2000 due to continuing financial problems, notably with the Internal Revenue Service.

As if Greg weren't busy enough in the fall of 1966, he managed to squeeze in extensive campaign appearances on behalf of the reelection of California's Democratic governor, Edmund G. "Pat" Brown.

After the election, which Brown won, the governor looked ahead to the 1968 campaign for the U.S. Senate seat held by Republican Thomas Kuchel and suggested Peck as a possible candidate. It wasn't such a far-fetched idea. Two years earlier, actor-dancer George Murphy, a Republican, had captured the state's other Senate seat. Moreover, Peck had demonstrated through his various charitable efforts that he was a forceful public speaker. He had an agenda about which he cared deeply, and he was willing to work tirelessly on behalf of these causes.

But Peck wasn't interested in political office. He issued his definitive statement on the subject in 1970, when the gubernatorial victory of another movie actor, Republican Ronald Reagan, reignited interest in Greg as a candidate. "I am far from indifferent to the idea of public service," Peck explained, adding that, "like many men of my age who have enjoyed some success, I am interested in making myself useful in as many ways as I can in helping to solve public problems. But I am not interested in seeking elective office. I have had enough of the limelight to last for a lifetime. I am not tempted by the idea of political power. I would not lend myself to politics as a front man nor would I capitalize on any 'electability' I might have because of experience as a professional performer. I like my present job and hope to continue making films as long as audiences will tolerate me. Aside from that, and up to the limits of my available time and capacity, I am willing to work on projects for the public welfare and to serve in appointive office."

In 1967, however, Peck did accept two high offices within his profession: he was elected president of the Motion Picture Academy of Arts and Sciences, and he became the first chairman of the Board of the American Film Institute.

Two years in the planning, the AFI was officially incorporated in spring 1967, with George Stevens Jr. as the organization's first director. He and Peck held a press conference in Washington, D.C. "At the 1967 announcement ceremony," recalled Stevens, "Greg spoke of the urgent need to save America's film heritage from neglect. He also expressed concern over the excessive commercialism 'that has become so unfortunately identified with American film,' and he called for the creation of an Advanced Study Center, where young filmmakers could master their craft. Idealism was never a hot ticket in Hollywood and Gregory Peck's willingness to raise his voice and lend his stature to an institution devoted to the cultural worth of film and television gave needed strength to the fledgling organization." Peck would serve as chairman of the AFI's board of trustees through 1969.

In contrast to the new and as-yet-untested film institute, the Academy of Motion Picture Arts and Sciences was a very prestigious organization. To be elected president, as Peck was on June 13, 1967, required a majority vote of the members of the board of governors. He was the eighteenth chief executive in the organization's history and the sixth to come from the Actors branch (the others were Douglas Fairbanks Sr., Conrad Nagel, Bette Davis, Jean Hersholt, and Wendell Corey).

Like the AFI, the Academy had an executive director, in the person of the formidable Margaret Herrick. But the president had considerable power, and Peck was determined to put his authority behind what he considered some badly needed reforms.

His principal concern lay with the Oscars given by the Academy and the award telecast itself. Worried that large segments of the moviegoing public, especially younger audience members, were finding both increasingly irrelevant, he wanted to restore the dignity of the occasion and the importance of the result. To do this, he felt it important to bring fresh young blood to the Academy's voting membership and to the Board. Conversely, he hoped to eliminate the old, stodgy thinkers who were then dominating the organization.

He accomplished these objectives in several ways. First, he encouraged younger, vital members of the various crafts to join the Academy so they could vote. He also retired members who'd not been active in the industry for decades, making them associate members. As such, they were accorded all of the other privileges of Academy association—invitations to film screenings and lectures, for example—but were not allowed to ballot for the Oscars. To modernize the board, several branches, including those of the Administrators and Executives, were eliminated, and an additional Governor was added from each of the remaining divisions. The new board members had to be under thirty-five and have no more than five years of industry experience. Finally, limitations were placed on the tenure of office-holders. "We believe," said President Peck near the end of his term, "that the new procedure will result in a board that will be increasingly responsive to contemporary attitudes and to the ideas of a new generation of film professionals."

Greg also sought to discourage the practice of lobbying for the awards. Recognizing that an Oscar win could add significantly to a picture's box-office earnings, studios had increasingly politicized the process since the mid-1950s, taking out expansive "For Your Consideration" advertisements in trade publications and offering voters various promotional gifts.

At Peck's behest, the board issued a letter to all members, warning them not be swayed by such tactics. As the actor later explained, "We are not the studios. The Academy is not synonymous with the industry. The studios may cash in on our awards, but that is not why we are here." The effort was noteworthy, but, on this front, Greg was unsuccessful; over time and with modern technology, the campaigning has become even more aggressive.

Peck's predecessor, Arthur Freed, produced the Oscar telecast during Greg's first year in office, but the new president had to make a crucial decision regarding the ceremony. On April 4, 1968, four days before the event was to be held at the Santa Monica Civic Center, Martin Luther King Jr. was assassinated in Memphis. Believing that it would be inappropriate to proceed until after the civil rights leader's funeral, Peck, with the board's approval, delayed the ceremony. Although the event had never been postponed in the Academy's history, it was rescheduled from April 8 to April 10, the day after King's burial. Greg opened the telecast by noting that two of the nominated films for Best Picture, *Guess Who's Coming to Dinner* and *In the Heat of the Night* (which won), involved racial tensions. "We must unite in compassion if we are to survive," he told the audience and TV viewers around the world.

Reelected two months later to a second term, Peck was then able to put into action the other principal element of his agenda, upgrading the quality of the awards telecast. He began by moving the event from the Santa Monica Civic Center to the newer, grander Dorothy Chandler Pavilion, part of the new Music Center in downtown Los Angeles. Then he hired the gifted Broadway director-choreographer Gower Champion to stage the festivities. The old standby emcee, Bob Hope, was replaced with a dozen "Friends of Oscar." These rotating hosts ranged from Frank Sinatra and Ingrid Bergman to Jane Fonda and Sidney Poitier. Finally, Peck made a major effort to ensure the presence of the acting nominees, the majority of whom did, in fact, attend. The result was a livelier, more sophisticated show. As Philadelphia reporter Harold Heffernan wrote, "Peck in two years has done more for the updating of its format and all around operation than anyone in the 40-year history of the group."

He would serve a third term as president, from June 1969 to June 1970, and then turn the job over to his second vice president, Daniel Taradash. The screenwriter was determined to build on Peck's accomplishments. "I was tremendously impressed with his point of view," Taradash recalled, "and what he wanted to do, and I tried to follow up on it. Everything he did was right on the nose, as far as I was concerned." Taradash added that the last few Academy presidents, including Karl

Malden, Fay Kanin, and Robert Rehme, were also in the Gregory Peck tradition. As a consequence, Taradash concluded, "The Academy today reflects, I think, what Peck would have wanted it to be."

In the years between 1964, when he became the American Cancer Society's California fund-raising chairman, and 1970, when he completed his tenure as president of the Motion Picture Academy of Arts and Sciences, Gregory Peck devoted himself to a range of civic, political, and nonprofit professional endeavors that were arguably without precedent in Hollywood history. Without concern for personal aggrandizement, he did a tremendous amount of good for a large number of people. Little wonder, then, that in 1967 his fellow Academy governors voted to bestow on him an honorary Oscar, the prestigious Jean Hersholt Humanitarian Award. On January 20, 1969, he was accorded even greater recognition. Just before leaving office, President Johnson awarded him the Presidential Medal of Freedom, calling him "an artist who had brought new dignity to the actor's profession," and adding, "He has given his energies, his talents, and his devotion to causes which have improved the lives of people. He is a humanitarian to whom Americans are deeply indebted." The following month, Greg's efforts were again acknowledged, this time by the Hollywood Foreign Press Association, which presented him with the Cecil B. DeMille Award for outstanding contributions to the entertainment industry during the annual Golden Globe Awards. Finally, on November 22, 1970, a few months after the end of his final term as Academy president, he was the recipient of the Screen Actor's Guild award for "outstanding achievement in fostering the ideals of the acting profession." The award was presented by the union's president, Charlton Heston, at the annual membership meeting.

This recognition was uplifting, but Peck's devotion to public service didn't come without a price. Between fall 1963 and spring 1967—approximately three and a half years—he spent only seven months before a motion picture camera, resulting in two features, one hit and one miss. Time is precious to a fifty-year-old leading man. As if to make up for the loss, Greg would star in six features during the next two and a half years, beginning in May 1967, an amazing output, particularly since he continued to serve as president of the Academy, chairman of the board of the AFI, and a member of the National Council on the Arts at the same time.

Unfortunately, the pictures produced during this period were among the least memorable of his entire oeuvre.

CHAPTER 18

Changing Times

For his return to features, Peck joined forces with the studio (Columbia), producer-screenwriter (Carl Foreman), and director (J. Lee Thompson) of one of his biggest hits, *The Guns of Navarone.*

This time around, the team chose a Western. Based on the novel *Mackenna's Gold* by Will Henry, the story involved the hunt for a mythical cache of gold. The title character—a former prospector turned marshal—is impressed into the search by a charming but deadly outlaw named John Colorado and Colorado's band of cutthroats. Also on the scene are a group of "reputable" townsfolk, including a myopic shopkeeper and a fanatical preacher; a tribe of bloodthirsty Apaches; and a troop of U.S. cavalrymen, led by an unsavory sergeant.

It is axiomatic in Hollywood that people who share successful ventures want to join forces again, but Peck was not eager to star in *Mackenna's Gold.* Nor was he Foreman's first choice. The producer wanted Steve McQueen, then at the peak of his popularity. It was only after McQueen and several other candidates rejected the role of the marshal that Foreman approached Peck. Greg agreed to do it because he wanted to show his gratitude to the producer for *Navarone.*

Like *Duel in the Sun, The Big Country,* and *How the West Was Won, Mackenna's Gold* was conceived as an epic, boasting a budget of $14.5 million. It was to be shot in 70-mm Panavision with a star-studded cast that, in addition to Peck, included Omar Sharif as the outlaw Colorado, Telly Savales as the cavalry sergeant, and, as gold-hungry townsfolk, Lee J. Cobb, Raymond Massey, Burgess Meredith, Anthony Quayle, Edward G. Robinson, and Eli Wallach. On the distaff side, Camilla Sparv and Julie Newmar were featured in more or less decorative roles.

Arguably, the real star of the picture was cinematographer Joseph MacDonald. Between May 16, 1967, when the shoot began and September 29, when the picture wrapped, MacDonald's camera captured awesome vistas of the American West, among them the rushing waters of the

Rogue River in Oregon, the rugged terrain around Arizona's historic Canyon de Chelley (pronounced "Shay"), the lush valleys of Kenab, Utah, and, finally the arid, forbidding Mojave Desert near Palmdale, California.

But scenery alone can't make a film, and this one had little else going for it. "*Mackenna's Gold* was a *terrible* Western," Peck conceded a few years later, "just wretched." Few disagreed with him when the picture was released on May 10, 1969—a long twenty months after filming ended. Lacking style, interesting characters, and a novel point of view, the screenplay was well below par for the man who crafted *The Guns of Navarone,* not to mention one of the greatest Westerns of all time, *High Noon.* Kevin Thomas of the *Los Angeles Times* summed up the critical reaction: "Not in recent years has a Western arrived with such advance ballyhoo and landed with a more resounding thud."

Moviegoers were not persuaded by the big-name cast or outsized production. Consequently, *Mackenna's Gold* took in a mere $3.1 million at the box office, to rank thirty-first among the hits of 1969.

By the time *Mackenna's Gold* premiered, another Peck Western had already come and gone from the nation's movie screens.

Like Columbia's ill-fated epic, *The Stalking Moon* reunited Greg with the producer and director of one of his biggest hits—in this case, Alan J. Pakula and Robert Mulligan of *To Kill a Mockingbird.* It also featured some beautiful scenery. But, unlike the Foreman-Thompson offering, this Western operated on a more intimate scale.

Based on a novel by Theodore V. Olsen, the screenplay by Alvin Sargent centered on a veteran army scout named Sam Varner who decides to retire to his ranch in New Mexico. A white woman, Sarah Carver, recently rescued from the Apaches after many years of captivity, accompanies him on his journey. With her is a young boy, her son by the fearless warrior, Salvaje. After reaching Sam's ranch, the three loners find common ground but, before they can build a life together, they have to deal with the boy's relentless father, who has tracked them down.

National General, which had acquired the chain of movie theaters formerly owned by Fox, produced the film, in association with Peck's Brentwood Productions and Pakula-Mulligan Productions.* With a modest budget of $5 million, the picture was shot primarily in the area around Las Vegas, including the Valley of Fire, beginning on January 8, 1968, a

*The Supreme Court had prohibited movie studios from owning chains of theaters, but there was nothing to prevent a theater chain from producing a film. Before going out of business, National General bankrolled a total of sixteen features.

little more than three months after *Mackenna's Gold* wrapped. While on location, Greg and Veronique rented the Vegas home of late-night comic Johnny Carson. At first, they took full advantage of the city's night life, gambling at the casinos and catching the shows on the Strip. Then, the novelty wore off, and they spent their evenings quietly enjoying the desert surroundings of the Carson abode.

Greg's costar was Eva Marie Saint, the sensitive Oscar-winning actress of *On the Waterfront* as well as *A Hatful of Rain, Raintree County, North by Northwest,* and *Exodus.* Like Peck, she hadn't been seen on the nation's movie screens since 1966. Hardly the gushing type, Saint actually wrote Greg what she called "a fan letter, the only one I've ever written," after seeing *To Kill a Mockingbird.* "There are certain people an actress wants to work with," she said shortly after the release of *The Stalking Moon,* "and he's one of them." She described him as "shy," but, like *Mirage*'s Diane Baker, enjoyed his sense of humor.

Opening in New York on January 29, 1969, *The Stalking Moon* was quickly seen as a departure from the usual shoot-'em-up. Not only were its principal characters—lonely, inner-directed people—somewhat deeper and more complex than the traditional genre archetypes, director Mulligan borrowed elements of the horror genre in the sequences involving the almost ghostlike Indian stalker, Salvaje. These built to moments of edge-of-the-seat tension. In between, however, were long stretches of slow-moving character study.

Like the film itself, Peck's performance had its supporters and its detractors. *Time* praised his "customary rigid dignity" that gave the rancher "an honest Abelike stature." However, the *New York Times*' Vincent Canby argued, "Peck is so grave and earnest it seems he must be thinking about his duties on the board of the American Film Institute, rather than on survival." Like its successor, *Mackenna's Gold, The Stalking Moon* failed to rouse the moviegoing public, earning little more than $1 million.

Peck would get two more cracks at the 1969 box-office sweepstakes. Five weeks after the debut of *Mackenna's Gold,* he could be seen in an espionage thriller called *The Chairman* and, just in time for Christmas, he was back in a sci-fi disaster tale called *Marooned.*

In *The Chairman,* Peck played a Nobel Prize–winning scientist, Dr. John Hathaway, a character not unlike David Pollack in *Arabesque.* The genial scholar is asked by the U.S. military to go to Red China and steal a formula for an enzyme that will allow food to be grown in any kind of climate. As an added wrinkle, a transmitter is implanted behind Hathaway's ear before his departure, thereby allowing his controllers to monitor his conversations thousands of miles away. In a mild understatement, Peck later called this plot device "a bit hard to swallow."

Based on a novel by Jay Richard Kennedy, the thriller was a joint venture of Arthur P. Jacobs and 20th Century–Fox, marking Peck's first association with the studio since breaking his contract seven years earlier. This time, however, his salary was $500,000 plus 10 percent of the gross, a marked improvement over his previous dealings with Fox.

Directed by Peck's old colleague J. Lee Thompson, principal photography took place between August 26 and December 3, 1968, at the Pinewood Studios in London and at a variety of locations in the British capital and in Wales. Taiwan substituted for China, where sentiment against the project was so great that Peck was burned in effigy prior to the company's arrival in Asia.

Although the role of the intrepid, slightly ironic scientist played directly into the Peck persona, the plot of *The Chairman* simply lacked enough twists and turns to intrigue audiences for its 104-minute running time. As *Cue* asserted upon the thriller's New York debut on June 25, 1969, "The film is patently absurd and, worse, dull." As a consequence, it landed in forty-first place among the year's releases—behind *Mackenna's Gold*—with earnings of $2.5 million.

Marooned was rooted in a much firmer sense of reality than *The Chairman.* Released less than four months after the historic Apollo 11 moon landing, Mayo Simon's screenplay anticipated by just a few years the advent of the space shuttle and by only a few months the near-disastrous mission of Apollo 13.

Based on the novel by Martin Caidin, the story postulated a serious operational failure aboard a three-man command module (populated by Richard Crenna, Gene Hackman, and James Franciscus) after being docked to a space shuttle for five months. In desperation, NASA patches together a rescue mission piloted by a lone astronaut (David Janssen). Peck played the mission control chief, Charles Keith, a cold-blooded technocrat who reluctantly approves the rescue attempt.

As with *The Guns of Navarone* and *Mackenna's Gold,* Greg was toplining a big-budget Columbia epic, this one costing approximately $10 million. The studio placed this sum in the hands of independent producer M. J. Frankovich, a former Columbia executive, and director John Sturges, an experienced hand at large-scale popular entertainments, with *The Magnificent Seven, The Great Escape,* and *Ice Station Zebra* among his sixties hits.

Marooned went into production while Greg was in London filming *The Chairman.* He joined the Columbia company on February 3, 1969.

Although his efficient, almost robotlike character placed minimal demands on his talent, he had a good reason for accepting the assignment: $600,000—a substantial increase over his salary for *The Chairman*—plus profit participation.

As NASA cooperated with the production, Greg and the rest of the company spent several weeks at the launch site, Cape Kennedy, Florida, and at NASA's facility in Houston. Filming also took place at a variety of southern California locations and at Columbia, where a detailed replica of the space agency's Mission Control Center was created.

Premiering at the Ziegfeld Theatre in Manhattan on December 11, 1969, the sci-fi thriller drew generally negative notices. Although the climactic rescue attempt contained some suspense, the filmmakers were so enamored of their state-of-the art special effects (which won an Oscar) and so eager to show the nuts-and-bolts of the space program that the result was, in the words of *New York*'s Judith Crist, a "long, lugubrious spectacle." Aside from Hackman's cowardly astronaut, the acting was strictly perfunctory. The most interesting observation about the film's stars came from the *New Yorker*'s Pauline Kael, who asked readers, "Who in his right mind would cast the three leads with Gregory Peck, Richard Crenna, and David Janssen, when anybody can see they're all the same man?"

Marooned managed to take in $4.1 million at the box office (released at the end of the year, most of its revenues were earned in 1970). It outperformed *Mackenna's Gold, The Stalking Moon,* and *The Chairman,* but the quartet's grosses—about $10.7 million—looked woeful compared to their combined costs, approximately $30 million.

That Peck's 1969 output proved so disappointing was due, first and foremost, to the films themselves; they simply weren't very good. But they were also old-fashioned, woefully out of step with the themes, characters, and styles coming to the fore at the end of the 1960s.

Indeed, the motion picture industry—and, for that matter, America as a whole—had changed dramatically in the three years since Peck's prior film, *Arabesque,* had graced the nation's movie screens. In that interval, much of the nation's youth, spurred by a growing opposition to the war in Vietnam, had created a counterculture epitomized by long hair, kinky clothing, psychedelic music, a liberal attitude toward sex, and a pervasive use of drugs—notably pot, hash, and LSD. Violence—from the assassinations of Martin Luther King Jr. and Robert Kennedy to the riots in the streets of Chicago during the 1968 Democratic national convention—suggested that the conflict at home was as divisive and dangerous as the one in far-off Asia.

Hollywood soon reacted to the changing landscape. Since the mid-

1950s, when the Production Code lost its viselike grip on the industry, there had been a slow liberalizing trend in the depiction of sex and violence on the screen. This predisposition escalated dramatically amid the anything-goes attitude of the later sixties.* Peck didn't care for the new permissiveness. As early as 1964, he asserted, "Frankness has gone too far. . . . Most of the time it verges on plain vulgarity and it's degrading to the profession of acting." He added, "I prefer the suggestiveness of acting skill. . . . Give the people in the audience the right suggestions and they'll fill in the details. You don't have to sock 'em in the face."

Many in Hollywood agreed with him. But by the end of the decade, the biggest commercial hits, among them *Bonnie and Clyde, The Graduate,* and *Midnight Cowboy,* were on the cutting edge of sex and/or violence. Such films were also earning critical acclaim and numerous Academy Award nominations, including nods for Best Picture. *Midnight Cowboy,* the shocking X-rated story of an aspiring gigolo and a lowlife street hustler, even won the big prize in 1969.

Even more revolutionary was *Easy Rider,* a low-budget feature independently made by Peter Fonda and Dennis Hopper, about two drug dealers who travel by motorcycle from Los Angeles to New Orleans. Released in 1969, this unvarnished celebration of sex, drugs, and rock-and-roll demonstrated the growing power of teens and young adults at the box office. To be sure, previous films—from *Rebel without a Cause* to *I Was a Teenage Werewolf* to the Frankie-Annette beach movies—had built-in youth appeal. What distinguished *Easy Rider* was that it neither preached at, talked down to, or exploited young people. It addressed their values because it was *made* by young people. In a few years, the hottest filmmakers in the world would be baby boomers, with Steven Spielberg and George Lucas leading the way.

In such a climate, *Mackenna's Gold, The Stalking Moon, The Chairman,* and *Marooned* seemed terribly passé. Worse, if Gregory Peck's movies appeared irrelevant, the same might be said of the actor himself. A new generation of stars had come to the fore as the sixties progressed. Those who arrived first—Paul Newman, Steve McQueen, Robert Redford—combined a leading man's usual physical attributes with a new brand of cool, bordering on the aloof. Those who followed, Dustin Hoffman and Jack Nicholson, and shortly thereafter Al Pacino, Robert De Niro, Donald Sutherland, and Elliott Gould, played characters with

*As a guide for prospective moviegoers, the MPAA adopted a ratings system in 1968. The system encompassed four categories of films: "G" (general audiences), "PG" (all ages admitted but parental guidance suggested), "R" (restricted; youngsters under 17 admitted only in the company of a parent or guardian), and "X" (no one under 16 admitted).

much greater flaws. Moreover, these actors looked like just plain folks. Even their names—Hoffman, Pacino, De Niro—sounded real; no longer would Hollywood feel the need to sanitize ethnic identities, transforming the likes of Bernard Schwartz and Issur Danielovitch into Tony Curtis and Kirk Douglas.

Compared to the newcomers like Hoffman and Nicholson, Gregory Peck was decidedly out-of-date, as much a throwback to the past as Ronald Colman or Adolph Menjou had been when he first came on the scene. He wasn't alone. Burt Lancaster, Robert Mitchum, and the other stars of the postwar era, most of whom were now in their fifties, had to confront the same reality. To be sure, previous generations of stars had fallen victim to time. But, as the 1960s redefined what it took to be a leading man, the situation became far more perplexing and precipitous. Stars of the previous generation, like Clark Gable and Cary Grant, had been able to churn out smash hits into their sixties. Now, only John Wayne seemed immune to the changing standard. As long as he stuck to Westerns, a middle-American staple with well-established conventions, he remained on top.

Greg made a dramatic change with his next film. Instead of playing the conventional hero of his 1969 Westerns and thrillers, he chose instead to address the middle-age angst afflicting many members of his generation as they watched their sons and daughters and, indeed the world itself, pass understanding.

Returning to the rural South of *To Kill a Mockingbird,* albeit in a modern context, Greg played Henry Tawes, a competent small-town sheriff who's bored with his routine, with his ambitious redneck deputy, and with his frumpy "happy homemaker" wife. As a consequence, he falls head-over-heels in love with a sexy and savvy, but uneducated, young woman named Alma McCain. Just as the unlikely duo are about to run off together, Alma leaves Henry flat; thereafter, he discovers that she was simply distracting him all along at the behest of her father so that the unscrupulous moonshiner could pursue his illegal trade.

With a screenplay by *The Stalking Moon*'s Alvin Sargent from the novel *An Exile* by Madison Jones, *I Walk the Line*'s guiding force was its director and coproducer, John Frankenheimer. A veteran of numerous live TV dramas of the 1950s, Frankenheimer was best known by the late sixties for his suspenseful, politically oriented features, *The Manchurian Candidate, Seven Days in May,* and *The Train.* But his previous project, *The Gypsy Moths*, starring Burt Lancaster and Deborah Kerr, was also a study of middle-aged angst.

Frankenheimer put together a distinguished supporting cast for *I*

Walk the Line. This included Charles Durning as the deputy sheriff, Ralph Meeker as the moonshiner, Lonny Chapman as an aggressive federal agent, and Estelle Parsons, an Oscar-winner for her portrayal of Blanche Barrow in *Bonnie and Clyde,* as the sheriff's wife.

But the genuine standout was Tuesday Weld as Alma. Although she'd gone to work as a child model at the age of three, graduating to TV at the age of thirteen and then features, the twenty-six-year-old honey-blonde beauty had only recently emerged from B-film sex-kitten and nymphet roles to display a genuine acting talent. While the part of Alma played to her established screen persona, she imbued the moonshiner's daughter with a lively curiosity and a hint of vulnerability, thereby leaving a shred of doubt as to the character's real purpose in pursuing the sheriff.

"Tuesday Weld is most unusual," Peck said a few years later. "A totally honest actress. I liked working with her." According to Charles Durning, the costars could often be seen between setups huddled over their scripts, engaged in earnest conversation. The thirty-six-year-old character actor, making his second screen appearance in this film, was impressed by the professionalism of both. He described Peck as "really a hardworking guy" who would often ask Frankenheimer for retakes, even when the previous take seemed fine. Off-camera, Durning recalled, the star would occasionally spin wry but entertaining anecdotes about his past. "He has this kind of professorial approach to life," Durning explained.

Even better than his sense of humor, Peck could swim—as Durning discovered one very important day. During the course of the picture, the deputy is killed and his body is dumped in the river, weighted down with chains. After the sequence was shot, Frankenheimer called "Cut. Print," and prepared to move on to the next setup, "forgetting," in Durning's words, "that I was still out there in the water." As the rest of the company began readying the next scene, Peck noticed his costar's inability to make his way to shore. Fully clothed, Greg leaped into the water, swam out to the struggling actor, and pulled him in to safety. The film's publicist wanted to issue a press release highlighting the rescue mission, but Peck insisted that the incident be kept quiet.

The site of Durning's near-demise was Colusa County, California, but filming also occurred in the Cumberland Plateau area of Tennessee, the setting of the original novel. In total, the shoot, including the interiors that were filmed on the Columbia lot, lasted a mere two months—between October 14 and December 18, 1969. As Peck put it, the film "was made under the control of a tight budget, with a great deal of hustle and drive."

Ten months elapsed between the time the picture wrapped and its release on October 12, 1970. Peck, who had enjoyed working with Frankenheimer, felt that the director wasn't as meticulous in the cutting room as he had been on the set. The actor was particularly annoyed by the decision to eliminate a prologue and some scenes revealing the sheriff's back-story, having to do with the loss of his family's farm. These episodes gave the character a rootlessless, a world-weariness that made him receptive to an affair. Once the film was cut, Greg saw the sheriff reduced to what he called "a kind of middle-aged man with a stale marriage who got a crush on a teenage girl—you know, the oldest story in the book."

He also differed with Frankenheimer over the inclusion of several Johnny Cash songs, including "I Walk the Line," after which the film was named. He found the material "too heavy, too sentimental and too limited." He told the director, "Frankly, it seems to me a forced marriage," recommending the use of bluegrass music instead.

Although the Cash songs remained, Greg was generally pleased with *I Walk the Line.* Prior to its release, he told Frankenheimer that he thought the film was "gripping, unusual and very moving." The critics, for the most part, disagreed. They acknowledged the inclusion of some noteworthy elements, including the opening sequence in which the camera lovingly captures the weather-beaten faces and ramshackle homes of Cookeville, Tennessee, but found that overall the drama lacked tension, pacing, and punch. Moreover, the ending was unsatisfactory; it was downbeat and offered no resolution to the sheriff's story. As Pauline Kael observed in the *New Yorker,* "The movie is half over while you're still wondering when it's going to start, and finally it's over but never did get started. *I Walk the Line* has gone so far in deglamorizing everything that it forgets to give you a reason for watching it."

Some applauded Greg's departure from his screen persona. Howard Thompson, for example, told readers of the *New York Times,* "It was admirable of Peck to try such a role in a hillbilly context, after his usual expensive showcases. He performs with laconic restraint. . . ." By contrast, Phyllis Funke of the New York *Morning Telegraph* found it "unseemly for Peck with his stand-up-and-take-charge presence to grovel this low [in his pursuit of Weld's Alma]. No matter how miserable an expression he wears, he is not believable on his knees to anyone. And if his desperation can not be felt, it is hard for the film to gel."

Although some faulted Frankenheimer for miscasting the star, the director had actually wanted Gene Hackman, with whom he'd recently worked in *The Gypsy Moths.* It was Columbia who insisted upon Peck. In the director's opinion, this decision "killed the movie." He added, "Gregory Peck has been very good in certain movies and he's a very good actor, but having him play a Tennessee sheriff just shot credulity to hell. . . . The audience just wouldn't accept him in the part."

In this, Frankenheimer was correct. The strange conundrum facing Greg in 1970 was that, while he was growing a bit too old to continue in his traditional vein, he was still too fit and strong for characters like the lost, lovesick dupe in *I Walk the Line.* All he could do, if he wanted to continue acting, was pick roles that interested him and hope that sooner or later a mass audience would find something it liked.

In the meantime, such was his faith in the potential of *I Walk the Line* that after the film disappeared from America's movie screens without a ripple at the box office, he offered to recut it. He would pay, he told Columbia, to restore the prologue and references to the sheriff's past, and replace Johnny Cash's songs with a more suitable score. He also offered to actively promote the rerelease overseas. But Columbia and/or Frankenheimer turned him down. Why? "Because they couldn't admit they were wrong," he asserted a few years later. "If I made a success out of it, the whole series of blunders would be there for everybody to see."

While his gloomy Southern drama was still in production, Peck ended 1969 and, for that matter, the decade, on a lighter note. In a guise as unfamiliar as that of the middle-aged sheriff, he became a song-and-dance man for his TV debut. Airing on NBC on December 3, the show, a Jack Benny special entitled *Jack Benny's New Look,* featured Greg, his host, and Benny's close friend, George Burns, in a soft-shoe number called "Steamboat Whistles Blowing." The trio billed themselves as "Two Bushels and a Peck."

Greg had a ball. Said Benny, "I can't tell you how he loved it—he didn't want to stop rehearsing. When I got tired, he said, 'Go home, I'll keep working.' "

As a result of this appearance, Peck and Benny became close friends. "We were an odd couple," Greg confessed, "but somehow I could make Jack laugh. We had a very nice friendship."

When in doubt, do a Western. Although Peck had followed that adage without success the previous year, the prospect of doing a shoot-'em-up with Henry Hathaway augured for a better outcome. In 1969, the principal director of *How the West Was Won* had scored a bull's-eye—commercially and critically—with *True Grit.* It also brought its star, John Wayne, his only Oscar.

As with *True Grit, Shoot Out,* the name of the Peck-Hathaway collaboration, was produced by Hal B. Wallis. Thirty years had passed since Wallis had caught Greg's Broadway debut in *The Morning Star* and urged his then-boss Jack Warner to sign the youngster to a contract. In the interim, Wallis had become one of the most successful independent producers in the business, credited with launching the film careers of Kirk Douglas, Burt Lancaster, Elvis Presley, and numerous others. After a long, mutually profitable relationship with Paramount, he'd recently partnered with Universal, for which *Shoot Out* was his third feature.

Not only did *Shoot Out* reteam the producer and director of *True Grit*, both films were crafted by the same screenwriter, Marguerite Roberts, and shared a somewhat similar plot. Each featured a tough, aging loner saddled with a feisty youngster while in pursuit of some bad guys. In the case of *Shoot Out*, the crusty veteran is Clay Lomax, a bank robber who's just been released from prison and wants to find the partner who double-crossed him during a job. Along the way, Lomax "inherits" a six-year-old girl. Meanwhile, a team of young toughs hired by his ex-partner dog his trail. The film was based on a novel called *The Lone Cowboy* by veteran Western author Will James.

Reflective of his current box-office standing, Peck agreed to play Lomax without a guaranteed salary, accepting a percentage of the profits instead. "I've not had to do this before," the actor confessed at the time, "though I've worked free-lance rather than under contract to a studio for the past fifteen years."

Without the burden of a big-star salary, Wallis was able to keep the budget to a very tight $1.19 million. Obviously, the shooting schedule had to be brief. Hathaway was given forty days—between October 12 and December 2, 1970—but fell a bit behind. Thus, the picture didn't wrap until December 16. All but the last three weeks were spent on location in the Santa Fe–Los Alamos area of New Mexico.

Hathaway was his usual cantankerous self during filming. He was deferential with Greg but tended to pick on other company members. When the director started in on an actor or member of the crew, Greg would often intervene. "C'mon, Henry," he'd say gently but firmly, causing the director to stop the harassment. He also didn't care for Hathaway's attempts to model him after John Wayne, urging him to in effect re-create Duke's manner in *True Grit*. "I remember he was really disgusted by that," said Jeff Corey. Greg's *Only the Valiant* costar played a crippled bartender in *Shoot Out*.

The Western debuted on October 13, 1971. It may have played to the formula of *True Grit*, but, aside from some equally compelling visuals, it clearly lacked the strengths of its predecessor—novel, interesting characters, crisp dialogue, and plenty of action. As Michael Kerbel observed in the *Village Voice*, "At times, the film does capture something of *True*

Grit's surface quality, but the humor and charm are missing and what remains—a predictable revenge story—becomes tiresome."

That this was another in a string of disappointing Peck features wasn't lost on the critics, who devoted considerable space to the sorry state of Greg's career. As the *Los Angeles Times*' Charles Champlin put it, *Shoot Out* served "mostly as a glum reminder of the inadequate use the movies have lately made of one of their principal personalities, Gregory Peck. . . . It would be nice to see Peck again in a role that matches his gifts and his persona." Others wondered why Greg would be involved with such unworthy material in the first place. As Paine Knickerbocker of the *San Francisco Chronicle* put it, "Peck, m'boy, what the hell are you doing here?"

The answer was simple and very human: acting was what Greg did and what he loved to do. He was accustomed to going from film to film with relatively short breaks in between. Without giving the situation much thought, he perpetuated his modus operandi by simply taking the best of what was offered.

In the wake of *Shoot Out* and its immediate predecessors, however, he reassessed his options. "I did several pictures that I probably shouldn't have done," he acknowledged a few years later. "I didn't do them only for the money—it took me a while to rid myself of the habit of getting up early in the morning and going to the studio. I'm talking about things like *Mackenna's Gold, Marooned.* . . . I knew they weren't worth much when I read the scripts, but as soon as I started work on them, damned if I didn't start believing in them! It just goes to prove you can't be an actor and Pauline Kael at the same time."

The wake-up call came when he found himself experiencing an emotion he'd not felt before as a star, embarrassment. As he put it, "It was humiliating to work in mediocre films—not that I ever felt a lowering of self-esteem, but it was embarrassing to know that people who had liked my earlier work weren't enjoying my latest movies." Furthermore, he realized that the potboilers were hurting his chances for better roles in better projects. "You see, producers, directors and financial backers consider you a kind of leper if you have a string of losers," he explained. "How did Jack Kennedy say it? 'Failure is an orphan, success has a thousand fathers.' That's what happened to me."

Finally, he recognized that he was caught in an awkward middle ground. He was no longer suited to play the romantic leading man but hadn't made the transition to character actor. His solution was to just stop working so much and, in his words, "sit back and reflect a while." In the interim, he also thought he might try his hand at producing. Who knew where that might lead?

CHAPTER 19

Mr. Producer

He started not with a feature film but with a gala.

Since becoming chairman of the endowment campaign for the Motion Picture & Television Fund in 1965, Peck had helped raise a significant sum. But the ultimate goal, $40 million in fifteen years, was still a long way off.

So, in 1970, as the Fund looked toward its fiftieth anniversary, Greg conceived a bold money-raising idea: to stage an all-star gala at the Los Angeles Music Center, involving all three of its theaters—the Ahmanson, the Dorothy Chandler Pavilion, and the Mark Taper Forum. He volunteered to produce the event and, on April 27, 1970, the organization's board of trustees gave him the authorization to proceed.

Greg threw himself into the massive undertaking, supervising every detail, from arranging traffic control permits for the big night to the layout of the playbill. Most important, he personally appealed to some of the biggest names in show business to lend their talents to the festivities, including Frank Sinatra, Barbra Streisand, Pearl Bailey, Jack Benny, the Fifth Dimension, Mitzi Gaynor, Bob Hope (and the Gold Diggers), and Bobby Sherman. Rock Hudson, Jack Lemmon, Joe Namath, David Niven, and Don Rickles came on board as "guest stars," Ali MacGraw, Ryan O'Neal, Rosalind Russell, and James Stewart agreed to introduce acts, and screenwriter I. A. L. Diamond and playwright Leonard Gershe contributed humorous introductory material. The program was directed by Vincente Minnelli, and Princess Grace was the guest of honor.

With tickets priced at $100, $150, and $250, the grand affair took place on June 13, 1971. The entertainment started at the Dorothy Chandler Pavilion. A half hour later, the festivities began anew at the Ahmanson. Throughout the long evening, the stars shuttled over to the next theater to entertain a fresh audience after completing their turn before the first. Separate orchestras, under the direction of Nelson Riddle and David

Rose, kept things moving in each setting. Meanwhile, a block party with several combos was held on the Music Center Plaza and, in the small Mark Taper Forum, audiences could catch a continuously running retrospective of film clips, put together under the supervision of George Cukor. This tribute, covering the best of Hollywood from the silent era to 1970, was so successful that it inspired ABC to produce two two-hour specials along the same lines, with the profits benefiting the Fund.

The gala was a resounding success, one of those glittering evenings that those in attendance would fondly remember for many years. It netted $850,000 for the endowment, slightly exceeding even producer Peck's financial goal.

Clearly, a gala like the one in 1971 can happen only rarely. While it remained the highlight of the long endowment campaign, Peck stayed the fifteen-year course, and the target goal of $40 million was met.

In August, two months after the gala, Greg turned his attention toward a more personal affair, the wedding of his second son, Stephen, to Kimi Felene Moore, the daughter of a Bel-Air engineering consultant. Unlike Greg's own small, private weddings, this one took place with the usual pomp at St. Alban's Episcopal Church in Westwood followed by a reception at the home of friends of the bride's family.

The groom, born the year that Greg made *The Macomber Affair,* was now twenty-five. Four years earlier, after graduating from Northwestern University, where he majored in public speaking, theater, and communications, he'd been commissioned a lieutenant in the Marine Corps and served in a combat division in Vietnam. Upon his return, he studied cinema at UCLA, eventually becoming a documentary filmmaker.

His older brother, Jonathan, twenty-seven that August, had also been in the Marine Corps, albeit the reserves. Following his 1966 graduation from Occidental College, where he'd been a track star, Jon joined the Peace Corps, serving two years in Tanzania. Thereafter, he considered careers in law and teaching, but instead became a political speechwriter. "Politics was exciting," he said later, "but what I found more to my liking was working with the press. I made up my mind to get a job as a newsman." For eighteen months, he labored in the audio department of UPI in New York. Shortly before his brother's marriage, he returned to L.A. to work as a reporter for a local radio station, KNX.

Meanwhile, Stephen's younger brother, Carey, twenty-one that June, had just graduated from Georgetown University where he'd been a student in the foreign studies program. His half-brother and half-sister, Anthony and Cecilia, were in high school and junior high, respectively.

* * *

Given his friendship with Lyndon Johnson, Peck was initially ambivalent about the war in Vietnam. "I knew what his dreams were for the country," the actor recalled. "I saw the disaster of Vietnam overtake him and destroy him. . . . So, I had strong feelings about it." Stephen's tour of duty exacerbated his concern.

By 1971, two years into Richard Nixon's presidency, Peck's opposition to the war had solidified. "I had been searching for a way to say what I thought about our country's involvement in Vietnam," the actor explained, "and I suppose I felt I was a bit overage for carrying placards, marching in the streets, and lying down in front of the Justice Department in Washington." Then, he caught a performance of a play called *The Trial of the Catonsville Nine* at the Mark Taper Forum.

Three years earlier, on May 17, 1968, Father Philip Berrigan, his brother, Father Daniel Berrigan, and seven others had removed the files of 378 young men classified as 1-A from the offices of Selective Service Board #33 in Catonsville, Maryland, and ignited those files in trash bins outside the building. They then joined hands and prayed while awaiting arrest. At their trial, which took place that October, they pleaded not guilty, maintaining that they had burned the draft records as a matter of conscience. Nevertheless, on October 9, 1968, they were convicted and sentenced to prison terms ranging from two to six years. The play, by Daniel Berrigan, was drawn from the transcript of the trial.

"It was stimulating, emotionally engaging," Peck said of the stage performance. "I found that my wife and I discussed it on and off for several days. We found it quite moving that a group of people would put their freedom on the line, would perform a symbolic act which involved breaking the law, knowing they'd be arrested."

He decided to produce *The Trial of the Catonsville Nine* as a motion picture, his contribution to the antiwar effort. After acquiring the screen rights to the play, he met with the executives of several studios in the hope of arranging a partnership, but no one would back the venture. Estimating the need at $250,000, he supplied about 40 percent of the capital out of his own pocket and obtained the rest from friends, including the director of the Kennedy Center, Roger Stevens, and film producer Ray Stark.

Given the production's limited means, Peck had little choice but to shoot it as a stage play rather than opening it out in the more traditional fashion. Gordon Davidson, the artistic director of the Mark Taper Forum and the director of the drama in New York as well as in Los Angeles, was the obvious choice to direct the film, even though he'd had no prior feature experience. Before shooting began, Peck arranged for Davidson to watch several pictures with courthouse settings: *Twelve Angry Men, The Caine Mutiny,* and Greg's own starring vehicle, *The Paradine Case.* Peck also gave the director an extremely talented cinematographer, Haskell Wexler, who had won an Oscar for his work on *Who's Afraid of Virginia Woolf?*

Peck briefly considered portraying Philip Berrigan but decided that his presence would detract from the verisimilitude of the drama. For the same reason, he refused to cast other Hollywood stars, even though some volunteered to work for scale. Instead, he and Davidson drew from members of the New York and Los Angeles stage companies. William Schallert, who played the judge, was familiar to television viewers as the dad in *The Patty Duke Show,* but most of his costars were unknown. Several, including Ed Flanders, Richard Jordan, Donald Moffat, and Peter Strauss, would subsequently establish notable film and TV careers. Each cast member was paid the Screen Actors Guild minimum plus one percent of the profits. Davidson and Haskell Wexler also took a percentage in lieu of salary. As Peck put it, "Everybody had a stake in the outcome."

The company rehearsed for a week, followed by eight days of filming starting on October 5, 1971. Two scenes were improvised that were not in the play: the opening, which depicted the precipitating incidents at the Catonsville draft board office, and a discussion among the defendants during a recess in the court proceedings. The latter was shot in the studio lunchroom while the actors themselves were eating.

For Peck, the process of making *The Trial of the Catonsville Nine* represented a new experience. He had previously participated in matters such as casting, script development, editing, and, even to a certain extent, budgeting, but in the other films produced under his auspices, he'd been the star. Someone else had always taken care of the day-to-day concerns of producing. With *Catonsville Nine,* the responsibility was solely his.

While he was often present during principal photography, he essentially let Davidson and Wexler shoot the picture as they wished. After the director delivered his cut, however, Peck made substantial changes. Davidson wasn't terribly pleased with the alterations. As a consequence, there were moments of tension between the producer and the director. Looking back, Davidson said, "He wasn't the antagonist. He wasn't being overbearing. He felt he was doing what is expected of him in that moment." Ultimately, Peck restored some of the director's choices, and Davidson accepted some of the producer's changes, and their relationship was preserved.

The film was finished, but the major studios were no more interested in distributing the result than they had been in financing the project in the first place. The response of Paramount's president, Frank Yablans, was typical. After a screening set up by Peck, Yablans said, "This film must be distributed, but not with my *Godfather* money," a reference to his studio's current megahit about the Mafia.

Finally, David Rugoff, owner of a small chain of theaters, offered to play the film in New York, Washington, D.C., Los Angeles, and Boston, and it opened on May 19, 1972. The reviews were respectful but not ecstatic. Several critics faulted the decision to film the drama in the fashion of a stage play. "What created magic and poetry in theatrical circumstances," noted William Wolf in *Cue,* "simply is wrong for the movie medium. . . . However, those who didn't see the play . . . may nevertheless be moved."

Concurrent with the picture's opening in New York was its screening at the annual international film festival in Cannes. There it received a warm reception. Back home, however, it faired poorly. During its first week at Rugoff's Cinema II in Manhattan, where the cost of operation was $5,000 per week, ticket sales amounted to a mere $6,300. By the third week, the gross had fallen to $5,300. In Boston, the opening week's take was only $1,400. And the Los Angeles debut at the Crest Theatre generated a paltry $2,700 against $4,500 in operating expenses. Clearly, there was no point in opening the film in other venues.

Peck was philosophical about the result. "Very few people saw it," he said a few years later, "but it was widely talked about in the press. All things considered, it may have shortened the war by about fifteen minutes." Producing the film also earned him a spot on Richard Nixon's enemies list. Said Peck, "I have no regrets, but I doubt if I'll do any more of the 'agitprop' kind of thing."

In fact, he already had another, far more commercial project in mind, having hired a fulltime reader to sift through properties then making the studio rounds. Three months before the premiere of *The Trial of the Catonsville Nine,* he had settled on *The Dove,* Robin Lee Graham's memoir about his five-year, 32,786-mile journey in a twenty-four-foot sailboat, a journey that he initiated at the age of sixteen. Peck liked, in his words, "the rather simple, straightforward concept of a young man with a dream to sail around the world alone, in a tiny boat. As a pure adventure story, as a character builder—man alone against the elements—it appealed to me." Also, Graham had met a girl on his journey, and that love story resonated for Greg.

This time, he was able to get studio backing. First, he hooked up with a British company, EMI, which put up the front money for the project in return for the U.K. rights. Then, he returned to Paramount. Unlike with *Catonsville Nine,* Frank Yablans said yes to *The Dove.*

With studio support in place, Greg formed a new company, which he called St. George Productions, and hired *Catonsville Nine*'s executive producer, Joel Glickman, to help him run it. He also brought in a technology and management consultant named Milton Forman as the film's associate producer, Graham's coauthor Derek Gill to write the screenplay, and Charles Jarrott to direct. Although the British director had previously helmed two historical dramas, *Anne of the Thousand Days* and *Mary Queen of Scots,* Peck chose him primarily on the strong word-of-mouth for his musical version of *Lost Horizon,* which was not yet released (it would not be a hit).

For the all-important role of Robin, Peck and Jarrott surveyed the pool of young actors in Hollywood. The director was keen on Richard Thomas, but Thomas had signed to star in a new TV series, *The Waltons.* Also considered were David Cassidy and Edward Albert, son of Peck's three-time costar Eddie Albert, but ultimately the role went to Joseph Bottoms, marking his feature debut. The nineteen-year-old actor, who came to Peck's attention via a TV production of *Winesburg, Ohio* with Eva Marie Saint, was one of three talented brothers. Tim, his senior by three years, had already starred in two major films, *The Last Picture Show* and *The Paper Chase.* For Robin's love interest, California girl Patti Ratteree, they chose a Los Angeles–born model, Deborah Raffin, who had one film comedy, *40 Carats,* to her credit.

As with any feature, *The Dove* required months of preproduction work. While Peck's team—Jarrott, Forman, Gill, and Glickman—readied the adventure story, their producer decided to make a brief return to acting. The project he selected was arguably the strangest Western of his career—and his last.

Billy Two Hats is the story of two unusual outlaws—the title character, a morose, young half-breed, and his friend, an aging, free-spirited Scot named Arch Deans. On the run from a grizzled veteran marshal, they encounter an old farmer with a beautiful young wife whom he purchased for $100. The relationships among these five characters—the outlaws, the marshal, the farmer, and the wife—play out in the West of the late 1890s, a time when the frontier's raucous days were coming to an end.

The screenplay for *Billy Two Hats* was the first script by a young Scottish writer named Alan Sharp, who grew up watching Hollywood shoot-'em-ups by John Ford and Ford's contemporaries. He recognized the mythic nature of the American frontier experience, but at the same time, he treated the genre as an outsider, a European. Not only were his plots and characters far more quirky than the standard fare, he sometimes used the Old West to address contemporary issues. *Billy Two Hats,* for example, dealt with racism. Another Sharp Western, *Ulzana's Raid,* served as a metaphor for the United States' involvement in Vietnam.

Ulzana's Raid and a third Sharp screenplay, *The Hired Hand,* were written after *Billy Two Hats* but filmed and released by the time producer-director Norman Jewison decided to put the writer's initial effort into production. In addition to Peck, Jewison cast veteran Jack Warden as the marshal, Sian Barbara Allen as the farm wife, and Desi Arnaz Jr. as Billy.

Budgeted at a conservative $1.1 million, *Billy Two Hats* couldn't be shot in the United States. While Italy and Spain had become the substitutes of choice by the early seventies, Jewison opted for a most unusual alternative, Israel. "The Israeli Government is very eager to get film production going there," he explained at the time, "and they're subsidizing about 20 percent of *Billy Two Hats.* Besides they've built a Western set in Tel Aviv that's as good as anything that could be done in a Hollywood studio, and they've got all those locations that look just like Arizona."* Moreover, Jewison was planning on directing the rock opera *Jesus Christ Superstar* in Israel. Making the Western there at the same time seemed sensible.

While Jewison would oversee *Billy Two Hats,* he couldn't direct two feature films concurrently. So he chose a forty-one-year-old Canadian, Ted Kotcheff, to helm the Western.

Filming began on October 15, 1972, in the newly built Western "town" near Tel Aviv and continued through December 13 in the desert around Ashkelon and near the Red Sea port of Eilat. Said Peck, "You wouldn't have known had it not said in the titles at the beginning that this was made entirely in Israel." He added, "We were actually filming on some sites where King David was supposed to have battled against neighboring tribes and nations in biblical times." The irony wasn't lost on him. When he'd made *David and Bathsheba* more than twenty years earlier, Arizona had substituted for those sites. Now, Israel was substituting for Arizona.

Peck enjoyed working on the film and on his role. Thinking perhaps

*Sarcoville, as the Western set was called, was the brainstorm of a Chicago group called Sarco Westerns International, Ltd. Designed by Fernando Career, it featured a group of typical Old West structures in an appropriate geographical setting about a thirty-minute drive from Tel Aviv. The investors hoped to attract numerous makers of Westerns to the location because a production unit could be put together there for about a quarter of the cost of an American crew.

this could lead to other character parts, he went full out, portraying the outlaw with long hair and a thick mustache and beard; moreover, he rendered his dialogue in a heavy Scottish burr. Ted Kotcheff arranged for a Scots actor to record all of the character's lines in the dialect of a late nineteenth-century Glasgow laborer, and Greg practiced assiduously with the tape, before the start of principal photography and all during filming. He later boasted of his accent, "Well, it was absolutely authentic—right down to the last syllable and diphthong."

Desi Arnaz Jr., only nineteen but a veteran actor, having appeared in one of the sitcoms of his mother, Lucille Ball, and several films, was awed by Peck's dedication. "He was really interested in doing it," Arnaz recalled, "in getting that character right. He would go back into his dressing room after each scene, and he just kept going back over that accent. He was obsessed as an actor." Arnaz was also impressed with Greg's demeanor, saying, "He couldn't have been more selfless. Not a star. None of that. Couldn't have been easier to work with, couldn't have been nicer to me."

Eleven months after the end of principal photography, the Western was cut and scored. Jewison's partner, United Artists, even screened it for critics, including *Variety,* which published a very positive review on November 7, 1973. Then the director, concerned that the quirky, character-driven comic-drama would be lost in the large number of end-of-the year releases, asked for a postponement, and UA complied. Thus, the picture wasn't seen around the country until May 1974.

Unfortunately, the *Variety* review wasn't a portent of things to come. Lacking the edge of Alan Sharp's subsequent scripts, the writer's first Western came across as oddball and artsy but to little purpose. Even Peck, while credible as the old rogue, was too straightforward and diligent. Called "an international mishmash . . . as gloomy and pretentious as it is perfectly awful" by *New York*'s Judith Crist, *Billy Two Hats* quickly disappeared from view.

Once again, Peck was philosophical about the failure. "We thought it was an interesting little Western anecdote to tell," he said, "but we must have been wrong. But you write those things off when that happens and you think, 'Well, we did our best.'" But he'd had seven disappointments in a row as an actor. As he went back to work on *The Dove,* he wondered if he had a career left. Nearly three years would pass before he would step in front of a feature film camera again.

It took four writers to translate Robin Lee Graham's seafaring adventure into a workable screenplay. But only two, Peter Beagle, author of the novel *The Last Unicorn,* and Adam Kennedy, received credit.

The screenplay still wasn't finished when the shoot began in the Fiji Islands on May 25, 1973. But Charles Jarrott's contract specified an outside start date, so, ready or not, the cameras started to turn. Based in London, the home of EMI, Peck continued to massage the script. On some occasions, he had to phone in new dialogue to a secretary in some far-off clime. After it was transcribed, it was given to the actors and Jarrott for the following day's work.

Budgeted at $1.5 million, the picture, then called *Here There Be Dragons,* was shot in twelve locations, including Australia, South Africa, Mozambique, Brazil, Panama, the Galapagos Islands, and Hollywood. Nine sloops, modeled after Graham's own, were constructed and stationed at various ports so the company didn't have to transport its principal set from one locale to the next.

Peck was present during much of principal photography, but he had to return to London periodically to oversee the script rewrites and to view the rushes. He racked up an incredible amount of airtime. Sometimes Veronique accompanied him on his travels, and sometimes he was joined by one of his kids, Anthony or Cecilia, who were then on summer break.

For the most part, filming progressed in an orderly fashion. But the initial budget was too conservative. Midway through the shoot, it became apparent that about $600,000 would be needed to finish. Paramount came through with the additional capital, enabling principal photography to conclude—in Del Mar, California—on September 28, 1973.

After six months of editing, the film was released, under its original name, *The Dove,* on a staggered basis starting in May 1974 (It opened in Los Angeles in October and in New York the following February). Cinematographer Sven Nykvist drew raves for his stunning seascapes, sunsets, and other impressive visuals, but otherwise the critics judged the picture harshly, finding it poorly acted and scripted. Part adventure story, part love story, and part sociological study of two young dropouts, it covered a lot of bases without much drama. Although it performed poorly in the United States, it was a hit in Australia, New Zealand, and Japan, and thus wound up in the black.

Peck blamed himself for the result. Agreeing to a forced production start had been a mistake, as was his assessment of the original material. He wouldn't select another project, he said in 1976, "until I had done a very thorough job indeed of examining every aspect of the story. I think I would reject and reject and reject until I found something that would be consistently exciting, suspenseful, funny—whatever it was supposed to be—throughout, from start to finish, which is more than we achieved with *The Dove.*"

He had enjoyed the creative decision-making associated with the production—the work on the script, the casting, the choice of locations, the editing, and so forth. As he put it at the time of the picture's release, "I feel I play a role in every scene, if I don't direct it or act in it. I helped to shape it. I made the thing happen in the first place. Whatever has happened over the last two years, I've certainly known I've been alive." But he was less enamored of the other facets of producing. "I got terribly stifled," he said, "with sitting six, eight months in an office. . . . [I]t didn't suit my nature, to sit though endless hours of budget meetings and discussing logistics and travel plans and equipment. . . . After doing it a couple of times, I could hardly wait to get away from it."

Thus, by 1975, as he neared the age of sixty, Greg removed another option from the table. Having previously determined to be selective in his choice of material as an actor, he now decided against producing as a fulltime career alternative. Essentially, he was back to his original profession but waiting for the right vehicle to present itself. He had no idea how long that would take.

In the meantime, he kept busy in a variety of ways. At the beginning of November 1974, he was the honoree at the USA Film Festival in Dallas. The following month, he was in Hartford, Connecticut, to shoot commercials and training films for Travelers Insurance, having signed a four-year contract with the company. It was his first time as a TV pitchman. "I've had some offers over the years," he confided to the Associated Press' Bob Thomas at the time, "but none appealed to me until this one. It seemed like good honest work for a good, honest company."

His job with Travelers left him plenty of time for other pursuits. As he told reporter Bart Mills, "My life isn't entirely centered on work. I like to travel, read. I'm interested in all of the arts. I have children to watch as they grow up. I've got a helluva fine wife with whom I get along very well." With months of leisure at their command, Greg and Veronique enjoyed long intervals at their house in southern France, just, in Greg's words, "reading, living, conversing, listening to music, lying in the sun, swimming, bicycling, having a social life." He enjoyed those holidays immensely.

But his relaxation at Cap Ferrat was shattered in June 1975 when he experienced what he later called "the tragedy of my life." On the twenty-seventh of that month, he learned that his oldest son had committed suicide.

Six months previous to this, at the beginning of 1975, Jonathan had left his job at KNX radio in Los Angeles. He opted instead for an on-camera spot with KCOY, a television station in a southern California farming community called Santa Maria. His job was to cover the much larger city of Santa Barbara, about a hundred miles away.

Working for this small station wasn't easy. The thirty-one-year-old reporter was required to come up with a trio of on-camera stories every day and have the footage for all three on a bus to Santa Maria by one o'clock in the afternoon. To unearth newsworthy nuggets, he had to keep in touch with a wide variety of sources—policemen, hospital personnel, religious leaders, city officials, instructors at the local university, members of the artistic community, and so forth. He had to schedule his own interviews and conduct them. He was also his own cameraman and sound mixer. When he told his father that the pace was killing him, Greg suggested that he tell his bosses on slow days that there simply was no news to report. Or at least get some help, a legman perhaps or a camera operator. But Jon rejected these options, saying that the station insisted upon three stories a day, and there was no money for additional personnel. Finally, Greg urged Jonathan to quit, but the young man refused to do so.

In addition to coping with job-related stress, young Peck had been dating a divorcée with two small children. When he asked her to move in with him, she turned him down, saying that she was still recovering from the breakup of her marriage. He took the rejection badly. Finally, there were health problems. According to the Associated Press' Bob Thomas, Jon had an enlarged heart and an early case of arteriosclerosis. The former champion runner must have found his physical condition particularly irksome. Still, as his other problems closed in on him, he grew listless and stopped exercising.

Greg thought counseling might help. Before departing for Fiji for *The Dove,* he gave his son some money and encouraged him to see a psychiatrist. Jon took his advice but, unknown to his father, he soon gave up on the sessions, which he found a waste of time and money.

Finally, on June 25, young Peck failed to file any stories with KCOY. When he missed a second day, a coworker stopped by his apartment to check on him. He discovered the reporter lying on the floor with a bullet wound in his head. Nearby lay a .44-caliber revolver.

Greg was devastated by the news. Although he knew about his son's problems at work and his disappointing love affair, he didn't realize the extent of Jon's pain. Flying home immediately—while Veronique stayed behind to close up the Cap Ferrat house—he brooded on what could have led to such a horrible, irrevocable deed and what he, as a father, might have done to prevent it. "I felt certain that if I had been in Los Angeles," the actor said later, "he would have called me because he often dropped in and talked things over with me. If only he could have picked up the phone and said: 'Things are just bearing down so much on me tonight, that I can't stand it,' I would have said, 'Stay where you are. I'll be there. Come on, we'll go off to Tahiti or somewhere.' "

In the immediate aftermath of the suicide, Veronique issued a statement on behalf of the family, saying, "The autopsy showed that Jonathan had a serious heart condition. We think that maybe the oxygen flow to his brain was cut down and—in an irrational moment—he shot himself not really realizing the importance of what he was doing." Most likely, however, the deed was done with Jon's full knowledge. Greg later acknowledged that his son's "greatest problem was that he set goals which were too high. Part of the reason he set such high goals was that he was the son of a famous man." A friend, Nancy Stesin, concurred, saying, "Poor Jonathan. He was always the son of Gregory Peck. When people introduced him they didn't even say his first name. And he was desperately trying to find himself. He had to resolve the question of who he was—and I don't think he could ever come to terms with it."

After the funeral, Greg fell into a profound depression, repeatedly reviewing his behavior as a father to access his share of the blame for his son's demise. Ultimately, he was unable to find a fatal error. "When you look back on your life," he said, "there are a number of things you say you might do differently. But with Jon, if he were born to me tomorrow, I would raise him the same way."

Of course, that didn't ease the pain. For comfort, he turned, naturally, to Veronique. "The fact that he survived this," said his wife, "was a great expression of his love for us, for me, for Anthony and Cecilia. I believe he surmounted something which was insurmountable because of us."

His depression lasted for months; his pain for the rest of his life. But, if nothing else, Gregory Peck is a survivor. A few months after the funeral, he was again ready to face the business of living. Moreover, work had always been his best tonic, and he'd finally found the project that he'd been searching for as an actor. How ironic that, in the wake of the worst tragedy of his life, would come the biggest hit of his career.

CHAPTER 20

Bankable Again

Gregory Peck in a horror film? At first glance, the idea seems absurd. The genre had traditionally been the purview of a few specialists. Over the years, these included Lon Chaney, Bela Lugosi, Boris Karloff, Vincent Price, and Christopher Lee. But, by the mid-seventies, horror had entered the mainstream, thanks, in large part, to two spectacular hits, 1968's *Rosemary's Baby* and 1973's *The Exorcist.*

Like these popular predecessors, *The Omen* posited supernatural evil, not in a remote castle or quaint Middle European village, the genre's traditional strongholds, but in a modern, urban setting, amid well-educated, sophisticated people. In this case, the U.S. ambassador to the Court of Saint James, Robert Thorn, and his wife, Katherine, find themselves parenting a malevolent boy named Damien, their adopted child.

Unlike *Rosemary's Baby* and *The Exorcist,* which were based on bestselling novels, *The Omen* was written directly for the screen. The author was David Seltzer, who had scripted *The Hellstrom Chronicle,* but the power behind the project was independent producer Harvey Bernhard. It was Bernhard's idea do a movie about the birth of Satan's son, the precipitating incident in the final confrontation between good and evil—Armageddon—as foretold in the Bible.

The Antichrist, as Seltzer's script was called, was optioned by Warner Bros., producer of *The Exorcist.* But the project languished while the studio considered a sequel to its already established hit (*Exorcist II: The Heretic* was released in 1977). Just as Warners' option was about to lapse, television director Richard Donner read the screenplay and loved it. He convinced his friend, Alan Ladd Jr., then head of production at Fox, to review it before it went on the open market. Ladd snapped it up.

Donner, whose credits included a made-for-TV movie entitled *Portrait of a Teenage Alcoholic* and dozens of episodic dramas, realized that *The Antichrist* represented a major opportunity to move up to features permanently.* He was determined to leave nothing to chance. "David and Harvey and I sat for days," the director recalled, "and we actually charted that film—from zero to 120 minutes." The key to success, Donner felt, lay in the pacing. As he put it, "With this picture you must lull the audience and then shock them," then even things out for a time and then "hit them *again.*" As a consequence, the final cut would contain several much-discussed set pieces—the frenzy of a band of baboons at an animal park visited by Damien; the impaling of a priest during a rainstorm; the fall of the ambassador's wife from a second-story balcony; the attack of a pack of wild dogs in a Jerusalem cemetery, and, finally, the decapitation of a photographer investigating the boy's history. Donner also prepared his shooting schedule with extreme care; if anything went wrong anywhere along the line, he had backup plans.

The first choice for the role of the ambassador was Charlton Heston. It was only after negotiations with Peck's *Big Country* costar fell through that the script was sent to Greg. "I saw it for what it was," Peck said, "a well-constructed, well-conceived horror thriller. But I didn't see any harm in it; I thought, 'This is entertainment, too.' " He liked the loving relationship between the ambassador and his wife, Katherine; she was to be played by Lee Remick, whom he admired. And he was intrigued by Thorn's character, whom he saw as a "well organized and well disciplined man" who finds his life "coming apart at the seams."

His only serious objection was the film's opening, in which the distraught ambassador agrees to take a newborn whose mother died in childbirth in place of his own dead infant—without telling his wife what he's done. "Personally, I thought that Thorn was far too intelligent to accept a substitute child," Peck said, "without even asking to see his own dead child, and without looking into the background of the adoptee, and certainly he would have told his wife about it." He would have preferred a later scene in which Satan's cohorts arranged to substitute the demon for the original boy. Then, he explained, the Thorns "would have been innocent victims of the conspiracy." Donner and Bernhard acknowledged the logic of his argument but preferred the original sequence. In their view, it opened the picture on a more ominous note, and Thorn's guilt gave him a strong motivation for opposing Damien later on.

Although Peck would continue to lobby for this change during filming—as a concession, the sequence was shot both ways—it was hardly a

*Donner realized this ambition. Since the release of *The Omen,* he has worked steadily in features. His credits include *Superman, Maverick,* and the *Lethal Weapon* series.

deal-breaker. So he signed to do the picture. How far his stock had fallen can be seen by the terms he accepted—10 percent of the gross plus $250,000, less than half of his salary for *Marooned.*

The trickiest part of the casting came with the selection of Damien. According to Bernhard, the father of the original choice pulled his son out at the last minute because he didn't want the boy playing the devil. Thus, about two weeks before filming began, auditions for a new demon child had to be scheduled. "One day," Bernhard recalled, "in comes this little towhead, a tough little Cockney son of a bitch—his name was Harvey [Stephens]. I liked him, but Dick didn't think much of him." Bernhard persuaded Donner to at least test the boy. "So," the producer continued, "Dick takes the kid out to Pynford Court, which is a big estate in England, and he says to him, 'Now, when I yell action, I want you to come at me and try to beat me up, and when I yell cut, you stop. Right?' The kid's eyes brighten up, Dick yells action—and the kid hits him right in the nuts. Absolutely right in the balls! Knocks him to the ground and just kicks the shit out of him!" After Donner recuperated, he said, "Dye his hair black. That's the kid."

Produced for a modest $2.8 million, *The Omen* was shot over eleven weeks starting on October 6, 1975. The night before filming began, Greg sent Lee Remick two dozen pink roses. The accompanying note read, "At last we get to work together. And in such a jolly little subject."

The company began at the Shepperton Studios outside of London, then moved on to Pynford Court. Serving as the ambassador's residence, this magnificent estate included a sixty-room, eighteenth-century-style mansion. Filming also took place in Jerusalem and in Rome, marking the first time Peck had shot a feature in the Eternal City since *Roman Holiday.*

Greg relished his return to acting after a three-year hiatus. "The main feeling I have is it's hardly like work," he told reporter Fred Robbins shortly after the picture wrapped. "When you have to worry about the script and the casting and the schedule and the logistics and the union problems . . . as a producer and then you come back to this, where you learn your lines and say them the best way you know how and then go home, it seems like a vacation for me. But it is also like getting back on the old job. It's a nice familiar feeling."

Moreover, making *The Omen* was fun. "We were kidding the damn thing all the time on the set," Peck said shortly after the film's opening. "We joked and laughed about the script, and about those horrible effects." When the camera turned, however, everyone got serious.

The company took a break over the holidays, enabling Greg to spend Christmas with his family in Los Angeles, a badly needed respite in the wake of Jonathan's death only a few months earlier. He returned to London after New Year's, where the picture wrapped on January 9, 1976. Donner's intense preparations had paid off. "We finished principal photography on schedule, on budget, with no problems," reported executive producer Mace Neufeld.

As was his custom, Greg sent Donner, Neufeld, and Bernhard extensive editing suggestions while the picture was being cut. He also met with Alan Ladd Jr. and other Fox executives to encourage changes. "You may choose to think," Greg wrote Donner at one point, "that I am overstepping the bounds and being meddlesome; on the other hand, please remember that it takes some kind of courage to stick my neck out in this way. I could just keep quiet and hope for the best and not put my judgment on the line. In addition, I am quite sincere when I say that I will support the picture and do all I can to help it whether or not I agree with the way it is cut." Donner and Bernhard replied, "We appreciate the candor of your letter and certainly do not feel that you have over-stepped your bounds. You have contributed so much to this picture that it would be ridiculous for you not to express yourself fully and clearly." They even tried some of Peck's suggestions—including the alternative opening sequence for which he continued to fight—but, in their opinion, it didn't work. "We are sorry that we could not be more in accord with your line of reasoning, Greg," they concluded, "but we have been with this picture a long time and have seen it many hundreds of times. We feel as strongly about our position as you feel about yours."

Today, almost every summer release is a would-be blockbuster, whose opening is preceded by a huge, costly promotional campaign. In 1976, however, the trend was in its infancy. *The Omen,* in fact, contributed significantly to this practice, for early in the film's postproduction period, Alan Ladd Jr. became convinced that he had a potential megahit on his hands. He wanted to create the same sort of frenzied anticipation that had greeted the openings of *Jaws* and *The Exorcist.* Accordingly, he authorized the expenditure of a then-massive $2.8 million advance promotional blitz, even though Fox was in the midst of a severe financial crisis. For several months preceding the picture's opening, filmgoers were deluged with well-made, enticing trailers. In addition, sneak previews were held in 547 theaters, and nearly half of the PR budget was used to plug these events. As a consequence, virtually every venue enjoyed standing-room-only, sending hundreds of thousands of satisfied moviegoers out to tell their friends and relatives about the coming must-see picture. Finally, a novelization of David Seltzer's screenplay was commissioned, and the book, a paperback original, was released shortly before the film's debut. It quickly climbed to the top of the nation's paperback best-seller lists, racking up sales of more than 3.5 million copies by the end of the year.

Ladd's gamble paid off. Such was the interest in *The Omen* that when the picture finally debuted at 516 theaters in 316 cities on June 24, 1976, it grossed a then-staggering $4.3 million in its first three days, making it the biggest opening in Fox's forty-one-year history. By year's end, another $23.5 million had landed in the studio's coffers. *The Omen* became the third-biggest hit of the year, just behind the Oscar-winning *One Flew Over the Cuckoo's Nest* and *All the President's Men.*

Although it was virtually critic proof, the horror film drew its fair share of praise. Among others, Richard Schickel told readers of *Time,* "*The Omen* is, like *Jaws,* a brisk, highly professional thriller in which an implausible tale is rendered believable by the total conviction with which it is told."

By the seventies, commercial hits invariably spawned sequels, and *The Omen* was no exception. Three additional films carried the story through Damien's adulthood, each chapter featuring new stars and a new director. None displayed the creativity or enjoyed the popularity of the original.

As Greg's character was killed at the end of *The Omen,* he wasn't a candidate for the sequels. But, with 10 percent of the original's gross, he reaped more than enough financial reward from his association with one. However, the money was a secondary consideration as far as he was concerned. Far more important was that the horror film changed his status in Hollywood.

It wasn't due to his acting. Like most modern highly commercial vehicles, *The Omen* didn't make serious demands on the talent of its stars. It was enough, in Peck's case, that he brought his well-honed brand of humanistic heroism to his performance. But the success of the film was *his* success as well. "Up to that point," he confessed, "the only pictures I had been offered were a couple of Yugoslavian-Italian quickies." Now, suddenly, he was associated with a hit, one aimed squarely at the large pool of teen and young-adult ticket-buyers. He loved the fact that, as he put it, "so many young people now see me again as a current performer rather than someone they vaguely remember from their childhood or someone they see on the television. It sort of brings me up to date."

The offers started pouring in. He was bankable again!

For his follow-up to *The Omen,* Peck chose a biopic of General Douglas MacArthur, the enormously capable but egotistical commander of the Allied forces in the Pacific during World War II and military governor of Japan during the postwar occupation. MacArthur was also in charge of the United Nations forces during the police action in Korea—until he was relieved of that command by the U.S. president, Harry Truman. By a strange coincidence, *MacArthur* would mark the first of five films in a row in which Gregory Peck portrayed characters drawn from real life.

As with *The Guns of Navarone* and *Arabesque*, *MacArthur* was designed to capitalize on a remarkably successful predecessor, in this case *Patton.* The 20th Century–Fox release was the runaway hit of 1970, earning $21 million and winning seven Oscars, including one for Best Picture and one for Best Actor (George C. Scott).

Patton's driving force was its producer, Frank McCarthy, a former brigadier general. McCarthy was the producer of *MacArthur* as well. This time he was joined by Richard Zanuck, son of Greg's old boss, Darryl F. Zanuck, and David Brown. Executives at Fox when *Patton* was made, Zanuck and Brown had since formed a successful production company whose credits included *The Sting* and *Jaws.* Instead of going to Fox, they took their new film to Universal.

The producers had hoped to reteam with George C. Scott. But they and the star couldn't agree on the direction of the screenplay, which, like *Patton,* would cover only its subject's mature period. For several years the project sat on the shelf. Then, finally, in mid-1975, it was given the green light and nine months after that, in February 1976, Peck was announced for the title role. To direct, the producers selected Joseph Sargent. Like Richard Donner, Sargent had come from TV where his credits included such notable telefilms as *Sunshine, Tribes,* and *The Marcus-Nelson Murders.* Sargent had also directed a successful action feature, *The Taking of Pelham One Two Three.*

For Peck, playing Douglas MacArthur represented a major opportunity. He knew what *Patton* and winning the Oscar had done for Scott's career. The part of the five-star general was also an enormous challenge. Always a meticulous researcher, Peck investigated MacArthur with a thoroughness unprecedented even for him. He read virtually everything there was to read about his subject, including several major biographies. He also studied photos and 16-mm footage. "I think he knew more about MacArthur than Mrs. MacArthur," joked Richard Zanuck. "He really became an authority on this guy."

Greg decided early on that he didn't want to do an impersonation of the general, nor was he concerned about establishing an exact physical resemblance. "After I'd tried on rubber nose No. 1," he said, "rubber nose No. 2, rubber nose No. 3, and all the rubber jowls, I said, 'Fellows, I just can't do it—I feel unnatural; I feel like a ham.' They were very understanding and actually I think they were somewhat relieved." He settled for shaving his hair in front to give him MacArthur's high forehead and creating a bald spot at the back of his crown. That and the costuming, which featured the general's trademark sunglasses, corncob pipe, and battered gold-braided hat, did, indeed, create the proper effect. But, of far greater importance to Greg, was the acting. As he put it, "I wanted to get inside the man's head."

That wouldn't be an easy task. To begin with, the general was a political reactionary, the antithesis of the liberal Peck. Moreover, the man was full of contradictions and complexities. Greg naturally started by distrusting MacArthur, particularly his controversial decisions in Korea. But as he investigated his subject, his attitude changed. "The more I studied," he explained, "the many myths about him turned out to be just gossip. The truth is, his career is almost unblemished, a total success. Militarily, he was right in Korea; the Russians weren't about to have World War III start there."

With his newfound regard for his subject, Peck became a factor to be reckoned with as the screenplay went through several preproduction revisions. As he discovered interesting tidbits about his character, he passed them on to Frank McCarthy. In reading one biography, for example, he learned that the general and his superior, George Marshall, were very different personalities who didn't understand one another. "I think we should consider the Marshall-MacArthur relationship very seriously," Peck wrote the producer, adding, "We can make drama out of it without attempting to provide the final answer as to who was right or wrong."*

Most important, while Greg wasn't out to whitewash the general's character, he wanted to ensure that the man didn't come off as a villain, a genuine possibility in the liberal environs of Hollywood. Looking back, Joseph Sargent acknowledged Peck's influence over the screenplay in this regard. "Greg had a lot of input," asserted the director, "to say the least. I mean, he fought like a tiger as he got deeper and deeper into MacArthur's needs to maintain a balance as he called it, between the negative and the positive."

Greg continued to agitate for changes once filming began on August 19, 1976. In numerous memos to McCarthy, Sargent, Zanuck, and Brown, he pointed out elements in the general's character that the screenplay overlooked and moments when MacArthur's opinions were either misrepresented or unstated. For example, in the scene where the general confronts President Truman on Wake Island, he felt that the for-

*Peck's advice wasn't taken; *MacArthur* doesn't deal in any way with the relationship between the general and the Chairman of the Joint Chiefs and subsequent Secretary of State and Defense.

mer's positions were poorly expressed. "Whoever wrote this scene," he argued, "seems determined to set MacArthur up as a clay pigeon." Specifically, he felt that the general's brash dismissal of the Chinese was vastly inflated. "I have read enough," Peck told the director and the producers, "to know that MacArthur qualified at least some of these assertions. . . . The scene is too much of a setup. It is oversimplified and doesn't play well."

Regarding another scene, which showed MacArthur routing an army of protesting veterans in Washington, D.C., in 1932, Peck wrote, "MacArthur wore no special uniform, nor did he wield a saber, nor did he at any time charge into the Bonus Marchers on a white horse. If we were to stage this scene, it would come under the heading of perpetuating a myth, something I think we are trying to avoid."*

Some of Peck's suggestions were helpful, but the truth was that he'd lost all objectivity when it came to MacArthur. "I truly identified with this man," he later acknowledged. "My emotions were wide open to every situation in which he found himself. I was angry when he was angry . . . torn when he was torn . . . grief-stricken when he was grief-stricken. I found some identification in his lack of a normal home life and my own as a child. . . I found identification in the fact that he had an unsuccessful first marriage, so did I, and his second was close to ideal, and so it has been with me. I found identification in his total obsession with his job of military leadership and my love of acting. It's as if I'd come back to my own thing, this picture."

Proportional to Peck's identification with the general was his increasing intolerance for any slurs against MacArthur by other characters in the picture. As Sargent saw it, "He didn't willfully sit back as Gregory Peck and say, 'I'm going to change the content of this film to suit my needs.' He was literally reacting as the character, as General Douglas MacArthur, who was taking offense at certain conditions and statements that were being made about him. And I'll tell you, it enriched his performance tremendously." But, Sargent added with a chuckle, "it remained for the other characters to say these things . . . out of earshot."

Clearly, in the midst of filming, when everyone is working on a tight schedule and a lot of money is at stake, it was taxing for the director and producers to wade through long memos from the star and to hold lengthy discussions about his requested changes. But they respected Peck's diligence and perspective. As David Brown put it, "How many times do you get an actor who really gives a damn? Other than the paycheck. Greg really cared

*There is no scene in the final cut that shows MacArthur's attack on the Bonus Marchers.

about *MacArthur.* He wanted to get it right, and we respected that. There comes a point when you have to say, 'This is a movie, not a book.' But it was never done cynically that I recall." Richard Zanuck added, "There was never any time when we said to him, 'Greg, we're going to shoot this, and you have to say these lines. I don't care what you think.' We tried to iron out whatever differences there may be one by one."

Aside from the script, another major issue rankled during filming. When Peck signed to do the picture, it was budgeted at $12 million and much of it was to be shot in Asia (although not in the original locations; they no longer looked as they did in the forties and fifties). But, by the time principal photography began, the budget had been slashed to $7 million, and the company never left the United States. The Japanese surrender was restaged on the actual ship where it took place, the USS *Missouri,* which was berthed in Bremerton, Washington, and Peck delivered MacArthur's 1962 West Point speech at the military college in New York, but otherwise sites in the southern California area were made to do.* For example, Greg's boyhood vacation retreat, Catalina Island, served as Corrigidor; an old subway near downtown Los Angeles was used for the tunnel to which MacArthur retreated before leaving the Philippines; and the Japanese gardens at the Huntington Library near Pasadena became the American embassy in Tokyo. Joseph Sargent found the substitutions challenges to his ingenuity, part of the magic of making movies, but Peck thought the whole thing was shoddy, made on the cheap.

Disgruntled and frustrated as he was at times, Peck nevertheless enjoyed making *MacArthur.* He particularly appreciated filming at West Point. "It was quite an inspiring moment," he later said, "to stand there and deliver his words in the same spot that he had done it and to get that reaction from the boys—the same cheering and stamping ovation that they gave him."

There were also a few light moments during the shoot, as when the company was filming the scene in which MacArthur returns to the Philippines, dramatically stepping out of a boat, wading ashore, and announcing "I have returned" to members of the press. In Peck's case, he stepped out of the boat during the first take, put his foot in an unseen pothole, and promptly disappeared beneath the water. "We saw it in the dailies," said Richard Zanuck, "and just howled." No one thought it was funnier than Greg himself.

He also derived a side benefit from playing the commander. For some

*This speech serves as the opening and closing of the film, which otherwise covers the years between 1942 and 1951.

time, he and Veronique had been looking for a new home, a place where they could spend the rest of their lives. One day while Greg was filming, he got a call from his wife. She had found what she thought was the perfect estate on North Carolwood Drive in the Holmby Hills area of Los Angeles. The only problem, she explained, was that an offer for the house was already pending. If they wanted it, they would have to grab it that day. Greg agreed to tour the estate on his lunch break. Arriving at the appointed time dressed from head to toe in his uniform, he surveyed the two-level, five-bedroom Norman-style home and the four acres of grounds, which included a swimming pool, a tennis court, and wooded environs. Then, instead of following his own slow, deliberative nature, he remained true to his film character. With the decisiveness of a five-star general, he turned to his wife and said, "Buy it."

After a very quick fifty-day production schedule, *MacArthur* wrapped. Not surprisingly, Peck continued to lobby for his character and his point of view while the picture was being edited. He was upset that the dramatic heart of the story, the MacArthur-Truman controversy, didn't dominate the picture. As far as he was concerned, the sequences pertaining to World War II and its aftermath could have been eliminated entirely. Moreover, he thought the picture lacked the fire and passion that had made *Patton* so popular. Audiences expecting a similar kind of electricity, he warned, were going to be disappointed. Worst of all, from his perspective, the film was reduced to a relatively short 130 minutes. By contrast, *Patton* ran 169 minutes. As a result, little moments were cut that together added up to what he hoped would be his crowning achievement as an actor. As he wrote to the producers and Sargent, "Before we started, we all agreed that we did not want a typical Gregory Peck performance. We wanted idiosyncratic behavior, vanity, pomposity, stubbornness, a man sure of his own opinions, and all the rest of it. In the effort to shorten the picture, those are exactly the qualities that have been lost, it seems to me, and what we have, without the solo arias and the other characteristics that were lost . . . is more or less a Gregory Peck performance." He added, "If George Scott or anyone else were playing it, and I were producing it, I would feature him and even coddle him in the cutting, to build as great a star performance as I could possibly achieve with him. It is expected, anticipated, demanded even that the actor playing this role be in contention for the Academy Award. I wish that it were not so, that there were three or four other strong characters to share the load. But it is *MacArthur* and we can't change that."

It is impossible to know, of course, what Peck's performance would have been like had the film been cut to his satisfaction. He didn't, in fact, receive an Oscar nomination, but, following the opening of the film on

July 10, 1977, he earned mostly respectful reviews. The *New York Times*' Vincent Canby summed up the majority opinion, asserting "Gregory Peck is remarkably good. He not only looks and sounds like the general, he also makes the character disgracefully appealing, even when he is being his most outrageous. Though he's a well-known libertarian, Mr. Peck has a kind of lofty manner—even when he's being humble—that well suits MacArthur. In addition, the actor displays a wit that gives an edge to the performance and humanity to a character who it might well have been impossible to be around."

The response to the picture was less fulsome. As Greg feared, it was invariably compared to 1970's Oscar-winner and found wanting. "Unlike the snappy, smartly executed *Patton*," observed Kathleen Carroll in the New York *Daily News*, "*MacArthur* is so stiff-necked and generally undistinguished that it leaves one wishing that Hollywood had allowed this old soldier to fade away quietly."

Not surprisingly, the film failed to come close to *Patton*'s commercial success, earning only $8.16 million in its initial release, to place thirty-fifth among the box-office hits of 1977. The following year, NBC paid $4.5 million to air a two-part version of the picture. Some of the footage that Peck fought for was restored for this expanded edition, but additional scenes were shot as well. These countered MacArthur's actions during World War II with those of the Japanese high command.

For Peck, who had embarked on the project with such high hopes and lofty ambitions, the finished product and its reception provided a cruel aftermath. He was proud of his portrayal of the general, saying, "I thought I got pretty close to him. There are occasional moments where I think I hit him dead on." But he considered the picture itself "a lost opportunity." It was the biggest disappointment of his career.

After starring in two films in 1976, *The Omen* and *MacArthur*, Peck took a year off. He passed the time pleasantly, relaxing at his new home in Holmby Hills and at his retreat in Cap Ferrat. Then, at the end of October 1977, he traveled to Portugal where his next feature, *The Boys from Brazil*, commenced filming on the thirty-first.

Published by Random House in 1976, *The Boys from Brazil* was the fourth in a string of best-selling novels by Ira Levin, the author of *Rosemary's Baby*. The protagonist of Levin's thriller is an elderly Nazi-hunter, Yakov Lieberman (changed to Ezra in the film), a character based on the real-life Simon Wiesenthal. Lieberman's principal nemesis is Josef Mengele, the former Auschwitz doctor whose experiments on concentration camp victims earned him the nickname the "Angel of Death." From his hideout in Paraguay, Mengele has launched an audacious scheme: he has cloned ninety-four boys from the DNA of Adolf Hitler and has placed his protégés in a variety of countries with parents of similar ages and backgrounds as those of the Führer. In the hope that like experiences will yield like results, he has launched a mission to kill the fathers of the clones as they reach their sixty-fifth birthdays, thereby re-creating Hitler's boyhood loss.

A joint venture of the Producers Circle, 20th Century–Fox, British producer Sir Lew Grade, and ITC, *The Boys from Brazil* featured a first-class team headed by director Franklin T. Schaffner, the Academy Award–winning director of *Patton, Planet of the Apes, Nicholas and Alexandra,* and *Papillon.* The supporting cast boasted an unusually distinguished group of veterans—James Mason, Uta Hagen, Lilli Palmer, Denholm Elliott, and Rosemary Harris—plus newcomers Steve Guttenberg and John Rubinstein. And for Lieberman, the producers signed Laurence Olivier. Ironically, the legendary actor had earned an Oscar nomination the previous year for his portrayal of a Mengele-like war criminal in *Marathon Man.*

The opportunity to work with Sir Laurence, whom he'd known since the early fifties, was a primary reason behind Peck's decision to portray Mengele, the first genuine villain of his career. He also hoped that creating a character so far from his established persona might open new doors for him. He knew the role was a major stretch. But, as he told *Parade* magazine's Cleveland Amory, "that's where the whole challenge of acting comes in—and of life too. You just can't always take the easy way."

He researched Mengele with the same zeal that he'd pursued with Douglas MacArthur, but, not surprisingly, he failed to gain empathy for his character this time. "This man is loathsome, evil," the actor proclaimed during filming. To give himself a more sinister air, he died his hair jet black, grew what he called "a miserable little mustache," and worked on his German accent with a dialogue coach, Bob Easton. As a Method actor he normally built characters from the inside out, but finding so little in the Angel of Death with which to identify, he resorted in this case to technique.

Principal photography on the $12 million production began in Lisbon, where a refurbished saltwater lagoon about twenty-five miles to the south substituted for the jungles of Paraguay, Mengele's hideaway. Finishing in mid-November, the company traveled to Lancaster County, Pennsylvania, where the home of one of the Hitler clones becomes the site of the final confrontation between Mengele and Lieberman. The original plan had been to film the entire sequence in Lancaster, but Olivier had fallen ill shortly before filming began. Wishing to spare the sixty-eight-year-old actor a long overseas journey, Lew Grade ordered the construction of a duplicate interior in Vienna, where Olivier had other scenes scheduled.

Greg shot the first half of the sequence, that involving the Hitler clone in Lancaster, and then returned to Los Angeles for the holidays. In January, he rejoined the company in Austria for what he called "my big confrontation scene with Larry." Still in poor health, the British star found even shaking hands painful. As the scene with Peck included a demanding fight to the death, great care was taken to minimize Olivier's discomfort. "Of course, it was all choreographed," Peck explained. "We would do three or four gouges and a kick, and then stop for a while. Then we'd do a punch and a scratch across the face with a quick knee to the groin before taking another break." In total, the sequence took about three or four days to film. Most of the time, Peck recalled, he and Olivier "were lying around on the floor" laughing at the absurdity of playing such a *mano-a-mano* confrontation at their advanced ages.

The friends shared time away from the set. "We went to the Vienna Opera together," Peck recalled, "and Larry had a dinner one night at the Hotel Sacher for Veronique and myself with Lilli Palmer and her husband." Greg was particularly struck by the difference between Olivier's private and public personas. En route to the opera house, for example, he recalled that "Larry had been laughing and joking and making rude noises," but as soon as they arrived at the theater, the actor out-regaled even the real-life royals in attendance.

The Boys from Brazil opened on October 5, 1978, about seven and a half months after the picture wrapped. Although Harold Schonberg encouraged readers of the *New York Times* to "get a bag of popcorn, check your brains at the door, and have a good time," most of his colleagues advised moviegoers not to bother. Tom Allen of the *Village Voice* called the thriller "a painful monstrosity" while *Time*'s Richard Schickel termed it "a penny dreadful fantasy."

Moreover, Greg's performance, a portrait of unremitting evil raised to the level of grand opera, was the object of considerable disdain. As Pauline Kael put it in the *New Yorker*, "Peck appears to relish his fling at villainy so much that he doesn't recognize that his performance will go down in the annals of camp. . . . It's such a dumb idea to begin with." David Denby even likened him to "Sessue Hayakawa in a leisure suit," a reference to the short stocky Japanese star of several Kurasawa films and the villain of *The Bridge on the River Kwai.* Olivier's performance was equally over the top. Nevertheless, the British actor earned an Oscar nomination for his performance.

Greg took the abuse in stride. A few years later he noted that "sometimes critics are hard to sway, they like you to play the same role over and over. . . . And if you come up with something surprising with a whole different hat on, they're just not ready to accept it." He added that he was "very pleased with" his work in *The Boys from Brazil*, that he thought he had stretched his "range." A few years after that, however, he reconsidered, saying, "You stub your toe once in a while, I suppose, and then you regain your footing and proceed. I don't expect I'll be doing any more sadistic Nazis."

The Boys from Brazil performed poorly at the box office, finishing in fortieth place for the year with earnings of only $7.6 million.

Between the time that the thriller wrapped and its premiere, Peck was a busy man. A month after returning to Los Angeles from Vienna, he and Veronique joined Frank and Barbara Sinatra and several other friends on a junket to Israel for the dedication of the Frank Sinatra International Student Center at Hebrew University. While in Jerusalem, Greg turned sixty-two.

Back home at the end of April, Greg's twenty-nine-year-old son, Carey, was married. His bride, Kathy Katz, age twenty-five, was the manager of a Westwood art gallery. It was her second marriage. Two months later, the Pecks attended another wedding, this one in Monaco, where Princess Grace's twenty-one-year-old daughter, Princess Caroline, wed Phillipe Junot. Among the other guests were Peck's friends Cary Grant, David Niven, Frank and Barbara Sinatra, and Ava Gardner.

Around this point, Greg and Veronique decided to sell their nearby Cap Ferrat home. "We didn't feel that we wanted to spend every summer there for the rest of our lives," he later explained, "and we felt we had had all the lunches and dinners and champagne and fireworks and house guests that we wanted. It was all wonderful, our Scott-and-Zelda period, if you like, but finally we'd had enough."

That September the actor was in New York, taping an NBC special entitled *Rockette: A Holiday Tribute to Radio City Music Hall*, which was broadcast on December 14. As the host of the special, which also featured Ann-Margret, Diahann Carroll, Greer Garson, Jack Jones, Beverly Sills, and Ben Vereen, Greg returned to the role of tour guide that he'd first held in the summer of 1939, taking a much wider audience this time around the venerable picture palace. He even read part of the spiel that he'd given to tourists forty years earlier. Later, he joined Ann-Margret for a rendition of "Have Yourself a Merry Little Christmas."

Doing the special was fun, but the biggest event on Greg's calendar that fall was Carey's candidacy for the U.S. House of Representatives from California's twenty-seventh district, in the Los Angeles area ranging from Pacific Palisades in the north to Palos Verdes in the south. Although he'd never held elective office, Carey had served as an aide to U.S. senator John Tunney of California and on the staffs of the U.S. Senate committees on education and energy. Young Peck's opponent was incumbent Robert K. Dornan, a conservative Republican who'd won the seat by 20,000 votes in 1976, following a bitter campaign against Gary Familian, a liberal from a wealthy Los Angeles family.

Greg had helped his son kick off the campaign earlier in the year with a star-studded party at his and Veronique's home. Other friends and liberal members of the Hollywood community lent their support as well. Liza Minnelli performed at a dinner at the posh Beverly Wilshire Hotel, Warren Beatty and Cheryl Ladd cohosted a cocktail reception at a club in Marina Del Rey, and Hugh O'Brian cohosted a gathering with political cartoonist Paul Conrad at the home of Mrs. Kevin Cox Vanderlip. Greg's reach even extended to Washington, D.C., where his American Film Institute colleague, George Stevens Jr., held a fundraiser at his Georgetown home. Among those who paid $100 a couple to hobnob with the aspiring congressman and his father were the George McGoverns, the Edward M. Kennedys, and the Alan Cranstons.

A former radio and TV talk show host, Dornan also had show-biz supporters, including Debbie and Pat Boone, John Wayne, Bob Hope, Gene Autry, and Dornan's uncle, Jack Haley. "I've got more stars than he has," Carey joked at one point during the campaign. "He has Danny Thomas and I've got Marlo and I think that just about tells the story."

Although the press dubbed the contest "Star Wars," the race was about more than who had the best and wealthiest celebrity backers. The candidates met seventeen times during the campaign, including participating in a series of televised debates in which they expressed divergent views on a variety of issues. On election day, Dornan won the heavily Republican district by a tiny margin, 1.5 percent. The victor claimed that he had not only run against Carey Peck but also Carey's dad, who was in charge of the campaign's finances. "I think too much is made of this 'celebrity father' issue in the race," Greg replied. "I have not determined the course of the campaign. . . . I am in the position of an affectionate father and loyal supporter." Terry Pullan, Carey's campaign manager, added that Dornan "did not debate Gregory Peck and he did not run against him."

Two years later, Carey challenged Dornan again, saying, "The first time was like *Star Wars.* Now it's going to be like *Star Wars II* with a bit of *Rocky* thrown in on the side." This time, however, Dornan's margin of victory was much wider. Carey blamed his defeat on President Jimmy Carter's concession to Ronald Reagan before the polls closed in California. As a result, many Democrats who hadn't voted yet simply stayed home. But, after two tries, young Peck gave up on his quest for political office and entered private life. Today he works for the Municipal Transport Authority. He and his second wife, artist Lisa Albuquerque, have a son, Christopher. Carey also has a daughter from his first marriage, Marisa, and two stepdaughters, Jasmine and Isabelle.

While Greg was campaigning for his son, a high-adventure thriller called *The Wild Geese* was cleaning up at box offices around the world. In the tradition of Peck's own *Guns of Navarone,* the drama featured Richard Burton, Richard Harris, and Roger Moore as mercenaries who rescue a kidnapped African leader.

As is so often the case with a runaway hit, the film's creators—producer Euan Lloyd, director Andrew V. McLaglen, and screenwriter Reginald Rose—decided to reteam in the hope of duplicating the magic. For their second outing, they chose an adventure story drawn from real life. As recounted in the book *The Boarding Party* by James Leasor, the Indian port of Goa was under neutral Portuguese control during part of World War II. Thanks to a local spy network that fed information to the *Ehrenfels,* a ship berthed in the port, German U-boats were able to sink British ships in the Indian Ocean with great accuracy. In 1943, two English officers, Lieutenant Colonel Lewis Pugh and Captain Gavin Stewart, launched a daring mission to sink the *Ehrenfels.* For political reasons, they couldn't use British regulars, so they drew on elderly volunteers from the Calcutta Light Horse, a unit that had last seen action forty years earlier during the Boer War.

The filmmakers' original intent had been to reunite the stars of *The Wild Geese* for what was eventually called *The Sea Wolves.* But, in the end, only Roger Moore signed on. He played the younger of the two British intelligence officers. Peck, who was friends with Moore from his Cap Ferrat days, agreed to play the senior man, Lewis Pugh (the real Pugh served as one of the picture's technical advisors). Greg and Roger arranged for the hiring of a mutual chum, David Niven, as the third star. Niven played Colonel Bill Grice, the commander of the elderly ex-soldiers.

In a repeat of *The Paradine Case* three decades earlier, Peck again found himself playing a Brit in the company of genuine English actors. Bob Easton, who had coached him for *The Boys from Brazil,* helped him try to blend in vocally with his colleagues. As with past performances, however, Greg ultimately opted for a hint of British inflection rather than a full-blown accent. To add to the effect, he grew a swooping mustache and puffed on a pipe from time to time. He looked the part, but soft-pedaling the accent was distracting in the finished film. When Peck interacted with Moore, Niven, and the other authentic Brits, one couldn't help but notice the difference in their vocal mannerisms.

With a budget of $11.5 million, *The Sea Wolves* was shot on location in New Delhi and Goa over three months starting on November 26, 1979. Although the heat was often oppressive, Peck, Moore, and Niven basked in the opportunity to work together—Greg and David for the first time since *The Guns of Navarone*—and to transfer the good times they'd known in the South of France to the west coast of India. The only cloud over principal photography was Niven's occasional difficulty moving and speaking. The actor didn't know it at the time, but he had developed a degenerative muscular disorder popularly known as Lou Gehrig's disease. *The Sea Wolves* would turn out to be his last film.

The Sea Wolves opened in Great Britain in August 1980, but due to a change in the distributor, it was not seen in the United States until June 1981. Although it met with some success elsewhere, it failed to connect with American audiences. With *Raiders of the Lost Ark* and *Superman II* topping the box-office charts, the stiff-upper-lip derring-do of an aging generation of stars was decidedly passé, particularly since Reginald Rose's script failed to give those actors much in the way of scintillating dialogue, diverting romance, or rousing action.

The Sea Wolves brought to an end the string of major Gregory Peck features initiated with *The Omen*. After five years and three box-office disappointments in a row, the momentum from the 1976 horror film was gone. Indeed, in a town like Hollywood, where a star is only as good as his or her last picture, Peck had made the moment last as long as possible. While a few major features remained in his future, other people would be the principal stars of those ventures, save one. That was okay with Greg. Having turned sixty-four in 1980, he was content to let a new generation carry the ball. For him it was enough to take on an interesting role every once in a while—wherever one could be found.

CHAPTER 21

Character Actor

Such an opportunity was provided by the director of *The Sea Wolves,* Andrew V. McLaglen. The son of actor Victor McLaglen, the director had about two dozen features to his credit, several of which starred either John Wayne or James Stewart. But he'd gotten his start in episodic television, working on such series as *Perry Mason, Gunsmoke,* and *Have Gun, Will Travel.*

In the early 1980s, McLaglen prepared to return to his TV roots, by taking the helm of the most expensive project in CBS's history to that point, a $17-million, eight-hour miniseries called *The Blue and the Gray.* Developed by historians John Leekley and Bruce Catton and scripted by *Roman Holiday's* Ian McLellan Hunter, the drama featured two principal characters: a *Harper's Weekly* artist named John Geyser, to be played by soap opera star John Hammond, and Jonas Steele, an army scout and bodyguard of President Abraham Lincoln, in the person of Stacy Keach. During the course of their adventures, Geyser and Steele between them would witness many of the principal events of the Civil War era and encounter a number of its outstanding figures, including John Brown, Ulysses S. Grant, George Meade, and Robert E. Lee. These individuals and several lesser lights would be portrayed by guest stars, including Colleen Dewhurst, Lloyd Bridges, Sterling Hayden, Robert Vaughn, Rory Calhoun, Paul Winfield, Geraldine Page, and Rip Torn.

McLaglen asked Gregory Peck to play Abraham Lincoln. Although the role wasn't the largest in the sweeping saga, the character would appear throughout the drama, encompassing about twenty-three minutes of airtime. Audiences would see the president in a variety of guises, from devoted husband and father to yarn-spinning politician to wartime commander-in-chief.

Like most movie stars, Peck had refused previous television roles. The occasional hosting job or variety-show gig was one thing, but acting on the tube was another matter. Not only was the pay scale for episodic programming and telefilms far below the standard for features, the pace of the work was much swifter. Where a feature company would typically shoot about three or four script pages a day, a television cast and crew would cover about eight or ten.

But with his options for big-screen roles narrowing, Greg was willing to amend his previous position. Moreover, he'd been hoping for an opportunity to portray Lincoln for a long time. "He's the ideal American," Peck asserted, "the one that we think embodies the best of us all."

Although he was tempted by McLaglen's offer, Greg refused to commit to *The Blue and the Gray* until the director and its producers, Hugh Benson and Harry Thomason, agreed to two conditions: first, that he be allowed to deliver the Gettysburg Address in its entirety, and second, that he be made up to resemble Lincoln as closely as possible. McLaglen and the producers agreed to Peck's terms.

To get the makeup right, Greg started with James Melton's definitive photographic collection, *The Face of Lincoln.* As when he played General MacArthur, he shaved his hairline back. But he also put putty behind his ears to make them stand out, had a latex nose constructed along with a latex lower lip, and used makeup to sink in his cheeks and create a mole. He even used special contact lenses to change his hazel eyes to the appropriate shade of blue-gray. The lenses were so painful that he could only wear them for ten or fifteen minutes at a time. The one thing he refused to do was approximate Lincoln's voice, which was reportedly high-pitched; he felt that audiences would have a hard time accepting such a radical departure from his well-known baritone.

Testament to the swiftness of TV production, the entire miniseries—six and a half hours of running time before the addition of commercials—was shot over seventy-seven days, between September and December 1981. The center of activity was Fayetteville, Arkansas. A local courtroom served as the locus of John Brown's trial; Civil War–era locomotives were found at a tourist attraction in Eureka Springs; and the battle sequences were staged, using Civil War reenactors, at the Prairie Grove Battlefield State Park, site of an actual 1862 engagement.

Peck's scenes were shot in two blocks of time. "He would come onto the set each morning, " recalled Cal Zinzer, a Prairie Grove Park historian, "already in makeup, already in costume, and already in character. It was quite an experience. I still don't feel that I've ever talked to Gregory Peck. I feel more like I've talked to Abraham Lincoln." Stacy Keach added, "In makeup he was eerie. It was as if the spirit of Lincoln filled him."

Although Greg knew what to expect, he still found television's pace a bit disconcerting. "If we were shooting the Gettysburg Address for a feature," he told *TV Guide,* "we'd want to shoot Lincoln from half-a-dozen different angles, get shots of the others on the platform, crowd and individual reactions. The thing would take two or three days. So I was a little surprised when I saw they had it down for one morning."

As usual, he'd prepared assiduously, concentrating in particular on defamiliarizing the words in the address that he'd memorized as a boy. "Because I knew it so well," he explained, "it was hard to put myself in the position of a man who was saying it in public for the first time; perhaps even saying it aloud for the first time. . . . I had to go over it hundreds of times to find the meanings fresh, and to get out of my head the rhythms of something I had learned by rote more than fifty years ago."

After the first take, McLaglen was satisfied. It was nice that the director was pleased, but Greg been hoping for another run at the speech, just for the thrill of it. "The thing zinged by before I was ready to let go of it," he confessed.

The Blue and the Gray aired over three evenings in 1982—Sunday, November 14; Tuesday, November 16; and Wednesday, November 17. "If you're expecting Catton's intricate political-military nuances and narrative lyricism," Harry F. Waters warned *Newsweek*'s readers, "get thee to a library. But if all you're seeking is pulpy diversion served with splashes of historical substance, *The Blue and the Gray* makes for a cozy Little House on the Shenandoah." Walters considered the combat sequences first-rate but most of the characterizations paper-thin. Agreeing with him, Kay Gardella of the New York *Daily News* likened the plot to "a soap opera story that would be laughed off daytime television."

John Hammond drew the worst fire for his wooden portrayal of the young *Harper's Weekly*'s artist, while Stacy Keach received considerable praise for what *Variety* called the "program's strongest performance." The trade paper had kind words for Peck as well, noting that he delivered the Gettysburg Address "in a direct, no-nonsense way that seems the likeliest approach to the original style." Overall, the performance brought Greg some of his best notices in years.

Peck hoped for another crack at his hero someday. "I'm pleased with those little scenes," he explained, "but strictly speaking I still haven't played him. I regretted I didn't have more to do, didn't show more sides of him. Frankly, I'd like to do an eight-hour piece on Lincoln alone, go into it exhaustively." Unfortunately, the opportunity never came.

By the time *The Blue and the Gray* aired, Peck already had another television project in the can. *The Scarlet and the Black* enabled him to add yet another historical portrait to his back-to-back portrayals of Douglas MacArthur, Josef Mengele, Lewis Pugh, and Abraham Lincoln.

One of the lesser-known heroes of World War II, Hugh O'Flaherty was an Irish monsignor assigned to the Holy Office in the Vatican. With the help of other clergymen and nuns, Italian nobles and intellectuals, and foreign dignitaries, he quietly enabled thousands of Allied prisoners of war turned loose by Mussolini's Fascists to escape the clutches of the Gestapo following the German occupation of Italy in 1943. Even after he aroused the suspicion of the Third Reich's commanding officer in Rome, Colonel Herbert Kappler, who placed him under round-the-clock surveillance, he continued his mission, eluding his watchers by donning various disguises. After the war, the monsignor returned to his native Ireland, where he died in 1965. Two years later, J. P. Gallagher told his story in a book entitled *The Scarlet Pimpernel of the Vatican.*

Far from a staid, religious ascetic, O'Flaherty was an engaging fellow. Journalist Cecil Smith described him as a "playboy priest who loved to box and go to parties, possessed a wit much prized by Roman hostesses, was a sportsman who seemed much more interested in his golf handicap than the war against Hitler." David Butler skillfully captured the multifaceted monsignor in his teleplay, which Peck responded to immediately. "When I read this script," he said, "I felt a little the way I felt when I got my hands on *To Kill a Mockingbird.* I felt that I knew this fellow O'Flaherty, just from reading the script, just as I knew Atticus Finch and had known him always." The monsignor even reminded the actor of his father. In a very meaningful way, O'Flaherty enabled Greg to connect with his roots.

Peck had already developed a keen sense of his heritage at the end of the 1960s, when he and Veronique visited his ancestral home in County Kerry. There he found members of the Ashe family, the clan with whom his dad had lived for several years in the 1880s. In fact, his father's cousin, Thomas Ashe, still resided on the family farm that Gregory Peck Sr. had called home. The old man fondly remembered his boyhood chum, the cousin who lost part of his finger in a silly game.

In Dingle, Greg met other relatives. He also studied the parish records in the local church, records that included the birth of his grandmother, Catherine Ashe, in 1864. Attending mass on Sunday, he looked around and experienced a realization unimaginable in polyglot America—the close-knit townsfolk, with their dark hair and piercing dark eyes, all looked like him!

As with Josef Mengele and Lewis Pugh, Greg developed an accent for his portrayal of O'Flaherty. This time, the character's Irish brogue came naturally. Indeed, he found that in every respect playing the monsignor was "a comfortable thing to do, like slipping into a comfortable old jacket."

Backed by a budget of $5 million, lavish by the standards of television films, *The Scarlet and the Black* was shot entirely in Rome during the summer of 1982, the hottest summer on record there since 1934.

As usual, the pace was swift; the entire picture, which would run three hours including commercials, was filmed in a mere thirty-five days. "Television acting," Peck said shortly thereafter, "is like running the mile, while movie acting is a series of fifty-yard dashes." He added, "To do this sort of film you have to simply cut seven weeks out of your life and let nothing get in the way of the work. My wife Veronique and I accept no invitations, go nowhere, see no one."

But even he was unprepared for the pace of filming in Saint Peter's Square. This world-famous gathering place served as the backdrop for about thirty short scenes, including shots of Peck in the different disguises O'Flaherty donned to escape Gestapo surveillance. In part because of the costume changes, the production company asked the Vatican for a three-day shooting permit. Initially, the request was granted. Then, for security reasons, the time was reduced to two days and, finally, to one.

To film thirty scenes in a single day, with time for Peck to change clothes between setups, seemed impossible. But having Saint Peter's Square as a backdrop was essential to the authenticity of the production. If he were to have even a prayer of getting the job done, the film's director, Jerry London, determined that he would need three camera units. While one shot, the other two would set up. As soon as the first one finished, it would move to the next location in the Square. Meanwhile work would commence with unit two. And so on through the day.

But the scheme couldn't work without Peck's cooperation. Not only was he on camera in virtually all of the setups, he would also have to submit to about two dozen very rapid wardrobe changes in between. "Can you do it?" London asked his sixty-six-year-old star. "Jerry," Peck replied, "if you can do it, I can do it." London was pleased but not surprised. "That's the kind of guy he was," the director said. "He was just in with the group. It was like, 'Okay, guys, let's make a great film. What do you need?' . . . There was none of this star arrogance. Here is a top-notch, A-one movie star. But he didn't act like one."

The day went just as planned. "I never worked so hard in my life," London recalled. "I did seventy setups that day.* I'll tell you, it almost killed me. But Greg was such a trouper. He would change his clothes real fast and he was out there, ready to go. Complete cooperation. Without that, we couldn't have done it."

*Although London needed to shoot roughly thirty scenes, some would require several different camera angles, hence seventy setups.

Peck and London also filmed at the Coliseum, site of the climactic night encounter between O'Flaherty and Kappler, played by Christopher Plummer. "So we got out there," said London, "and here we are—the crew, the two of them, and myself. It was a seven-page scene, and I shot from I think about twelve or fourteen different angles. And I printed take one on every take because they were perfect. There was no reason to say, 'Okay, do it again,' because they couldn't have done it any better. It was very exciting."

Looking back, the director, whose credits included the TV miniseries *Chiefs* and *Shogun,* considered that scene emblematic of the entirety of *The Scarlet and the Black.* "I'll tell you," he said chuckling, "this picture was problem free. When we shot it, it looked good. When we cut it, it looked good. And we finished it, it looked good."

The critics thought so as well. When the film aired on CBS on February 2, 1983, Kay Gardella of the New York *Daily News* called it "the finest drama to come along this season on television. I urge you not to miss it." She called the performances of Peck, Plummer, and John Gielgud as Pope Pius XII "riveting."

Although *The Scarlet and the Black* would earn Emmy nominations for editing, sound mixing, and graphic design, it was inexplicably overlooked in the major categories. The lack of recognition for Peck was particularly unfortunate, as he was most effective in this engaging role. Plummer was good as well, but it is O'Flaherty's outrage, leavened by his wit, which drives the picture, and Peck infused every scene with passion, dignity, and humor. Overshadowed perhaps by Greg's work in features, this performance is among the best of his mature period. At last, he was a full-fledged character actor.

Four years would pass before Peck took on another acting assignment. But it wasn't for lack of effort. He invested a considerable amount of time trying to launch Sinclair Lewis' *Dodsworth,* which, in the 1930s, had been made into a Broadway play and film starring Walter Huston. To produce the project, Greg had formed an association with producer Fred Levinson and the Producers Circle's Martin Richards and Mary Lea Johnson. At various times, they considered adapting the novel for the stage, for features, and for television, but the project never got off the ground. Eventually, Greg sold his interest in the property to Steve Ross of Warner Bros.

In August 1984, Greg signed to portray a Jewish doctor in *The Miracle,* from the novel by Irving Wallace, but this project also failed to materialize. And the following year, he was slated to return to the big screen in

Judgment Day, written by Pete Hamill with William Friedkin directing. Then Friedkin withdrew, and the project fell apart. Greg later brought suit against the producers, New Century Productions and SLM Inc., for breach of contract; the suit was eventually settled out of court.

Greg also spent some time looking backward, having reached the age where career retrospectives were becoming commonplace. In February 1984, the Los Angeles County Museum of Art launched one such tribute, which ran for six weeks and included twenty-eight films. Peck was present on February 17 to kick off the series with *Roman Holiday.*

He also spent a fair amount of time in New York, as his son Anthony, and his daughter, Cecilia, were living in the city—upon graduation from Amherst and Princeton, respectively. Raising a second set of kids hadn't always been easy, particularly in the turbulent 1960s and early 1970s. With Anthony, as with his older sons, Greg had been relatively indulgent. "I like a boy who raises a little hell," he once explained. "If a boy isn't adventurous, it isn't right." Cecilia, however, found him "a strict, old-fashioned father," which occasionally brought the two into conflict. Greg himself admitted that he was "uptight" during his daughter's teenage years, when she blossomed into a genuine beauty. "I was concerned about her vulnerability as a young girl," the star explained, "and the mistakes a young girl can fall into." But eventually he learned to trust her good sense, recognizing that, in any event, what she did with her life was "her business." In time, he became quite close with his kids, who developed a tight bond with one another as well. "They used to battle a bit growing up," Greg recalled, "but they've gone through all that, now they sort of admire each other and like being together and miss each other."

If a child's decision to follow in his or her parent's footsteps represents the sincerest form of flattery, Peck had reason to feel pleased, for both of his youngest children were pursuing acting careers. Where Tony was studying at Juilliard and with the noted teacher Stella Adler, Cecilia was honing her craft with Herbert Berghof, the head of HB Studios. Anthony's decision reflected an ongoing interest, but for Cecilia, performing was something new. "Cecilia's sudden decision to act," Greg said, "after devoting so much time to writing and photography came as a great surprise to us but we feel she has the talent for it so we are delighted." She would make her Broadway debut in April 1987 in *Sleight of Hand,* a play by John Pielmier. That year, she could also be seen in Oliver Stone's hit film *Wall Street.*

Before that, in July 1986, Greg made another trip to New York. This time, however, the visit wasn't mandated by the presence of his kids. Rather, he had been tapped for a singular honor—to introduce French

President François Mitterrand during the opening ceremonies for the one-hundredth birthday of the Statue of Liberty. It was an appropriate job, given Greg's wife's country of origin.

The following month, he finally went back to work, playing a president himself—in fact, the president of the United States.

Amazing Grace and Chuck was written and produced by David Field, a longtime executive for United Artists, Fox, and Columbia. Field had never tackled a screenplay before, but, as a child of the Cold War who could remember hiding under his desk during air-raid drills in school, he had strong feelings about the threat of nuclear extinction. His fablelike screenplay opens with the decision of a Little League pitcher named Chuck Murdock to give up baseball until all nuclear weapons are destroyed. A Boston Celtics basketball star, known as Amazing Grace Smith, reads a newspaper article about the boy's selfless act and joins the crusade. Professional athletes in other sports and in other nations follow until eventually the American president and the Soviet general secretary are forced to confront the situation.

Completed in 1983, the screenplay was rejected by studio after studio. "It was a very hard movie to get made," Field conceded, "because it's a goofy premise. It doesn't have any overt magic. There's no E.T. coming down from outer space. The magic of the fable is really the magic of the human heart—which is harder to believe in than an extra-terrestrial or a magician. And it tackled a very serious subject."

Told the script lacked a professional gloss, Field asked a friend, Ron Bass, whose credits included *Rain Man,* to help him out. For about two weeks, they examined the material page by page, primarily polishing the dialogue—with Bass working for free. Sadly, the Writers Guild refused to allow Field to give his friend screen credit.

Finally, after about three years, a new company, Tri-Star, for which Field was serving as a consultant, agreed to take the project on, providing it could be produced for the incredibly low sum of $5 million. "The only way it could be made for $5 million," Field explained, "was if things happened like I wrote and produced it for free and the director and all the actors worked for scale."

Salary wasn't much of an issue when it came to casting the title characters, for the roles went to first-time actors—a Minnesota seventh-grader named Joshua Zuehlke as Chuck and the All-Star forward of the Denver Nuggets, Alex English, as Amazing Grace Smith. Then, Jamie Lee Curtis, the popular young star of *Halloween* and *Trading Places* and the daughter of Greg's *Captain Newman, M.D.,* costar, Tony Curtis, agreed to play Amazing's manager for scale. Peck followed suit. "They couldn't legally work for free," Field said. "If they could have, they would have."

Field and his director, Mike Newall, a Brit whose credits included *The Man in the Iron Mask* with Richard Chamberlain, *The Awakening* with Charlton Heston, and *The Good Father* with Anthony Hopkins, almost bypassed Greg, thinking the star, then seventy, had retired. After all, he hadn't been seen in anything since *The Scarlet and the Black* aired in 1983. But they decided to send him the screenplay anyway, and the gamble paid off. "When I read the script," Greg said, "I felt my hair stand up a bit. I felt like cheering. It touched me." It reminded him of the movies of Frank Capra with, as he put it, the "little people overcoming the rich and the powerful and the corrupt." What's more, the antinuclear theme would enable him to reinforce the message conveyed by *On the Beach* decades earlier.

Although the company filmed briefly in Boston, most of the thirty-nine-day production schedule centered around two Montana towns, Livingston and Bozeman, as well as nearby Paradise Valley. Peck was needed on July 24, 1986, for the Little League ballgame that marks the film's finale. The rest of his scenes were shot between August 11 and 16, with a set erected in a local warehouse serving as the White House.

Field and Bass' script didn't provide many clues to the president's personality or history. He isn't even given a name. So Greg created a biography for his character—his schooling, family life, and so on—just as he'd learned to do decades earlier at the Neighborhood Playhouse. What he devised so closely resembled his own nature that he had merely to play himself, more or less, when the cameras turned. As he put it, "Why should I inflict any thespian trickery on the audience when I can actually be this man? It's a means of letting the audience know what sort of fellow I consider myself to be."

After such a long hiatus, he was delighted to be working again. So much so that on his final day, he asked Field—half-jokingly—to draft another scene for him. "I don't want to leave," he told the screenwriter. "I'm having a good time."

While the picture was in production, Tri-Star experienced a change of administration. As often happens in such circumstances, the new executives had little interest in the projects of their predecessors, particularly Field and Newall's quirky little fable. Consequently, when *Amazing Grace and Chuck* premiered on May 22, 1987, it was essentially an orphan. It was given minimal exposure—sixty theaters throughout the entire United States—with a total advertising budget of about $1 million, a tiny sum by the mid-eighties. "They guaranteed that it wasn't going to get seen," Field asserted.

In Los Angeles, the film debuted on the Memorial Day weekend—at one venue, the United Artists multiplex in Westwood. According to Field, the theater was given two prints and both were damaged. With the distributor closed for the holiday weekend, the theater manager decided on Saturday morning to cancel all screenings until the problem could be rectified the following Tuesday, a situation that was totally unacceptable to Field. Calling a friend at Tri-Star, he discovered that two copies of the picture were on private loan in the Los Angeles area, to studio executive Sherry Lansing and to Michael Jackson. Field knew Lansing but couldn't reach her by phone. He didn't know Jackson but remembered that Peck and the entertainer were friends. So he called Greg. Greg, in turn, called Jackson, who agreed to let the theater have his print. "Great," Field told Peck, "just give me the address and I'll go get it." But the actor replied, "Actually, they won't release it to you, 'cause they don't know you. Why don't you come to my house and we'll go together."

Field hopped in his car and drove to Carolwood Drive. Transferring to Peck's green Bentley, they proceeded to Jackson's estate in the San Fernando Valley, where several very muscular bodyguards gave them the cans of film. En route to the theater, Field profusely thanked Greg for helping him out of a jam. The actor looked at him with a twinkle in his eye and replied, "You know, you're an interesting kid. First, you get me to work for free and now you've got me delivering film."

They arrived in Westwood, where a crowd had gathered outside the cineplex. "The manager," Field recalled, "had obviously warned the people waiting for the show that a new print might be on the way." When the moviegoers saw Peck, they gave him a thunderous ovation. "And he actually blushed," said Field, "which was indeed sweet."

Field's story makes a cute anecdote, but it also illustrates the extent to which Peck remained committed to his projects. It is difficult to imagine many other seventy-one-year-old movie stars exerting themselves as he did that Saturday morning.

Unfortunately, *Amazing Grace and Chuck* didn't justify the effort. Most of the critics treated the picture with downright disdain. *People* magazine's Ralph Novak pointed to its "many moments of horrendous naivete and egregious sentimentality," and *Variety* called it as "amazingly bad as it is audacious."

Peck's personal notices were more respectful. Ralph Novak said that he "masterfully creates a complex character" while the New York *Daily News*' Chris Chase, one of the few critics to like the picture, argued that he made "a perfect President."

Given its poor notices and limited release, the film rapidly vanished.

* * *

Eight months after the premiere of *Amazing Grace,* Greg completed a major personal project, an unabridged audiocassette version of the King James Bible. Converting his guesthouse into a recording studio, he spent fourteen months making the tapes with his son Stephen, who acted as producer and engineer. "I'd say that for every hour we spent recording," Peck recalled, "we'd spend three hours on research so that I was absolutely clear on the geography, the very old place names, the cross references to the Old Testament, that sort of thing. I had to be clear in my own head if I had any hope of making it clear to the audience." They chose the King James Version of the New Testament because, in Greg's opinion, it offered the "most fulsome and poetic and rich" use of language. The collection of sixteen cassettes was originally sold through *The Hour of Power,* Robert Schuller's weekly religious broadcast, and later through the Sears Roebuck catalogue. At present, the set is distributed by Dove Audio.

The following year, 1987, the actor undertook two major international excursions. In February, he went to Moscow at the invitation of the Soviet government to participate, appropriately enough, in an international forum on nuclear disarmament. Other guests included Gore Vidal, Norman Mailer, and twenty Nobel Prize–winning scientists plus businesspeople and members of numerous religious orders. On the final day, the participants were invited to the Kremlin, where the Soviet president, Mikhail Gorbachev, spoke. Impressed by what he heard, Peck told a high-ranking member of the government that he thought it would be helpful if Gorbachev could address a joint session of the U.S. Congress. "Can you fix it?" the official asked. "I don't have too high a standing with the Reagan administration," the liberal Democrat confessed. "Neither do we," the Soviet replied.

Seven months later, on September 11, Greg and Veronique landed in Beijing for a ten-day visit to China. The trip was sponsored by the United States Information Agency, Ford Motor Company, the China Film Association, and the Cultural Section of the American Embassy in Beijing. "We made certain," an official named Chen Mei reported, "that Mr. Peck had the opportunity to meet a cross-section of Chinese film actors, directors, and scholars from different backgrounds and age groups. We hosted screenings of his films and engaged him to meet the audience." He also attended several seminars, screenings of Chinese pictures, and receptions where he met local artists. He didn't have much time for sightseeing, but, according to Chen Mei, he and his wife did spend a few hours searching for Chinese brush paintings and seeing a bit of the capital city.

Shortly after his return to the United States, Peck received the George Eastman Award for "Distinguished Contributions to the Art of Film" in a ceremony held on October 24 at the International Museum of Photography, George Eastman House, in Rochester, New York. The evening, which benefited the museum, included a screening of *Duel in the Sun* followed by a question-and-answer session with the star. Audrey Hepburn showed up as a surprise guest. She was in Rochester visiting relatives of her fiancé, Rob Wolders.

When he wasn't traveling or being feted, Greg enjoyed the quiet life. He and Veronique dined out two or three times a week, sometimes by themselves, sometimes with old friends. Among their closest pals were Cary Grant and his wife Barbara, whom Grant had married a few years earlier. In fact, Greg and Veronique had been instrumental in bringing them together. In 1976, they were in Cap Ferrat with the Sinatras as their houseguests, and Grant was staying at the nearby Monaco palace. One evening, the quintet went to dinner together. Although Cary had a wonderful time, he confided that being with the two happy couples made him kind of lonely. "You're Cary Grant," Greg replied, "and you don't have a girlfriend?" "No," the debonair star replied, adding that he had dined a few times with a public relations executive for a London hotel. He liked her but wasn't sure how she felt about him. The Pecks and the Sinatras persuaded their friend to fly to London and bring her back for dinner the following evening. Peck recalled, "Barbara Harris came for dinner—and never went back. We liked her right away—she was very pretty with a good head on her shoulders."

Whether with friends or by themselves, the Pecks stayed busy. "We never seem to have time on our hands," the actor asserted, adding, "I'm quite happy in the fullness of my years."

But he would rather have been acting. "I love the work," he explained. "I'm addicted to it. There are a lot of compensations for getting older. Experience is something of value. You do find you can call on skills and take chances. I like to play flamboyant, strange, interesting characters because I love make-believe and I feel I'm better at it than ever. I'm not as young as I was, I'm not as useful as the leader of the cavalry troops, but I think I can be useful and perhaps do better work than I've ever done before."

Two months later, he was offered just what he was looking for, a "flamboyant, strange, interesting" character—Ambrose Bierce—in an important new feature.

In 1913, the real Bierce, an aging American journalist and novelist, entered northern Mexico and vanished, never to be heard from again. Seventy-two years later, the distinguished Mexican novelist, Carlos Fuentes, used the writer's disappearance as the starting point for a novel that considered relations between his native land and her powerful neighbor to the north. *Gringo Viejo* featured two other principal characters, Tomas Arroyo, a general under Pancho Villa, and Harriet Winslow, a thirty-one-year-old American woman who comes to Mexico to tutor the children of a wealthy landowner. The complex interrelationships among this trio play out against the turbulence of the Mexican Revolution.

Jane Fonda met Fuentes in California around 1978, seven years before the publication of *The Old Gringo,* as the novel was called in the United States. By the eighties, the two-time Oscar winner and political activist had become a major power in Hollywood; her independent production company had developed such hits as *Coming Home, The China Syndrome, Nine to Five,* and *On Golden Pond.* When she told Fuentes that she was interested in a project that would consider the relations between their countries, he told her what he was working on, and she expressed immediate enthusiasm. Thereafter, Fuentes fleshed out the character of Harriet Winslow with Fonda in mind.

Columbia Pictures, with whom the actress had a coproduction deal, optioned *The Old Gringo* for her. But bringing Fuentes' story to the screen required several years and involved numerous writers, including the novelist himself, playwright Luis Valdez, and the husband-and-wife team John Gregory Dunne and Joan Didion. Finally, Aida Bortnik and Luis Puenzo crafted a workable screenplay. The Argentinians had previously collaborated on *The Official Story,* which Puenzo had also directed and which won the Oscar for Best Foreign Language Picture in 1985.

Essentially, Bortnik and Puenzo used Fuentes' novel as a starting point. As Bortnik explained, "Almost everything [in the book] is an interior monologue." It didn't lend itself easily to the medium of film. Therefore, most of the scenes had to be invented. However, they stayed true to the spirit, ideas, and characters of the original.

Among the screenwriters' inventions was the idea of telling the story through the eyes of Harriet Winslow. As they conceived it, the picture would open with the tutor on a train, accompanied by the body of the deceased Bierce, known by his Mexican alias Bitter. As she travels to the headquarters of General Pancho Villa seeking permission to return the corpse to the U.S., she thinks back on her experiences with the "old gringo" and with the fiery young general, Arroyo. En route, Bierce's corpse speaks to her. "It wasn't surrealistic," Bortnik explained, "it was Mexican. . . . For Mexicans, bodies talk. And people don't die immediately. People make a long trip until they arrive at death." Bortnik didn't think she'd get away with the concept, but to her great surprise, no one objected; not David Puttnam, who was running Columbia at that point, nor, for that matter, Puttnam's successor, Dawn Steele.

By the end of 1987, the screenplay had been polished, and principal photography was scheduled to begin after the New Year—with Burt Lancaster as Bierce/Bitter and Jimmy Smits, costar of the popular television series *L.A. Law,* as Arroyo. Then, a few days before Christmas, Fonda, who was rehearsing in northern Mexico where filming was to take place, learned that Lancaster couldn't get an insurance bond due to the potential impact of Mexico's high altitudes on his weak heart. Jane was willing to pledge her percentage of the film as a hedge against the seventy-four-year-old actor's ability to perform. But her offer was refused. Ironically, Lancaster himself was a replacement—for Paul Newman, who had withdrawn from the production for personal reasons.

To lose a principal actor in a pivotal role a few weeks before the start of filming is always devastating. In this case, the loss was even worse, because Lancaster had begun rehearsing the role and had endeared himself to Fonda, her partner, producer Lois Bonfiglio, and the other members of the company.

Back in Los Angeles for Christmas, Jane and Lois scrambled to find a new old gringo. "There were a handful of people who could have possibly played that part," Bonfiglio explained. "Of course, we wanted a mature actor and a brilliant actor and someone who would be magnetic on the screen, so that put a limit to it right away." Kirk Douglas and Robert Mitchum were among those under consideration, but their first choice was Gregory Peck.

Peck was already familiar with Fuentes' novel; at one point, he'd even considered optioning it himself. Before committing to the role, however, he called Burt, who graciously told Greg, "If they've offered you the part, go ahead and play it with my blessing." Shortly thereafter, Peck signed up.

"The chance to play Ambrose Bierce," he asserted, "is, at this stage of my career, an unanticipated but welcome challenge and a great opportunity." He knew the author's writings, having read some of his books in college and others in the decades since. "He fascinated me," Greg admitted, "he's an ideal character to play. He was sardonic, poetic, unpredictable, full of virtues and faults, arrogance and kindness. He punctured hypocrisy wherever he found it—whether religious, political, or social."

Budgeted at $24 million, *Old Gringo* went into production in mid-January 1988. Filming would take place at several locations, with interiors shot at the Churubusco Studios in Mexico City. But the biggest block of time—virtually half of the shoot—would be spent at Venta de Cruz, the remains of an eighteenth-century hacienda located in the desert north of Mexico City; it was extensively refurbished for the film.

Three weeks after being cast, Greg joined the company. He was a bit nervous, as the other cast members had had considerably more time to prepare than he. Moreover, he hadn't been in front of a feature camera in two and a half years. He went to Luis Puenzo and said, "I'm way behind, but I'm willing and I want to play this character. I don't want to be Old Greg in this. I want to be Ambrose Bierce. So I'm going to leave myself completely open to you, and I want as much help as you can give me." "They worked very closely together," Lois Bonfiglio recalled, "but Greg knew who Ambrose Bierce was. . . . He had a very clear picture of who this man was and what he was going to go for, I think."

Within short order, the veteran impressed everyone in the company with his ability to take on the complex writer. Bortnik recalled in particular a scene in which Bierce is thrust into a train compartment with a lively young prostitute. He is extremely uncomfortable, which Peck chose to indicate by talking very quickly, to use what Bortnik called "a wall of words" to protect himself. "It was such a magnificent idea," she said, "such a wonderful way to do the scene, that makes it seem completely different. Another rhythm. It was fantastic."

He was even more effective in a charming moment with Fonda as Harriet. It comes as Bierce, sitting astride a white horse, subtly romances the teacher. "Oh, once, once, the women sighed," he tells her, "swelled out their chests. How beautiful they were. I thought they'd always be there, sighing into my mustache, admiring my every glance, just waiting for a sigh from me. But they're all gone. They didn't wait. I suppose I didn't inspire enough love. In any of them." His hair completely white and boasting a black mustache, Peck clearly relished the poetic language, virtually cooing to an entranced Fonda. The heartthrob of a generation of women moviegoers, he could have just as easily been speaking about himself, save for the love of Veronique. Looking back on that scene, Fonda said, "It was magical. I loved the experience of shooting that scene with him. I loved the way he played it."

As the Pecks and Jane's father, Henry Fonda, were social acquaintances, she knew Greg somewhat before filming began, but they weren't close friends. However, a bond formed between them during the making of *Old Gringo.* "I think it was an amazing relationship that he had with Jane," said Lois Bonfiglio. "I think Jane adored him, as I did. And I think she felt he was somewhat of a father figure for her—and yet he was enough of a rascal that he could bring out the flirtatiousness. I mean, he's a gorgeous, gorgeous man. So actually it was a very rich relationship, extremely so."

Fonda also developed respect for Peck the actor. "There's something about him," she later said, "that walks this thin line between safe and familiar and warm and welcoming, and that which is dangerous and sexual and mysterious. Greg has not lost the hunger to take big risks. He never plays it safe." When the picture wrapped on April 29, after eighty-eight days of filming, Jane and the rest of the company were certain that he would earn an Oscar nomination for his performance.

But during the film's postproduction period the vision of those involved in its creation became blurred and confused. This may have been due, in part, to the inexperience of Puenzo as a director. Also, there was a change of administration at Columbia following Sony's acquisition of the company, and the new executives had no faith in the project. To enhance its commercial potential, they wanted to tell the story in the most direct, least complicated fashion possible.

As a consequence, the talking corpse and other surrealistic elements were dropped, and a linear treatment replaced the flashback concept. Peck, as usual, made extensive notes and comments during the postproduction period.

Although he initially favored the linear approach, feeling that the mystical elements weren't working, he changed his mind after viewing a subsequent cut. "In my opinion," he wrote Puenzo, Fonda, and Bonfiglio on December 12, 1988, "the picture has to be a memory piece, seen and heard from the perspective of Harriet Winslow as she is years after the events of the story." He remembered some unused footage that showed the tutor inside a car with the dead body of Bierce, and felt that that scene could serve in place of the train material, with some voice-over narration added. The result, he argued, would be somewhat reminiscent of *Out of Africa,* the Oscar-winning film of 1985, about the past experiences of another writer, Isak Denison, in another foreign clime. "Like that picture," he concluded, "ours is not a tight story, cause and effect. Everything cannot be made to link perfectly. Obviously it was not written that way."

The argument made sense. Thus, Bortnik was brought to L.A. from her home in Buenos Aires. She quickly dashed off the voice-over narration for Fonda to record.

The problem of the film's structure having been solved, Peck turned his attention to his own performance. "After looking at the cassette [of the latest cut] several times," he noted on January 10, 1989, "I see clearly that Bitter's character does not come over the way I had hoped." He felt that efforts to shorten the picture's running time had resulted in the deletion of dialogue that enriched his performance. As he put it, "Most of the lines which Bitter lost in the cutting were seen as character lines, not plot lines, therefore expendable. I think that the result was to flatten out Bitter's character, to take the juice out of him. It comes over to me as too straight a performance. He comes over as rather a sad old man."

This time, the situation went unresolved to his satisfaction. He was so upset by the lack of change that, on April 10, he wrote his agents, "I find it very hard to live with decisions that unnecessarily diminish the character of Bitter. In my opinion, the cuts have the effect of making my performance look inept, colorless, too straight, un-Bitter-like." He was determined, however, to remain a gentleman. "I'll never say anything against the picture," he told his agents. "There will be no visible signs of discontent, no leaks to the press."

He remained true to his word, appearing in May at Cannes, where the picture was shown during the annual film festival. He also promoted it in the United States at the time of its release on October 5. Indeed, at that point, he told Sandra McElwaine of the New York *Daily News,* "Hopefully a lot of people will go out to see it. And hopefully it will get out some of the more discerning people other than the kids who love these stunt shows," referring to current hits like *Batman* and *Ghostbusters II.* He added, "Maybe some of the more discerning critics will see something that they haven't been getting recently. I think there's an effort to get some substance."

The "effort" was evident. Some individual scenes and moments in *Old Gringo* were absolutely splendid—fresh, strange, intriguing—but so much had been compromised in the editing that overall the film was muddled and confusing, especially the interrelationships among the three major characters. Moreover, just enough footage of crowd scenes, sweeping landscapes, and twinkling nighttime skies had been shot and inserted into the final cut that the intimate personal stories were dwarfed by a kind of epic grandeur. In her well-reasoned review in the *New York Times,* Janet Maslin argued, "If *Old Gringo* were to work on the screen at all, it would have worked better on a smaller scale. Mr. Puenzo's film is overloaded with the kinds of artificial Hollywood touches that don't work well even in Hollywood hands. . . . Mr. Peck, Ms. Fonda, and Mr. Smits are all that holds *Old Gringo* together. And, despite the film's many difficulties, they are almost magnetic enough to do the job."

Peck's performance, despite his postproduction fears, was widely applauded. "Many bad movies have a bright spot," noted Julie Salamon in the *Wall Street Journal,* "and this one has Gregory Peck. In a marvelously loose and energetic portrayal of an old man who wants to die the way he wants to die." Other critics agreed.

Even with raves, the film's commercial potential would have been questionable. Given the critical response and the lack of advertising support from Columbia, it was a resounding failure, taking in a mere $2.3 million at the box office after three weeks of release. Shortly thereafter, it was gone from the nation's movie screens.

Oscar nominations rarely come from commercial disappointments. It was no surprise, therefore, that Peck's work in *Old Gringo* went unacknowledged by the members of the Academy. But he had done an extremely good job. His Bierce combines an outrageous disregard for life and limb with natural flamboyance and the poignant sensitivity of a romantic who hasn't lost his touch with women. At least he could content himself with that. As he told Charles Champlin of the *Los Angeles Times,* "[It] often happens that the parts are better than the whole, and you have to hope you're one of the parts." In this case, he was.

In March 1989, Greg was the beneficiary of the Lifetime Achievement Award of the American Film Institute, the organization that he'd helped to establish more than two decades earlier. Since then, the institute's annual tribute had become one of the signal honors accorded a member of the motion picture industry. Past winners included actors James Cagney, Bette Davis, Henry Fonda, James Stewart, Fred Astaire, Lillian Gish, Gene Kelly, Barbara Stanwyck, and Jack Lemmon, and directors John Ford, Orson Welles, William Wyler, Alfred Hitchcock, and Frank Capra. "I was genuinely surprised," Peck told *Variety,* when he learned that he'd been named the honoree for 1989. He added with wry humor, "[I] always saw this as an award for older people."

The dinner, held on March 9, was hosted by Audrey Hepburn, looking radiant in a black, off-the-shoulder gown. After recounting the milestones of Greg's early years, she recalled the help and support he'd provided her during the making of *Roman Holiday.* She told the celebrity audience, "I have waited thirty-seven years, not only to honor him, but to finally be able to say to him with all my heart and all my love, 'Thank you, dear Greg.'" The lavish applause that followed left Peck looking slightly embarrassed and perhaps a bit misty as well.

Interspersed with numerous film clips were other tributes—from Lauren Bacall, Anthony Quinn, Jennifer Jones, Jane Fonda, Robert Mulligan and Alan J. Pakula, Mary Badham, Angie Dickinson, Liza Minnelli, Dean Stockwell, Charlton Heston, Greg's daughter, Cecilia, and Sidney Poitier. Finally, George Stevens Jr. made the presentation. Greg accepted the award with typical grace and humor, but he also took a moment to encourage his Hollywood colleagues to elevate the quality of films and television shows. "Making millions is not the whole ballgame, fellas," he asserted. "Pride of workmanship is worth more. Artistry is worth more. The human imagination is a priceless resource. The public is ready for the best you can give them. It just may be that you can make a buck and, at the same time, encourage, foster, and commission work of quality and originality." The applause was loud and sustained.

Variety called the event "a thrilling, moving affair, buoyed by an outpouring of genuine emotion from friends and colleagues gathered to celebrate one of the greats of the business." An edited one-hour version of the tribute aired on NBC on March 21.

CHAPTER 22

The Nineties and Beyond

Other People's Money was the perfect play for the get-rich Reagan era. Written by Jerry Sterner, a forty-four-year-old businessman-turned-playwright, the wry drama centered on an aggressive corporate raider named Lawrence Garfinkle, better known as "Larry the Liquidator." Garfinkle has earned his nickname by gaining control of undervalued companies and selling off their assets. While his profits are considerable, the companies are destroyed in his wake. Setting his sights on a new target, New England Cable and Wire, he comes into conflict with the company's chairman and CEO, Andrew "Jorgy" Jorgenson, a pillar of old-fashioned business rectitude, and with Jorgenson's attorney, a Wall Street hotshot named Kate Sullivan. Beautiful and savvy, Sullivan is, like Garfinkle, more interested in the game than anything else. It just so happens that this time the client is family; her mother, Bea, has been Jorgy's lover for years. The play climaxes with Garfinkle and Jorgensen's respective appeals to the company's stockholders, which Garfinkle wins. Thereafter, we are told, Kate joins his firm, becomes his partner, and then his wife.

Opening off-Broadway at the Minetta Lane Theatre on February 16, 1989, *Other People's Money* featured Kevin Conway as Garfinkle (a character based, in part, on the real-life corporate raider, Britain's James Goldsmith), Mercedes Ruehl as Kate, and Arch Johnson as Jorgy. Only Sterner's second dramatic effort, it went on to earn three Outer Critics Circle Awards, including one for Best Off-Broadway Play.

The screen rights were acquired by independent producer Ellen Krass. She took the project to Warner Bros. and to Peck's *Billy Two Hats* producer, Norman Jewison, who elected to direct as well as produce the picture. His recent credits included two other adaptations of successful plays, *A Soldier's Story* and *Agnes of God.*

Although Wall Streeters had loved the sharp satire of *Other People's Money,* particularly Garfinkle's unabashed greed, Jewison felt that the comedy needed a softer touch for the broader movie audience. Accordingly, Oscar-winning screenwriter Alvin Sargent, author of Peck's *The Stalking Moon* and *I Walk the Line,* kept the play's basic plot but blurred Lawrence's rough edges. On stage Conway had played the character so broadly that virtually every critic had likened him to the Jewish comic Jackie Mason. For the film, all traces of his ethnicity were eliminated; even his name was changed to the slightly less obvious Garfield (like the cuddly cartoon cat). At the same time, the character was made far more vulnerable; his sexual banter with Kate, a major factor in the play, would now underscore genuine longing, such that Larry tenderly proposes marriage to her on the eve of the stockholders' meeting (but is gently rebuffed). In more conventional fashion, Sargent also opened the play up, adding numerous minor characters, including Lawrence's chauffeur, his droll assistant, and his fleet of associates and lawyers, as well as a few employees of Jorgenson's factory.

Initially, Jewison had hoped to cast Dustin Hoffman as Garfield and Michelle Pfeiffer as Kate, but the roles went instead to Danny DeVito and Penelope Ann Miller. The balding, pudgy, diminutive DeVito had made a career playing lovable rogues, from Louie DePalma, the dispatcher in the television sitcom *Taxi,* to the businessman who refuses to pay a ransom for his kidnapped wife in *Ruthless People* to the unscrupulous aluminum-siding salesman in *Tin Men.* A more unusual choice was Miller, an attractive young blonde who specialized in sweet innocents, as in her roles in *Biloxi Blues* and *Kindergarten Cop.* "[W]e knew that we needed someone who was both fresh and talented," explained Jewison's coproducer Ric Kidney. "And while doing research, Norman and I discovered that an awful lot of the high-powered lawyers on Wall Street are surprisingly young. So we met all the up-and-comers in New York and Hollywood, and Penelope Ann Miller was the one who knocked us out."

Although Jewison had wanted Paul Newman for Jorgy, casting Peck as the voice of business ethics made perfect sense. The star brought five decades of portraying upstanding decent Americans with him to the role. As Jewison put it, "Gregory represents real values to an audience. You feel safe when he is in the picture." Moreover, Peck campaigned for the opportunity. "I saw the play twice," the actor recalled, "and when I read that Norman Jewison had acquired it, I wrote him and said, 'I'm the one for you.' I really wanted to play that part."

The shoot began in New York City, Larry and Kate's home base, on October 26, 1990. About two weeks later, the company moved to Connecticut—standing in for Rhode Island in the film. The work was concentrated at two mills about forty miles apart. The first was the Gilbert & Bennett Manufacturing Company in Georgetown. Founded in 1818, it was shut down shortly before principal photography began (although the company had functioning mills elsewhere). The second was the Seymour Specialty Wire Company, a copper and brass firm in Seymour, whose employees served as extras in the film (the mill would close in June 1992).

Dean Jones, cast as Jorgy's second-in-command, Bill Coles, recalled that at one point in Seymour, he and Greg were asked to walk through the plant and say hello to the employees. As the mill extended over several floors, a considerable amount of strolling and climbing was involved. "So we were walking around," Jones recalled, "people coming up. Greg had been on his feet all day and here he's got a break for an hour, and we're walking through being talked to by the employees—who were very gracious, very sweet—but the point is maybe a guy his age would have liked to sit down and relax for that hour. I was constantly amazed at his gracious behavior."

While filming in Connecticut, Greg missed a personal milestone, the marriage of his son Anthony, thirty-five, to his longtime girlfriend, thirty-four-year-old supermodel Cheryl Tiegs. Since completing his acting training, Tony had appeared as a Spanish lord in Roman Polanski's *Pirates;* had a featured role in the NBC miniseries *Poor Little Rich Girl* starring Farrah Fawcett; played the title role in *Hollywood Detective,* a series on the Arts & Entertainment cable network; and costarred with Brooke Shields in the 1990 film *Brenda Starr.* The spur-of-the-moment ceremony was held in the garden of Frank Sinatra's Palm Springs estate. On October 3, 1991, shortly before *Other People's Money* opened, Tiegs gave birth to a boy, whom they named Zackary, making Greg a grandfather for the first time.

After about four weeks in Connecticut, the cast and crew of *Other People's Money* returned to Los Angeles to film the interiors, including the climactic stockholders' meeting, for which the company rented a warehouse and hired a host of extras. Not since *To Kill a Mockingbird* had Peck been given such a long, well-written speech—which came directly from Sterner's play. "A business is worth more than the price of its stock," the CEO tells his shareholders. "It's a place where we earn our living, meet our friends, dream our dreams. It is in every sense the very fabric that binds our society together."

Articulating these sentiments came naturally to Peck. "I'm for Jorgy," he said. "I think he's right and Danny's wrong. Danny in his role as Larry the Liquidator represents the loss of traditional values, the loss of concern for people. . . . I think the traditional values do count, and sooner or later we'll come back to them, otherwise we'll trivialize ourselves right out of existence."

It is not uncommon for elderly stars to require strategically placed cue cards as memory aids, since even the best of actors suffer from a loss of concentration with advancing years. But the seventy-four-year-old Peck needed no such assistance. Time and again, he delivered the lengthy monologue without difficulty. "To see him go through it," recalled the film's assistant director, Marty Ewing, "and with ease it appeared, was a great moment."

Indeed, the septuagenarian dazzled his coworkers throughout the eleven weeks of filming. "I have never worked with a more professional performer," asserted Dean Jones. "I was so impressed and, at times, awestruck at the way he professionally ruled himself." To Penelope Ann Miller, he was "everything that you see on the screen. He's so handsome, he's such a gentleman, he is so funny and charming. I mean, he walks into the room and you just melt!" And to Piper Laurie, who played Bea, he was her youthful crush in the flesh. As she put it, "Growing up, I had been such a fan of his, seen everything he'd done and fallen in love with him. And there he was! And, of course, he remained through the years a very imposing, beautiful person, physically. He just looked so elegant. The whole package was just breathtaking." She also found him "very creative and open and vulnerable."

According to Laurie, Alvin Sargent rewrote the script throughout principal photography. The tinkering continued during postproduction, particularly after the film was tested in previews. To Peck's dismay, numerous scenes between Jorgy and Bea were cut, giving greater focus to Garfield and Kate. "I regret very much the loss of that human dimension," Greg told reporter Bob Campbell. "Some scenes went because of market testing. . . . Apparently six or eight guinea pig audiences were impatient with the subplot." Given these deletions, the picture contains an underlying tension between Jorgy and Kate that is never explained. (By contrast, in the play, the audience learns that she knew her mother was cheating with Jorgy while her dad was alive.) Worst of all, perhaps, the ending was altered. Garfield still triumphs at the stockholders' meeting, but the company is saved at the eleventh hour by a Japanese firm that contracts the mill to manufacture automobile airbags. It seemed like a cop-out.

Upon its opening on October 18, 1991, Jewison's kinder, gentler *Other People's Money* failed to take off at the box office. The acting was fine, with DeVito as the principal standout in the largest and juiciest role, and the picture had a wonderful texture in terms of the New York and the New England settings. But it wasn't funny enough, biting enough, or romantic enough to rouse either moviegoers or film critics. As Julie Salamon noted in the *Wall Street Journal,* "Mainly, Mr. Jewison and his screenwriter, Alvin Sargent, decided to transform this story of money love into boy-girl love. . . . Though the sexual side of corporate gamesmanship was an ingredient in the play, the movie seems to be little else besides a long, leering flirtation. . . . And instead of showing us how Wall Street plays hardball, the film plays kneesies with us."

One month after the opening of *Other People's Money,* Peck could be seen in another feature film, albeit in a cameo role. *Cape Fear* was a remake of Greg's 1962 thriller, with Nick Nolte taking over as the beleaguered attorney Sam Bowden plus Jessica Lange as his wife, and Robert De Niro as the psychopath Max Cady.

Although the idea of the remake had originated with Steven Spielberg, the director cooled on the project. He swapped with his friend and fellow director, Martin Scorsese, for a project about the holocaust, *Schindler's List,* that Scorsese had been developing.

Noted for his hard-edged dramas about social outcasts, including *Mean Streets, Taxi Driver, Goodfellas,* and *Raging Bull,* for which he won an Oscar, Scorsese was intrigued by the idea of taking what he called "a psychologically realistic thriller to a movie landscape where the main characters battle it out in a sort of movieland apocalyptic vision." Along the way, he and screenwriter Wesley Strick made the harmonious Bowden family dysfunctional, with Sam a repentant adulterer and their daughter, played by the edgy Juliette Lewis, a rebellious nymphet. They also gave Cady a stronger motivation for revenge by making Sam not simply a witness to his crime, but his attorney, one who arranged to lose the case. As film critic Peter Travers observed, "In the first *Cape Fear,* Cady was the only walking time bomb; in the Scorsese version, everyone is ticking."

"I didn't want to do the cameo," Peck said upon the film's release. "I don't want to play little supporting parts. You can't get your teeth in it. You've got to have some horses to ride, some meat on the bones to make it fun to do. But Scorsese and De Niro were persistent." Offered his choice of small roles, he chose that of the attorney who represents Cady at a hearing at which the ex-con is, ironically, seeking a restraining order against Bowden. "I took the one I thought was an amusing twist," Peck said, "the lawyer who defends De Niro instead of prosecuting him." Two of his original costars also had cameos; Martin Balsam, the sheriff in the 1962 version, portrayed the judge in the hearing with Peck, and Mitchum played the equivalent of the sheriff, a much smaller role this time around.

Decked out in a white three-piece suit with blue shirt, bow tie, and black mustache, Peck spent only a day in Fort Lauderdale, Florida, filming his short scene. In fact, he was still shooting *Other People's Money* at the time. But he enjoyed working with Scorsese. "I'd like to work with him again," he noted, "not in another cameo, though."

Unlike the original thriller, Scorsese's remake was a huge commercial and critical success, accurately called a "punishing, sock-it-to-'em thriller that makes the audience feel as worked over as a punch-drunk fighter," by Kathleen Carroll of the New York *Daily News*. The *New York Times'* Vincent Canby called Greg's appearance a "brief but surprisingly effective performance."

So far, Peck's hoped-for reunion with Scorsese hasn't materialized. Indeed, his twin releases in the fall of 1991 have most likely brought an end to his feature career. Each in its own way offered a fitting epitaph. *Cape Fear* is, in part, an homage to the original thriller and, by extension, its star and producer. Moreover, as a Southern lawyer, Peck made a fleeting reference to the most celebrated of his roles, Atticus Finch in *To Kill a Mockingbird*. Likewise, *Other People's Money* gave him an Atticus-like speech, calling upon Americans to find the best in their natures. Envisioning a world where businesspeople take pride in their work and in their coworkers, Greg also offered a modern articulation of the ideal sought by Tom Rath in *The Man in the Gray Flannel Suit* thirty-five years earlier. It wasn't a bad note on which to exit.

Peck back on Broadway? After an absence of forty-eight years? When Greg's friend, *Mirage* and *Arabesque* screenwriter Peter Stone, suggested the idea the actor told him it was impossible; he was far too old. Nevertheless, when *The Will Rogers Follies* opened on May 1, 1991—a few months before *Other People's Money* and *Cape Fear*—the movie star was among the featured players.

Actually, Peck was in the audience watching that night. But his voice resonated throughout the venerable Palace Theatre.

The idea behind the show was unusual—to portray the life of the great comic-actor-writer Will Rogers as if it were being presented on the stage by the legendary showman Florenz Ziegfeld, producer of the Ziegfeld Follies for which Rogers had been a major star. The reason for this format, Stone explained, was that Rogers' life "was unremarkable in almost every way." By telling the entertainer's story through the medium of the Follies, Stone could change whatever he wanted without attempting to deceive the audience. For example, in real life, Rogers met his wife at a train station in a small town in Oklahoma. Ziegfeld rejects this unprepossessing locale, staging the encounter on—believe it or not—the moon instead.

As Stone knew, Ziegfeld had an office in his theater with a glass window in the floor, a device that enabled him to view the activities on the stage below. Thus, the playwright decided to have the showman direct the action of the musical from his office, as an unseen but very powerful presence. "He would have been smaller than life had he appeared," Stone explained. This decided, he needed a commanding voice, issuing directions to the actors like "the voice of God." Peck's stentorian tones seemed ideally suited to the job. Hiring the old-time movie star had yet another benefit. "It added a kind of glamour," pointed out Betty Comden, who wrote the lyrics for the musical numbers with her partner, Adolph Green. "Don't forget it's a Ziegfeld Follies. It's a very up kind of show-biz entertainment."

As with *Cape Fear,* Peck took a bit of time from his work on *Other People's Money* to record his lines for *The Will Rogers Follies.* Present during the taping at a Manhattan sound studio were Stone, the musical's director Tommy Tune, and the actors who interact with Ziegfeld, including Keith Carradine starring as Rogers. That way, Stone explained, Peck's readings weren't "flat. There was some give and take" with the other players. Each of the showman's speeches was looped separately, to be controlled by a sound engineer at the back of the theater during each performance. Consequently, the actors on stage weren't locked into a fixed time frame for their responses.

The entire recording session, Stone asserted, took a few hours, but Peck drew a hefty paycheck for each and every week of the show's very respectable 983-performance run.

With a Broadway musical and two feature films bearing his name, Peck was a rather visible presence in 1991. He ended the year with another important public appearance. On December 8, he was one of the recipients of the Kennedy Center Honors.

Since their inception in 1978, the awards given by the John F. Kennedy Center for the Performing Arts were highly prestigious. The list of honorees reads like a Who's Who of American performing artists in the last quarter of the twentieth century, from composers and musicians to dancers and choreographers to dramatists and directors. The previous Hollywood recipients included Fred Astaire, Henry Fonda, James Cagney, Helen Hayes, Lillian Gish, Gene Kelly, Frank Sinatra, and James Stewart. Sharing the honor with Greg were his *Will Rogers Follies* colleagues Betty Comden and Adolph Green; conductor Robert Shaw; the tap-dancing Nicholas Brothers, Harold and Fayard; and country music singer-producer Roy Acuff.

The segment honoring Peck featured a tribute by Audrey Hepburn, who called her friend "the most authentic actor of our time." On a personal note, she added, "For your courage and integrity, you have my deepest respect. For your friendship, your goodness, and your humor, you have all my love." Acknowledging Peck's Irish heritage, his friend, violinist Isaac Stern, performed "Londonderry Air." In customary fashion, the program, hosted by Walter Cronkite, was taped and broadcast on CBS on December 26.

Like *Other People's Money, The Portrait* was an adaptation of an off-Broadway play. Entitled *Painting Churches,* Tina Howe's drama begins when Margaret "Mags" Church, a promising Manhattan artist, returns to the Boston home of her youth to help her elderly parents, Gardner and Fanny, vacate their lifelong home and move to a summer cottage. She also wants to paint their portrait for an upcoming exhibition of her work. During the course of the drama, Howe explored the delicate bonds among the three—Gardner, a recently retired college professor and well-regarded poet, is slipping into senility; Fanny still loves her husband but resents the care his condition requires; and Mags wants her parents to accept her for what she is, a talented, competent adult. Like her characters, Howe, author of several other well-regarded plays, including *Museum* and *The Art of Dining,* hailed from Boston. Her mother was a painter and her father a newsman. "When people ask me how much do the Churches resemble my family," she said, "I always answer: all of it is true, but none of it happened."

Produced by the Second Stage company, *Painting Churches* opened at the South Street Theater on Manhattan's West Forty-second Street on January 25, 1983, with Frances Conroy as Mags, Donald Moffat as Gardner, and Marian Seldes as Fanny. It moved to the Lambs Theatre, where it enjoyed a run of 206 performances and won an Obie for Best Off-Broadway Play.

Although a taped version of the drama aired on PBS in 1986, with Moffat, Roxanne Hart as Mags, and Sada Thompson as Fanny, Peck acquired the screen rights through his most recent company, Atticus Productions. To finance the $4 million film, he joined forces with Robert Greenwald Productions and TNT, one of Ted Turner's cable stations. "It is very much an actor's piece," Peck said of the drama, adding, "It is exactly what blockbuster movie types would disparagingly call 'a picture with relationships.' It is kind of a dirty word for them. For that reason, TV is the right medium."

One of the property's principal attractions, as far as Greg was concerned, was that Mags offered a strong role for his daughter, Cecilia. By this point, her career had included numerous film and TV appearances, and stage roles in Los Angeles as well as New York. She had also been a dancer with the company of her father's Neighborhood Playhouse teacher, Martha Graham. He asked his friend Lauren Bacall to play Fanny and engaged the noted stage and film veteran, Arthur Penn, to direct. The director had gotten his start in the live TV dramas of the fifties before tackling such features as *The Miracle Worker, Bonnie and Clyde,* and *Little Big Man.*

Peck decided to play Gardner only after Jack Lemmon turned the role down. Boasting long, snow white hair, a full, mostly white beard, and a black mustache, he endowed the academic with a bit of panache. But he was clearly at home in the character's shoes, having played so many men of similar intellectual bent throughout his career—although Church's incipient senility introduced a new wrinkle. Moreover, the poet's hobby, rowing, enabled him to display the form that had earned him his athletic letter at Cal so many years before, and he was able to reunite with his old screen partner, Lauren Bacall. Most important perhaps, Gardner's touching relationship with Mags allowed him to capture on film something of his real-life bond with his daughter.

Lynn Roth, who adapted the play, made significant alterations to Howe's drama. She invented much of the dialogue and many of the episodes and added numerous characters, including academic colleagues of Gardner, Mags' ex-boyfriend, and a stuffy son of family friends with whom the artist attends a concert. Most important, perhaps, Roth softened Fanny's character, slightly downplayed the state of Gardner's senility, and made central to the drama Mags' sense of being an outsider in her parents' extremely close relationship.

Roth also opened up the drama from the confines of the Church home. Hence, a college backdrop was needed for filming. As principal photography would start on the last day of March 1992 (following several weeks of rehearsal in Los Angeles and New York), the likelihood of inclement weather made a New England location inadvisable. Peck and Penn instead selected Duke University in North Carolina. The company took full advantage of the location, shooting at sixteen different sites in the Raleigh-Durham area. But the heart of the action remained the Church home, for which they found a charming two-story Victorian-style house, complete with a spacious front porch and gazebo, in an historic section of Raleigh.

Peck and Bacall were delighted to be working together again, thirty-six years after their original pairing. "We like one another," the actress said. "There is good chemistry between us. Greg is a loving human being. He is not like most actors. He is interesting and intelligent." As for playing opposite his daughter, Greg found the experience a "total, unmitigated joy." Cecilia was pleased as well. "It's a treat spending time together," she told reporter Ann Green. "Even though we are close and stay in the same city [at this point, she was living in Los Angeles], we never get to spend so much time together. He is great fun on the set. Between him and Ms. Bacall, I have not stopped laughing."

The old veterans also appreciated the contributions of their director. As Peck put it, "Arthur Penn is an asset to this picture in very special ways—the subtleties and his knowledge of human behavior." Bacall added, "Arthur has been very helpful. I have not felt that I have had to protect myself. When actors don't trust a director, they pull in and give safe performances because they are afraid of making fools of themselves. With this, I have gone for broke."

During filming, Peck took time out for yet another homage. On April 13, he flew to New York where the Film Society of Lincoln Center presented *A Tribute to Gregory Peck.* In association with the gala, the Film Society screened a series of the actor's movies between April 11 and April 28 at Lincoln Center's Walter Reade Theater.

The day after the tribute, Greg returned to North Carolina, where, on April 24, *The Portrait* wrapped—after twenty-one days of filming. A month after completing the family drama, the actor suffered a major personal loss, the death of his mother. Bernice was ninety-seven.

Although Peck and Penn came into conflict with TNT executive Alan Sabinson over the nuts-and-bolts editing of *The Portrait,* the actor-producer remained satisfied with the result. "I think it is pleasant to watch," Greg wrote his director in July, "quite funny, with moments of pathos without sentimentality, and that the ending is going to wrap it up in style with a good emotional kick. A dynamite piece it is not. But I think the critics are going to approve. It has style, and there is nothing second rate or embarrassing about it."

He was right. When the picture debuted on February 13, 1993, Tony Scott of *Variety* called the film "an effective study of aging, loving parents and the adult daughter they've shut out all these years," likening it to the popular feature *On Golden Pond.* Fran Wood of the New York *Daily News* agreed. She found Roth's teleplay "poignant and funny" and described Peck and Bacall as "terrific, demonstrating that talent endures and no effort to find worthy vehicles for Hollywood legends is too great." Cecilia Peck was equally engaging as their charming, vulnerable daughter, a performance that earned her a Golden Globe Best Supporting Actress (TV) nomination.

Gardner Church will probably prove to be the last major role of Gregory Peck's career. In the wake of the TV drama, he wanted to continue acting, but he recognized that the Hollywood of the nineties wasn't his Hollywood. "I admire very many of the new filmmakers and the work they do," he told *Los Angeles Times* critic Charles Champlin in 1991, "but I don't know them. They have their own gatherings of people of their own generation. . . . We still have a lot of friends here. But we're not in the vortex anymore." He added with a smile, "But that's the natural order of things."

So he stopped reading the trade papers, no longer concerned himself with what he called "the little world of who's doing what and what did what at the box office and what pictures are moving up to the front burner." If, by chance, a good opportunity came along, he'd grab it. But, in the meantime, there were plenty of other things to do.

Fortunately, his health allowed him to do them. Although he turned seventy-six while *The Portrait* was in production, he had no major physical problems. His daily regimen even included what he described as "a little exercise and two glasses of red wine."

Still, as he acknowledged wryly, he had "four or five doctors I call by their first names." And there *were* a few health-related incidents over the next few years. In August 1994, he underwent ankle fusion surgery, thanks to the injury he had suffered from a falling horse in 1948. Four months later, on December 20, he experienced what was later described as "stomach distress" while dining in a restaurant near his home. An ambulance ferried him to Cedars-Sinai Medical Center, where he improved quickly and was released the following day. About a year and a half after that, on July 13, 1996, he was again hospitalized, this time in Karlovy Vary, a spa town in Czechoslovakia, about eighty miles west of Prague, where he was attending a film festival. Diagnosed with appendicitis, he was rushed into surgery. After about a week, he was released minus his appendix. He and Veronique flew to Paris, where he further recuperated before returning to the States.

These incidents aside, Peck went about his business—traveling, participating in numerous industry-related events, even indulging in a bit of work.

Between 1993 and the end of 1999, for example, he was feted by the Berlin Film Festival, a gathering of the French Film Academy, and the Chicago Film Festival, taking home a lifetime achievement award on each occasion. He was also accorded the second annual Marion Anderson Award from the city of Philadelphia in recognition of his humanitarian work. And in October 1998, he, along with Fats Domino, Philip Roth, Gwen Verdon, and others received the National Medal of the Arts from President Bill Clinton.

Greg not only received awards and tributes, he gave them. At the Oscar ceremonies in 1993, he presented the Jean Hersholt Humanitarian Award posthumously to Audrey Hepburn. And, twice, he was a presenter at the Kennedy Center Honors—in 1992, for cellist-conductor Mstislav Rostopovich; and in 1997, for singer-songwriter Bob Dylan.

Also in 1997, he accepted an invitation from the Czech government to attend a four-day gathering in Prague called Forum 2000. Among the participating artists, statesmen, and religious leaders were the Dalai Lama, Czech president Vaclav Havel, and author Elie Weisel. At a concert during the festivities, Peck, along with Lynn Redgrave and James Earl Jones, read words by Churchill, Twain, and other great thinkers.

When significant occasions didn't beckon, Greg and Veronique often went traveling for the mere pleasure of it. Ireland had become a favorite destination. In 1994, Greg established a scholarship for young filmmakers at the University College Dublin, and he liked to visit the college from time to time. In 2000, the institution bestowed upon him an honorary doctorate of literature.

Ireland was refreshing, but Veronique's birthplace, Paris, remained home away from home. Greg was virtually an adopted son of France, having been made a Chevalier of the Legion d'Honneur under President Mitterand and a Commandeur under President Chirac. The Pecks were, in fact, in the City of Lights, on December 31, 1995, to mark their fortieth wedding anniversary, and again the following April 5, when Greg turned eighty.

In addition to his televised participation in the Kennedy Center Honors in 1992 and 1997, Peck maintained an occasional presence on the small screen during the nineties. In 1991, he narrated an episode of PBS's *American Masters* series entitled "Frederic Remington: The Truth of Other Days." The following year, he participated in the segment of the Cinemax series *Crazy About the Movies* that profiled Ava Gardner, and he served as the voice of explorer John Wesley Powell for an episode of PBS' *Nova* called "Rafting Through the Grand Canyon." In 1993, he paid tribute to his *Roman Holiday* costar in the PBS documentary *Audrey Hepburn Remembered.* He also participated in an NBC special hosted by Katie Couric entitled *Legend to Legend,* in which a variety of celebrities honored another accomplished individual in his or her field. Peck paid tribute to Jimmy Stewart. Finally, in 1994, he could be heard on the Arts & Entertainment cable network, narrating an episode of the series *Time Machine* devoted to the pursuit of the Nazi war criminal Adolf Eichmann, and as the voice of Connie Mack, the legendary owner-manager of the Philadelphia Athletics, in the epic PBS/Ken Burns documentary *Baseball.*

Of course, none of these TV appearances were acting assignments. They were fun and sometimes lucrative, but by 1996, Greg had had enough. As he turned eighty that April, he formally announced his retirement, saying "I've had a fifty-year run, and I don't want to wear out my welcome." Then he quickly amended his remarks, saying, "No actor retires totally. If a great role comes along, I'd come charging out of the barn, snorting!"

The following year he did just that, playing Father Mapple in a four-hour adaptation of *Moby Dick*. As with Martin Scorsese's *Cape Fear*, Greg's casting was, in part, an homage to a noteworthy predecessor, in this case the John Huston version of the Melville classic. But the role of the clergyman, played by Orson Welles in the 1956 feature, was a challenge in its own right, and Peck treated it as such. He spent weeks in preparation. He also rewrote much of Mapple's six-minute sermon about Jonah and the whale, referring back to both Melville's novel and the original biblical account.

The filming of *Moby Dick* took place near Melbourne, Australia, between May and August 1997. The $20 million epic, produced by Robert Halmi Sr., Francis Ford Coppola, and Fred Fuchs, and directed by Franc Roddam, featured Patrick Stewart—who had played Jean-Luc Picard of *Star Trek: The Next Generation*—as Ahab, and *E.T.: The Extra-Terrestrial*'s Henry Thomas as Ishmael. The result aired over two nights, March 15 and 16, 1998, on the USA cable channel, where it drew the largest basic-cable audience to that point for a nonsports or news program. Peck and most critics found this new four-hour adaptation (including commercials) an improvement over the feature film, if not wholly satisfying. Caryn James of the *New York Times* called Peck's presence "a warm bit of casting" and noted that his voice was "still incomparably rich."

Greg's brief appearance required only one day of filming, but, on January 24, 1999, he was amply rewarded for his effort. The Hollywood Foreign Press Association accorded him a Golden Globe for Best Supporting Actor in a Series, Miniseries, or Movie Made for Television. He tied with Don Cheadle, for his portrayal of Sammy Davis Jr. in the HBO movie *The Rat Pack*.

In the wake of his performance in *Moby Dick*, Peck remained open to other possible acting opportunities. "I get sent scripts," he said in 1998. "But, on the whole, the kinds of roles that are written for someone my age are mostly character roles, and they are not very interesting. You know, grandfathers, old uncles. I don't want to bow out doing that kind of thing." Instead he devoted the bulk of his attention to two projects that he had initiated in 1995.

The first was a program to support the Los Angeles Public Library.

Called the Gregory Peck Reading Series, the events, held at the Central Library's Mark Taper Auditorium six to eight times a year, typically spotlight two celebrities per evening, reading material of their own choosing. These have ranged from Peck's old friends and colleagues, including Norman Lloyd, the late Walter Matthau, Piper Laurie, and Charlton Heston, to such younger stars as Richard Dreyfuss, Angelica Huston, Kathy Bates, Billy Bob Thornton, and Laura Dern. Occasionally, Peck is one of the featured performers; otherwise, he serves as host, with the late Roddy McDowell substituting for him on a couple of occasions.

Even more ambitious than the reading series was the second venture that Peck initiated in 1995, a lecture-circuit offering that he called *A Conversation with Gregory Peck.* The idea was suggested by Cary Grant, who'd created a similar program in his later years.

"I resist calling what I do lectures," the actor explained. He preferred to think of the program as "an entertainment." Typically, he opened with a selection of clips, which ran about twenty-eight minutes. Then he would appear on stage, take a seat in a lone chair, and tell a series of well-honed anecdotes. Finally, he would open the floor to questions. "That's my favorite part of the program," he said in 1997. "It's always interesting to see what people remember."

Meeting fans all around the country was an energizing experience. It wasn't quite the same as returning to his theater roots, but, as Peck put it, "there's a live audience and when you come out on the stage, you have to keep 'em interested for an hour and a half." He hadn't lost his stage fright over the decades. Phillip Alford—Jem from *To Kill a Mockingbird*—who joined Peck for a few such appearances, said, "When he's waiting in the wings to go on, he's nervous to the point of trembling. Scared about it. . . . But, once he's out there, he's as smooth as silk."

After launching *A Conversation with Gregory Peck* in Miami in January 1995, Greg accepted about fifteen or twenty bookings a year. Finally, in early 2000, a few months before his eighty-fourth birthday, he rang down the curtain. The show's final engagement came on February 20 at the Elsinore Theater in Salem, Oregon, a town he had first played five decades earlier while touring *The Doctor's Dilemma.*

Elements of *A Conversation with Gregory Peck* were preserved in a documentary bearing the same name, which aired in October 1999 on the premium cable channel Turner Classic Movies.* The Oscar award–winning documentary filmmaker Barbara Kopple and her camera operators had covered the actor's engagements in Boston; Buffalo;

*The documentary was rebroadcast on PBS in spring 2001 as part of the network's *American Masters* series.

Galveston; Greeley, Colorado; and Abingdon, Virginia—where he returned to the Barter Theater nearly sixty years after performing there in summer stock. They also captured him backstage at these events—in his dressing room, in the wings waiting to go on, and greeting guests after the performances.

But the documentary also offered glimpses of Peck in a variety of personal settings—at home with his boisterous family; enjoying Paris with Veronique and Cecilia, including a lively dinner with the president of France, Jacques Chirac; in his hotel suite in Washington, D.C., where he and his wife are joined by their very pregnant daughter (who coproduced the documentary) and her significant other, Daniel Voll; the White House ceremony the following day where President Clinton presented him with the Medal of the Arts; a private chat between Greg and Cecilia in a small, quiet Manhattan park; the actor speaking out against gun control at a 1999 rally in Philadelphia; and a ceremony in Dublin, where Greg presented a check to university officials to support the film studies program. Interspersed with the live footage are stills, film clips, and Greg's voice-over recollections of his youth, the death of his son Jonathan, and other significant events.

A mixture of many elements, the documentary provided a rare opportunity for fans to get past the performances and public appearances and glimpse the actor as a human being. He comes across as what, in fact, he is—a dignified, unpretentious, intelligent, and gentle man, with a dry, self-deprecating sense of humor, no longer young but still full of life. As the *TV Guide* critic noted, "I never felt much need to know the real Gregory Peck. The one in *To Kill a Mockingbird* and *Roman Holiday* is perfectly satisfying. But this sweet film . . . enhances the legend. . . . Peck is unfailingly warm and witty. . . . This is a valentine, and it makes you feel as good as a valentine."

Since completing the documentary, the Pecks have lived relatively quietly, spending somewhat more time at their "dream house" on Carolwood Drive than in years past. Greg toils in his extensive gardens, reads, and carves out time for business matters in his home office with the assistance of his longtime secretary, Barbara Russel (until her retirement in summer 2001). During the summer of 2000, Anthony and his son Zackary came for a long visit, as did Cecilia, Daniel Voll, and their son, Harper (named for author Harper Lee), who was born at New York's Lenox Hill Hospital on February 27, 1999. Peck spent as much time as possible with his visiting family. "Anything else," he said, "looks like work to me."

He also continues to produce his reading series on behalf of the Los

Angeles Public Library. On November 14, 2000, the Library Foundation acknowledged the fifth anniversary of the program with a gala held at the Regent Beverly Wilshire Hotel. The evening was in support of the Gregory Peck Literary Endowment, established with a gift of $100,000 from the William Randolph Hearst Foundation. Appropriately, there were readings by Angelica Huston, Patrick Stewart, Sally Field, and the late Jack Lemmon.

Nearly five months later, on April 5, 2001, Gregory Peck turned eighty-five. He has in all likelihood put his career to rest. Taking home the Golden Globe for his portrayal of Father Mapple enabled him to go out a winner. Moreover, he was able to close the book with—unbelievably—the exact same vehicle that enticed him into acting in the first place all those years ago at the University of California, *Moby Dick*.

How far he has come since the days when he was an eager college kid, basking in the spotlight for the first time and causing the ladies in the audience to sigh over his awesome good looks. Were he to look back, perhaps he would fondly remember himself as an ernest apprentice, soaking up all he could from teachers like Sandy Meisner and old pros like Katharine Cornell and Guthrie McClintic. Or as the new Broadway sensation, determined to make his career on the stage. Or as the hottest heartthrob in films since Clark Gable. Or, finally, as the handsome movie star whose indelible screen presence and commitment to his craft kept him at the forefront of his profession from the golden age of the studio system to the advent of cable TV.

Those who know him recall the consummate professional, meticulous in his preparation, not short of opinions but lacking a star's outsized ego. Through nearly sixty years of stardom, he has never given less than his best. Sometimes the project wasn't worthy of such an effort. Sometimes he was miscast. And, yes, sometimes he failed to rise to the occasion. But, whatever the result, he made the journey with a full heart and an open mind.

Along the way, he forged a celluloid gallery of heroes—writers, lawyers, military men, political figures, corporate executives, and rugged archetypes of the Old West—real flesh-and-blood human beings. They have flaws, but they surmount their defects as events or conscience—or both—demand. From the simple priest in *The Keys of the Kingdom* to the wily monsignor in *The Scarlet and the Black*, from the crusading journalist in *Gentleman's Agreement* to the old-fashioned businessman in *Other People's Money*, he has embodied the best in the human character and shown us ourselves as we'd like to think we'd be if we were tall, handsome, and dignified too.

For that, people the world over have come to love him. And because they sense in the man, perhaps without even knowing why, the essence of the characters they've admired on the screen, they respect him even more. He's part of what Tom Brokaw calls "The Greatest Generation." Appreciating the good things that have come his way while working hard to earn them, he's given back at least as much as he's gotten—lending his support to important political and social causes, laboring tirelessly on behalf of the arts, and, perhaps best of all, living his life by a set of principles in which honor, decency, a person's word, and love of family, friends, and country count for something.

Love of family above all.

Arguably, the highlight of the ninety-minute documentary *A Conversation with Gregory Peck* comes at the end, with the birth of Cecilia's child. Shortly thereafter, the infant is presented to his tired grandfather, who cuddles the little boy while murmuring, "Just thankful. Cecilia is well. She's fine." Then he tells the unseen camera operator, "The boy has a loud voice—like his granddad, I guess. Just happy."

It's a moving moment, for it underscores the fact that the fondest wish of a lonely boy named Eldred Peck has come true. He is finally surrounded by people he loves and who love him. A warm, supportive home life is, and always has been, his first concern. "I'd like to be remembered by my children and my grandchildren as a good father and grandfather," he once said. "And I'd like to be remembered by my wife as someone who's made her life as happy as she's made mine."

He doesn't have to worry on either score.

Filmography

Dates of feature films and Broadway shows reflect the openings in New York City. A * denotes a film's availability on videotape. A † denotes a film's availability on DVD.

Feature Films

1. *Days of Glory* (RKO). June 16, 1944. Produced by Casey Robinson. Directed by Jacques Tourneur. Screenplay by Robinson, from the story by Melchior Lengyel. Cinematography by Tony Gaudio. With Tamara Toumanova, Alan Reed, Maria Palmer, Lowell Gilmore, Hugo Haas, Dena Penn. 86 minutes. b&w.
2. *The Keys of the Kingdom* (20th Century–Fox). December 28, 1944. Produced by Joseph L. Mankiewicz. Directed by John M. Stahl. Screenplay by Mankiewicz and Nunnally Johnson, from the novel by A. J. Cronin. Cinematography by Arthur Miller. With Thomas Mitchell, Vincent Price, Rosa Stradner, Roddy McDowell, Edmund Gwenn, Sir Cedric Hardwicke. 137 minutes. b&w.*
3. *The Valley of Decision* (MGM). May 3, 1945. Produced by Edwin J. Knopf. Directed by Tay Garnett. Screenplay by John Meehan and Sonya Levien, from the novel by Marcia Davenport. Cinematography by Joseph Ruttenberg. With Greer Garson, Donald Crisp, Lionel Barrymore, Preston Foster, Gladys Cooper, Dean Stockwell, Jessica Tandy, Dan Duryea. 111 minutes. b&w.*
4. *Spellbound* (Selznick International/Vanguard Films/United Artists). November 1, 1945. Produced by David O. Selznick. Directed by Alfred Hitchcock. Screenplay by Ben Hecht, from the novel *The House of Dr. Edwardes* by Francis Beeding. Cinematography by George Barnes. Dream Sequence designed by Salvador Dalí. With Ingrid Bergman, Leo G. Carroll, Michael Chekhov, Rhonda Fleming, Donald Curtis. 111 minutes. b&w.* †
5. *The Yearling* (MGM). January 23, 1946. Produced by Sidney Franklin. Directed by Clarence Brown. Screenplay by Paul Osborn, from the novel by Marjorie Kinnan Rawlings. Cinematography by Charles Rosher, Leonard Smith, and Arnold Arling. With Jane Wyman, Claude Jarman Jr., Chill Wills, Clem Bevans, Margaret Wycherly. 134 minutes. color.*
6. *The Macomber Affair* (United Artists). April 20, 1947. Produced by Benedict Bogeaus and Casey Robinson. Directed by Zoltan Korda. Screenplay by Robinson and Seymour Bennett, from the story "The Short Happy Life of Francis Macomber" by Ernest Hemingway. Adaptation: Seymour Bennett, Frank Arnold. Cinematography by Karl Struss. With Robert Preston, Joan Bennett, Reginald Denny, Earl Smith, Jean Gillie. 89 minutes. b&w.
7. *Duel in the Sun* (Vanguard/Selznick Releasing Organization). May 7, 1947. Produced by David O. Selznick. Directed by King Vidor. Screenplay by David O. Selznick, suggested by the novel by Niven Busch. Cinematography by Lee Garmes, Hal Rosson, and Ray Rennahan. Narrated by Orson Welles. With Joseph Cotten, Jennifer Jones, Lionel Barrymore, Lillian Gish, Walter Huston. 138 minutes. color.* †
8. *Gentleman's Agreement* (20th Century–Fox). November 11, 1947. Produced by Darryl F. Zanuck. Directed by Elia Kazan. Screenplay by Moss Hart, from the novel by Laura Z. Hobson. Cinematography by Arthur Miller. With Dorothy McGuire, John Garfield, Celeste Holm, Anne Revere, June Havoc, Albert Decker, Jane Wyatt, Dean Stockwell. 118 minutes. b&w.* †
9. *The Paradine Case* (Vanguard/Selznick Releasing Organization). January 8, 1948.

Produced by David O. Selznick. Directed by Alfred Hitchcock. Screenplay by Selznick, from the novel by Robert Hichens. Cinematography by Lee Garmes. With Charles Laughton, Charles Coburn, Ann Todd, Ethel Barrymore, Louis Jourdan, Valli. 132 minutes. b&w.* †

10. *Yellow Sky* (20th Century–Fox). February 1, 1949. Produced by Lamar Trotti. Directed by William A. Wellman. Screenplay by Trotti, based on a story by W. R. Burnett. Cinematography by Joe MacDonald. With John Russell, Richard Widmark, Charles Kemper, Henry Morgan, Robert Adler, Anne Baxter. 98 minutes. b&w.
11. *The Great Sinner* (MGM). June 29, 1949. Produced by Gottfried Reinhardt. Directed by Robert Siodmak. Screenplay by Ladislas Fodor and Christopher Isherwood, from a story by Fodor and René Fülöp-Miller. Cinematography by George Foley. With Ava Gardner, Melvyn Douglas, Walter Huston, Ethel Barrymore, Frank Morgan. 110 minutes. b&w.
12. *Twelve O'Clock High* (20th Century–Fox). January 26, 1950. Produced by Darryl F. Zanuck. Directed by Henry King. Screenplay by Sy Bartlett and Beirne Lay Jr., from their novel. Cinematography by Leon Shamroy. With Hugh Marlowe, Gary Merrill, Dean Jagger, Millard Mitchell, Robert Arthur. 132 minutes. b&w.* †
13. *The Gunfighter* (20th Century–Fox). June 23, 1950. Produced by Nunnally Johnson. Directed by Henry King. Screenplay by William Bowers and William Sellers, from a story by Bowers and André De Toth. Cinematography by Arthur Miller. With Helen Westcott, Millard Mitchell, Jean Parker, Karl Malden, Skip Homeier, Richard Jaeckel. 84 minutes. b&w.*
14. *Only the Valiant* (Warner Bros.). April 11, 1951. Produced by William Cagney. Directed by Gordon Douglas. Screenplay by Edmund H. North and Harry Brown, from the novel by Charles Marquis Warren. Cinematography by Lionel Linden. With Barbara Payton, Ward Bond, Gig Young, Lon Chaney Jr., Neville Brand, Jeff Corey, Steve Brodie, Warner Anderson, Michael Ansara. 105 minutes. b&w.*
15. *David and Bathsheba* (20th Century–Fox). August 14, 1951. Produced by Darryl F. Zanuck. Directed by Henry King. Screenplay by Philip Dunne. Cinematography by Leon Shamroy. With Susan Hayward, Raymond Massey, Kieron Moore, James Robertson Justice, Jayne Meadows. 153 minutes. color.*
16. *Captain Horatio Hornblower* (Warner Bros). September 13, 1951. Produced by Gerry Mitchell. Directed by Raoul Walsh. Screenplay by Ivan Goff, Ben Roberts and Aeneas MacKenzie, from the novels *Ship of the Line, Beat to Quarters,* and *Flying Colors* by C. S. Forester. Cinematography by Guy Green. With Virginia Mayo, Robert Beatty, James Robertson Justice, Moultrie Kelsall, Terence Morgan, Richard Hearne, James Kenney, Ingeborg Wells. 117 minutes. color.*
17. *The Snows of Kilimanjaro* (20th Century–Fox). September 18, 1952. Produced by Darryl F. Zanuck. Directed by Henry King. Screenplay by Casey Robinson, from a story by Ernest Hemingway. Cinematography by Leon Shamroy. With Susan Hayward, Ava Gardner, Hildegard Neff, Leo G. Carroll, Torin Thatcher, Ava Norring, Helene Stanley. 117 minutes. color.* †
18. *The World in His Arms* (Universal-International). October 9, 1952. Produced by Aaron Rosenberg. Directed by Raoul Walsh. Screenplay by Borden Chase, from the novel by Rex Beach. Cinematography by Russell Metty. With Ann Blyth, Anthony Quinn, John McIntire, Andrea King, Carl Esmond, Eugenie Leontovich. 104 minutes. b&w.*
19. *Roman Holiday* (Paramount). August 27, 1953. Produced and directed by William Wyler. Screenplay by Ian McClellan Hunter and John Dighton, from a story by Hunter. Cinematography by Franz F. Planer and Henri Alekan. With Audrey Hepburn, Eddie Albert, Hartley Power, Laura Solari, Harcourt Williams. 119 minutes. b&w.* †
20. *Night People* (20th Century–Fox). March 12, 1954. Produced and directed by Nun-

nally Johnson. Screenplay by Johnson, from a story by Jed Harris and Thomas Reed. Cinematography by Charles G. Clarke. With Broderick Crawford, Anita Bjork, Rita Gam, Walter Abel, Buddy Ebsen, Hugh McDermott. 93 minutes. color.

21. *Man with a Million* (*The Million Pound Note* in United Kingdom) (J. Arthur Rank Organisation/United Artists). June 28, 1954. Produced by John Bryan. Directed by Ronald Neame. Screenplay by Jill Craigie, from the story "The Million Pound Bank Note" by Mark Twain. Cinematography by Geoffrey Unsworth. With Jane Griffiths, Ronald Squire, Joyce Grenfell, Reginald Beckwith, Hartley Power, A. E. Matthews, Wilfred Hyde-White. 92 minutes. color.
22. *The Purple Plain* (J. Arthur Rank Organisation/United Artists). April 10, 1955. Produced by John Bryan. Directed by Robert Parrish. Screenplay by Eric Ambler, from the novel by H. E. Bates. Cinematography by Geoffrey Unsworth. With Win Min Than, Bernard Lee, Maurice Denham, Ram Gopal, Brenda De Banzie, Lyndon Brook, Anthony Bushell. 100 minutes. color.
23. *The Man in the Gray Flannel Suit* (20th Century–Fox). April 12, 1956. Produced by Darryl F. Zanuck. Directed by Nunnally Johnson. Screenplay by Johnson, from the novel by Sloan Wilson. Cinematography by Charles G. Clarke. With Jennifer Jones, Fredric March, Marisa Pavan, Lee J. Cobb, Ann Harding, Keenan Wynn, Gene Lockhart, Gigi Perreau, Arthur O'Connell. 153 minutes. color.*
24. *Moby Dick* (Moulin/Warner Bros.). July 4, 1956. Produced and directed by John Huston. Screenplay by Ray Bradbury and Huston, from the novel by Herman Melville. Cinematography by Oswald Morris. With Richard Basehart, Leo Genn, Orson Welles, James Robertson Justice, Harry Andrews, Bernard Miles, Noel Purcell, Fredrich Ledebur. 116 minutes. color.*
25. *Designing Woman* (MGM). May 16, 1957. Produced by Dore Schary. Directed by Vincente Minnelli. Screenplay by George Wells, from a suggestion by Helen Rose. Cinematography by John Alton. With Lauren Bacall, Dolores Gray, Sam Levene, Tom Helmore, Mickey Shaughnessy, Jesse White, Chuck Connors. 118 minutes. color.*
26. *The Bravados* (20th Century–Fox). June 25, 1958. Produced by Herbert B. Swope Jr. Directed by Henry King. Screenplay by Philip Yordan, from the novel by Frank O'Rourke. Cinematography by Leon Shamroy. With Joan Collins, Stephen Boyd, Albert Salmi, Henry Silva, Kathleen Gallant, Barry Coe, Lee Van Cleef. 99 minutes. color.*
27. *The Big Country* (United Artists). October 1, 1958. Produced by William Wyler and Gregory Peck. Directed by Wyler. Screenplay by James R. Webb, Sy Bartlett, and Robert Wilder, from the novel by Donald Hamilton. Cinematography by Franz Planer. With Jean Simmons, Carroll Baker, Charlton Heston, Burl Ives, Charles Bickford, Alfonso Bedoya, Chuck Connors, Chuck Hayward, Buff Brady. 166 minutes. color.* †
28. *Pork Chop Hill* (Melville/United Artists). May 29, 1959. Produced by Sy Bartlett. Directed by Lewis Milestone. Screenplay by James R. Webb, from the book *Pork Chop Hill: The American Fighting Man in Korea, Spring 1953* by Brigadier General S. L. A. Marshall. Cinematography by Sam Leavitt. With Harry Guardino, Rip Torn, George Peppard, James Edwards, Bob Steele, George Shibata, Woody Strode, Norman Fell, Robert Blake, Biff Elliot, Barry Atwater. 97 minutes. b&w.* †
29. *Beloved Infidel* (20th Century–Fox). November 17, 1959. Produced by Jerry Wald. Directed by Henry King. Screenplay by Sy Bartlett, from the book by Sheilah Graham and Gerold Frank. Cinematography by Leon Shamroy. With Deborah Kerr, Eddie Albert, Philip Ober, Herbert Rudley, John Sutton, Karin Booth, Ken Scott, Buck Class. 123 minutes. color.*
30. *On the Beach* (United Artists). December 17, 1959. Produced and directed by Stanley Kramer. Screenplay by John Paxton, from the novel by Nevil Shute. Cinematog-

raphy by Giuseppe Rotunno. With Ava Gardner, Fred Astaire, Anthony Perkins, Donna Anderson, John Tate, Lola Brooks, Guy Doleman, John Meillon, Harp McGuire, Lou Vernon. 134 minutes. b&w.* †

31. *The Guns of Navarone* (Highroad/Columbia). June 12, 1961. Produced by Carl Foreman. Directed by J. Lee Thompson. Screenplay by Foreman, from the novel by Alistair MacLean. Cinematography by Oswald Morris. With David Niven, Anthony Quinn, Stanley Baker, James Darren, Anthony Quayle, Irene Papas, Gia Scala. 157 minutes. color.* †
32. *Cape Fear* (Melville/Talbot/Universal-International). April 18, 1962. Produced by Sy Bartlett. Directed by J. Lee Thompson. Screenplay by James R. Webb, from the novel *The Executioners* by John D. MacDonald. Cinematography by Sam Leavitt. With Robert Mitchum, Polly Bergen, Lori Martin, Martin Balsam, Jack Kruschen, Telly Savalas, Barrie Chase. 105 minutes. b&w.*
33. *To Kill a Mockingbird* (Pakula-Mulligan/Brentwood/Universal). February 14, 1963. Produced by Alan J. Pakula. Directed by Robert Mulligan. Screenplay by Horton Foote, from the novel by Harper Lee. Cinematography by Russell Harlan. With Mary Badham, Phillip Alford, John Megna, Frank Overton, Rosemary Murphy, Ruth White, Brock Peters, Estelle Evans, Paul Fix. 129 minutes. b&w.* †
34. *How the West Was Won* (MGM/Cinerama). March 27, 1963. Produced by Bernard Smith. Directed by Henry Hathaway ("The River," "The Plains," "The Outlaws"), John Ford ("The Civil War"), and George Marshall ("The Railroad"). Screenplay by James R. Webb, from the *Life* magazine series *How the West Was Won.* Cinematography by William H. Daniels, Milton Krasner, Charles Lang Jr., and Joseph La Shelle. With (Peck episode) Debbie Reynolds, Robert Preston, Thelma Ritter. Narrated by Spencer Tracy. 155 minutes. color.* †
35. *Captain Newman, M.D.* (Brentwood/Reynard/Universal). February 20, 1964. Produced by Robert Arthur. Directed by David Miller. Screenplay by Richard L. Breen, Phoebe Ephron, and Henry Ephron, from the novel by Leo Rosten. Cinematography by Russell Metty. With Tony Curtis, Angie Dickinson, Eddie Albert, Bobby Darin, James Gregory, Robert Duvall, Bethel Leslie, Larry Storch, Dick Sargent. 126 minutes. color.*
36. *Behold a Pale Horse* (Brentwood/Highland/Columbia). August 13, 1964. Produced and directed by Fred Zinnemann. Screenplay by J. P. Miller, from the novel *Killing a Mouse on Sunday* by Emeric Pressburger. Cinematography by Jean Badal. With Anthony Quinn, Omar Sharif, Mildred Dunnock, Raymond Pellegrin, Paolo Stoppa. 112 minutes. b&w.*
37. *Mirage* (Universal). May 26, 1965. Produced by Harry Keller. Directed by Edward Dmytryk. Screenplay by Peter Stone, from the novel *Fallen Angel* by Walter Ericson. Cinematography by Joseph MacDonald. With Diane Baker, Walter Matthau, Leif Erikson, Kevin McCarthy, Jack Weston, George Kennedy, Walter Abel. 108 minutes. b&w.*
38. *Arabesque* (Universal). May 5, 1966. Produced and directed by Stanley Donen. Screenplay by Julian Mitchell, Stanley Price, and Pierre Marton, from the novel *The Cipher* by Gordon Cotler. Cinematography by Christopher Challis. With Sophia Loren, Alan Badel, Kieron Moore, John Merivale, Carl Duering. 105 minutes. color.*
39. *The Stalking Moon* (Pakula-Mulligan/National General). January 22, 1969. Produced by Alan J. Pakula. Directed by Robert Mulligan. Screenplay by Alvin Sargent, from the novel by Theodore V. Olsen. Cinematography by Charles Lang. With Eva Marie Saint, Robert Forster, Noland Clay, Russell Thorson, Frank Silvera, Lonny Chapman. 111 minutes. color.
40. *Mackenna's Gold* (Highroad/Columbia). May 10, 1969. Produced by Carl Foreman and Dimitri Tiomkin. Directed by J. Lee Thompson. Screenplay by Foreman, from the novel by Will Henry. Cinematography by Joseph MacDonald. With Omar Sharif,

Camilla Sparv, Telly Savalas, Keenan Wynn, Julie Newmar, Ted Cassidy, Lee J. Cobb, Raymond Massey, Burgess Meredith, Anthony Quayle, Edward G. Robinson, Eli Wallach. 128 minutes. color.* †

41. *The Chairman* (*The Most Dangerous Man in the World* in the United Kingdom) (Apjac/20th Century–Fox). June 25, 1969. Produced by Mort Abrahams. Directed by J. Lee Thompson. Screenplay by Ben Maddow, from the novel by Jay Richard Kennedy. Cinematography by John Wilcox. With Anne Heywood, Arthur Hill, Alan Dobie, Conrad Yama, Zienia Merton. 104 minutes. color.
42. *Marooned* (Columbia). December 11, 1969. Produced by M. J. Frankovich. Directed by John Sturges. Screenplay by Mayo Simon, from the novel by Martin Caidin. Cinematography by Daniel Fapp. With Richard Crenna, David Janssen, James Franciscus, Gene Hackman, Lee Grant, Nancy Pruett, Mariette Hartley, Scott Brady. 133 minutes. color.*
43. *I Walk the Line* (John Frankenheimer Productions/Edward Lewis Productions/Halcyon Productions/Columbia). October 12, 1970. Produced by Edward Lewis and Harold D. Cohen. Directed by John Frankenheimer. Screenplay by Alvin Sargent, from the novel *The Exile* by Madison Jones. Cinematography by David M. Walsh. With Tuesday Weld, Estelle Parsons, Ralph Meeker, Lonny Chapman, Charles Durning. 95 minutes. color.
44. *Shoot Out* (Hal B. Wallis Productions/Universal). October 13, 1971. Produced by Hal B. Wallis. Directed by Henry Hathaway. Screenplay by Marguerite Roberts, from the novel *The Lone Cowbow* by Will James. Cinematography by Earl Rath. With Pat Quinn, Robert F. Lyons, Susan Tyrell, Jeff Corey, James Gregory, Rita Gam, Dawn Lyn. 95 minutes. color.* †
45. *Billy Two Hats* (Algonquin/United Artists). October 19, 1973. Produced by Norman Jewison and Patrick Palmer. Directed by Ted Kotcheff. Screenplay by Alan Sharp. Cinematography by Brian West. With Desi Arnaz Jr., Jack Warden, David Huddleston, Sian Barbara Allen, John Pearce. 80 minutes. color.*
46. *The Omen* (Harvey Bernhard–Mace Neufeld Productions/20th Century-Fox). June 24, 1976. Produced by Mace Neufeld and Harvey Bernhard. Directed by Richard Donner. Screenplay by David Seltzer. Cinematography by Gil Taylor. With Lee Remick, David Warner, Billie Whitelaw, Leo McKern, Harvey Stephens, Patrick Troughton. 111 minutes. color.* †
47. *MacArthur* (A Richard D. Zanuck–David Brown Production/ Universal). July 10, 1977. Produced by Frank McCarthy. Directed by Joseph Sargent. Screenplay by Hal Barwood and Matthew Robbins. Cinematography by Mario Tosi. With Ed Flanders, Dan O'Herlihy, Ivan Bonar, Ward Costello, Marj Dusay. 128 minutes. color.*
48. *The Boys from Brazil* (Producers Circle/20th Century–Fox). October 5, 1978. Produced by Robert Fryer, Martin Richards, Stanley O'Toole. Directed by Franklin J. Schaffner. Screenplay by Heywood Gould, from the novel by Ira Levin. Cinematography by Henri Decae. With Laurence Olivier, James Mason, Lilli Palmer, Uta Hagen, Steven Guttenberg, Denholm Elliott, Rosemary Harris, John Dehner, John Rubinstein, Anne Meara, Jeremy Black. 182 minutes. color.* †
49. *The Sea Wolves* (Lorimar/United Artists) June 5, 1981. Produced by Chris Chrisafis and Euan Lloyd. Directed by Andrew V. McLaglen. Screenplay by Reginald Rose, from the book *The Boarding Party* by James Leasor. Cinematography by Toni Imi. With Roger Moore, David Niven, Trevor Howard, Barbara Kellerman, Patrick Macnee. 120 minutes. color.* †
50. *Amazing Grace and Chuck* (Turnstar/David Field /TriStar/Rastar). May 22, 1987. Produced by David Field. Directed by Mike Newell. Screenplay by Field. Cinematography by Robert Elawit. With Jamie Lee Curtis, Alex English, William L. Peterson, Joshua Zuehlke, Lee Richardson, Alan Autry, Dennis Lipscomb, Frances Conroy. 115 minutes. color.*
51. *Old Gringo* (Fonda Films/Columbia). October 5, 1989. Produced by Lois Bonfiglio.

Directed by Luis Puenzo. Screenplay by Aida Bortnik and Puenzo, from the novel *Gringo Viejo* by Carlos Fuentes. Cinematography by Felix Monti. With Jane Fonda, Jimmy Smits, Patricio Conteras, Jenny Gago, Gabriel Roel, Sergio Calderon. 119 minutes. color.*

52. *Other People's Money* (Yorktown/Warner Bros). October 18, 1991. Produced by Norman Jewison, Ric Kidney. Directed by Jewison. Screenplay by Alvin Sargent, from the play by Jerry Sterner. Cinematography by Haskell Wexler. With Danny DeVito, Penelope Ann Miller, Piper Laurie, Dean Jones. 101 minutes. color.*
53. *Cape Fear* (Amblin/Cappa/Tribeca/Universal). November 13, 1991. Produced by Barbara DeFina. Directed by Martin Scorsese. Screenplay by Wesley Strick, from the screenplay by James R. Webb and the novel *The Executioners* by John D. MacDonald. Cinematography by Freddie Francis. With Robert De Niro, Nick Nolte, Jessica Lange, Juliette Lewis, Joe Don Baker, Robert Mitchum. 123 minutes. color.*

Television Appearances (Major Acting Roles)

1. *The Blue and the Gray* (CBS-TV). November 14–17, 1982. Produced by Hugh Benson, Harry Thomason. Executive Producers: Larry White, Lou Reda. Directed by Andrew V. McLaglen. Teleplay by Ian McLellan Hunter, from a story by John Leekley and Bruce Catton, based on the writings of Bruce Catton. Cinematography by Al Francis. With John Hammond, Stacy Keach, Colleen Dewhurst, Lloyd Bridges, Diane Baker, Kathleen Beller, Penny Peyser, Michael Horton, Cooper Huckabee, Dan Shor, Julia Duffy, Robin Gammell, Davis S. Haroer. Eight hours. color.*
2. *The Scarlet and the Black* (ITC Productions/CBS-TV). February 2, 1983. Produced by Bill McCutchen. Directed by Jerry London. Teleplay by David Butler, from the book *The Scarlet Pimpernel of the Vatican* by J. P. Gallagher. Cinematography by Giuseppe Rotunno. With Chrisopher Plummer, John Gielgud, Raf Vallone, Kenneth Colley, Walter Gottell, Barbara Bouchet, Julian Holloway. 180 minutes. color.*
3. *The Portrait* (Robert Greenwald Productions/Atticus/TNT). February 13, 1993. Produced by Philip Keinbart. Executive Producers: Robert Greenwald, Gregory Peck, Carla Singer. Directed by Arthur Penn. Teleplay by Lynn Roth, from the play *Painting Churches* by Tina Howe. Cinematography by Dick Quinlan. With Lauren Bacall, Cecilia Peck, Paul McCrane, Donna Mitchell, Joyce O'Connor, Mitchell Lawrence, William Prince. 120 minutes. color.*
4. *Moby Dick* (A Whale/Nine Network Australian Production and United Kingdom/Australia coproduction in association with USA Pictures). March 15–16, 1998. Produced by Franc Roddam, Kris Noble, Steve McGlothen. Executive Producers: Robert Halmi Sr., Francis Ford Coppola, Fred Fuchs. Directed by Roddam. Teleplay by Anton Diether and Roddam, from the novel by Herman Melville. Cinematography by David Connell. With Patrick Stewart, Henry Thomas, Ted Levine, Piripi Waretini, Hugh Keays-Byrne, Shane Feeney, Michael Edward-Stevens. 240 minutes. color.*

Broadway Productions

1. *The Morning Star.* September 14, 1942. Produced and directed by Guthrie McClintic. Written by Emlyn Williams. With Brenda Forbes, Gladys Gooper, Jill Esmond, Cecil Humphreys, Rhys Williams, Wendy Barrie, Nicholas Joy. 24 performances.
2. *The Willow and I.* December 10, 1942. Produced by Donald Blackwell, Raymond Curtis, and David Merrick. Directed by Blackwell. Written by John Patrick. With Martha Scott, Barbara O'Neil, Amanda Randolph, R. Davis Williams, Edward Pawley, Cora Witherspoon, Robert Harrison. 28 performances.
3. *Sons and Soldiers.* March 4, 1943. Produced by Max Reinhardt, Norman Bel-Geddes, and Richard Meyers. Directed by Reinhardt. Written by Irwin Shaw. With Geraldine Fitzgerald, Herbert Rudley, Millard Mitchell, Jack Willet, Joan Sweeney, Ted Donaldson, Karl Malden, Stella Adler, Jesse White. 22 performances.

4. *The Will Rogers Follies.* May 1, 1991. Produced by Pierre Cossette, Martin Richards, Sam Crowthers, James M. Nederlander, Stewart F. Lane, Max Weitzenhoffer in association with Japan Satellite Broadcasting, Inc. Directed by Tommy Tune. Book by Peter Stone. Music by Cy Coleman. Lyrics by Betty Comden and Adolph Green. With Keith Carradine, Dee Hoty, Dick Latessa, Cady Huffman (only Peck's voice was featured in the production). 983 performances.

Notes

Research for this book was based on three principal sources: 1) Interviews and correspondence conducted by the author, principally during the summer and fall of 2000, with the friends, relatives, schoolmates, and colleagues of Gregory Peck whose names are cited in the Acknowledgments section of this book. Unless otherwise indicated below, all quotes and information attributed in the text to these individuals was derived from the author's communication with them. All quotes attributed to Peck himself, however, are cited below; 2) Books and periodicals. Those works referenced in the bibliography are identified below by the author's last name followed by a "P" for periodical and "B" for book. Two books are attributed in the bibliography to the British biographer Michael Freedland, but all of the citations below refer to Freedland's biography of Peck. Reviews, announcements, and articles of no more than passing interest only are cited below; and 3) Primary source materials. Of particular importance to this project was the collection of scripts and documents donated by Gregory Peck to the Academy of Motion Picture Arts and Sciences and housed in the Academy's Margaret Herrick Library. It is designated herein as the Gregory Peck Collection (GPC). Included in this collection is the manuscript of a lengthy interview Peck gave to journalist Gregory Speck. As this interview is cited several times below, it has been given the abbreviation (Speck/GPC). Other documents in the Peck Collection are identified below in full. Also in the Margaret Herrick Library are the Gladys Hall Collection (GHC), the Hedda Hopper Collection (HHC), and a lengthy oral history with Peck conducted by Professor Ronald L. Davis between 1974 and 1980 as part of the Southern Methodist University Oral History Project (Davis). The 20th Century–Fox Collection (TFC), including the files of the Fox legal department, is housed in the Department of Special Collections, University Research Library, University of California, Los Angeles. At the University of Southern California's Cinema-TV Library are the Universal Pictures Collection (UPC), the Jerry Wald Collection (JWC), the Jack L. Warner Collection (JLWC), and the Warner Bros. Collection (WBC). At the Louis B. Mayer Library of the American Film Institute are an oral history with Casey Robinson conducted in 1974 by Josh Greenberg as part of the Louis B. Mayer/American Film Institute Film History Program (Greenberg) and an oral history with Henry King conducted in 1970–71 by Tom Stempel under the auspices of the Darryl F. Zanuck Research Project, American Film Institute, Louis B. Mayer Foundation (Stempel/OH). Also at the AFI are an audiocassette recording of a Q&A session between Peck and the school's students hosted by George Stevens Jr. and held on March 6, 1989 (Peck/AFI); the program of the AFI Lifetime Achievement Award gala honoring Peck on March 9, 1989, which includes brief remembrances from a variety of Peck's friends, relatives, and colleagues (AFI); and the undated transcript of an interview Peck gave to Jane Ardmore (Ardmore). The Neighborhood Playhouse graciously allowed me to review its file on Peck, which included documents pertaining to his student years (NPF). Finally, a few quotes are drawn from two television documentaries: *Gregory Peck: His Own Man,* which was produced by Wombat Productions in association with Devillier/Donegan Enterprises and aired on the premium cable Cinemax on August 24, 1988, as part of the series *Crazy about the Movies* (Wombat), and *A Conversation with Gregory Peck,* which was produced by Barbara Kopple, Cecilia Peck, and Linda Safire and began airing on the premium cable channel Turner Classic Movies in October 1999 (TCM).

Notes

Introduction

"the ultimate movie" (Wombat); "The first thing" (Vernon Scott, unidentified publication); "It's a little like" (Freedland/B); "He represented, I" (Wombat); "No. Sometimes I've" (Grant/P); "withdrawn and introverted" (Brown); "He is a" (Freedland/B).

Chapter 1: The Jewel

"Quite a settlement" (Schaelchlin/B); "a blonde of" (unidentified publication); "My mother was" (Amory/P); "He was a" (Shearer/P); "You want to" (Buckley/P); "too good-natured" (Ibid.); "How dare you" (Freedland/B); Bernice Peck's first divorce petition (Complaint *Bernice Mae Peck, Plaintiff, v. Gregory Pearl Peck, Defendant,* Superior Court, County of San Diego, State of California, February 3, 1921); "interfering with the" (Restraining Order and Order to Show Cause, Superior Court, County of San Diego, State of California, February 11, 1921); Bernice Peck's withdrawal of her initial divorce petition (Dismissal, Superior Court, County of San Diego, State of California, February 16, 1921); Gregory Peck's reasons for his parents' estrangement (Jeanne Stein/P); "Nothing like that" (Peck letter to author, July 26, 2001); Bernice's second divorce petition (Consent to Setting for Trial, Superior Court of the County of San Diego, filed July 25, 1921); The terms of the Pecks' divorce (Interlocutory Judgment, Superior Court of the County of San Diego, filed July 30, 1921); "I remember my" (Peck letter to author, September 8, 2000) "I wasn't scared" (Ibid); "My parents were" (Speck/B); "the happiest time" (TCM); "We adopted each" (McIntyre/P); "For the next" (Freedland/B); "We spent a" (McIntyre/P); "After his second" (Ibid); "a lean, leathery" (Ibid); "There were maybe" (CBS press release for *The Blue and the Gray,* September 7, 1982); "None of us" (McIntyre/P); "We played games" (Ibid); "We always had" (Ibid); "I got my" (Melton/P); "I was positively" (unidentified publication); "We would take" (*Newsweek*/1999); "orange paint on" (Haver/P); "not so much" (Burkett/P); "I never remember" (Wombat); "I was lonely" (Darrach/P).

Chapter 2: A Lonely Boy

"As I recall" (McIntyre/P); "I suffered agonies" (*Photoplay,* ca. 1945–46); "Maybe my mother" (Wombat); "the nearest thing" (*San Diego Tribune,* n.d.); "We had to" (Speck/GPC); "his whims and" (St. John's Military Academy brochure, 1928–1929); "From the time" (Molyneaux/B); "I got very" (Speck/GPC); "I shouted at" (Freedland/B); "One of the" (AFI); "It was apparently" (Peck letter to the author, September 8, 2000); "Little by little" (Amory/P); "When my turn" (McIntyre/P); "I was too" (*Photoplay,* ca. 1945–46); "I had supposed" (McIntyre/P); "I remember Peck's" (Erickson); "He never made" (Ibid); "He had dark" (Ibid); "Boy, that was" (Jones, 1947/P); *Time* magazine's account of when Peck met Kathie Jones (*Time*/P).

Chapter 3: The Awakening

"a basic knowledge" (*General Catalogue,* 1935–36, University of California, Berkeley, California, September 1, 1935); "I once made" (Laura Cunningham, unidentified publication); "I distinctly remember" (Freedland/B); "I was the" (Laura Cunningham, unidentified publication); "Anyone who's rowed" (Freedland/B); "a great place" (Speck/B); "I was a" (Ibid.); "I was at" (Ardmore); "I don't know" (Haver/P); "I don't know" (Freedland/B); "I was terrible" (Amory/P); "agonizing." (Ibid.); "I suppose part" (Battelle/P); The university yearbook response to *Anna Christie* (*The Blue & Gold,* 1938–39); "almost endangered the" (*The Daily Californian,* March 20, 1939); "You'll be broke" (Buckley/P); "I had a" (Peck letter to the author, August 17, 2000); "Berkeley was in" (Speck/B).

Chapter 4: The Playhouse

"I didn't know" (Speck/GPC); "It was the" (Jory/P); "Fine looking, tall" (Peck's Neighborhood Playhouse admission application, NPF); "Looks like very" (Peck's scholarship application, Neighborhood Playhouse, July 30, 1939, NPF); "The foundation of" (Meisner/B); "emotional freedom . . . wrong" (Peck letter to Rebekah T. Dallas, July 30, 1940, NPF); "When I'd get" (Molyneaux/B); "For twenty cents" (Ibid.); "To have such" (Ed Duerr letter to Peck, July 3, 1940, GPC); "a Will Rogers" (manuscript of Gladys Hall interview with Peck, n.d., GHC); "We played one" (Ibid.); "It was in" (Robert Porterfield letter to *Time,* January 10, 1948, GPC); "splendid physical equipment" (Arnold Sundgaard letter to Peck, December 3, 1940, GPC); "Well, there was" (Ibid.); "come to me" (Robert Porterfield letter to *Time,* January 10, 1948, GPC); "I have had" (Peck letter to Rebekah T. Dallas, July 30, 1940, NPF); "I know you" (Ed Duerr letter to GP, July 3, 1940, GPC); "the most valuable" (*Long Beach Press Telegram*); "Here simply being" (Seidelman/P); "out the story" (Molyneaux/B); "I am sorry" (Behlmer/*Selznick*/B); "Afterward, I discovered" (Jones, 1947/P); "You cannot learn" (letter to Peck from "Fred," March 31, 1941, GPC); "Never run from" (Ed Duerr letter to Peck, November 3, 1940, GPC); "The lads have" (Duerr letter read to the author by John Brenneis).

Chapter 5: The Apprentice

"Communism was in" (Speck/GPC); "never occurred to" (Ibid.); "in one way" (Mosel/B); "a stalwart honor" (Ibid.); "The chance is" (Ed Duerr letter to Peck, June 29, 1941, GPC); "Can't understand you!" (Freedland/B); "Dear Greg, I" (Sanford Meisner letter to Peck, September 12, 1941, GPC); "When McClintic first" (Mike Strong letter to Peck, October 15, 1941, GPC); "I used to" (Jeanne Stein/P); "somehow it seemed" (*Photoplay,* ca. 1946–47); "I've always hated" (Ibid.); "We were on" (Morris/P); "Our entertainment after" (Ibid.); "just a gadget" (*Photoplay,* ca. 1946–47); "a happy feeling" (Ed Duerr letter to Peck, October 18, 1941, GPC); "Which wasn't much" (Helleur/P); "a little lost" (Molyneaux/B); "the complete actor" (Freedland/B); "God knows how" (Buckley/P).

Chapter 6: Broadway and a Bride

"an exciting director" (Morley/*Gladys Cooper*/B); "There is going" (Waters., *Variety,* September 9, 1942); "Before to-morrow night" (Sanford Meisner letter to Peck, September 13, 1942, GPC); "I was scared" (Champlin/P); "Especially praise must" (John Mason Brown, *New York World-Telegram,* September 15, 1942); "a superlative job" (John Anderson, *New York Journal-American,* September 15, 1942); "Gregory Peck plays" (Brooks Atkinson, *New York Times,* September 15, 1942); "To walk out" (Brown/B); "It may not" (Berg/P); Samuel Goldwyn's initial interest in Peck (Haver/P); Hal Wallis' initial interest in Peck (Wallis/B); "he kind of" (Greenberg); "We wanted it" (Morris/P); "There was no" (unidentified publication, ca. 1952); "Go out and" (ms. of Associated Press copy by Bob Thomas, April 15, 1970); "And when it" (Peck/AFI); Peck's purchase of *Willpower: the Dynamo's Secret* (Gladys Hall interview with Peck, n.d., GHC); "both radiant and" (Howard Barnes, *New York Herald-Tribune,* December 11, 1942); "enormously ingratiating" (Wilella Waldorf, *New York Post,* December 11, 1942); "poise," "good looks" (Burns Mantle, New York *Daily News,* December 11, 1942); "again and again" (Robert Coleman, *New York Daily Mirror,* December 11, 1942); "Just to talk" (Gladys Hall interview with Peck, n.d., GHC); "I had a" (Haver/P); "Sorry, Mr. Mayer" (Freedland/B); "God, Alfred Lunt" (Speck/B): "quiet, very sincere" (Gladys Hall interview with Peck, n.d., GHC); "kind of like" (Pete Martin/P); "I love your" (Greenberg); "was famous for" (Brown/B); the terms of Peck's contract with Robinson/RKO (TCF); "When I got" (unidentified publication, ca. 1952); "Hayward thought I" (Pete Martin/P); "some embers still" (Davis); "helped me throw" (Freedland/B); "sharply observant scenes" (Ward Morehouse, *New York Sun,* May 5, 1943); "Several of us" (Shnayerson/B).

CHAPTER 7: "THE PHANTOM STAR"

"go the whole" (Greenberg); "the first time" (Delehanty/P); "You feel like" (Davis); "Greg, can't you" (Ibid.); "I got the" (Ibid.); "devil-may-care" (Rosalind Shaffer, Associated Press, n.d.); "always agreeable . . . not" (*Boston Post*/P); "This is the" (Delehanty/P); "succès d'estime" (Leo Mishkin, New York *Morning Telegraph,* June 19, 1944); "a slow, talky" (Kahn, *Variety,* September 3, 1944); "two new faces of" (Archer Winsten, *New York Post,* June 17, 1944); "destined for" (Kate Cameron, New York *Daily News,* June 17, 1944); "like a sure" (John T. McManus, *P.M.,* n.d.); "a classic demonstration" (unidentified publication); "You couldn't go" (Parsons/P); "the hottest thing" (Hedda Hopper, syndicated column, October 15, 1944); "That is unusual" (Creelman/P); The terms of Peck's first contract with Fox (TCF); "by the time" (Peck/*Saturday Evening Post*/P); "such range and" (Ibid); "I did it very" (Ibid.); *Variety*'s review of *The Keys of the Kingdom* is dated December 13, 1944; "interminable." (*New Yorker,* December 30, 1944); "human, dramatic and" (*Time,* January 1, 1945); The reviews of *The Keys of the Kingdom* in the New York dailies are dated December 29, 1944; "All I could" (Shay/*Kaleidoscope*/P); "I met everybody" (Friedland/B); Peck's first meeting with Gary Cooper (Ibid); "Not since Clark" (*New York Times*); "It was a" (Davis).

CHAPTER 8: THE HOTTEST GUY SINCE GABLE

How Selznick cast Peck for *Spellbound* (Leff/B); "I think Hitchcock" (Ibid.); "it took me" (Peck/AFI); "like to readjust" (Gow/P); Peck's flubs during the filming of *Spellbound* (Leff/B); "a very wonderful" (Speck/B); "I think you" (Ibid.); "Ingrid and Peck" (Leamer/B); "That is not" (Ibid.); "All I can" (Darrach/P); "We could not" (Behlmer/*Selznick*/B); "fascinating chase through" (Howard Barnes, *New York Herald-Tribune,* November 11, 1945); "the most mature" (Bosley Crowther, *New York Times,* November 11, 1945); "I respect it" (Shay/*Kaleidoscope*/P); "spotty" (James, 1992/P); "did things properly" (Davis); The terms of Peck's contract with MGM (*Time*/P); "first rate heart-throb" (*Life,* June 11, 1945); "Greer's audience would" (*Time*/P); "L. B. Mayer's" (Fox/P); "When it came" (Freedland/B); "small and quiet" (Troyan/B); "Peck had everything" (Buckley/P); "not [to] expect to find" (Bosley Crowther, *New York Times,* May 4, 1945); "a thumping box-office" (*New York Herald-Tribune,* May 4, 1945); "his best film" (*Cue,* May 5, 1945); "I did nothing" (Louella O. Parsons, syndicated column, n.d.); "I want this" (Thomas/B); "liked the idea" (Gow/P); "I know that" (Thomas/B); "Everything that had" (Vidor/*A Tree*/B); The length of the *Duel in the Sun* screenplay (Thomson/B); Selznick's use of a bartender as *Duel in the Sun* technical advisor (Thomas/B); "compared notes on" (Davis); "I never enjoyed" (Hopper, 1946/P); "took great pride"(Freedland/B); Sportin' Life as inspiration for Lewt McCanles (Vidor/*King Vidor*/B); "as flexible and" (Ibid.); "the kind of" (Davis); "He taught me" (Peck letter to author October 4, 2000); "I was having" (Dowd/B); "I want to" (Epstein/B); "In a bizarre" (Thomson/B); "a colorful Germanic" (Speck/B); The cost of making *Duel in the Sun* (*Time,* March 17, 1947); The film's publicity budget (Ibid.); "a munificent muddle" (Howard Barnes, *New York Herald-Tribune,* May 8, 1947); "biggest and emptiest" (Jesse Zunser, *Cue,* May 10, 1947); "I thought I" (Campbell/P).

CHAPTER 9: LITERARY PROPERTIES

"Oh, I thought" (Davis); "probably the best" (Ibid.); "It isn't very" (Bosley Crowther, *New York Times,* January 24, 1947); "I would have" (*Time*/P); "What a nightmare!" (Buckley/P); "I happened to" (Davis); "kind of an" (Ibid.); "there was just" (Griggs/B); "Well, what the" (Ibid.); "a brilliantly good" (*Time,* April 7, 1947); "the best and" (Davis); "ruthlessly lustful guide" (Alton Cook, *New York World-Telegram,* n.d.); "What he said" (*Screen Guide*/P); "Greg has great" (Ibid.); "on the stolid" (Molyneaux/B); "I stuck my" (*Screen Guide*/P); "greater honesty" (Jones, 1947/P); "something I hadn't"

(*Screen Guide*/P); "I feel better" (Ibid.); "I'm afraid of" (Gladys Hall interview with Peck, n.d., GHC); "He has a" (Rosalind Shaffer, Associated Press, n.d.); "a philosopher . . . with" (Ibid.); Peck's Sunday pursuits (*Photoplay,* ca. 1946–47); "neatly furnished" (Sidney Skolsky, syndicated column, April 20, 1946); "He never wants" (*Photoplay,* ca. 1946–47); "usually whoever feels " (Ibid.); "I ran to" (Ibid.); Hitchcock's interest in casting Peck in *The Paradine Case* (Leff/B); "really bored" (Ibid.); "I am on" (Behlmer/*Selznick*/B); "It is clear" (Ibid.); "So very often" (Davis); "What am I" (Taylor/B); "Well, it was" (Davis); Bosley Crowther and Howard Barnes' reviews of *The Paradine Case* are dated January 9, 1948; "I have goosed" (Leff/B); "impressively impassioned" (Bosley Crowther, *New York Times,* January 9, 1948); "Gregory Peck turns" (*Time,* January 12, 1948); "[I]t was the" (Buckley/P); "We had a" (Gardella/P); "Not only does" (Scheuer/P); "very closed off" (Young/B); "[W]hen I looked" (Kazan/B); "aggressive, dynamic . . . more" (Davis); "an extraordinary achievement" (Jesse Zunser, *Cue,* November 15, 1947); "brilliant and powerful" (Hobe, *Variety,* November 12, 1947); "unquestionably the finest" (Ibid.); "the perfect example" (Kazan/B); "I would like" (Custen/B); "His devotion to" (Peck letter to Roberta Ridgely, May 26, 1987, GPC); "The actors and" (William Sullivan/P); "The eight-week" (Peck letter to Maynard Morris, December 19, 1947, GPC).

CHAPTER 10: THE END OF A MOMENTOUS DECADE

"luckier, better looking" (*Time*/P); "By Hollywood standards" (Ibid.); The Peck home on San Remo Drive (*Architectural Digest*/P); Greta Peck's automobile accident (*Los Angeles Times,* May 7, 1948; June 24, 1948); "The payoff is" (Zanuck memo to Lamar Trotti, February 5, 1948, TCF); "like a small" (Davis); "someone got me" (20th Century–Fox press release, December 27, 1948); "[W]hen you start" (Thompson/B); "He yelled and" (Davis); Selznick's involvement in the La Jolla Playhouse production of *Serena Blandish* (Sullivan/P); La Jolla Playhouse's second season ticket sales (*San Diego Tribune-Sun,* September 3, 1948); "It doesn't take" (Bosley Crowther, *New York Times,* February 2, 1949); "pompous" (Freedland/B); "He was a" (Gardner/B); "There he goes" (Ibid.); "behaved like the" (Higham/B); "Come on, for" (Speck/GPC); "Son, always give" (Jeanne Stein/P); "taken on the" (Peck letter to Gottfried Reinhardt, January 29, 1949, GPC); The director who did the reshoots of *The Great Sinner* (Alpi/B); "I think that" (Peck letter to Gottfried Reinhardt, April 5, 1949, GPC); "dreary picture" (Bosley Crowther, *New York Times,* June 30, 1949); "Despite its impressive" (*Newsweek,* July 11, 1949); "There is more" (Freedland/B); The alleged Communist Front organizations with which Peck was affiliated (letter to Hedda Hopper from Michael O. Tuathail, Assistant Honorable Secretary, Catholic Cinema and Theatre Patrons' Assocation, December 2, 1949, HHC); "idealistic or humanitarian" (Davis); "I was not" (Ibid.); "You'll be so" (Freedland/B); "very pleasant person" (Shepard/B); "great fun" (Davis); "Once in a" (Coppedge/B); "We were somewhere" (Brown/B); "20th Century–Fox" (*Cue,* January 28, 1950); "rugged realism and" (Bosley Crowther, *New York Times,* January 28, 1950); "a topflight drama" (Brog., *Variety,* December 21, 1949); "Everybody broke up" (Vernon Scott, unidentifed publication); "Gregory, you cost" (Buckley/P); "We just worked" (Davis); "extremely convincing" (Howard Barnes, *New York Herald-Tribune,* June 24, 1950); "arresting and quite" (Bosley Crowther, *New York Times,* June 24, 1950); "relentless . . . and intense" (Brog., *Variety,* April 26, 1950); "I've learned more" (Jones, 1951/P); "Greg is a" (Vernon Scott, unidentified publication); "Greg wants to" (Brown/B); "the most anecdoteless" (*Time*/P); "Greg is not" (Shearer, 1956/P); "Yes, I believe" (Dean/P); "Sometimes I sense" (AFI); "For some days" (Louella O. Parsons, syndicated column, January 24, 1949); "Then I came" (Hopper/*Modern Screen*/P); "They had a" (Louella O. Parsons, syndicated column, n.d.).

CHAPTER 11: WORLD FILM FAVORITE

"Every day of" (Warner Bros. press release, WBC); "One of the" (Peck/AFI); "Did you, kid" (Ibid.); "a beautiful, sensitive" (*Focus on Film,* March 1981); "he studies each" (Ibid.); "Mr. Peck not" (*Britain To-Day,* July 1951); The La Jolla Playhouse's profits at the end of 1950 (minutes of Actors' Company meeting, December 21, 1950, GPC); "You lend yourself" (Davis); "effort to dig" (Jesse Zunser, *Cue,* April 14, 1951); "The starring role" (Dorothy Manners, *Los Angeles Examiner,* April 14, 1951); Peck's affair with Barbara Payton (Benson/P); "I felt like" (Speck/GPC); Peck's second contract with Fox (memo from Lew Schreiber to Frank Ferguson, August 26, 1955, TFC); "You could call" (Dunne/P); "He has a" (Dunne/B); "as completely enthusiastic" (Custen/B); "There are many" (Stempel/OH); "In the last" (Molyneaux/B); "an authoritative performance" (Andrew Weiler, *New York Times,* August 15, 1951); "Wake up, Greg" (Freedland/B); "[f]riendly rivalry. . . . T]here's" (Ibid.); "a boy's adventure" (Davis); "one of the" (Stempel/OH); "When I sold" (Ibid); Robinson's feelings about the casting of Peck in *The Snows of Kilimanjaro* (Greenberg); "I considered that" (Shepard/B); "a handsome and" (Bosley Crowther, *New York Times,* September 19, 1952); "a dull, long" (Hollis Alpert, *Saturday Review,* October 11, 1952); "She did things" (Gardner/B); "Of all the" (Ibid.); "He was picky" (Greenberg); "it was constantly" (Vincent Rogers, unidentified publication); "was experimenting with all." (Greenberg); "She struck me" (Sidney Skolsky, syndicated column, ca. April 1963).

CHAPTER 12: WORKING ABROAD

"You surprise me" (Herman/B); "I have no" (Ibid.); "I wanted a" (Madsen/B); "He was writing" (Herman/B); "The police couldn't" (Harris/*Audrey Hepburn*/B); "wonderful. An amazing" (Carmody/P); "You can't do" (Harris/*Audrey Hepburn*/B); "I don't really" (Davis); "Keeping her in" (Herman); "I was supposed" (Harris/*Audrey Hepburn*/B); "We can't stay" (Paris/B); "I've lost sixteen" (Newman/P); "Film-making is" (unidentified publication, ca. 1952); "a rather remarkable" (Paul V. Beckley, *New York Herald-Tribune,* August 28, 1953); Wyler's interest in making *Roman Holiday* in color from the outset (Madsen/B): "smooth and competent" (Hollis Alpert, *Saturday Review,* September 5, 1953); "the most gifted" (*Life,* August 24, 1953); "Greg was there" (Savoy/P); "Since he was" (Madsen/B); "an enchanting, petite" (Tornabene/P); "I was not" (Ibid.); The Pecks' fight at their French villa housewarming party (unidentified tabloid); "just too difficult" (Saunders/P); Peck's reaction to the sailing of Greta and his sons for America (Friedland/B); "doesn't spark with" (Bosley Crowther, *New York Times,* June 29, 1954); "sort of tough" (Davis); "his old competent self" (William K. Zinnser, *New York Herald-Tribune,* April 11, 1955); "Today's picture-making" (George Chasin cable to Peck, n.d., GPC); "I don't think" (Johnson/B); "a genuinely nice" (Stempel/B); "Most nights, he" (Parrish/B); "an ungodly scream" (Ibid); "We got it" (Ibid.); "Gregory has been" (Louella Parsons, syndicated column, June 14, 1954); Hedda Hopper's report of the Pecks' decision to divorce (Hedda Hopper, syndicated column, July 4, 1954); "most dangerous film" (Peck/1989–90/P); "We had decided" (*Saturday Review*/P); "saw something of" (Grobel/B); "John wove his" (Ibid.); Why Huston cast Friedrich Ledebur as Queequeg (Huston/B); "a marriage of" (Grobel/B); "Portuguese whalers still" (Huston/B); "stark . . . obsessed. Every scene" (notes in Peck's *Moby Dick* script, GPC); "tense and disenchanted" (Viertel/B); "Huston was not" (Haver/P); "Make it bigger" (William K. Zinsser, *New York Herald-Tribune,* n.d.); "Kid, if you" (Buckley/P); "Oh, my God" (Speck/B); Peck and Huston's visa problems during the making of *Moby Dick* (Grobel/B); "I've been to" (Zinsser/P); "one of the" (Bosley Crowther, *New York Times,* July 5, 1956); "may just be" (William K. Zinsser, *New York Herald-Tribune,* July 5, 1956); "say something cosmic" (Davis); "stiff and stagey" (Wanda Hale, New York *Daily News,* July 5, 1956); "I was unable" (Gow/P); "Greg Peck is" (Buckley/P); "Greg is one" (Huston/B); "Had it been" (Ibid.); "deceit . . . abandoned or" (Brown/B).

CHAPTER 13: BACK HOME

Greta Peck's testimony on behalf of her divorce petition (Muir/P); Peck's statement refuting Greta's allegations (*Los Angeles Times,* December 17, 1954); "As alimony, Mrs." (Ibid.); "wonderful father" (unidentified publication, September 17, 1953); "I want to" (unidentified publication); "One day, I" (Freedland/B); "In two years" (Louella O. Parsons, syndicated column, August 8, 1954); "I am very" (Valery/P); "I have no" (Louella O. Parsons, syndicated column, March 19, 1955): "She is entirely" (Louella O. Parsons, syndicated column, March 25, 1955); "just as a" (Halberstam/B); Christine Linn as a stand-in for the role of Betsy Rath (Crist/P); "She came out" (Johnson/B); "Peck does a" (Ibid.); "a mature, fascinating and" (Bosley Crowther, *New York Times,* April 13, 1956); "may turn out" (*Cue,* April 14, 1956); "there are enough" (William K. Zinsser, *New York Herald-Tribune,* April 13, 1956); "a wonderful sense" (Davis); "Greg . . . was raring" (Minnelli/B); "godsend" (Bacall/*By Myself*/B); "If you don't" (Freedland/B); "Betty Bacall is" (Peck, 1989–90/P); "Well, to me" (Gow/P); "a two-hour" (William K. Zinsser, *New York Herald-Tribune,* May 17, 1957); "[I]t took awhile" (TCM); "the continental woman's" (Block/P); "When he is" (Ibid.); "In the years" (Louella O. Parsons, syndicated column, August 3, 1958); "was the best" (Amory/P); "Gregory can be" (Mrs. Gregory Peck/P); "I don't have" (Sidney Skolsky, syndicated column, ca. April 1963); "We spent holidays" (Herman/B); "Everybody is doing" (Sheilah Graham, syndicated column, ca. 1956); "sort of a 'Grand" (*Newsweek*/1957/P); "At the meeting" (Baker/B); "cretin" (Haun/P); "I'll think about" (Ibid); "What are you" (Speck/B); "He'd be six" (Herman/B); Wyler's letter to Peck regarding the producer's credit for *The Big Country* (William Wyler letter to Peck, March 27, 1958, GPC); "I performed for" (Peck letter to William Wyler, April 8, 1958, GPC); "further time to" (William Wyler letter to Peck, April 16, 1958, GPC); Peck's ideas for the ending of *The Big Country* (Peck letter to Lew Wasserman, August 26, 1958, GPC); The reviews of *The Big Country* in the New York dailies are dated October 2, 1958; "I missed Willy" (Herman/B); "Congratulations, Willy, you" (Heston/B); Henry King's ending of *The Bravados* (Stempel/OH): "I was totally" (Collins/B); "I'm such a" (New York *Daily News*/P); "unbelievably grim and" (Coppedge/B); "I think my" (Brown/B); The reviews of *The Bravados* in the New York dailies are dated June 26, 1958.

CHAPTER 14: TWO FOR UNITED ARTISTS, TWO FOR FOX

"best writer of" (Alpert/P); "We wanted people" (*Los Angeles Examiner*/P); "Sy started screening" (Ibid.); "This is an" (Peck memo to Sy Bartlett et al., May 20, 1958, GPC); "Clemons taught me" (A. C. Green/P); "It's quite a" (Regelings/P); "Greg was generous" (*Los Angeles Examiner*/P); "a rather confused" (Millichap/B);"Milly had a" (Davis); "*Pork Chop Hill* became" (Millichap/B); "Hollywood has come" (Hift., *Variety,* May 6, 1959); *Time* magazine's high ranking of *Pork Chop Hill* (*Time,* January 4, 1960); "I like it" (James, 1992/P); "I have no" (Rogers, Cowan and Jacobs press release for Dorothy Kilgallen ostensibly written by Peck, written around the time of *The Big Country,* GPC); "Bearing in mind" (Kramer/B); "Fred Astaire spends" (Bella Rackoff letter to Sy Bartlett, March 2, 1959, GPC); "one of her" (Peck, 1989–90/P); "out of character" (*London Times*/P); "self-denial on" (Gardner/B); "I think we" (Ibid.); "The precision and" (AFI); "We flew to" (Davis); "[m]arvelous, glamorous experience" (Ibid.); "They loved us" (*Variety,* December 23, 1959); "a sentimental sort" (*Time,* December 28, 1959); "aims at something" (Arthur Knight, *Saturday Review,* October 24, 1959); "I wouldn't direct" (Hedda Hopper, syndicated column, April 8, 1959); "She has had" (Jerry Wald memo to Lew Schreiber, September 23, 1959, TFC); "I had never" (manuscript for an untitled article by Veronique Peck, ca. 1960, GPC); "I must have" (Peck letter to Jerry Wald et al., August 7, 1959, GPC); "We have had" (Peck letter to Jerry Wald, September 17, 1959, GPC); "He knocked himself" (Stempel/OH); "He scared Deborah" (Freedland/B); "I'd rather fight" (*Screen Stories,* January 1960); "Gregory

Peck . . . and" (Arthur Knight, *Saturday Review*, December 5, 1959); "After I got" (Stempel/OH); "With barely time" (manuscript for an untitled article by Veronique Peck, ca. 1960, GPC); The terms of Peck's contract for *The Billionaire* (TFC); "My part began" (Burkett/P); "I've always wanted" (Ibid.); "Peck's name on" (Shearer/1956/P); "I'd rather do" (transcript of Hedda Hopper radio show, June 1954, HHC).

CHAPTER 15: GOING COMMERCIAL

Carl Foreman's development of Peck's character in *The Guns of Navarone* script (Foreman letter to Peck, February 23, 1960, GPC); "tacked on" (Peck letter to Carl Foreman, February 9, 1960, GPC); "David Niven really" (Morley/*The Other Side*/B); The firing of Alexander Mackendrick from *The Guns of Navarone* (Peck cable to George Chasin, n.d., GPC); "frightened to death" (Davis); "a highly strung" (Ibid.); "a whim" (Quinn/B); "Nothing much happens" (Whitcomb/P); "all eyeing each" (Morley/*The Other Side*/B); "Here, on an" (Whitcomb/P); "We were in" (Davis); "But Greg would" (Morley/*The Other Side*/B); "were not due" (Davis); "There is no" (Archer Winsten, *New York Post*, June 23, 1961); "a textbook example" (Paul V. Beckley, *New York Herald-Tribune*, June 23, 1961); "making sure . . . best" (Peck, 1989–90/P); "equally commendable in" (Arthur Knight, *Saturday Review*, May 5, 1962); "a masochistic exercise" (Paul V. Beckley, *New York Herald-Tribune*, April 19, 1962); "In case you" (Brendan Gill, *New Yorker*, May 12, 1962); "We completely relax" (*National Enquirer*, July 1974/P); "Don't be silly!" (Speck/GPC); Peck's suggestion that Irene Dunne ask MGM to increase St. John's profit participation in *How the West Was Won* (Herb Stein/P); "a charming fellow" (Peck/AFI); "use of the" (Ibid.); "I didn't even" (Davis); "I found it" (Davis); The reviews of *How the West Was Won* in the New York dailies are dated March 28, 1963.

CHAPTER 16: ATTICUS

"God was smiling" (Peck, 1989–90/P); "I felt I" (Griggs/B); "If you want" (King/P): "He was a" (Louella O. Parsons, syndicated column, n.d.); "It was about" (*Film Review*/P); "While we were" (Ibid.); "Acting with Mary" (brochure published by the Motion Picture Association of America, 1963); "every little girl's" (*Film Review*/P); "Gregory Peck brought" (AFI); "Mary . . . never could" (Universal Press release, n.d.); "That was one" (*National Enquirer*, September 1974/P); "It's like getting" (*Film Review*/P); "I know, if" (John G. Rogers, unidentified publication); "Look, enough is" (*Film Review*/P); "It felt good" (King/P); "Atticus has no" (Peck memo to George Chasin, June 18, 1962, GPC); "I believe we" (Peck letter to Mel Tucker, July 6, 1962, GPC); Bosley Crowther's *New York Times* review of *To Kill a Mockingbird* is dated February 15, 1963); *Newsweek*'s review of the film is dated February 18, 1963); "a major film" (Tube., *Variety*, December 12, 1962); "As Atticus, Mr." (Leo Mishkin, New York *Morning Telegraph*, February 15, 1963); "In that film" (Freedland/B); "The movie is" (King/P); Darryl F. Zanuck's attempt to keep Peck from abrogating his contract with Fox (Zanuck letter to Peck, April 5, 1963, TFC); The Theatre Owners of America selection of Peck as the most popular actor of the year (*Motion Picture Exhibitor*, November 24, 1962); "Ah, yes, but" (Haun/P); "sharp," "rush," "relax," "Find the spots" (Peck's script notes for *Captain Newman, M.D.*, GPC); "I wasn't nervous" (Peck cable to Bob Thomas, April 9, 1962); "say anything mushy" (*Los Angeles Herald Examiner*/P); "Now when are" (Harris/*Sophia Loren*/B); "Having won it" (Block/P); "a landmark—you" (Shay/*Kaleidoscope*/P); "particularly for its" (Davis); The reviews of *Captain Newman, M.D.* in the New York dailies are dated February 21, 1964; "a continually interesting" (*Cue*, February 22, 1964); "restrained and intelligent" (Tube., *Variety*, October 23, 1963); "Not exactly, I" (John G. Rogers, unidentified publication); The initial casting of Peck and Quinn in *Behold a Pale Horse* (author interview with J. P. Miller); "I've got a" (*Seventeen*/P); "Except for film" (Woolfenden/P); "Do you like" (*New York Post*, May 20, 1963); "I was proud" (Ibid.); "It was a" (Davis); "planning and precision" (Davis); The reviews of *Behold a Pale Horse* in the New York dailies are dated August 14, 1964; "handsome, impressive picture" (*Newsweek,* August 24, 1964); "What is needed" (Richard Schickel, *Life,* August 21, 1964); "I think I" (Harris/P).

CHAPTER 17: PLAYING A PUBLIC ROLE

"I felt I" (Manners/P); "magnificent motion-picture tribute" (Bosley Crowther, *New York Times,* November 17, 1964); "This is the" (Block/P); "wonderful weeks of" (Manners/P); "It needed a" (Shay/*Kaleidoscope*/P); *Time* magazine's review of *Mirage* is dated May 28, 1965; *Life*'s is dated June 18, 1965, the *New York Times*' and the *New York Post*'s are dated May 27, 1965, *Newsweek*'s is June 14, 1965, *Cue*'s May 29, 1965, and *Variety*'s May 19, 1965; "Peck is everybody's" (Kathleen Carroll, New York *Daily News,* May 27, 1964); The original choice for the male lead in *Arabesque* was Cary Grant (Harris/*Sophia Loren*/B); The assertion that Peck suggested Loren for the female lead in *Arabesque* (Kate Cameron, New York *Daily News,* May 1, 1966); "Don't be embarrassed" (Harris/*Sophia Loren*/B); "a terrific woman" (Davis); "Stanley, there's only" (Silverman/B); "Stanley had a" (Ibid); "This is only" (Richard Schickel, *Life,* May 13, 1966); "gets lost in" (*New Yorker,* May 14, 1966); "brought me a" (Davis); "It was small" (Molyneaux/B); "I've had my" (unknown publication); "Dad doesn't like" (Darrach/P); "After nine years" (Hale/P); "an attraction of" (Cullen/P); "When I'm overtaken" (Ibid.); "After dinner we" (Peck letter to author, September 27, 2000); "I get a" (Dean/P); "I just participate" (Savoy/P); "beneath this 'I'm" (Ibid.); "We say cut" (undated draft of a speech for the American Cancer Society in Peck's handwriting, GPC); "There is no" (Joseph Papp letter to Peck, November 7, 1966, GPC); "In my years" (undated Peck appeal letter for the ICCC, GPC); The General Accounting Office's accusations against the ICCC (Robert L. Jackson, *Los Angeles Times,* n.d.); "I am far" (Peck's undated draft of a statement for the AP, GPC); "At the 1967" (AFI); "We believe that" (*Academy Report,* September 1970); "We are not" (Freedland/B); "We must unite" (Holden/*Behind the Oscar*/B); "Peck in two" (Harold Heffernan, *Philadelphia Daily News,* October 21, 1969); "an artist who" (unidentified publication).

CHAPTER 18: CHANGING TIMES

"*Mackenna's Gold* was" (Shaw/P); "Not in recent" (Kevin Thomas, *Los Angeles Times,* June 25, 1969); "a fan letter" (Bell/P); "customary rigid dignity" (*Time,* February 14, 1969); "Peck is so grave" (Vincent Canby, *New York Times,* January 23, 1969); "a bit hard" (Davis); "The film is" (Wolf, *Cue,* June 28, 1969); The reviews of *Marooned* in the New York dailies are dated December 19, 1969; "long, lugubrious spectacle" (Judith Crist, *New York,* December 22, 1969); "Who in his" (Pauline Kael, *New Yorker,* January 3, 1970); "Frankness has gone" (Rogers/P); "Tuesday Weld is" (Peck letter to Charles Jarrott, October 24, 1972, GPC); "was made under" (Eichelbaum/P); "a kind of" (Shaw/P); "Frankly, it seems" (Peck cable to John Frankenheimer, June 15, 1970, GPC); "gripping, unusual and" (Ibid.); "The movie is" (*New Yorker,* December 5, 1970); "It was admirable" (Howard Thompson, *New York Times,* November 19, 1970); "unseemly for Peck" (Phyllis Funke, New York *Morning Telegraph,* November 19, 1970); "killed the movie" (Frankenheimer/B); "Because they couldn't" (Mills/P); "I can't tell" (unknown publication); "We were an" (Freedland/B); "I've not had" (Eichelbaum/P); "At times, the" (Michael Kerbel, *Village Voice,* November 18, 1971); The reviews of *Shoot Out* in the New York dailies are dated October 14, 1971; "mostly as a" (Charles Champlin, *Los Angeles Times,* August 26, 1971); "Peck, m'boy, what" (Paine Knickerbocker, *San Francisco Chronicle,* June 29, 1971); "I did several" (Mills/P); "It was humiliating" (Beck/P); "sit back and" (Davis).

CHAPTER 19: MR. PRODUCER

"Politics was exciting" (Evans/P); "I knew what" (Haver/P); "I had been" (Woodside/P); "It was stimulating" (Berkvist/P); "Everybody had a" (Ibid.); "This film must" (Freedland/B); "What created magic" (William Wolf, *Cue,* May 20, 1972); The weekly grosses of *The Trial of the Catonsville Nine* in New York, Boston, and Los Angeles (Peck letter to the film's investors, June 9, 1972, GPC); "Very few people" (Mills/P); "the rather simple" (Shaw/P); "The Israeli Government" (Weiler/P); "You wouldn't have" (Shaw/P); "Well, it was" (Ibid.); The *Variety* review *of Billy Two Hats* is dated November 7, 1973; "an international mishmash" (Judith Crist, *New York,* May 5, 1974); "We thought it" (Griggs/B); The reviews of *The Dove* in the New York dailies are dated February 20, 1975); "until I had" (Pickard/P); "I feel I" (Mills/P); "I got terribly" (Davis); "I've had some" (Bob Thomas, Associated Press, February 16, 1975); "My life isn't" (Mills/P); "reading, living, conversing" (Davis); "the tragedy of" (TCM); Bob Thomas' report of Jonathan Peck's medical condition (Thomas/P); "I felt certain" (Freedland/B); "The autopsy showed" (Markfield/P); "greatest problem was" (Ibid.); "Poor Jonathan. He" (Ibid); "When you look" (Thomas/P); "The fact that" (Freedland/B).

CHAPTER 20: BANKABLE AGAIN

"David and Harvey" (Shay, *Cinefantastic*/P); "I saw it" (Davis); "Personally, I thought" (Shay, *Cinefantastic*/P); "One day, in" (Weaver/P); "At last we" (AFI); "The main feeling" (Robbins/P); "We were kidding" (Shay, *Cinefantastic*/P); "We finished principal" (*Hollywood Reporter,* January 14, 1976); "You may choose" (Peck letter to Harvey Bernhard and Richard Donner, April 8, 1976. The notes are dated March 26, 1967, GPC); "We appreciate the" (Harvey Bernhard and Richard Donner letter to Peck, April 21, 1976, GPC); "*The Omen* is" (Richard Schickel, *Time,* June 28, 1976); "Up to that point" (Lardine/P); "so many young" (Shaw/P); "After I'd tried" (Luce/P); "I wanted to" (Ibid.); "The more I" (Ibid.); "I think we" (Peck letter to Frank McCarthy, April 27, 1976, GPC); "Whoever wrote this" (Peck letter to Joseph Sargent et al., September 27, 1976, GPC); "MacArthur wore no" (Peck letter to Joseph Sargent et al., November 5, 1976, GPC); "I truly identified" (Ardmore); "It was quite" (Freedland/B); "Before we started" (Peck letter to Joseph Sargent et al., March 7, 1977, GPC); "Gregory Peck is" (Vincent Canby, *New York Times,* July 1, 1977); "Unlike the snappy" (Kathleen Carroll, New York *Daily News,* July 1, 1977); "I thought I" (Brown/B); "a lost opportunity" (Freedland/B); "that's where the" (Amory/P); "This man is" (Hall/P); "a miserable little" (Peck/AFI); "my big confrontation" (*Hollywood Reporter,* December 1, 1977); "Of course, it" (Speck/B); "were lying around" (Ibid.); "We went to" (Ibid.); "get a bag" (Harold Schonberg, *New York Times,* November 6, 1978); "a painful monstrosity" (Tom Allen, *Village Voice,* October 9, 1978); "a penny dreadful" (Richard Schickel, *Time,* October 9, 1978); "Peck appears to" (Pauline Kael, *New Yorker,* October 8, 1978); "Sessue Hayakawa in" (David Denby, *New York,* October 9, 1978); "sometimes critics are" (Davis); "You stub your" (Price/P); "We didn't feel" (Mann/P); "I've got more" (*Las Vegas Sun*/P); "I think too" (Merina/P); "did not debate" (Ibid.); "The first time" (*Interview*/P).

CHAPTER 21: CHARACTER ACTOR

"He's the" (*TV Guide*/P); "He would come" (Bennett/P); "In makeup he" (*People,* n.d.); "If we were" (*TV Guide*/P); "Because I knew" (Peck, *TV Guide*/P); "The thing zinged" (*TV Guide*/P); "If you're expecting" (Harry F. Waters, *Newsweek,* November 15, 1982); "a soap opera" (Kay Gardella, New York *Daily News,* November 11, 1982); "program's strongest performance" (*Variety,* November 17, 1982); "I'm pleased with" (*TV Guide*/P); "playboy priest who" (Smith/P); "When I read" (Ibid.); "a comfortable thing" (Ibid.); "Television acting is" (Ibid.); "the finest drama" (Kay Gardella, New York *Daily News,* February 2, 1983); "I like a" (Sheilah Graham, syndicated column, ca. 1956); "a strict, old-fashioned" (Darrach/P): "I was concerned" (White/P); "They used to" (Ardmore); "Cecilia's sudden decision" (*Hollywood Reporter,* March 7, 1984); Ron Bass' contributions to the screenplay of *Amazing Grace and Chuck* (author interview with David Field); "When I read" (Burden/P); "little people overcoming" (Tri-Star production notes for *Amazing Grace and Chuck*); "Why should I" (Price/P); "I don't want"

(*Tacoma News Tribune*/P); "many moments of" (Ralph Novak, *People,* June 8, 1987); "amazingly bad as" (Cart., *Variety,* April 1, 1987); "masterfully creates a" (Ralph Novak, *People,* June 8, 1987); "a perfect President" (Chris Chase, New York *Daily News,* May 22, 1987); "I'd say that" (Burkett/P); "most fulsome and" (Ibid.); "Can you fix" (Healy/P); "We made certain" (Chen Mei/P); "You're Cary Grant" (*The Star*/P); "We never seem" (Lois Armstrong, *People,* n.d.) "I love the" (Farley/P); "If they've offered" (Bennett/P); "The chance to" (Production notes for *Old Gringo*); "I'm way behind" (Hamill/P); "There's something about" (AFI); "In my opinion" (Peck letter to Puenza et al., December 12, 1988, GPC); "Like that picture" (Ibid.); "I see clearly" (Peck letter to Puenza et al., January 10, 1989, GPC); "I find it" (Peck letter to Nicole David and Arnold Rivkin, Triad Artists, April 10, 1989, GPC): "Hopefully a lot" (McElwaine/P); "If *Old Gringo*" (Janet Maslin, *New York Times,* October 6, 1989); "Many bad movies" (Julie Salamon, *Wall Street Journal,* November 2, 1989); "often happens that" (Champlin/P); "I was genuinely" (*Variety,* October 26, 1988); "a thrilling, moving" (Blue., *Variety,* March 29, 1989).

CHAPTER 22: THE NINETIES AND BEYOND

"[W]e knew that" (Production notes for *Other People's Money*); "Gregory represents real" (Ibid.); "I saw the" (Champlin/P); "I'm for Jorgy" (Macinnis/P); "everything that you" (Production notes for *Other People's Money*); "I regret very" (Campbell/P); The reviews of *Other People's Money* in the New York dailies are dated October 18, 1991; "Mainly, Mr. Jewison" (Julie Salamon, *Wall Street Journal,* October 24, 1991); "a psychologically realistic" (Jami Bernard, *New York Post,* November 12, 1991); "In the first *Cape*" (Peter Travers, *Rolling Stone,* November 28, 1991); "I didn't want" (Champlin/P); "I took the" (Ibid.); "I'd like to" (Macinnis/P); "punishing, sock-it" (Kathleen Carroll, New York *Daily News,* November 13, 1991); "brief but surprisingly" (Vincent Canby, *New York Times,* November 13, 1991); "the most authentic" (Paris/B); "When people ask" (Brenson/P); "It is very" (Ann Green/P); "We like one" (Ibid.); "total, unmitigated joy" (Ibid.); "Even though we" (Ibid.); "Arthur Penn is" (Ibid.); "Arthur has been" (Ibid.); "I think it" (Peck fax to Arthur Penn, July 1, 1992, GPC); "an effective study" (Tony Scott, *Variety,* February 8, 1993); "poignant and funny" (Fran Wood, New York *Daily News,* February 12, 1993); "I admire very" (Champlin/P); "the little world" (Ibid.); "a little exercise" (Associated Press, July 15, 1996); "four or five doctors" (Ibid.); "I've had a" (*Los Angeles Times,* April 5, 1996; "No actor retires" (*Variety,* April 10, 1996); "a warm bit" (James, 1998/P); "I get sent" (Dreifus/P); "I resist calling" (*New York Times,* March 4, 1997); "That's my favorite" (Blowen/P); "there's a live" (TCM); "I never felt" (*TV Guide,* October 16–22, 1999); "Just thankful. Cecilia" (TCM); "I'd like to" (Ibid.).

Bibliography

BOOKS

Alpi, Deborah Lazaroff. *Robert Siodmak.* Jefferson, N.C.: McFarland, 1998.
Andersen, Christopher P. *A Star, Is a Star, Is a Star! The Lives and Loves of Susan Hayward.* Garden City, N.Y.: Doubleday, 1980.
Bacall, Lauren. *By Myself.* New York: Alfred A. Knopf, 1979.
———. *Now.* New York: Alfred A. Knopf. 1994.
Baker, Carroll. *Baby Doll: An Autobiography.* New York: Arbor House, 1983.
Behlmer, Rudy. *Inside Warner Bros. (1935–1951).* New York: Viking, 1985.
Behlmer, Rudy, ed. *Memo from Darryl F. Zanuck: The Golden Years at Twentieth Century–Fox.* New York: Grove Press, 1993.
———. *Memo from David O. Selznick.* New York: Viking, 1972.
Bergman, Ingrid, and Alan Burgess. *Ingrid Bergman: My Story.* New York: Delacorte Press, 1972.
Braun, Eric. *Deborah Kerr.* London: W. H. Allen, 1977.
Brown, Dennis. *Actors Talk: Profiles and Stories from the Acting Trade.* New York: Limelight Editions, 1999.
Casper, Joseph Andrew. *Stanley Donen.* Metuchen, N.J.: Scarecrow Press, 1983.
Collins, Joan. *Second Act: An Autobiography.* New York: St. Martin's Press, 1997.
Coppedge, Walter. *Henry King's America.* Metuchen, N.J.: Scarecrow Press, 1986.
Cotten, Joseph. *Vanity Will Get You Somewhere.* San Francisco: Mercury House, 1987.
Crowley, Alice Lewisohn. *The Neighborhood Playhouse: Leaves from a Theatre Scrapbook.* New York: Theatre Arts Books, 1959.
Curtis, Tony, and Barry Paris. *Tony Curtis: The Autobiography.* New York: William Morrow, 1993.
Custen, George F. *Twentieth Century's Fox: Darryl F. Zanuck and the Culture of Hollywood.* New York: Basic Books, 1997.
Davidson, Bill. *Jane Fonda: An Intimate Biography.* London: Sidgewick & Jackson, 1990.
De Cordova, Fred. *Johnny Come Lately.* New York: Simon and Schuster, 1988.
Douglas, Kirk. *Climbing the Mountain: My Search for Meaning.* New York: Simon & Schuster, 1997.
Dowd, Nancy, and David Shepard, interviewers. *King Vidor: A Directors Guild of America Oral History.* Metuchen, N.J.: Directors Guild of America and Scarecrow Press, 1988.
Dunne, Philip. *Take Two: A Life in Movies and Politics.* New York: McGraw-Hill, 1980.
Durgnat, Raymond, and Scott Simmon. *King Vidor, American.* Berkeley: University of California Press, 1988.
Eells, George. *Robert Mitchum: A Biography.* New York: Franklin Watts, 1984.
Epstein, Edward Z. *Portrait of Jennifer: A Biography of Jennifer Jones.* New York: Simon & Schuster, 1995.
Flamini, Roland. *Ava.* New York: Coward, McGann & Geohegan, 1983.
Frankenheimer, John, with Charles Champlin. *John Frankenheimer: A Conversation.* Burbank, Calif.: Riverwood Press, 1995.
Freedland, Michael. *All the Way: A Biography of Frank Sinatra.* London: Weidenfeld & Nicholson, 1997.
———. *Gregory Peck.* New York: William Morrow, 1980.
Gardner, Ava. *Ava: My Story.* New York: Bantam Books, 1990.
Griggs, John. *The Films of Gregory Peck.* Secaucus, N.J.: Citadel Press, 1984.
Grobel, Lawrence. *The Hustons.* New York: Charles Scribner's Sons, 1989.
Guest, Kenneth L. *Pictures Will Talk: The Life and Films of Joseph L. Mankiewicz.* New York: Charles Scribner's Sons, 1978.

Gussow, Mel. *Don't Say Yes Until I Finish Talking: A Biography of Darryl F. Zanuck.* Garden City, N.Y.: Doubleday, 1971.
Halberstam, David. *The Fifties.* New York: Villard Books, 1993.
Harding, James. *Emlyn Williams: A Life.* London: Weidenfeld & Nicolson, 1993.
Harris, Warren G. *Audrey Hepburn: A Biography.* New York: Simon & Schuster, 1994.
———. *Cary Grant: A Touch of Elegance.* New York: Doubleday, 1987.
———. *Sophia Loren: A Biography.* New York: Simon & Schuster, 1998.
Herman, Jan. *A Talent for Trouble: The Life of Hollywood's Most Acclaimed Director, William Wyler.* New York: Putnam, 1995.
Heston, Charlton. *In the Arena: An Autobiography.* New York: Simon & Schuster, 1995.
Higham, Charles. *Ava.* New York: Delecorte, 1974.
Higham, Charles, and Roy Moseley. *Cary Grant: The Lonely Heart.* New York: Harcourt Brace Jovanovich, 1989.
Hobson, Laura Z. *Laura Z: A Life.* New York: Arbor House, 1983.
Holden, Anthony. *Behind the Oscar: The Secret History of the Academy Awards.* New York: Simon & Schuster, 1993.
———. *Laurence Olivier.* New York: Atheneum, 1988.
Hunter, Allan. *Gene Hackman.* London: W. H. Allen, 1987.
Huston, John. *An Open Book.* New York: Alfred A. Knopf, 1980.
Johnson, Nora. *Flashback: Nora Johnson on Nunnally Johnson.* New York: Doubleday, 1979.
Kazan, Elia. *A Life.* New York: Alfred A. Knopf, 1988.
Kemp, Philip. *Lethal Innocence: The Cinema of Alexander Mackendrick.* London: Methuen, 1991.
Kim, Erwin. *Franklin J. Schaffner.* Metuchen, N.J.: Scarecrow Press, 1985.
Kramer, Stanley, with Thomas M. Coffey. *A Mad, Mad, Mad, Mad World.* New York: Harcourt Brace, 1997.
LaGuardia, Robert, and Gene Arceri. *Red: The Tempestuous Life of Susan Hayward.* New York: Macmillan, 1985.
Leamer, Laurence. *As Time Goes By: The Life of Ingrid Bergman.* New York: Harper & Row, 1986.
Leff, Leonard J. *Hitchcock & Selznick: The Rich and Strange Collaboration of Alfred Hitchcock and David O. Selznick in Hollywood.* New York: Weidenfeld & Nicolson, 1987.
Levy, Emanuel. *George Cukor, Master of Elegance: Hollywood's Legendary Director and His Stars.* New York: William Morrow, 1994.
Linet, Beverly. *Susan Hayward: Portrait of a Survivor.* New York: Atheneum, 1980.
Macdonald, Kevin. *Emeric Pressburger: The Life and Death of a Screenwriter.* London: Faber and Faber, 1994.
Madsen, Axel. *William Wyler: The Authorized Biography.* New York: Thomas Y. Crowell, 1973.
Malden, Karl, with Carla Malden. *When Do I Start? A Memoir.* New York: Simon & Schuster, 1997.
Martin, Jeffrey Brown. *Ben Hecht: Hollywood Screenwriter.* Ann Arbor, Mich.: UMI Research Press, 1985, 1978.
Massey, Raymond. *A Hundred Different Lives: An Autobiography.* New York: Little, Brown, 1979.
McGilligan, Patrick. *George Cukor: A Double Life. A Biography of the Gentleman Director.* New York: St. Martin's Press, 1991.
Meisner, Sanford, and Dennis Longwell. *Sanford Meisner on Acting.* New York: Vintage Books, 1987
Millichap, Joseph R. *Lewis Milestone.* Boston: Twayne Publishers, 1981.
Minnelli, Vincente, with Hector Arce. *I Remember It Well.* Garden City, N.Y.: Doubleday, 1974.

Molyneaux, Gerard. *Gregory Peck: A Bio-Bibliography.* Westport, Conn.: Greenwood Press, 1995.

Morella, Joe, and Edward Z. Epstein. *Jane Wyman: A Biography.* New York: Delacorte, 1985.

Morley, Sheridan. *Gladys Cooper.* New York: McGraw-Hill, 1979.

———. *The Other Side of the Moon: The Life of David Niven.* New York: Harper & Row, 1985.

Mosley, Leonard. *Zanuck: The Rise and Fall of Hollywood's Last Tycoon.* Boston: Little, Brown, 1984.

Mosley, Roy. *Roger Moore.* London: New English Library, 1985.

Munn, Michael. *Gene Hackman.* London: Robert Hale, 1997.

Nelson, Nancy. *Evenings with Cary Grant: Recollections in His Own Words and by Those Who Knew Him Best.* New York: William Morrow, 1991.

Nolletti, Jr., Arthur, ed. *The Films of Fred Zinnemann: Critical Perspectives.* Albany, N.Y.: State University of New York Press, 1999.

Osborne, Robert. *65 Years of the Oscar: The Official History of the Academy Awards.* New York: Abbeville Press, 1989, 1994.

Paris, Barry. *Audrey Hepburn.* New York: Putnam, 1996.

Parker, Francine, interviewer. *Stages: Norman Lloyd.* A Directors Guild of America Oral History. Metuchen, N.J.: Directors Guild of America and Scarecrow Press, 1990.

Parrish, Robert. *Hollywood Doesn't Live Here Anymore.* Boston: Little, Brown, 1988.

Quinn, Anthony, with Daniel Paisner. *One Man Tango.* New York: HarperCollins, 1995.

Reynolds, Debbie, and David Patrick Columbia. *Debbie: My Life.* New York: William Morrow, 1988.

Schaelchlin, Patricia A. *La Jolla: The Story of a Community 1887–1987.* La Jolla, Calif.: Friends of the La Jolla Library, 1988.

Shepard, David, and Ted Perry. *Henry King Director: From Silents to 'Scope.* Los Angeles: Directors Guild of America, 1995.

Shipman, David. *Judy Garland: The Secret Life of an American Legend.* New York: Hyperion, 1993.

Shnayerson, Michael. *Irwin Shaw: A Biography.* New York: G. P. Putnam's Sons, 1989.

Silverman, Stephen M. *Dancing on the Ceiling: Stanley Donen and His Movies.* New York: Alfred A. Knopf, 1996.

Speck, Gregory. *Hollywood Royalty: Hepburn, Davis, Stewart and Friends at the Dinner Party of the Century.* New York: Birch Lane Press, 1992.

Spoto, Donald. *The Dark Side of Genius: The Life of Alfred Hitchcock.* Boston: Little, Brown, 1983.

———. *Laurence Olivier: A Biography.* New York: HarperCollins, 1992.

———. *Marilyn Monroe: The Biography.* New York: HarperCollins, 1993.

———. *Stanley Kramer, Film Maker.* New York: G.P. Putnam's Sons, 1978.

Stempel, Tom. *Screenwriter: The Life and Times of Nunnally Johnson.* San Diego: A. S. Barnes, 1980.

Swindell, Larry. *Body and Soul: The Story of John Garfield.* New York: William Morrow, 1975.

Taylor, John Russell. *Hitch: The Life and Times of Alfred Hitchcock.* New York: Pantheon Books, 1978.

Thomas, Bob. *Selznick.* Garden City, N.Y.: Doubleday, 1970.

Thompson, Frank T. *William A. Wellman.* Metuchen, N.J.: Scarecrow Press, 1983.

Thomson, David. *Showman: The Life of David O. Selznick.* New York: Alfred A. Knopf, 1992.

Tomkies, Mike. *The Robert Mitchum Story: "It Sure Beats Working."* Chicago: Henry Regnery, 1972.

Troyan, Michael. *A Rose for Mr. Miniver: The Life of Greer Garson.* Lexington, Ky.: University Press of Kentucky, 1999.

Vidor, King. *King Vidor on Film Making.* New York: David McKay, 1972.
———. *A Tree Is a Tree.* New York: Harcourt, Brace and Company, 1953.
Viertel, Peter. *Dangerous Friends: At Large with Huston and Hemingway in the Fifties.* New York: Doubleday, 1992.
Vilga, Edward. *Acting Now: Conversations on Craft and Career.* New Brunswick, N.J.: Rutgers University Press, 1997.
Wallis, Hal, and Charles Higham. *Starmaker: The Autobiography of Hal Wallis.* New York: Macmillan, 1980.
Walsh, Raoul. *Each Man in His Time: The Life Story of a Director.* New York: Farrar, Straus and Giroux, 1974.
Wayne, Jane Ellen. *Ava's Men: The Private Life of Ava Gardner.* New York: St. Martin's Press, 1990.
Whitelaw, Billie. *Billie Whitelaw . . . Who He?* London: Hodder & Stoughton, 1995.
Winecoff, Charles. *Split Image: The Life of Anthony Perkins.* New York: Dutton, 1996.
Young, Jeff, interviewer. *Kazan: The Master Director Discusses His Films.* New York: Newmarket Press, 1999.
Zinnemann, Fred. *A Life in the Movies: An Autobiography.* New York: Charles Scribner's Sons, 1992.

PERIODICALS

Alpert, Hollis. *Saturday Review,* May 16, 1959.
Amory, Cleveland. *Parade,* December 4, 1988.
Architectural Digest, April 1996.
Battelle, Phyllis. *Los Angeles Herald-Examiner,* January 14, 1962.
Beck, Marilyn. *Los Angeles Herald-Examiner,* December 27, 1977.
Bell, Joseph N. *San Jose Mercury News,* December 7, 1969.
Bennett, Ray. *TV Guide–Canada,* November 13–19, 1982.
Benson, N. E. *Confidential,* ca. 1955–56.
Berg, Louis. *This Week,* February 19, 1950.
Berkvist, Robert. *New York Times,* May 21, 1972.
Block, Jean Libman. *Good Housekeeping,* May 1966.
Blowen, Michael. *Boston Sunday Globe,* February 23, 1997.
Boston Post, April 2, 1944.
Brenson, Michael. *New York Times,* February 18, 1983.
Buckley, Michael. *Films in Review,* April 1984.
Burden, Martin. *New York Post,* May 14, 1987.
Burkett, Michael. *Orange County Register,* November 20, 1986.
Campbell, Bob. *Newark Star-Ledger,* October 20, 1991.
Carmody, Jay. *Washington Star,* May 31, 1959.
Champlin, Charles. *Los Angeles Times,* October 20, 1991.
Creelman, Eileen. *New York Sun,* December 27, 1944.
Crist, Judith. *New York Herald-Tribune,* October 12, 1955.
Cullen, Jenny. *Ladies' Home Journal,* November 1988.
Darrach, Brad. *People,* July 15, 1987.
Dean, Samantha. *Newsday,* September 4, 1977.
Delehanty, Thornton. *New York Herald-Tribune,* October 10, 1943.
Dreifus, Claudia. *New York Times,* May 4, 1998.
Dunne, Philip. *New York Herald–Tribune,* August 12, 1951.
Eichelbaum, Stanley. *San Francisco Examiner,* March 17, 1971.
Erickson, Joan. *El Campanario,* Midyear Issue, 1971–72.
Evans, Hal. *National Enquirer,* October 9, 1973.
Farley, Ellen. *Los Angeles Times,* "Calendar," October 22, 1978.
Film Review, April 1994.
Fox, Angela Dunn. *Page Up,* 1989.

Gardella, Kay. New York *Daily News,* August 24, 1988.
Gow, Gordon. *Films and Filming,* September 1974.
Grant, James. *Los Angeles Times,* June 2, 1994.
Green, A. C. *Abeline Reporter-News,* May 31, 1959.
Green, Ann. *Los Angeles Times,* "TV Times," February 7–13, 1993.
Hale, Wanda. New York *Daily News,* August 31, 1964.
Hall, William. *New York Post,* December 17, 1977.
Hamill, Pete. *Premiere,* October 1989.
Harris, Leonard. *New York World-Telegram and Sun,* August 17, 1964.
Haun, Harry. New York *Daily News,* May 17, 1987.
Haver, Ron. *American Film,* March 1989.
Healy, Michael. *Denver Post,* April 5, 1987.
Helleur, Stan. *Toronto Globe and Mail,* October 8, 1958.
Hopper, Hedda. *Chicago Sunday Tribune,* November 24, 1946
———. *Modern Screen,* May 1949.
Interview, October 1980.
James, Caryn. *New York Times,* March 13, 1998.
———. *New York Times,* April 12, 1992.
Johnson, Ted. *TV Guide,* October 9, 1999.
Jones, Lon. *Toronto Star Weekly,* ca. 1947.
———. *Toronto Star Weekly,* December 29, 1951.
Jory, Tom. *New York Post,* December 12, 1978.
King, Susan. *Los Angeles Times,* December 22, 1997.
Lardine, Bob. New York *Daily News,* October 31, 1976.
Las Vegas Sun, November 5, 1978.
London Times, December 16, 1959.
Long Beach Press Telegram, June 28, 1998.
Los Angeles Examiner, May 10, 1959.
Los Angeles Herald-Examiner, January 9, 1972.
Luce, William P. *New York Times,* July 11, 1977.
Macinnis, Craig. *Toronto Star,* October 11, 1991.
Mann, Roderick. *Los Angeles Times,* June 26, 1983.
Manners, Dorothy. *Los Angeles Herald-Examiner,* August 16, 1964.
Markfield, Alan. *National Enquirer,* August 19, 1975.
Martin, Pete. *Saturday Evening Post,* September 22, 1945.
McElwaine, Sandra. New York *Daily News,* October 1, 1989.
McIntyre, David. *San Diego Evening Tribune,* March 13, 1963.
Mei, Chen. *Chinese Literature,* Summer 1988.
Melton, Mary. *Los Angeles Times Magazine,* January 17, 1999.
Merina, Victor. *Los Angeles Times,* November 9, 1978.
Mills, Bart. *Chicago Tribune Magazine,* June 9, 1974.
Morris, Mary. *PM,* December 31, 1944.
Muir, Florabel. New York *Daily News,* December 30, 1954.
National Enquirer, July 23, 1974.
National Enquirer, September 14, 1974.
Newman, Larry. *The American Weekly,* November 9, 1952.
Newsweek, October 21, 1957.
Newsweek, June 8, 1999.
New York *Daily News,* May 2, 1958.
New York Times, January 7, 1945.
Parsons, Louella O. *Cosmopolitan,* ca. 1955.
Peck Gregory. *Saturday Evening Post,* March 22, 1947.
———. *Memories,* December 1989–January 1990.
Peck, Mrs. Gregory. *Hollywood Citizen-News,* June 3, 1961.

Pickard, Roy. *Films in Review,* April 1976.
Price, Michael H. *Fort Worth Star-Telegram,* April 26, 1987.
Regelings, Lowell E. *Hollywood Citizen-News,* August 5, 1958.
Robbins, Fred. *Celebrity,* March 1976.
Rogers, John G. *Los Angeles Times,* March 15, 1964.
Saturday Review, June 9, 1956.
Saunders, Marsha. *Modern Screen,* May 1953.
Savoy, Maggie. *Los Angeles Times,* December 18, 1967.
Scheuer, Philip K. *Los Angeles Times,* December 14, 1947.
Screen Guide, October 1946.
Seidelman, Arthur A. *After Dark,* January 1970.
Seventeen, December 1963.
Shaw, Don. *Focus On Film,* October 1977.
Shay, Don. *Cinefantastic,* Winter 1976.
———. *Kaleidoscope,* vol. 2, no. 3, 1967.
Shearer, Lloyd. *Toronto Star Weekly,* July 14, 1956.
Smith, Cecil. *Los Angeles Times,* November 27, 1982.
The Star. December 13, 1988.
Stein, Herb. New York *Morning-Telegraph,* March 13, 1963.
Stein, Jeanne. *Films in Review,* March 1967.
Sullivan, William. *San Diego Magazine,* May 1978.
Tacoma News Tribune, May 24, 1987.
Thomas, Bob. *New York Post,* April 2, 1982 (excerpted from Thomas' book, *Heartbreak Kids: The Tragedy of Hollywood's Children*).
Time, January 12, 1948.
Tornabene, Lyn. *Cosmopolitan Magazine,* October 1961.
TV Guide, November 13, 1982.
Valery, Bernard. New York *Daily News,* January 25, 1955.
Weaver, Tom. *Fangoria,* August 1991.
Weiler, A. H. *New York Times,* August 6, 1972.
Whitcomb, Jan. *Cosmopolitan Magazine,* January 1961.
White, Betty. *Saturday Evening Post,* January–February 1977.
Woodside, Gordon. *Take One,* December 10, 1972.
Woolfenden, John. *New York Times,* July 7, 1963.
Zinsser, William K. *New York Herald-Tribune,* July 1, 1956.

Index